My Little Monster

Robico

CONTENTS

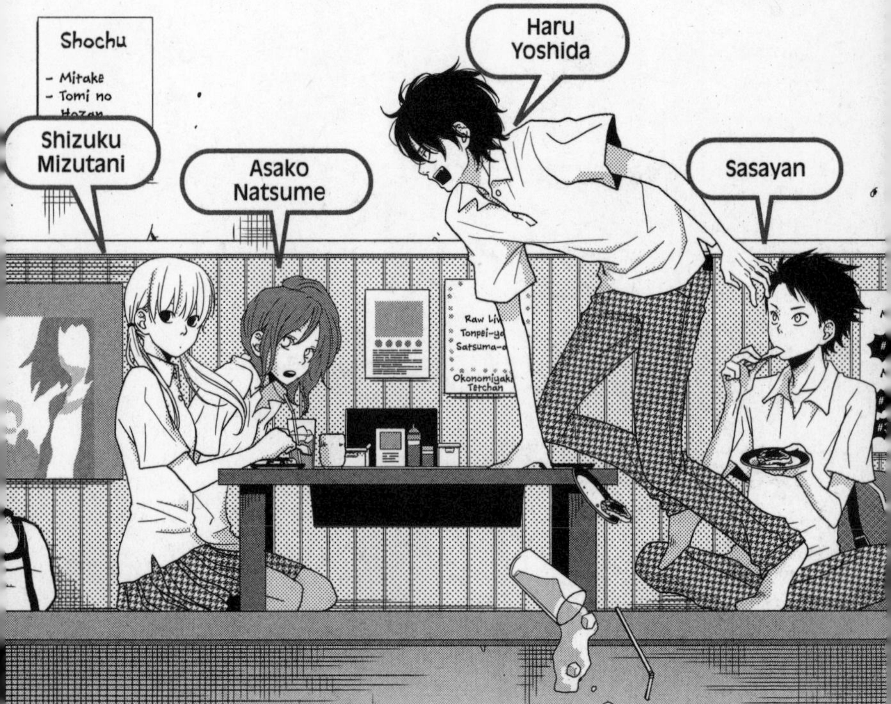

Haru Yoshida
Sasayan
Asako Natsume
Shizuku Mizutani
Shochu
- Mitake
- Tomi no Hozan
Okonomiyaki Tetchan

STORY

Shizuku Mizutani has a dream to earn 10 million yen a year,* and can't be bothered with the people (or animals) around her. One day, however, she does a favor for the mega-problem-child, Haru Yoshida, who sits next to her in school, and he ends up developing a crush on her.

At first she thought he was "incomprehensible and scary," but when she sees his innocent and kind side, she eventually falls for him, too.

When she tells him her feelings, though, he ends up turning her down!!

But still, he asks her to spend the night...?!

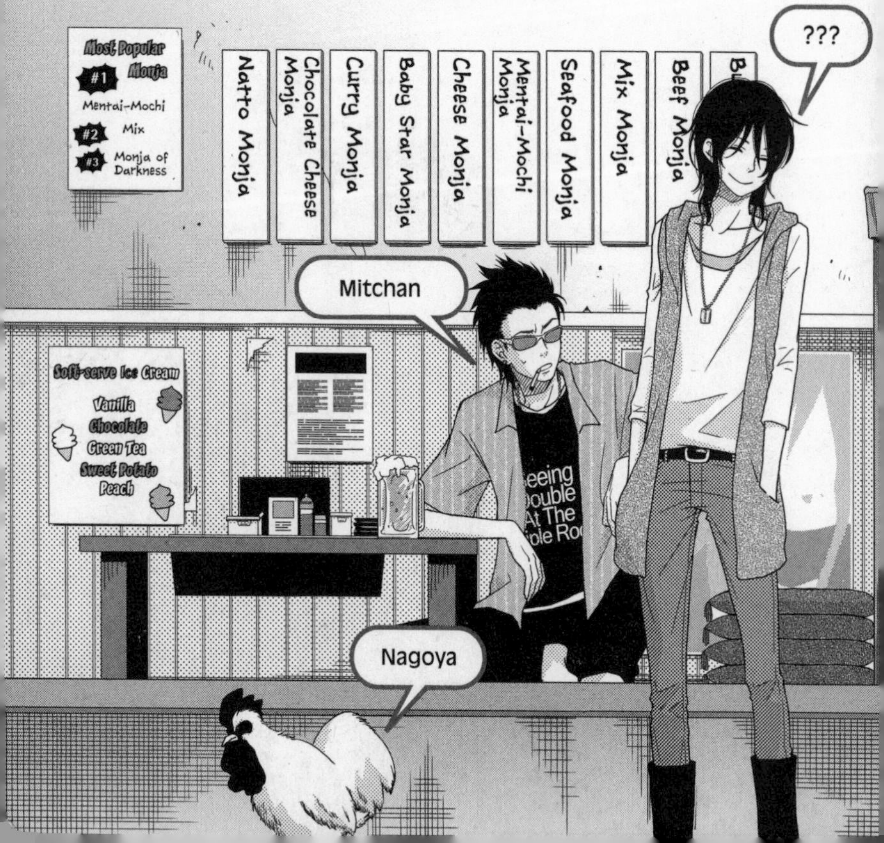

???
Most Popular Monja
#1 Mentai-Mochi
#2 Mix
#3 Monja of Darkness
Natto Monja
Chocolate Cheese Monja
Curry Monja
Baby Star Monja
Cheese Monja
Mentai-Mochi Monja
Seafood Monja
Mix Monja
Beef Monja
Mitchan
Soft-serve Ice Cream
Vanilla
Chocolate
Green Tea
Sweet Potato
Peach
Nagoya

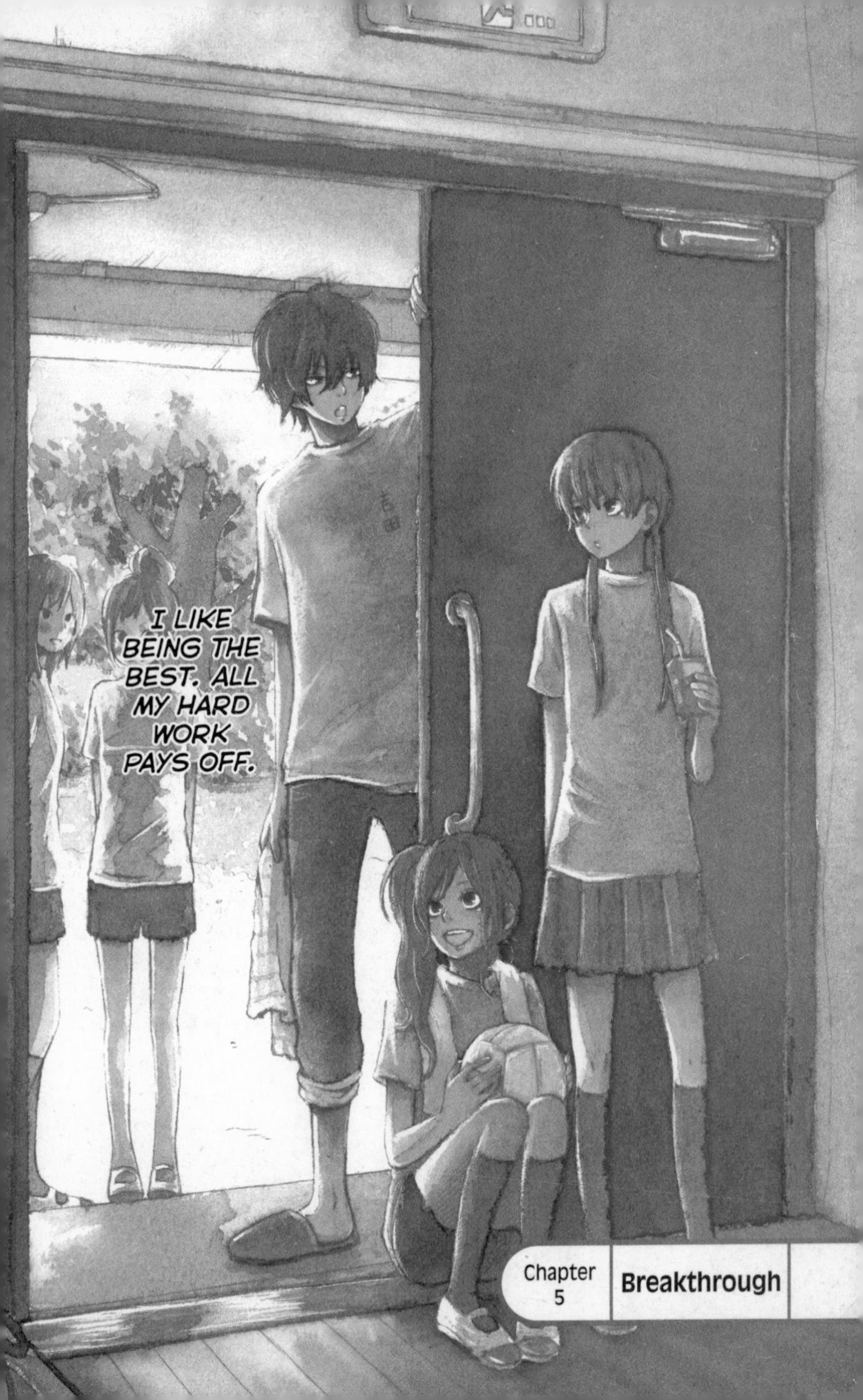
I LIKE BEING THE BEST. ALL MY HARD WORK PAYS OFF.
Chapter 5
Breakthrough

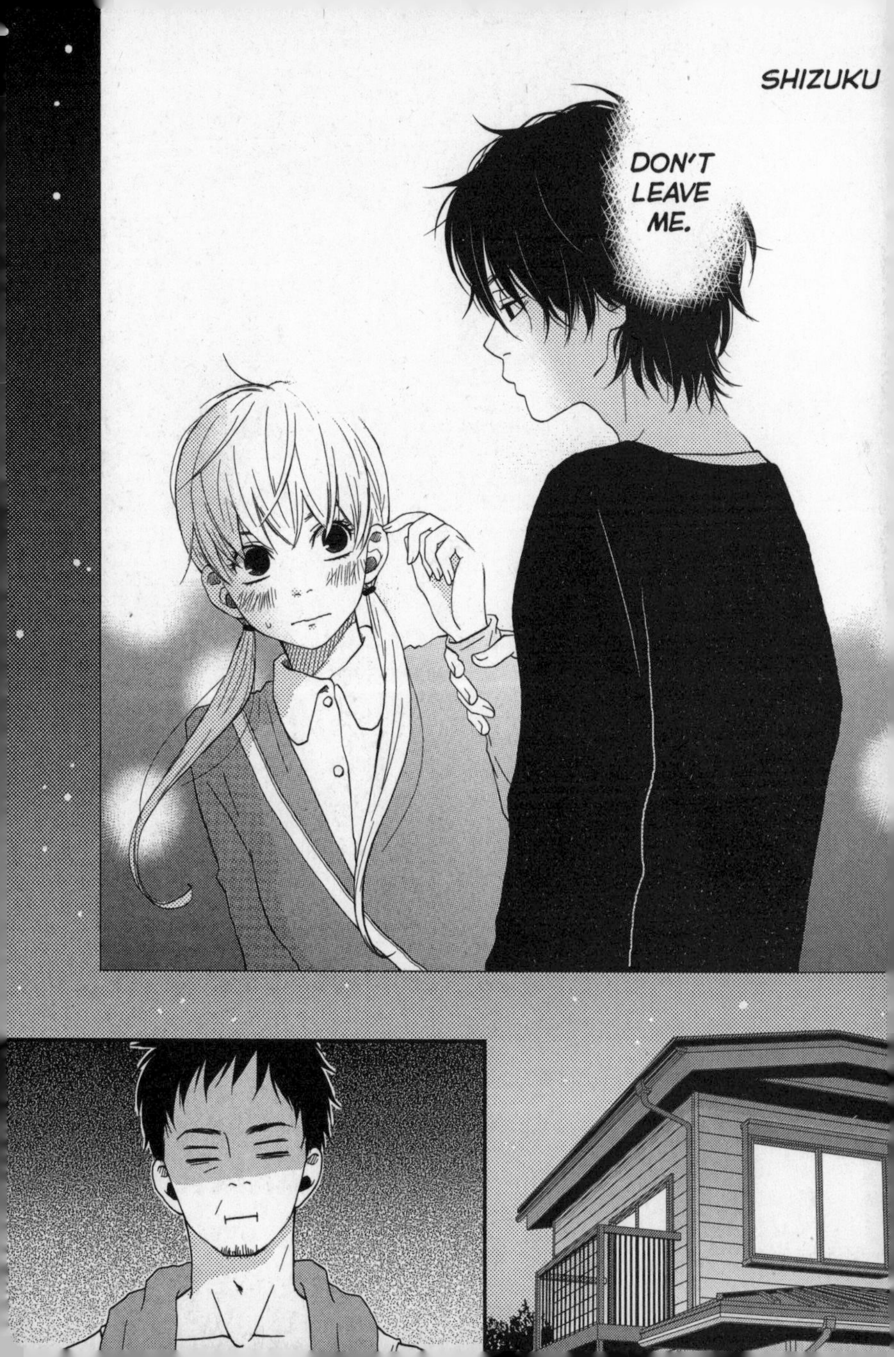
SHIZUKU
DON'T LEAVE ME.

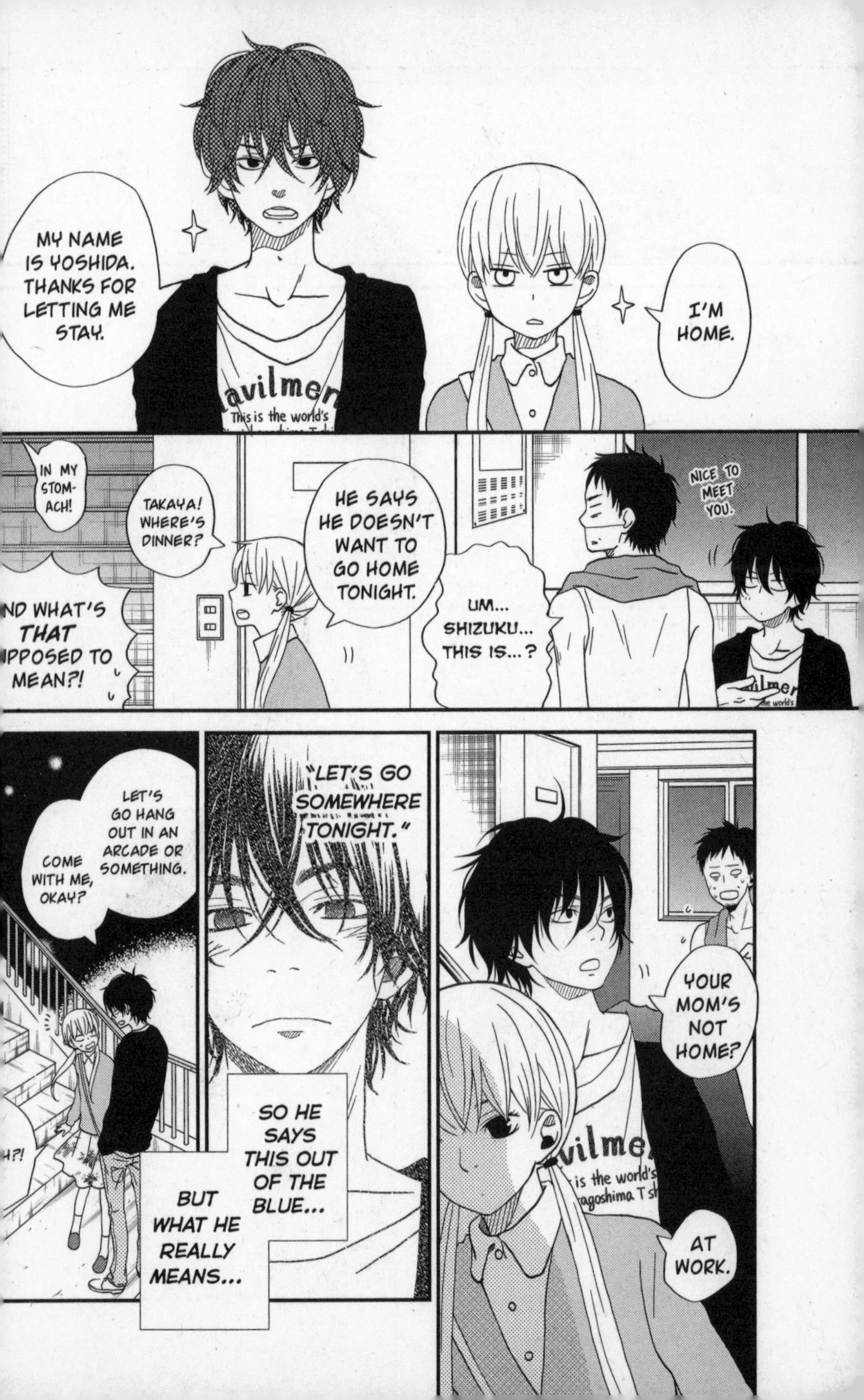
I'M HOME.
MY NAME IS YOSHIDA. THANKS FOR LETTING ME STAY.
NICE TO MEET YOU.
UM... SHIZUKU... THIS IS...?
HE SAYS HE DOESN'T WANT TO GO HOME TONIGHT.
TAKAYA! WHERE'S DINNER?
IN MY STOMACH!
ND WHAT'S THAT IPPOSED TO MEAN?!
YOUR MOM'S NOT HOME?
AT WORK.
"LET'S GO SOMEWHERE TONIGHT."
SO HE SAYS THIS OUT OF THE BLUE...
BUT WHAT HE REALLY MEANS...
LET'S GO HANG OUT IN AN ARCADE OR SOMETHING.
COME WITH ME, OKAY?
H?!

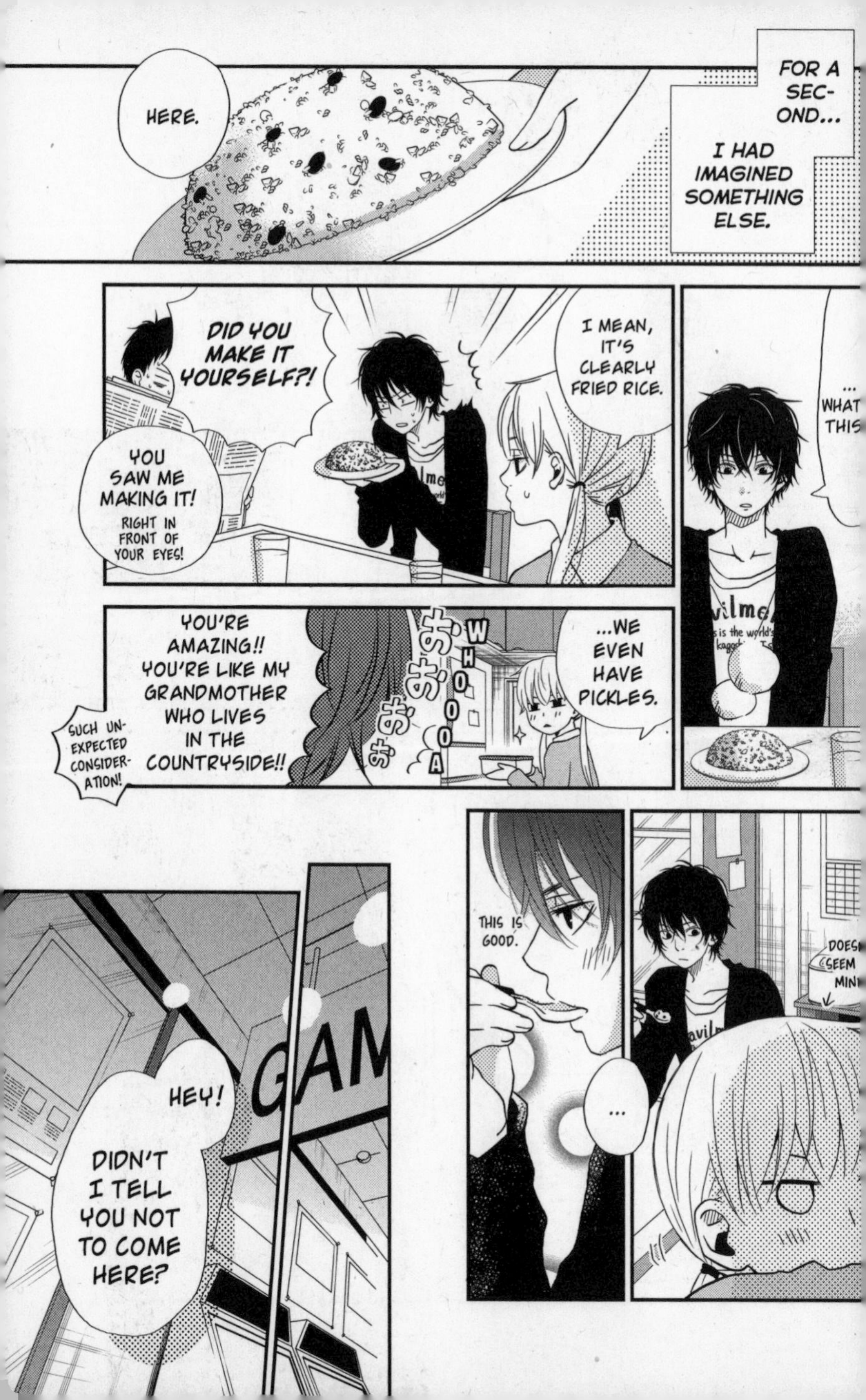
FOR A SEC-OND...
I HAD IMAGINED SOMETHING ELSE.
HERE.
...WHAT THIS
I MEAN, IT'S CLEARLY FRIED RICE.
DID YOU MAKE IT YOURSELF?!
YOU SAW ME MAKING IT!
RIGHT IN FRONT OF YOUR EYES!
...WE EVEN HAVE PICKLES.
おおおお
WHOOOOA
YOU'RE AMAZING!! YOU'RE LIKE MY GRANDMOTHER WHO LIVES IN THE COUNTRYSIDE!!
SUCH UN-EXPECTED CONSIDER-ATION!
DOES SEEM MIN
THIS IS GOOD.
...
GAM
HEY!
DIDN'T I TELL YOU NOT TO COME HERE?

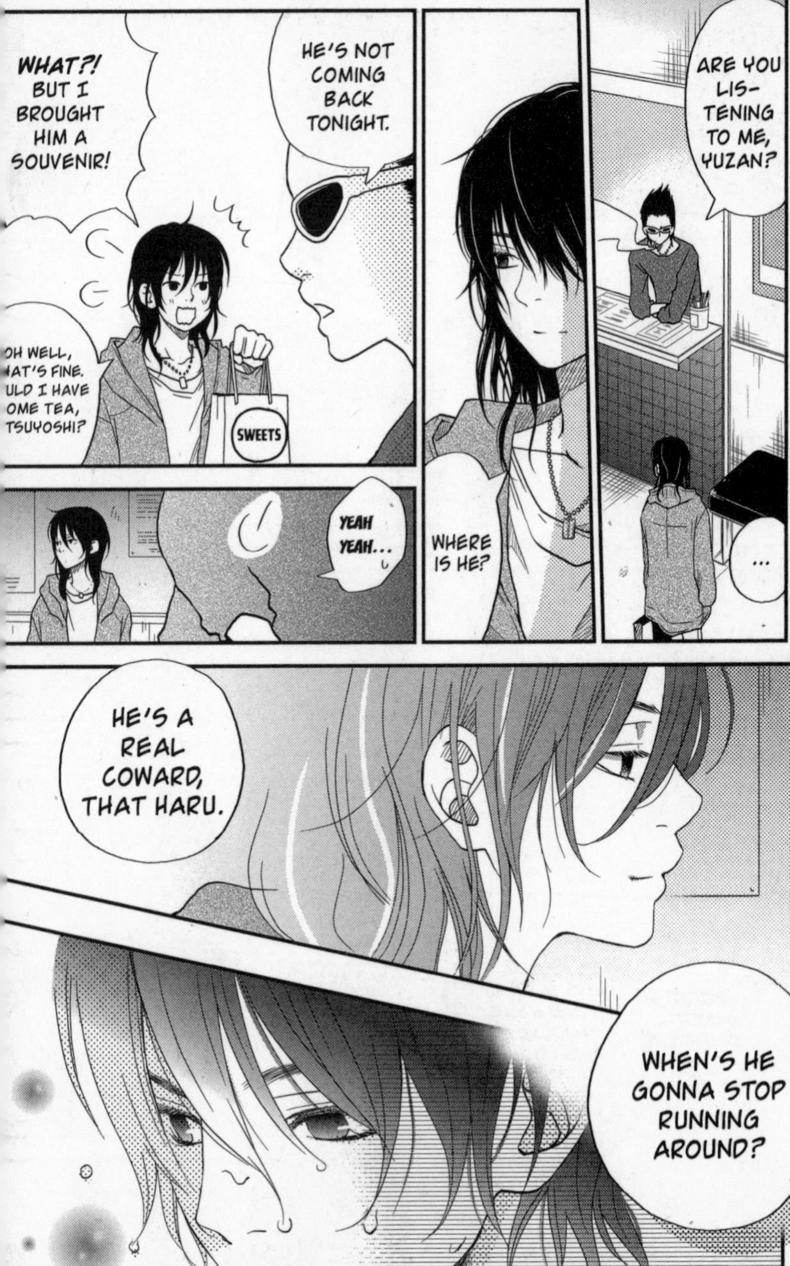
ARE YOU LIS- TENING TO ME, YUZAN?
...
WHERE IS HE?
HE'S NOT COMING BACK TONIGHT.
WHAT?! BUT I BROUGHT HIM A SOUVENIR!
SWEETS
OH WELL, HAT'S FINE. ULD I HAVE OME TEA, TSUYOSHI?
YEAH YEAH...
HE'S A REAL COWARD, THAT HARU.
WHEN'S HE GONNA STOP RUNNING AROUND?

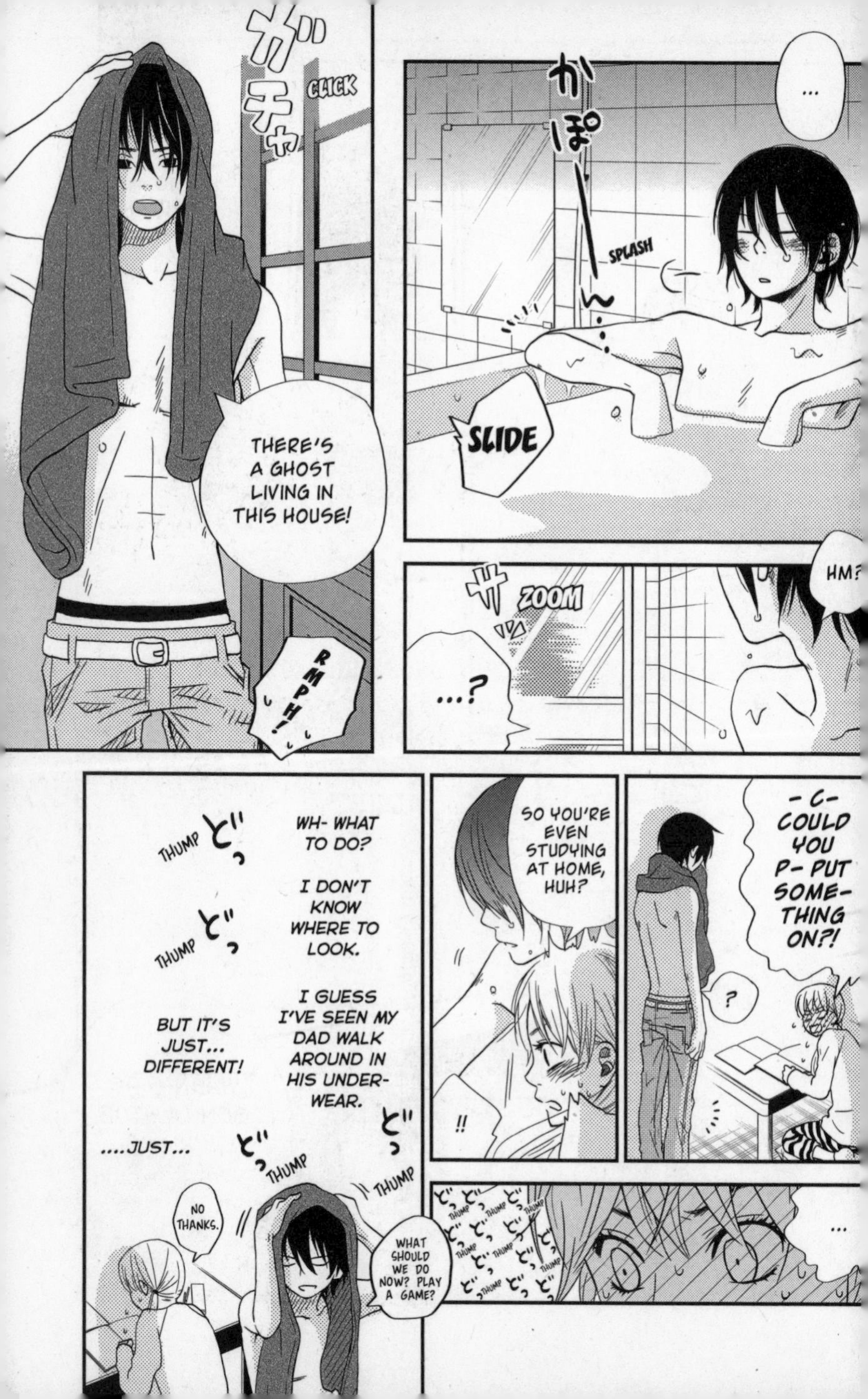
...
かぽーん
SPLASH
SLIDE
HM?
ザ
ZOOM
...?
ガチャ
CLICK
THERE'S A GHOST LIVING IN THIS HOUSE!
RMPH!
- C- COULD YOU P- PUT SOME-THING ON?!
?
SO YOU'RE EVEN STUDYING AT HOME, HUH?
!!
...
THUMP
WH- WHAT TO DO?
I DON'T KNOW WHERE TO LOOK.
THUMP
THUMP
I GUESS I'VE SEEN MY DAD WALK AROUND IN HIS UNDER-WEAR.
BUT IT'S JUST... DIFFERENT!
....JUST...
THUMP
THUMP
WHAT SHOULD WE DO NOW? PLAY A GAME?
NO THANKS.

JUST A PEEK...!!

THUMP THUMP

BLUSH

IF YOU'RE GOING TO SLEEP, SLEEP ON THE FUTON.

TEE-HEE-HEE

くか SNORE

devilment
This is the world's
first kagoshi-♥ t-shirt

devilment
This is the world's
first kagoshi-♥ t-shirt

...

JEEZ.

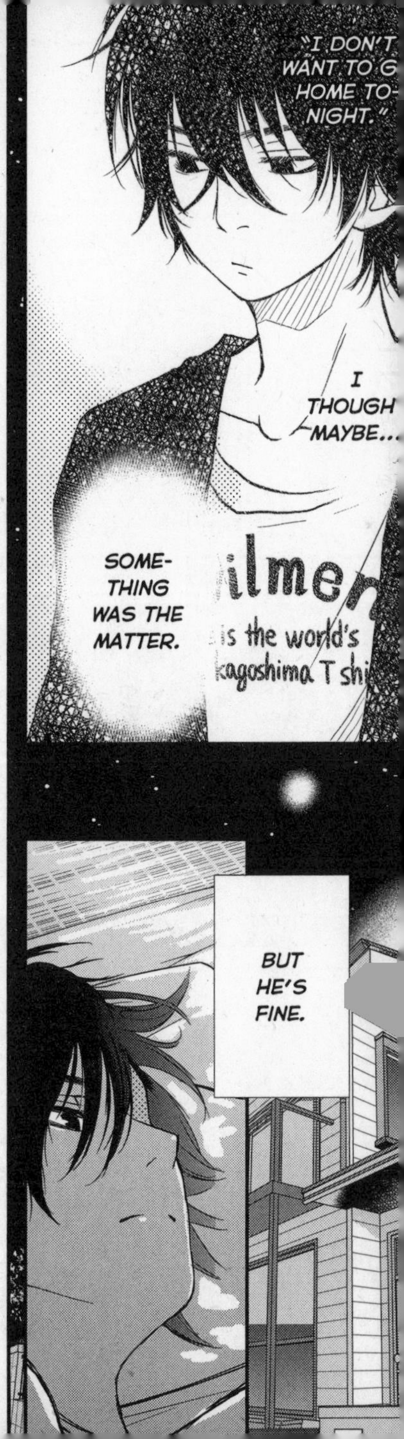
"I DON'T WANT TO G HOME TO-NIGHT."
I THOUGH MAYBE...
SOME-THING WAS THE MATTER.
is the world's
kagoshima T shi
BUT HE'S FINE.

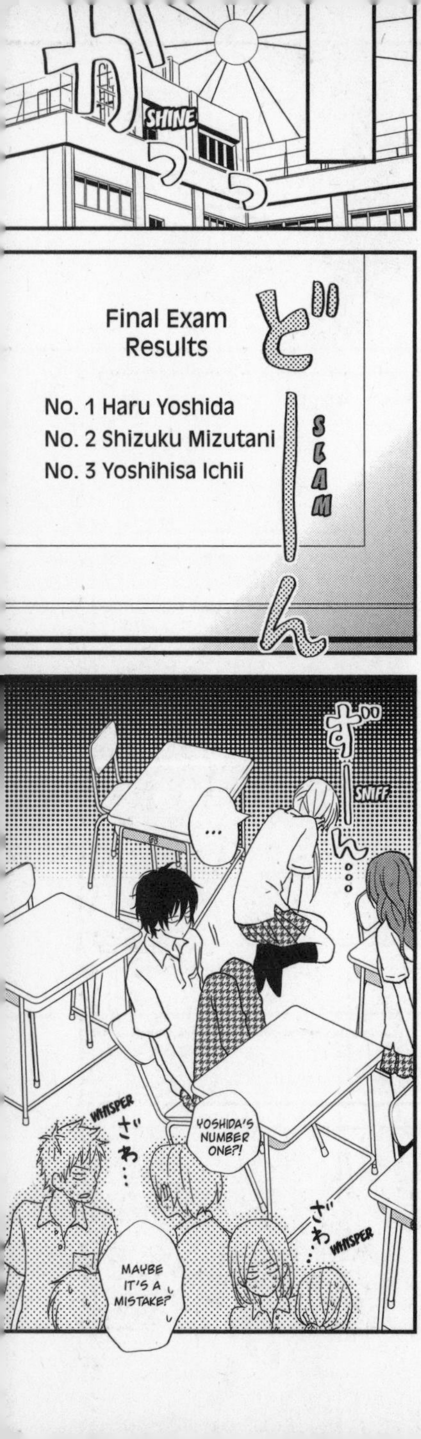
わっっ
SHINE
Final Exam Results
No. 1 Haru Yoshida
No. 2 Shizuku Mizutani
No. 3 Yoshihisa Ichii
どーん
SLAM
ずーん...
SNIFF
...
YOSHIDA'S NUMBER ONE?!
ざわ...
WHISPER
ざわ...
WHISPER
MAYBE IT'S A MISTAKE?

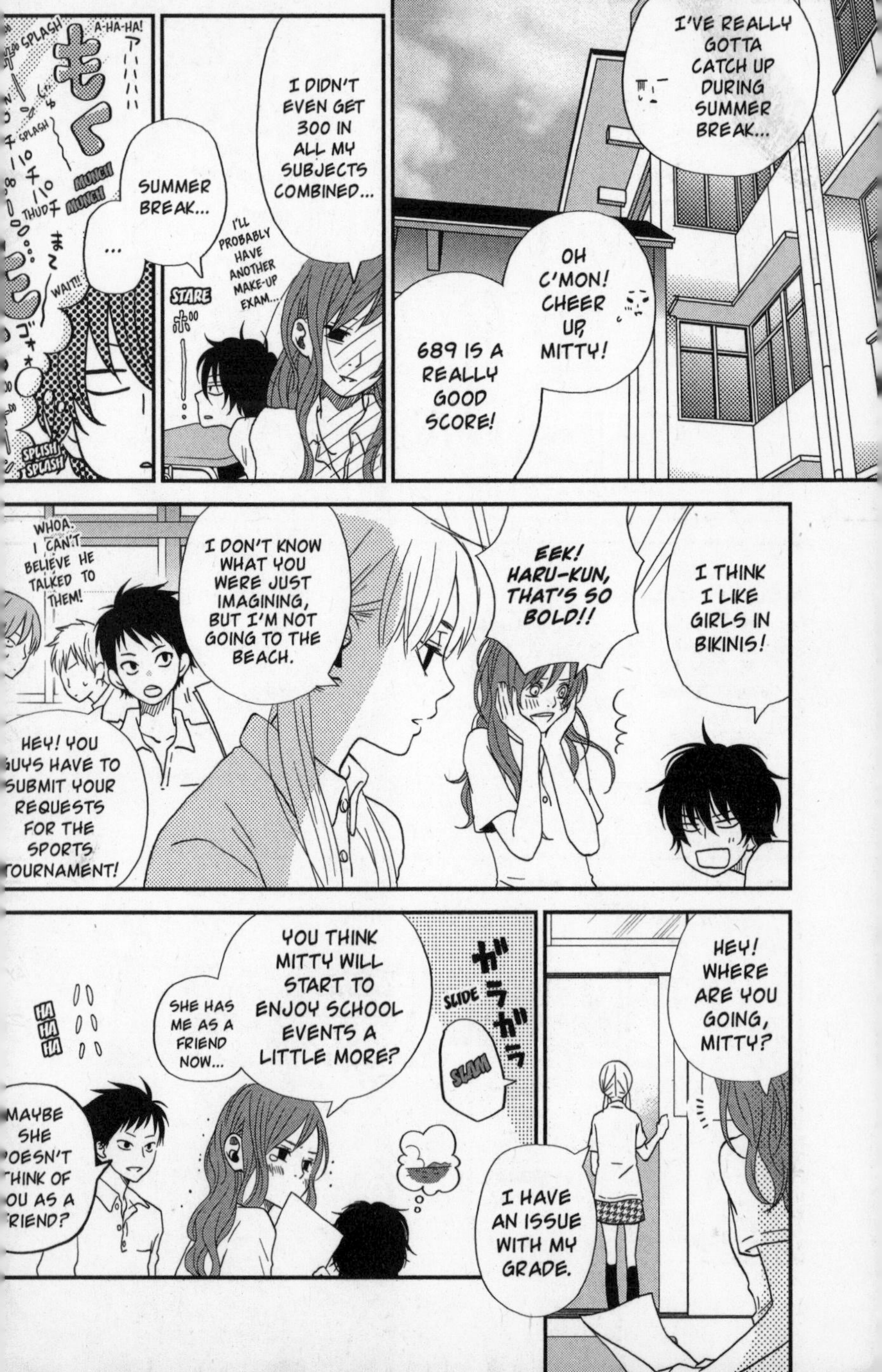
I'VE REALLY GOTTA CATCH UP DURING SUMMER BREAK...
OH C'MON! CHEER UP, MITTY!
689 IS A REALLY GOOD SCORE!
I DIDN'T EVEN GET 300 IN ALL MY SUBJECTS COMBINED...
I'LL PROBABLY HAVE ANOTHER MAKE-UP EXAM...
STARE
SUMMER BREAK...
...
A-HA-HA!
SPLASH
SPLASH
MUNCH MUNCH
THUD
WAIT!!
SPLASH SPLASH
I THINK I LIKE GIRLS IN BIKINIS!
EEK! HARU-KUN, THAT'S SO BOLD!!
I DON'T KNOW WHAT YOU WERE JUST IMAGINING, BUT I'M NOT GOING TO THE BEACH.
WHOA. I CAN'T BELIEVE HE TALKED TO THEM!
HEY! YOU UYS HAVE TO SUBMIT YOUR REQUESTS FOR THE SPORTS OURNAMENT!
HEY! WHERE ARE YOU GOING, MITTY?
I HAVE AN ISSUE WITH MY GRADE.
SLIDE
SLAM
YOU THINK MITTY WILL START TO ENJOY SCHOOL EVENTS A LITTLE MORE?
SHE HAS ME AS A FRIEND NOW...
HA HA HA
MAYBE SHE OESN'T THINK OF OU AS A RIEND?

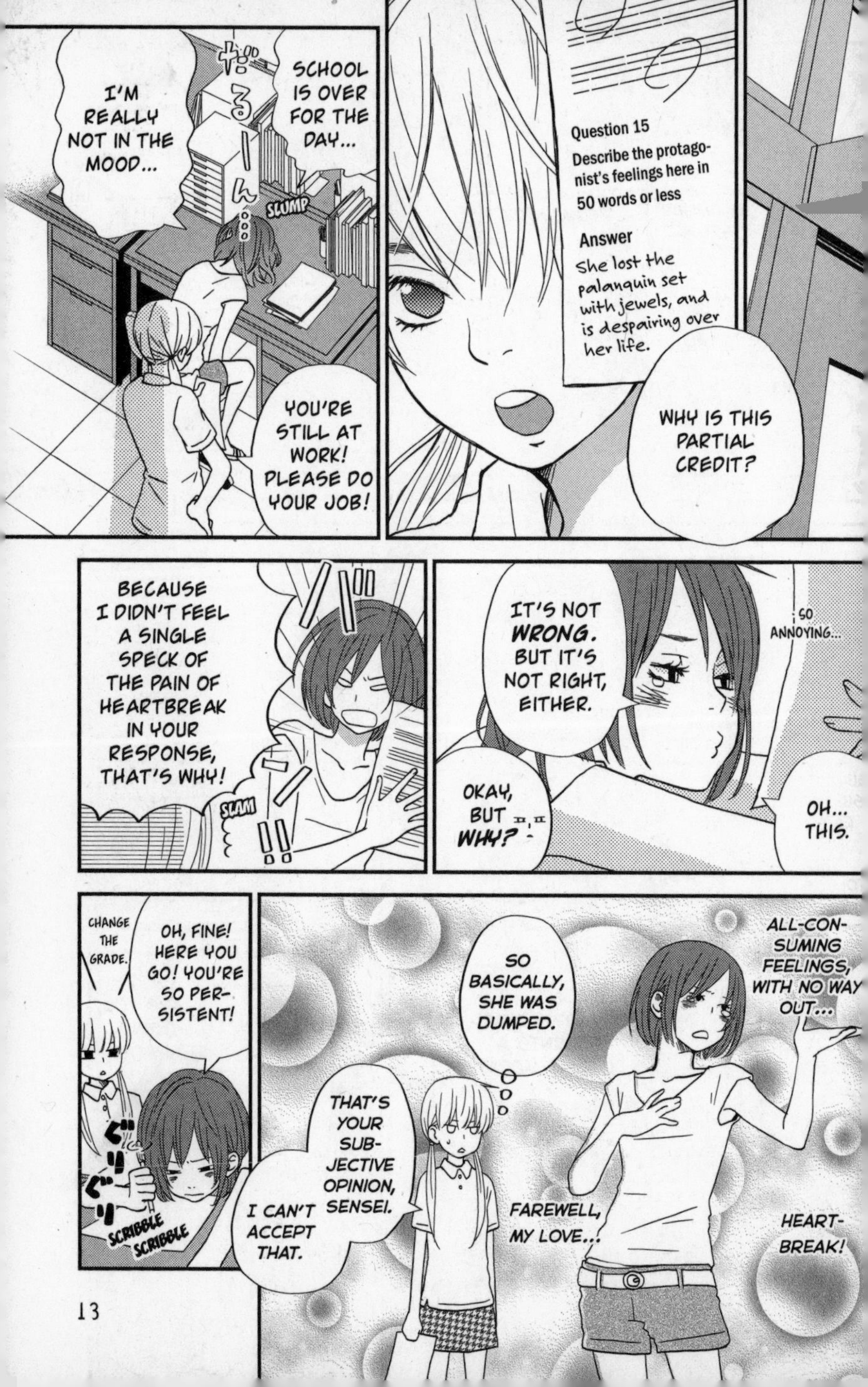
Question 15
Describe the protagonist's feelings here in 50 words or less
Answer
She lost the palanquin set with jewels, and is despairing over her life.
WHY IS THIS PARTIAL CREDIT?
SCHOOL IS OVER FOR THE DAY...
I'M REALLY NOT IN THE MOOD...
SLUMP
YOU'RE STILL AT WORK! PLEASE DO YOUR JOB!
SO ANNOYING...
IT'S NOT **WRONG.** BUT IT'S NOT RIGHT, EITHER.
OH... THIS.
OKAY, BUT **WHY?**
BECAUSE I DIDN'T FEEL A SINGLE SPECK OF THE PAIN OF HEARTBREAK IN YOUR RESPONSE, THAT'S WHY!
SLAM
ALL-CONSUMING FEELINGS, WITH NO WAY OUT...
SO BASICALLY, SHE WAS DUMPED.
HEART-BREAK!
FAREWELL, MY LOVE...
THAT'S YOUR SUBJECTIVE OPINION, SENSEI.
I CAN'T ACCEPT THAT.
OH, FINE! HERE YOU GO! YOU'RE SO PERSISTENT!
CHANGE THE GRADE.
SCRIBBLE SCRIBBLE

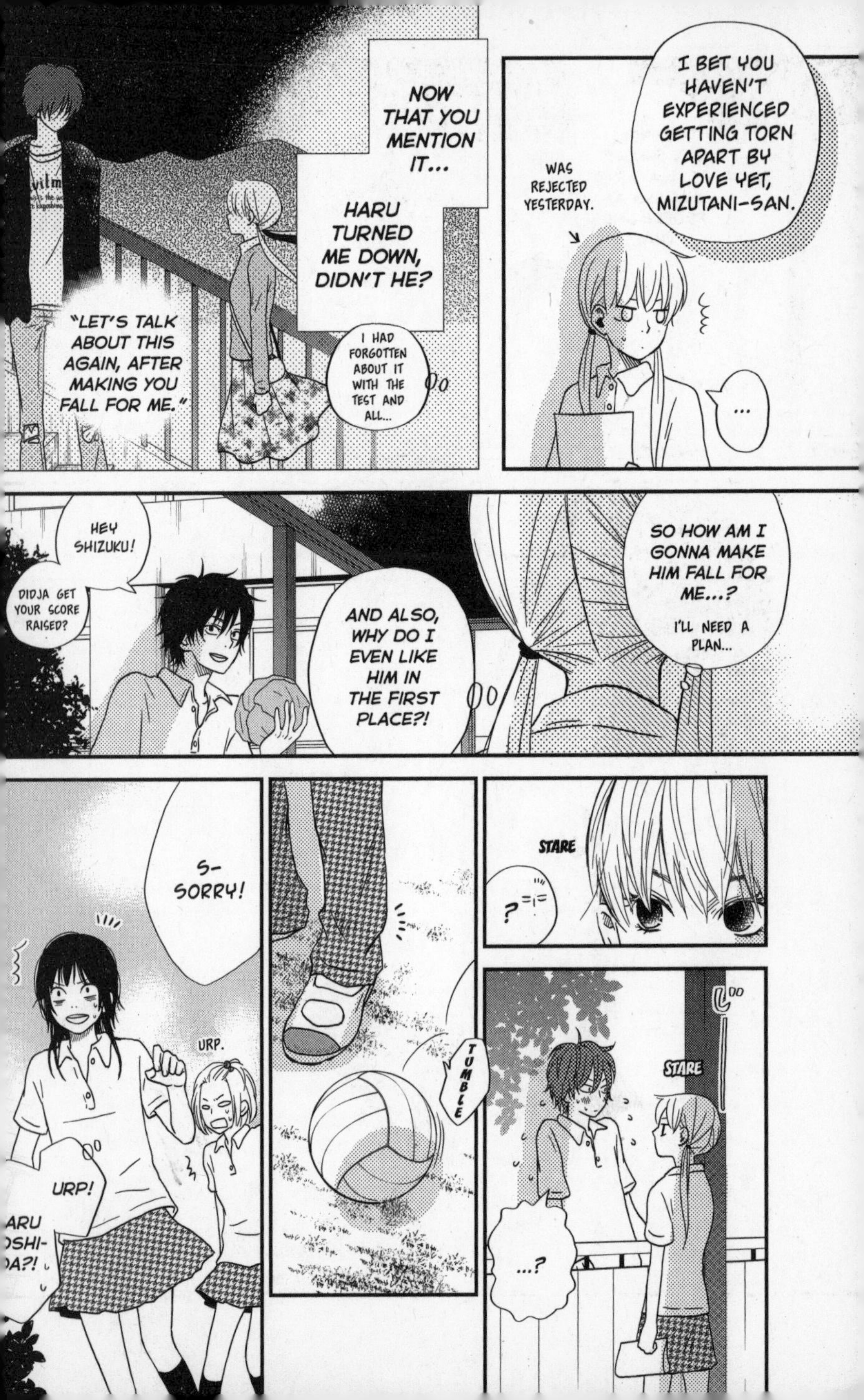
I BET YOU HAVEN'T EXPERIENCED GETTING TORN APART BY LOVE YET, MIZUTANI-SAN.
WAS REJECTED YESTERDAY.
...
NOW THAT YOU MENTION IT...
HARU TURNED ME DOWN, DIDN'T HE?
I HAD FORGOTTEN ABOUT IT WITH THE TEST AND ALL...
"LET'S TALK ABOUT THIS AGAIN, AFTER MAKING YOU FALL FOR ME."
SO HOW AM I GONNA MAKE HIM FALL FOR ME...?
I'LL NEED A PLAN...
AND ALSO, WHY DO I EVEN LIKE HIM IN THE FIRST PLACE?!
HEY SHIZUKU!
DIDJA GET YOUR SCORE RAISED?
STARE
?
STARE
...?
TUMBLE
S-SORRY!
URP.
URP!
ARU OSHI-DA?!

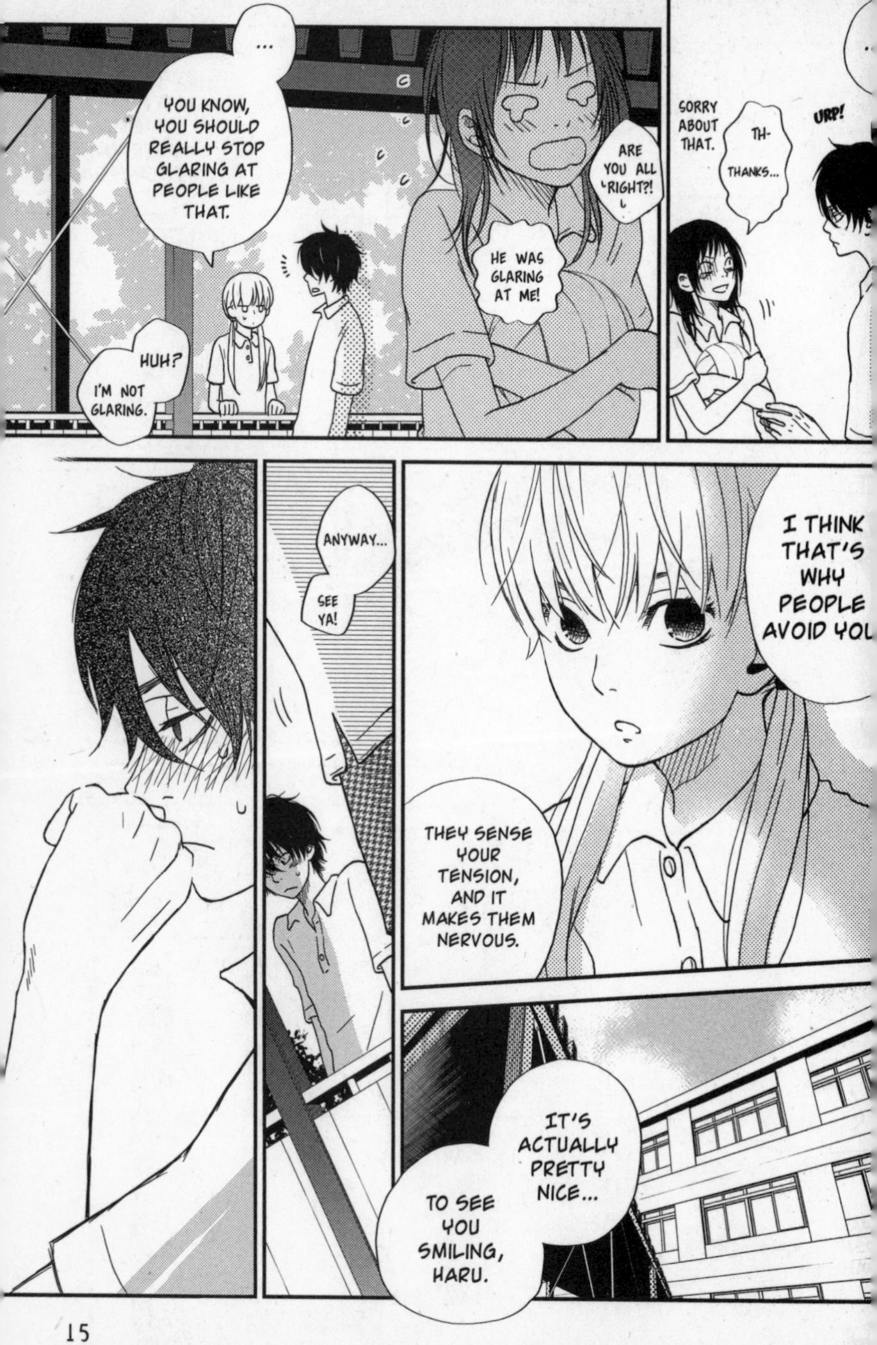
...
URP!
TH- THANKS...
SORRY ABOUT THAT.
ARE YOU ALL RIGHT?!
HE WAS GLARING AT ME!
...
YOU KNOW, YOU SHOULD REALLY STOP GLARING AT PEOPLE LIKE THAT.
HUH?
I'M NOT GLARING.
I THINK THAT'S WHY PEOPLE AVOID YOU
THEY SENSE YOUR TENSION, AND IT MAKES THEM NERVOUS.
IT'S ACTUALLY PRETTY NICE...
TO SEE YOU SMILING, HARU.
ANYWAY...
SEE YA!

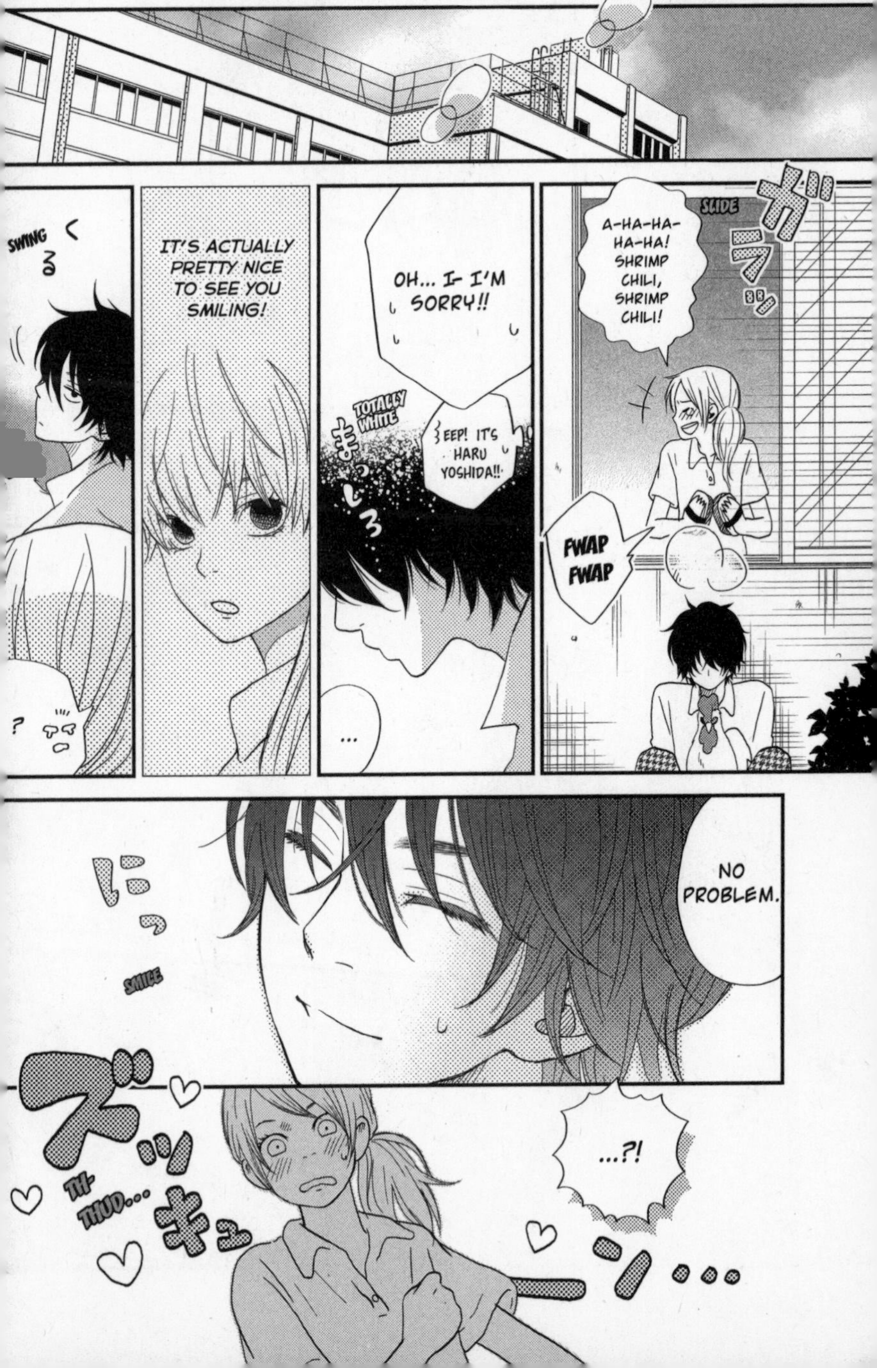
ガラッ
SLIDE
A-HA-HA-HA-HA! SHRIMP CHILI, SHRIMP CHILI!
FWAP FWAP
OH... I- I'M SORRY!!
EEP! IT'S HARU YOSHIDA!!
TOTALLY WHITE
まっしろ
...
IT'S ACTUALLY PRETTY NICE TO SEE YOU SMILING!
SWING
くる
?
NO PROBLEM.
にっ
SMILE
...?!
ズッキューン...
TH-THUD...

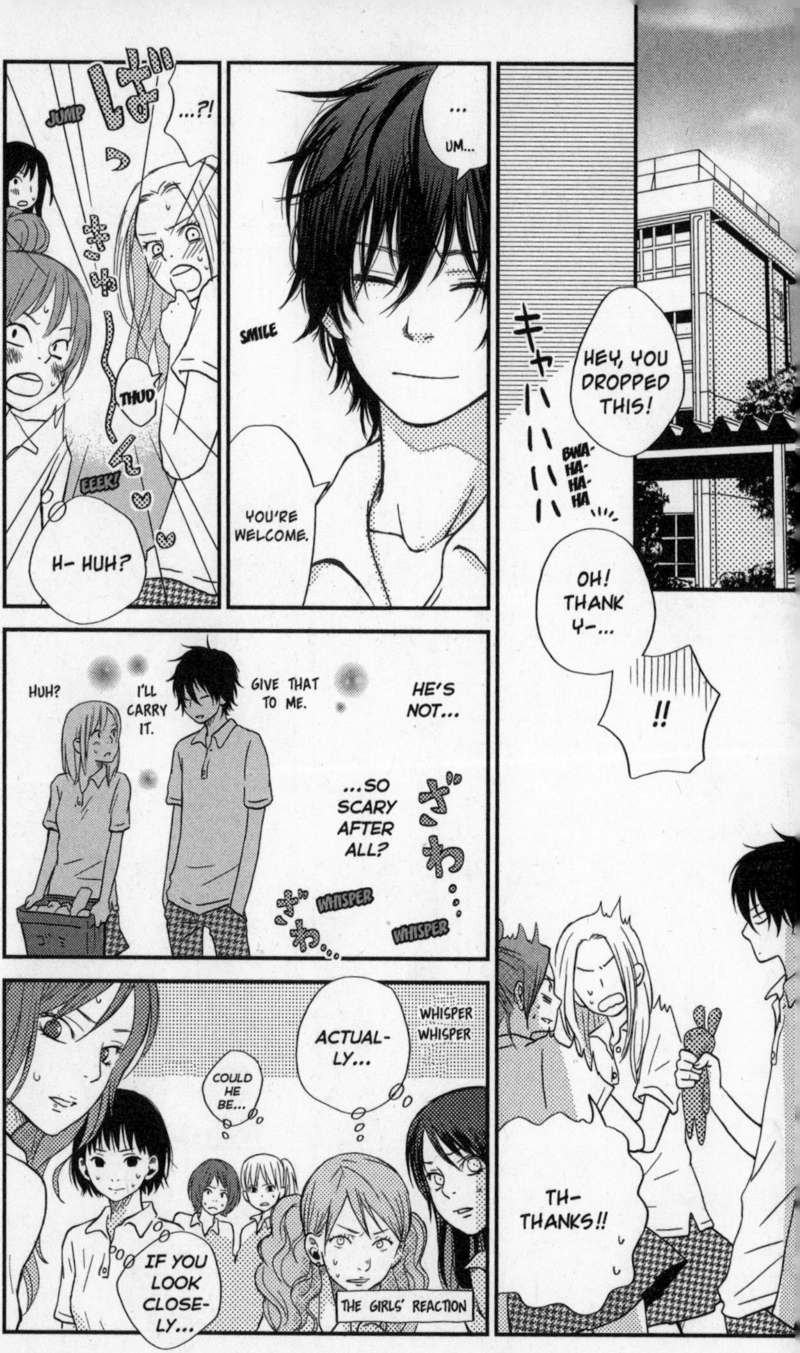
HEY, YOU DROPPED THIS!
キャハハハ
BWA-HA-HA-HA
OH! THANK Y-...
!!
TH-THANKS!!
...
UM...
SMILE
YOU'RE WELCOME.
JUMP
...?!
THUD
EEEK!
H- HUH?
HE'S NOT...
GIVE THAT TO ME.
I'LL CARRY IT.
HUH?
...SO SCARY AFTER ALL?
ざわ
WHISPER
ざわ
WHISPER
WHISPER WHISPER
ACTUAL-LY...
COULD HE BE...
IF YOU LOOK CLOSE-LY...
THE GIRLS' REACTION

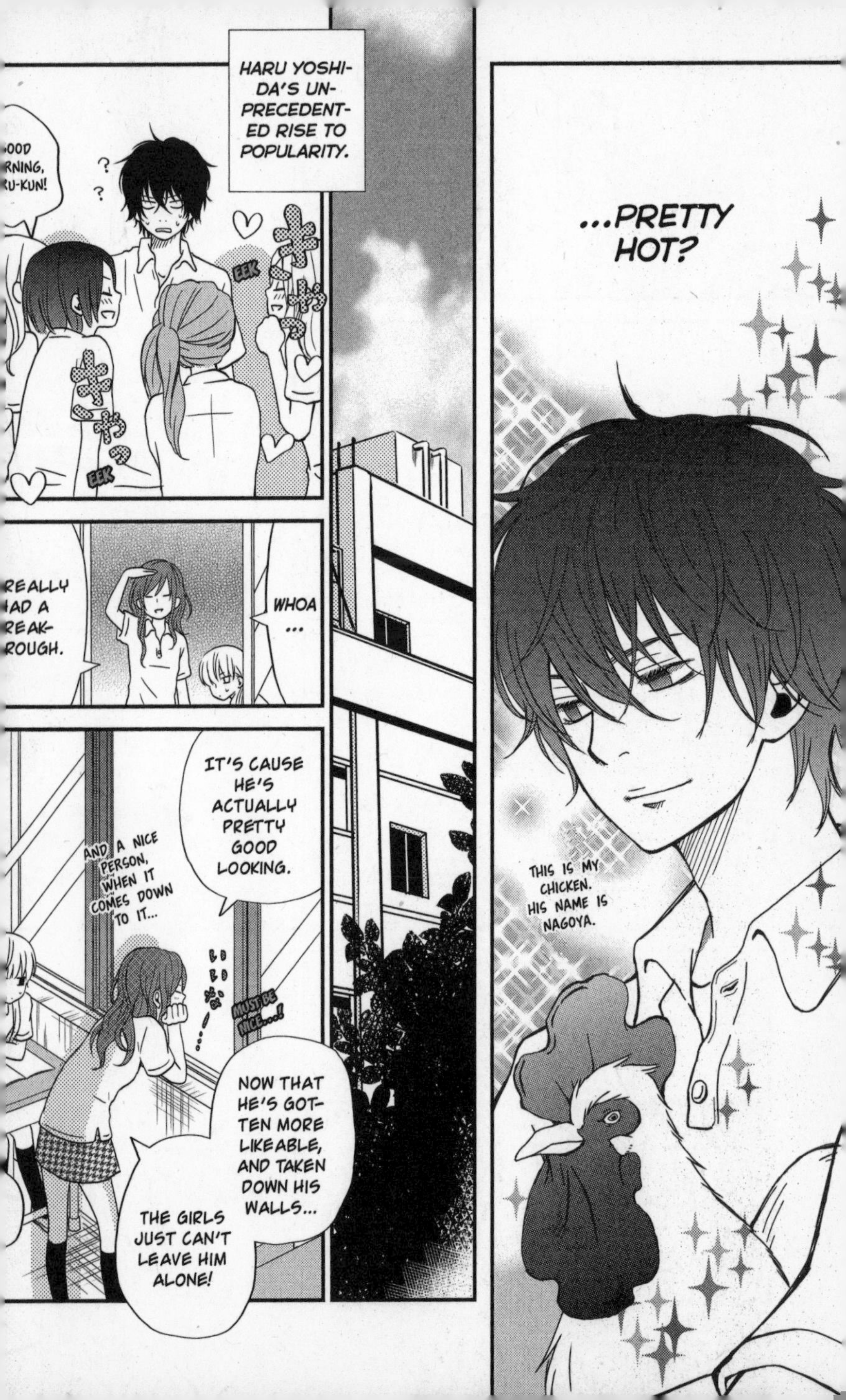...PRETTY HOT?
THIS IS MY CHICKEN. HIS NAME IS NAGOYA.
HARU YOSHIDA'S UNPRECEDENTED RISE TO POPULARITY.
OOD
RNING,
RU-KUN!
?
?
EEK
EEK
WHOA ...
REALLY
IAD A
REAK-
ROUGH.
IT'S CAUSE HE'S ACTUALLY PRETTY GOOD LOOKING.
AND A NICE PERSON, WHEN IT COMES DOWN TO IT...
MUST BE NICE...!
NOW THAT HE'S GOTTEN MORE LIKEABLE, AND TAKEN DOWN HIS WALLS...
THE GIRLS JUST CAN'T LEAVE HIM ALONE!

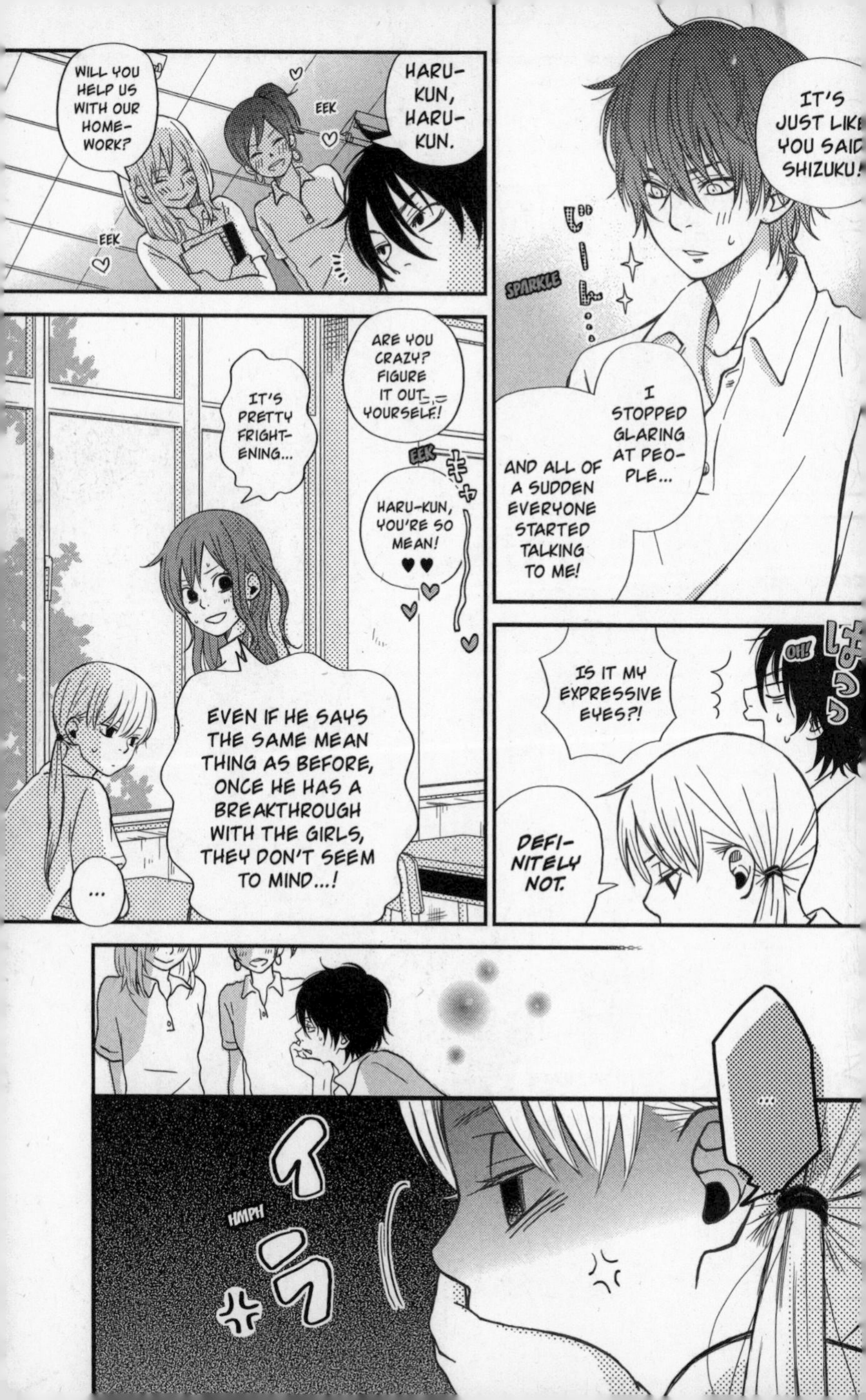

IT'S JUST LIKE YOU SAID SHIZUKU!
じーん…
SPARKLE
I STOPPED GLARING AT PEOPLE...
AND ALL OF A SUDDEN EVERYONE STARTED TALKING TO ME!
HARU-KUN, HARU-KUN.
EEK
WILL YOU HELP US WITH OUR HOMEWORK?
EEK
ARE YOU CRAZY? FIGURE IT OUT YOURSELF!
EEK
キャ
HARU-KUN, YOU'RE SO MEAN!
IT'S PRETTY FRIGHTENING...
EVEN IF HE SAYS THE SAME MEAN THING AS BEFORE, ONCE HE HAS A BREAKTHROUGH WITH THE GIRLS, THEY DON'T SEEM TO MIND...!
...
はっ
OH!
IS IT MY EXPRESSIVE EYES?!
DEFINITELY NOT.
...
イラ
HMPH

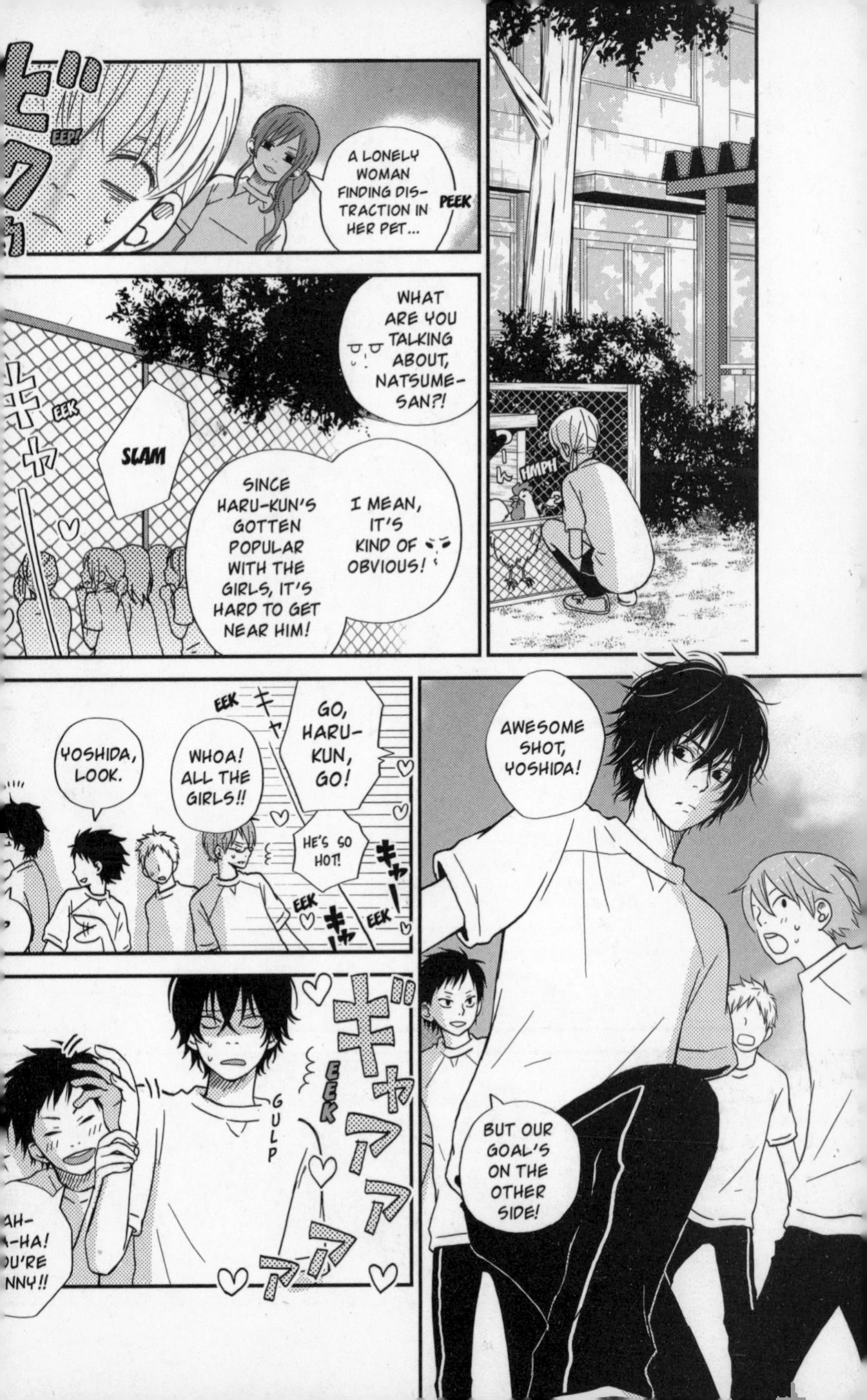
HMPH
EEP!
A LONELY WOMAN FINDING DISTRACTION IN HER PET...
PEEK
WHAT ARE YOU TALKING ABOUT, NATSUME-SAN?!
SLAM
EEK
I MEAN, IT'S KIND OF OBVIOUS!
SINCE HARU-KUN'S GOTTEN POPULAR WITH THE GIRLS, IT'S HARD TO GET NEAR HIM!
AWESOME SHOT, YOSHIDA!
BUT OUR GOAL'S ON THE OTHER SIDE!
EEK
GO, HARU-KUN, GO!
WHOA! ALL THE GIRLS!!
YOSHIDA, LOOK.
HE'S SO HOT!
EEK
EEK
EEK
GULP
AH-
-HA!
OU'RE
NNY!!

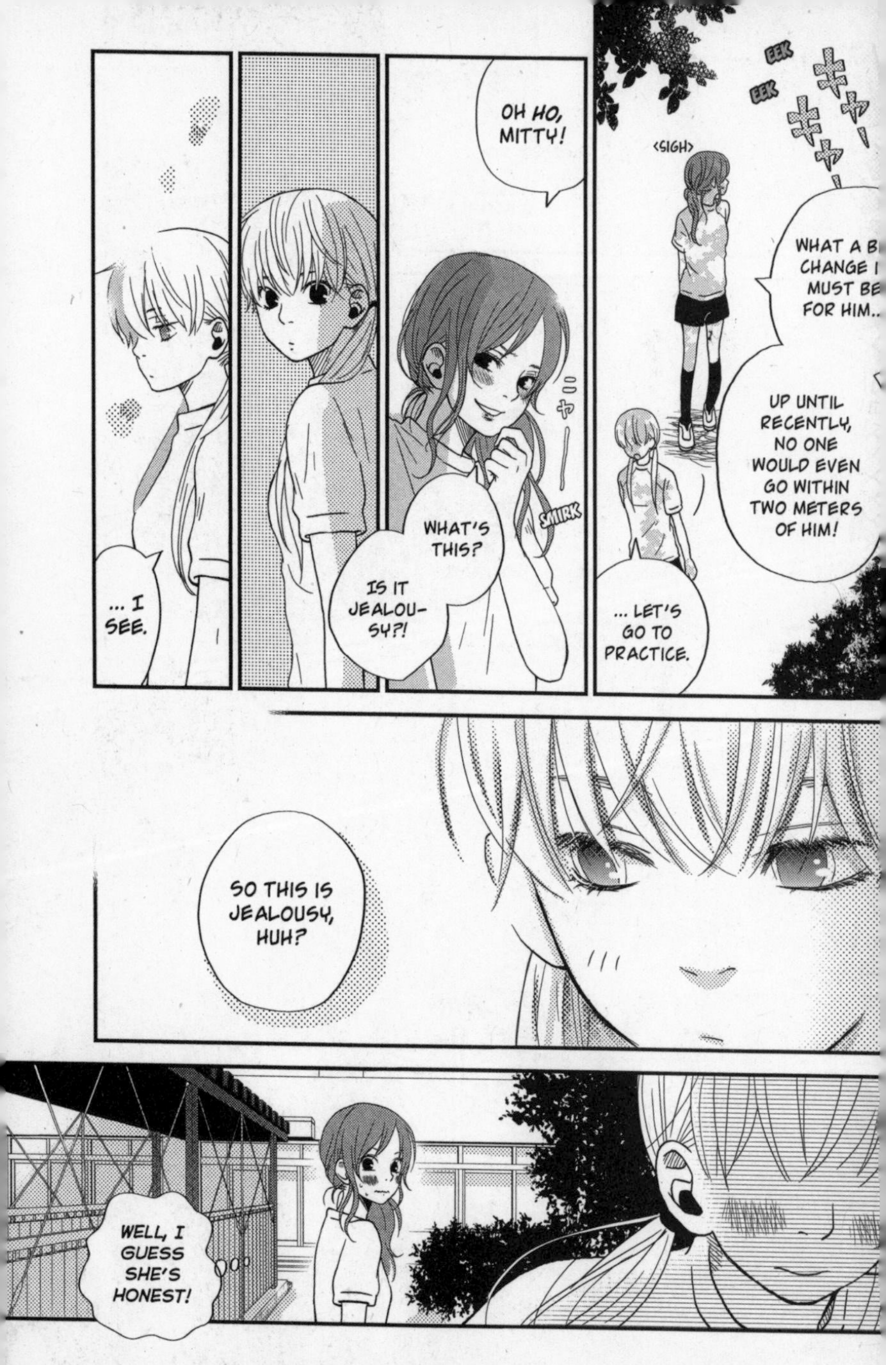
EEK
EEK
<SIGH>
WHAT A B CHANGE I MUST BE FOR HIM..
UP UNTIL RECENTLY, NO ONE WOULD EVEN GO WITHIN TWO METERS OF HIM!
... LET'S GO TO PRACTICE.
OH HO, MITTY!
SMIRK
WHAT'S THIS?
IS IT JEALOU-SY?!
... I SEE.
SO THIS IS JEALOUSY, HUH?
WELL, I GUESS SHE'S HONEST!

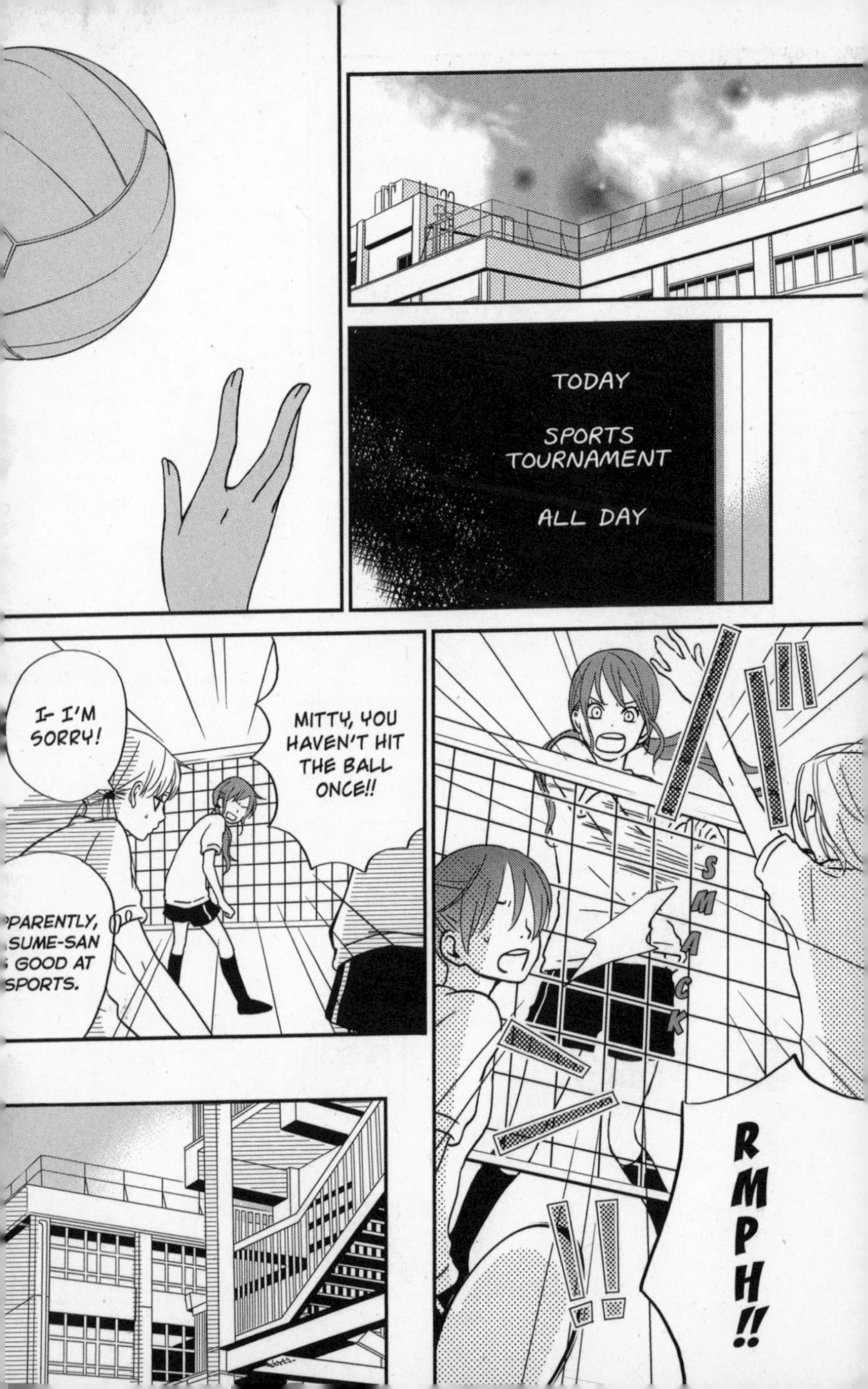
TODAY
SPORTS TOURNAMENT
ALL DAY
SMACK
RMPH!!
!!
MITTY, YOU HAVEN'T HIT THE BALL ONCE!!
I- I'M SORRY!
PPARENTLY,
SUME-SAN
GOOD AT
SPORTS.

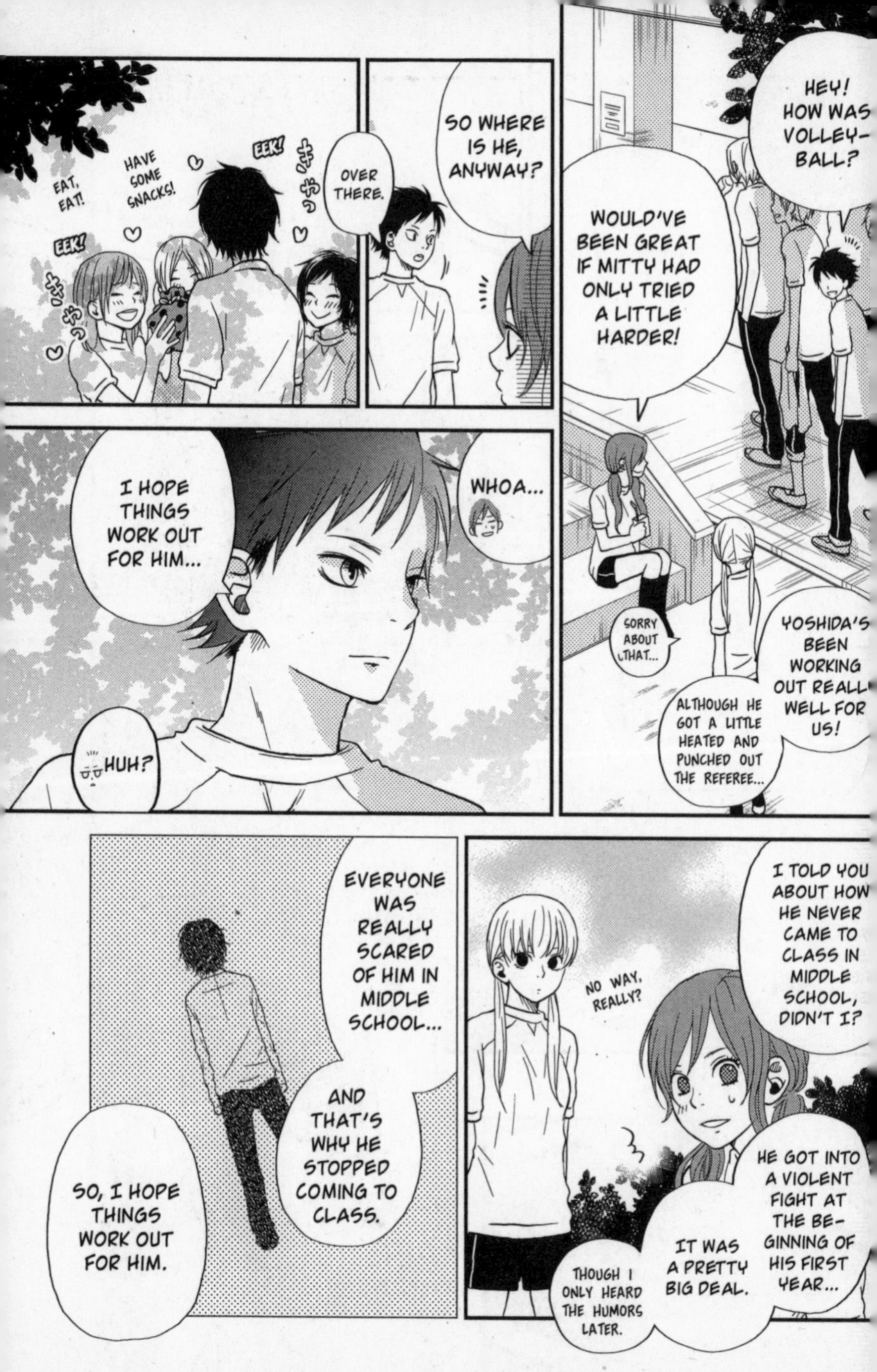
HEY! HOW WAS VOLLEY-BALL?
WOULD'VE BEEN GREAT IF MITTY HAD ONLY TRIED A LITTLE HARDER!
YOSHIDA'S BEEN WORKING OUT REALLY WELL FOR US!
ALTHOUGH HE GOT A LITTLE HEATED AND PUNCHED OUT THE REFEREE...
SORRY ABOUT THAT...
SO WHERE IS HE, ANYWAY?
OVER THERE.
EEK!
HAVE SOME SNACKS!
EAT, EAT!
EEK!
WHOA...
I HOPE THINGS WORK OUT FOR HIM...
HUH?
I TOLD YOU ABOUT HOW HE NEVER CAME TO CLASS IN MIDDLE SCHOOL, DIDN'T I?
NO WAY, REALLY?
HE GOT INTO A VIOLENT FIGHT AT THE BE-GINNING OF HIS FIRST YEAR...
IT WAS A PRETTY BIG DEAL.
THOUGH I ONLY HEARD THE HUMORS LATER.
EVERYONE WAS REALLY SCARED OF HIM IN MIDDLE SCHOOL...
AND THAT'S WHY HE STOPPED COMING TO CLASS.
SO, I HOPE THINGS WORK OUT FOR HIM.

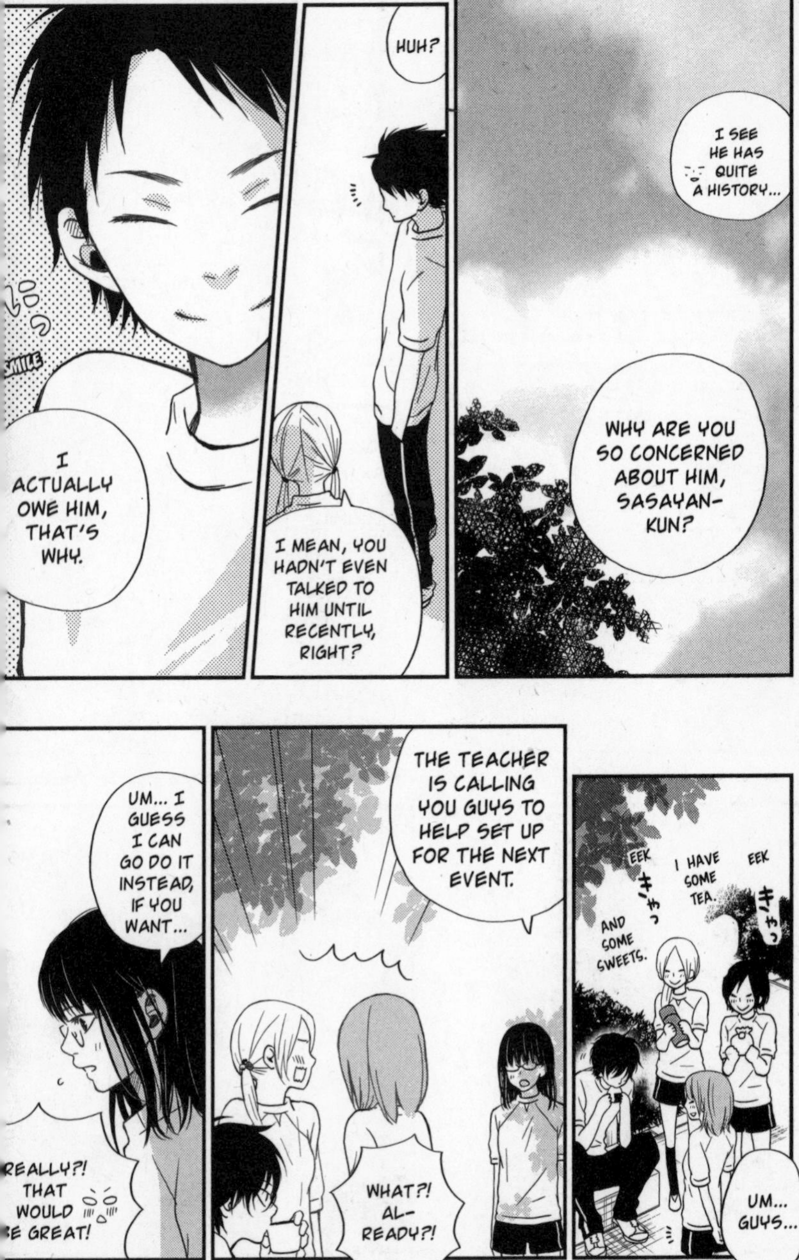
I SEE HE HAS QUITE A HISTORY...
WHY ARE YOU SO CONCERNED ABOUT HIM, SASAYAN-KUN?
HUH?
I MEAN, YOU HADN'T EVEN TALKED TO HIM UNTIL RECENTLY, RIGHT?
SMILE
I ACTUALLY OWE HIM, THAT'S WHY.
EEK
I HAVE SOME TEA.
EEK
AND SOME SWEETS.
UM... GUYS...
THE TEACHER IS CALLING YOU GUYS TO HELP SET UP FOR THE NEXT EVENT.
WHAT?! AL-READY?!
UM... I GUESS I CAN GO DO IT INSTEAD, IF YOU WANT...
REALLY?! THAT WOULD E GREAT!

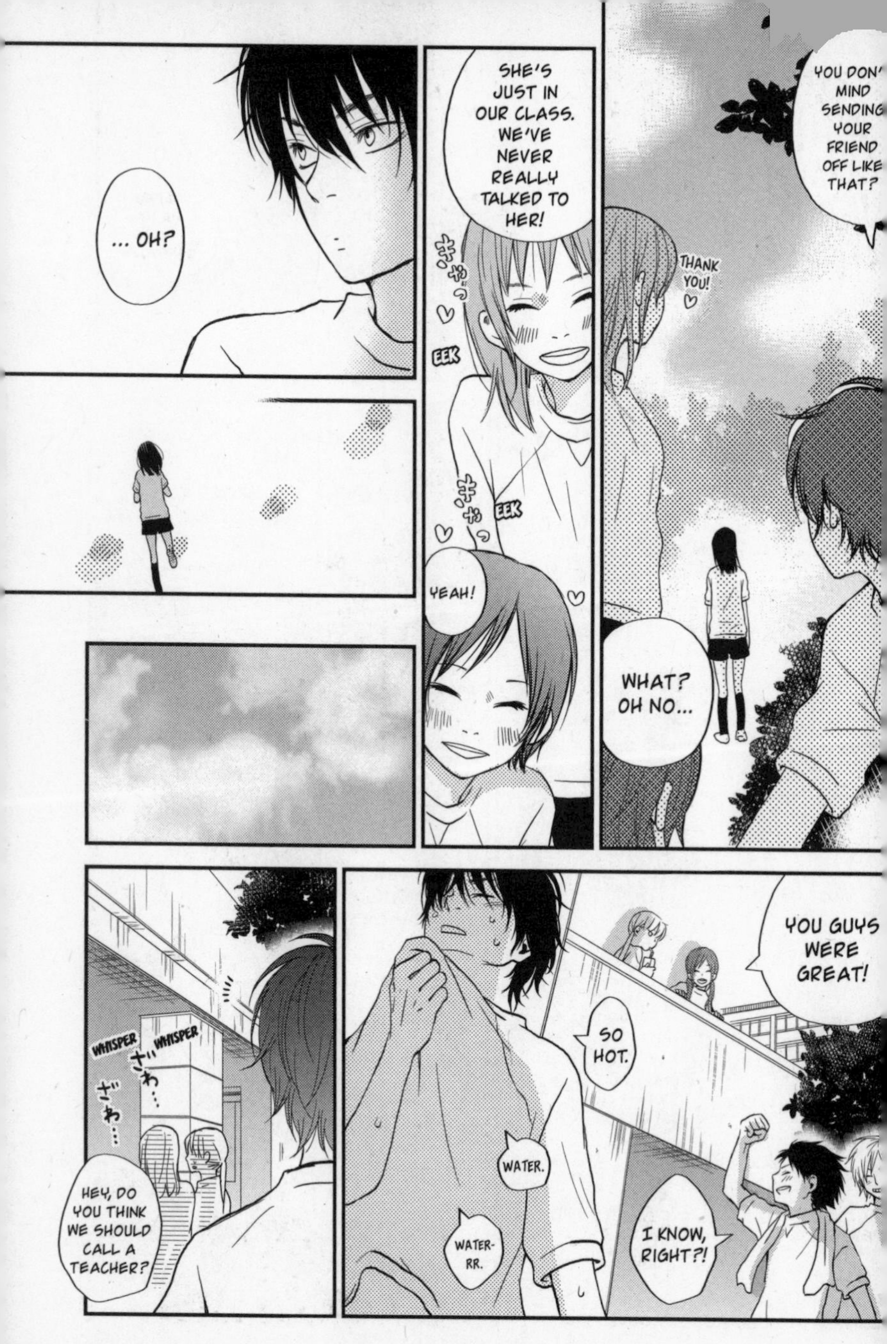
YOU DON'T MIND SENDING YOUR FRIEND OFF LIKE THAT?
THANK YOU!
WHAT? OH NO...
SHE'S JUST IN OUR CLASS. WE'VE NEVER REALLY TALKED TO HER!
EEK
EEK
YEAH!
... OH?
YOU GUYS WERE GREAT!
SO HOT.
I KNOW, RIGHT?!
WATER.
WATER-RR.
WHISPER
WHISPER
ざわ…
ざわ…
HEY, DO YOU THINK WE SHOULD CALL A TEACHER?

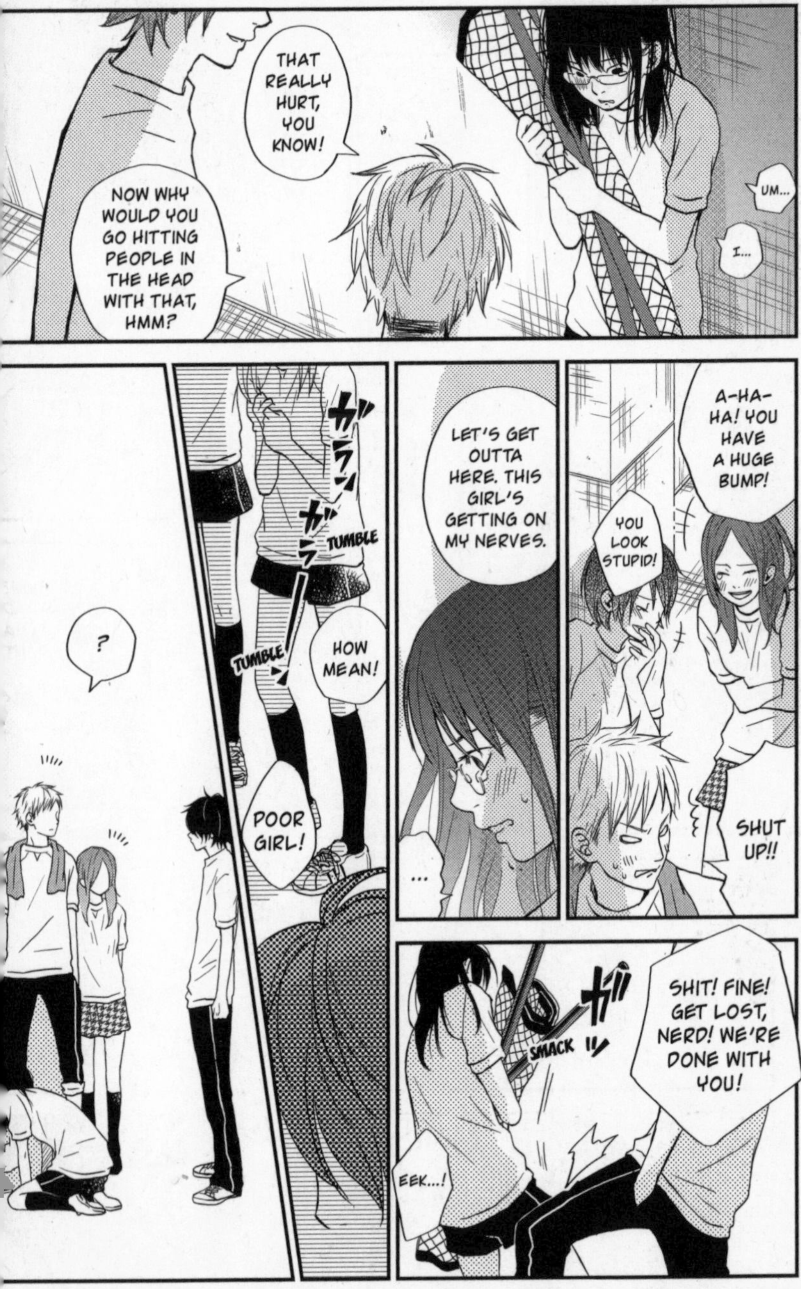
THAT REALLY HURT, YOU KNOW!
NOW WHY WOULD YOU GO HITTING PEOPLE IN THE HEAD WITH THAT, HMM?
UM...
I...
A-HA-HA! YOU HAVE A HUGE BUMP!
YOU LOOK STUPID!
SHUT UP!!
LET'S GET OUTTA HERE. THIS GIRL'S GETTING ON MY NERVES.
...
SHIT! FINE! GET LOST, NERD! WE'RE DONE WITH YOU!
SMACK
EEK...!
TUMBLE
TUMBLE
HOW MEAN!
POOR GIRL!
?

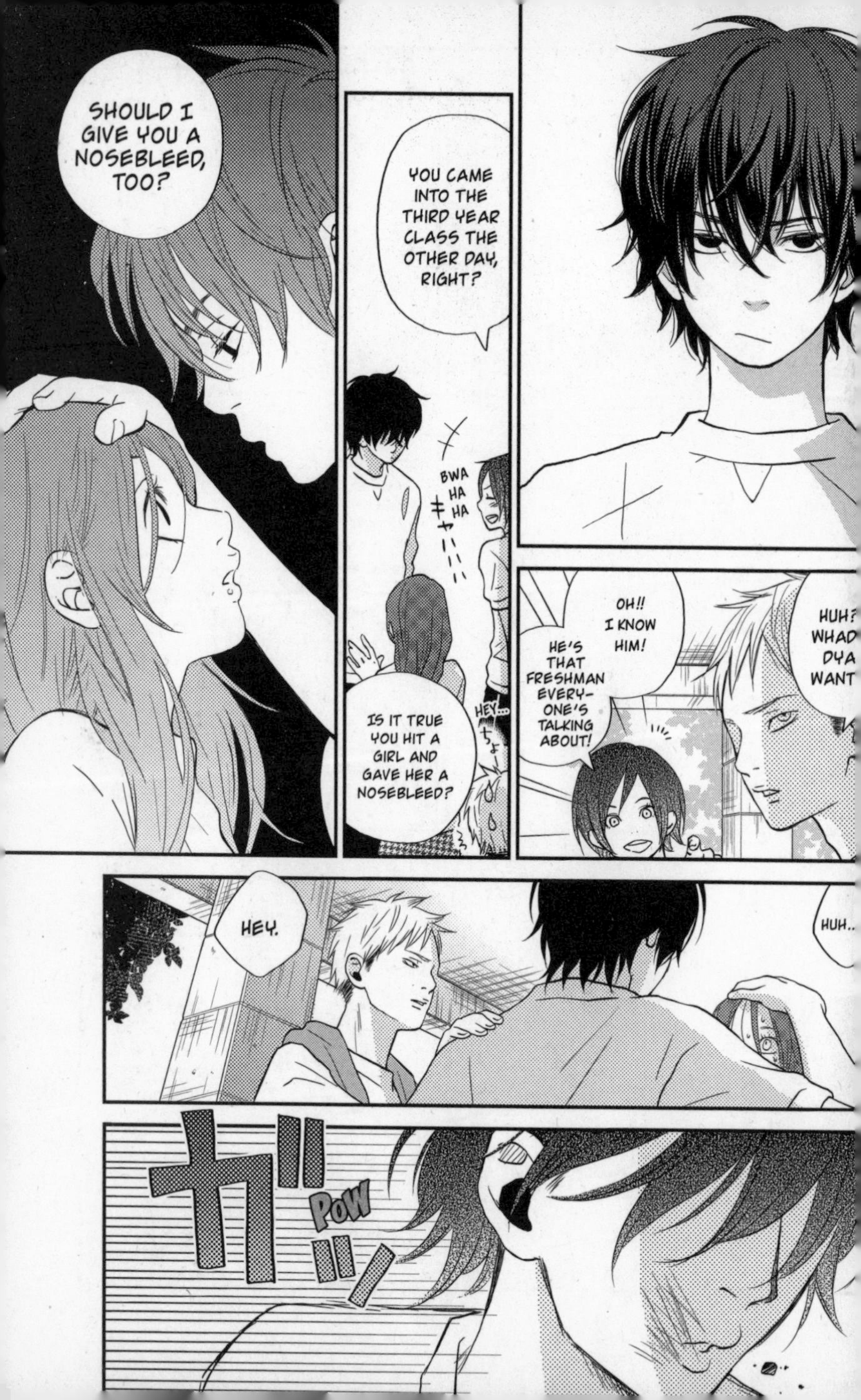
HUH? WHADDYA WANT
OH!! I KNOW HIM!
HE'S THAT FRESHMAN EVERY-ONE'S TALKING ABOUT!
YOU CAME INTO THE THIRD YEAR CLASS THE OTHER DAY, RIGHT?
BWA HA HA
HEY...
IS IT TRUE YOU HIT A GIRL AND GAVE HER A NOSEBLEED?
SHOULD I GIVE YOU A NOSEBLEED, TOO?
HUH..
HEY.
POW

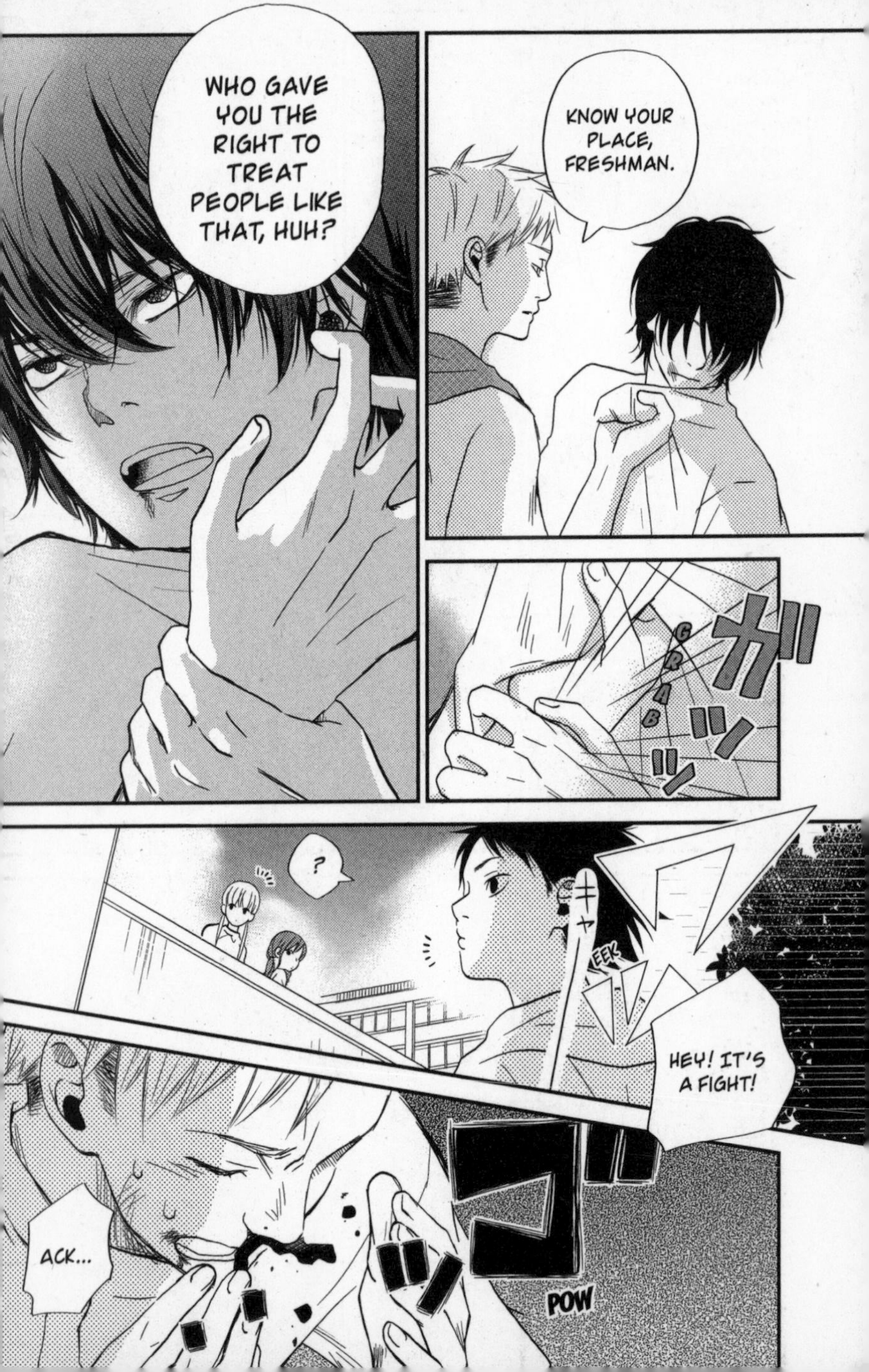

KNOW YOUR PLACE, FRESHMAN.
ガッ
GRAB
WHO GAVE YOU THE RIGHT TO TREAT PEOPLE LIKE THAT, HUH?
キャ
EEK
HEY! IT'S A FIGHT!
?
ゴッ
POW
ACK...

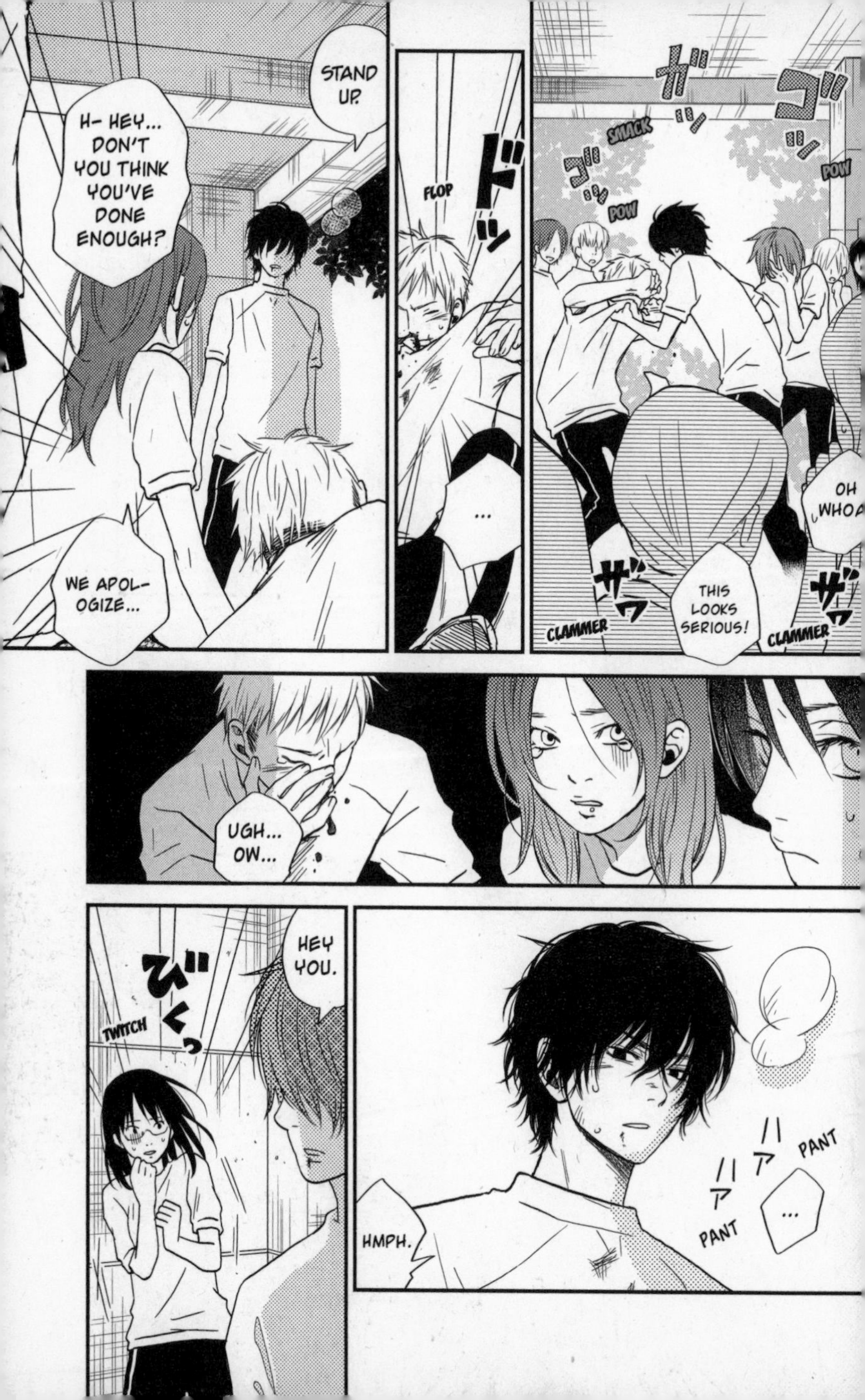

SMACK
POW
POW
OH WHOA
THIS LOOKS SERIOUS!
CLAMMER
CLAMMER
FLOP
...
STAND UP.
H- HEY... DON'T YOU THINK YOU'VE DONE ENOUGH?
WE APOLOGIZE...
UGH... OW...
PANT
PANT
...
HMPH.
HEY YOU.
TWITCH

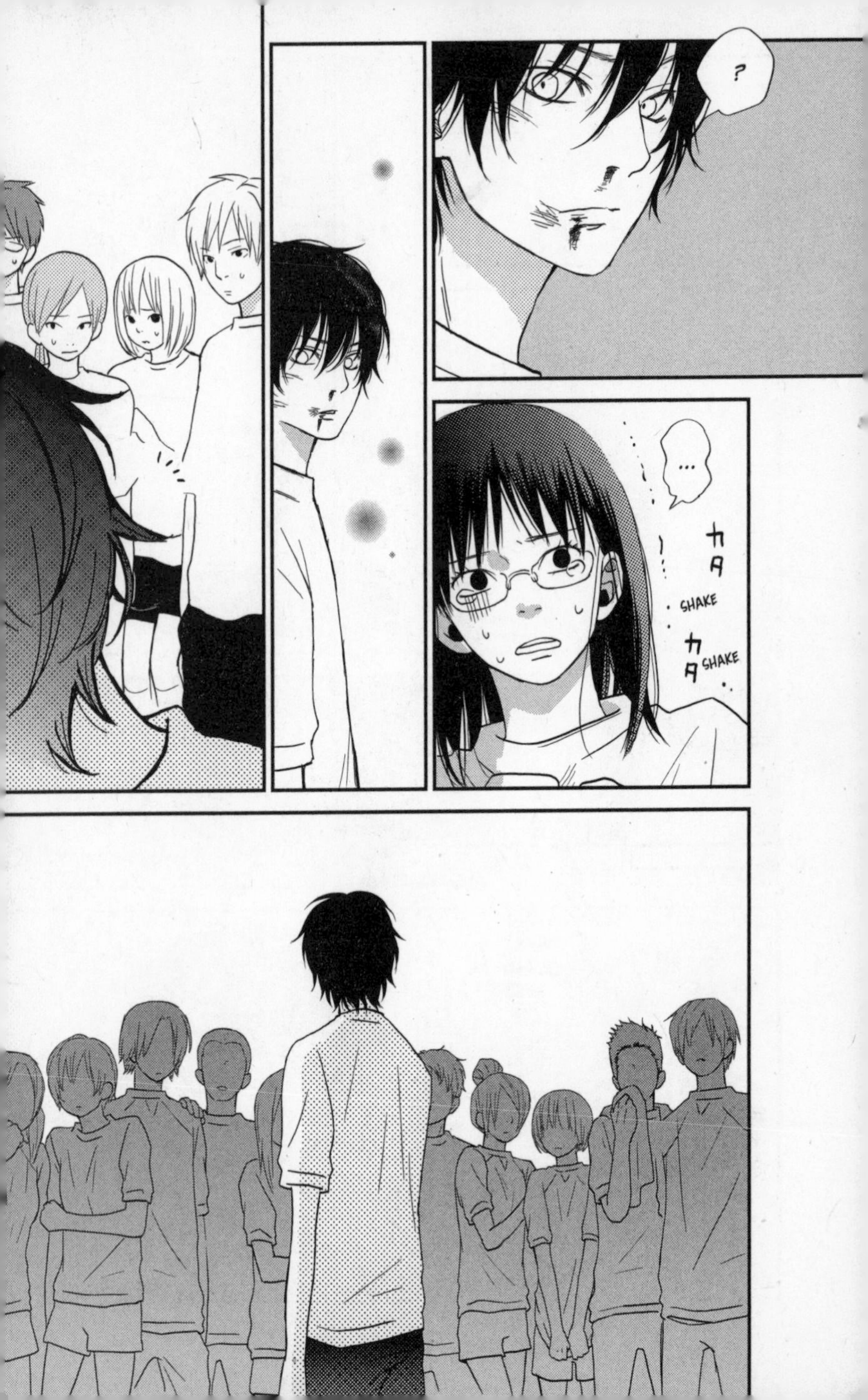
?
...
カタ SHAKE
カタ SHAKE

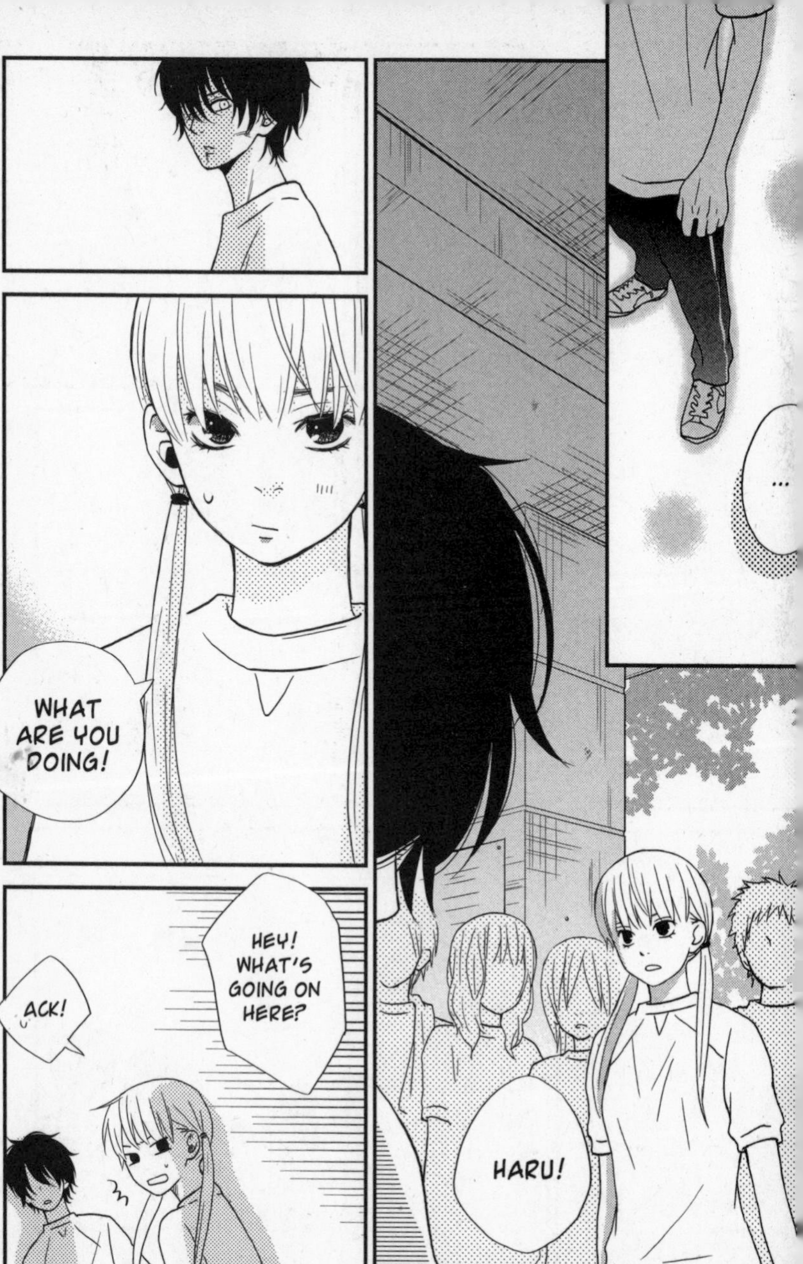
...
HARU!
WHAT ARE YOU DOING!
HEY! WHAT'S GOING ON HERE?
ACK!

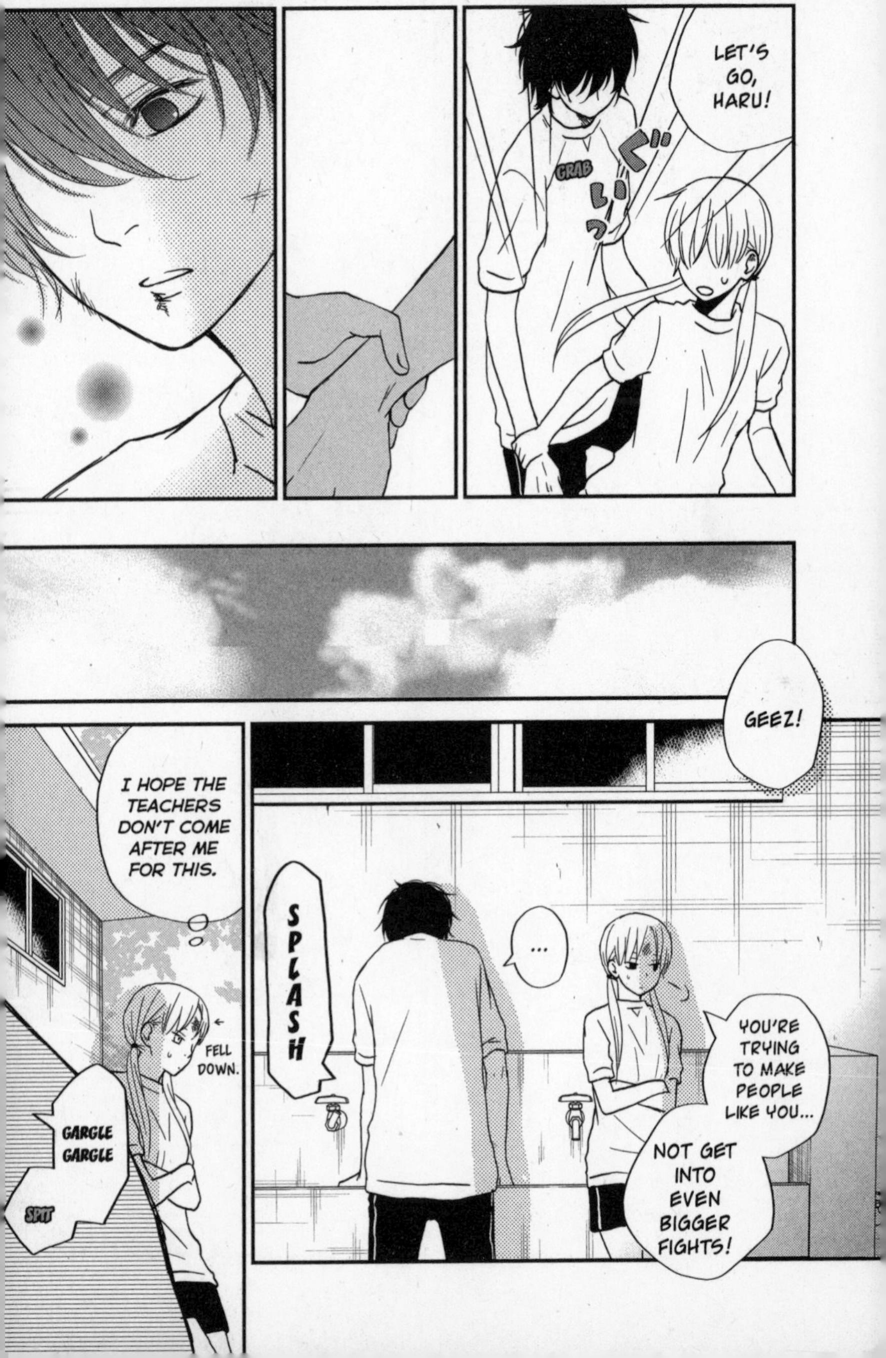
LET'S GO, HARU!
GRAB
GEEZ!
I HOPE THE TEACHERS DON'T COME AFTER ME FOR THIS.
YOU'RE TRYING TO MAKE PEOPLE LIKE YOU...
NOT GET INTO EVEN BIGGER FIGHTS!
...
SPLASH
FELL DOWN.
GARGLE GARGLE
SPIT

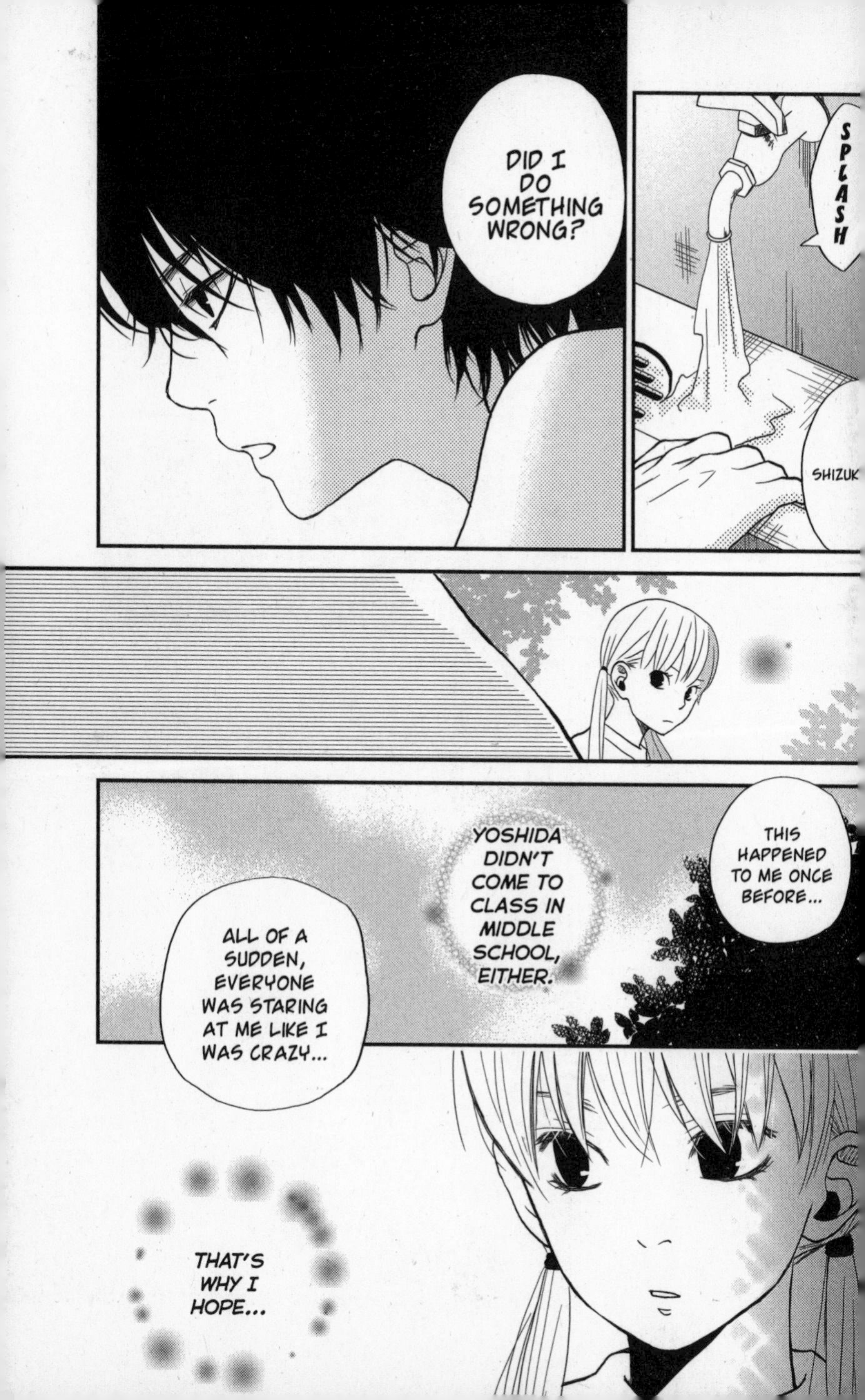
SPLASH
SHIZUK
DID I DO SOMETHING WRONG?
THIS HAPPENED TO ME ONCE BEFORE...
YOSHIDA DIDN'T COME TO CLASS IN MIDDLE SCHOOL, EITHER.
ALL OF A SUDDEN, EVERYONE WAS STARING AT ME LIKE I WAS CRAZY...
THAT'S WHY I HOPE...

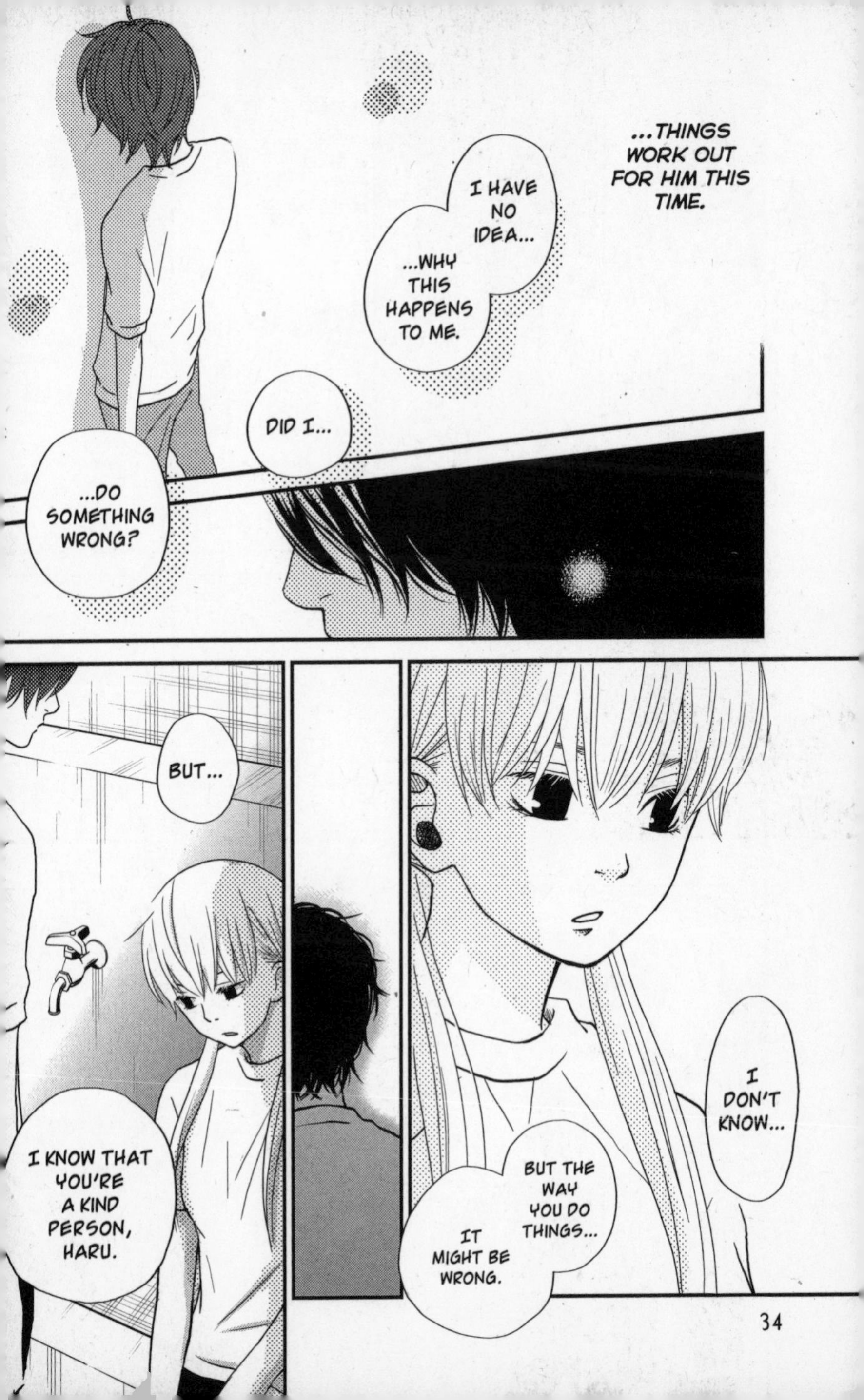
...THINGS WORK OUT FOR HIM THIS TIME.
I HAVE NO IDEA...
...WHY THIS HAPPENS TO ME.
DID I...
...DO SOMETHING WRONG?
I DON'T KNOW...
BUT THE WAY YOU DO THINGS...
IT MIGHT BE WRONG.
BUT...
I KNOW THAT YOU'RE A KIND PERSON, HARU.

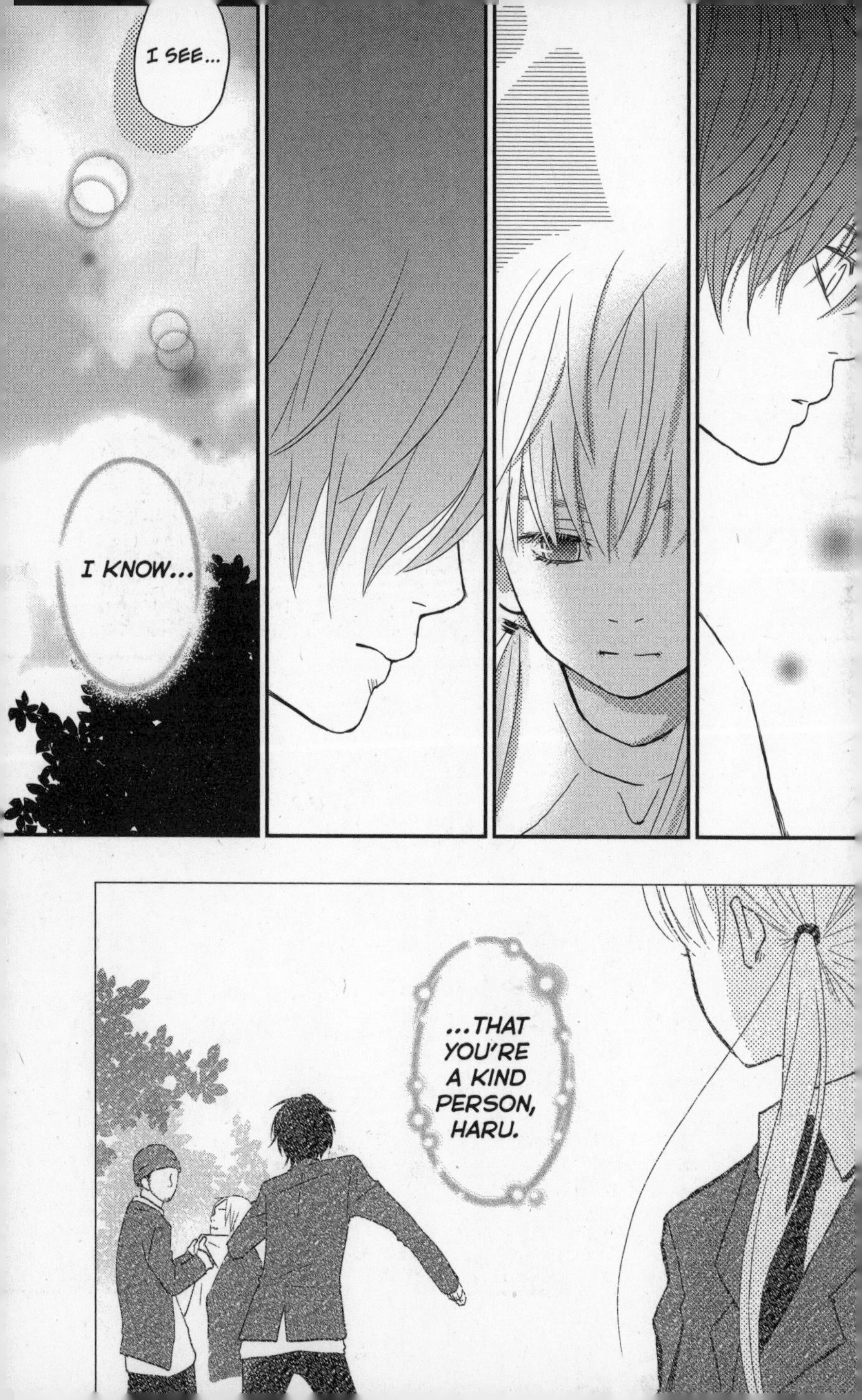
I SEE...
I KNOW...
...THAT YOU'RE A KIND PERSON, HARU.

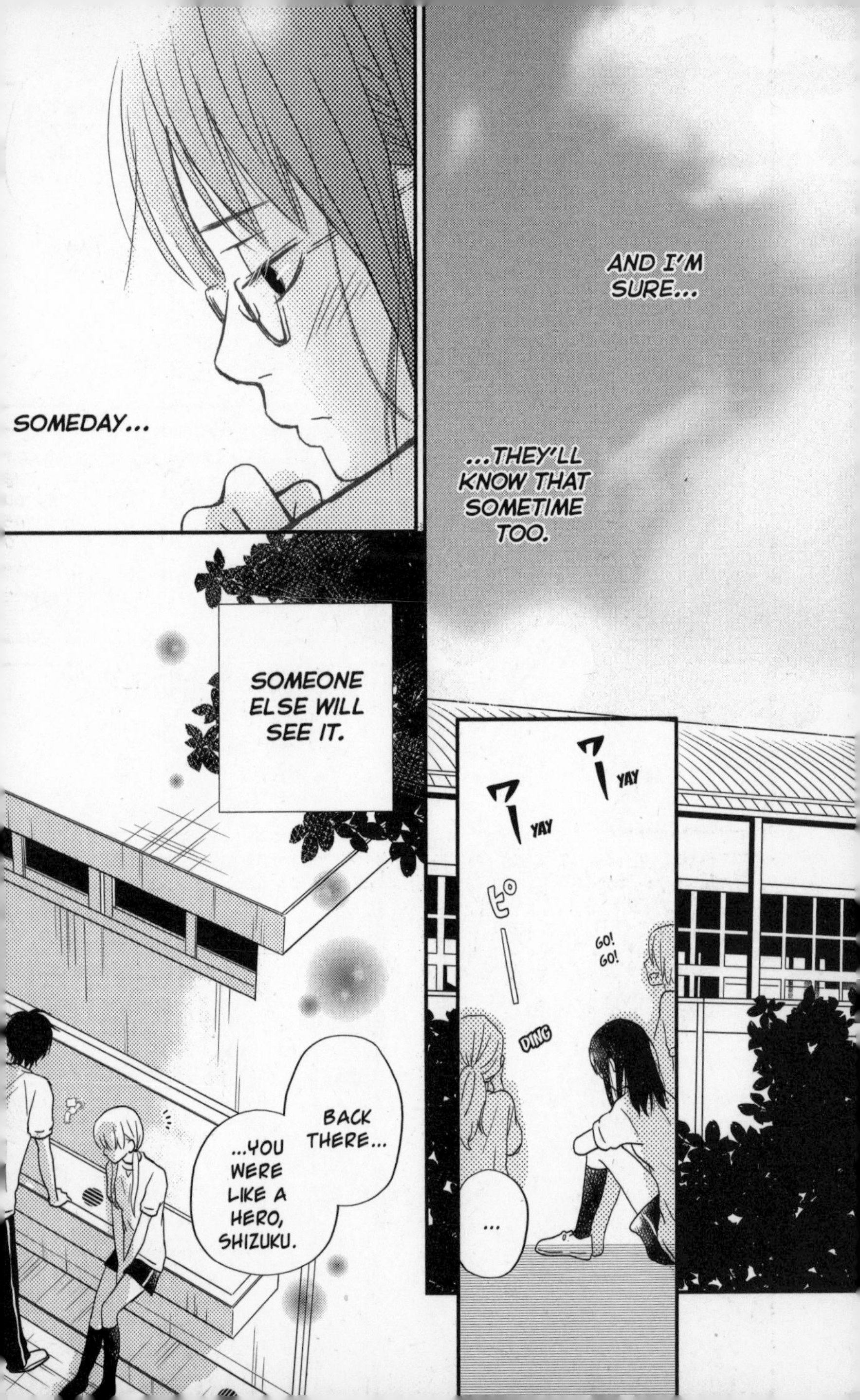

AND I'M SURE...
...THEY'LL KNOW THAT SOMETIME TOO.
SOMEDAY...
SOMEONE ELSE WILL SEE IT.
YAY
YAY
DING
GO! GO!
...
BACK THERE...
...YOU WERE LIKE A HERO, SHIZUKU.

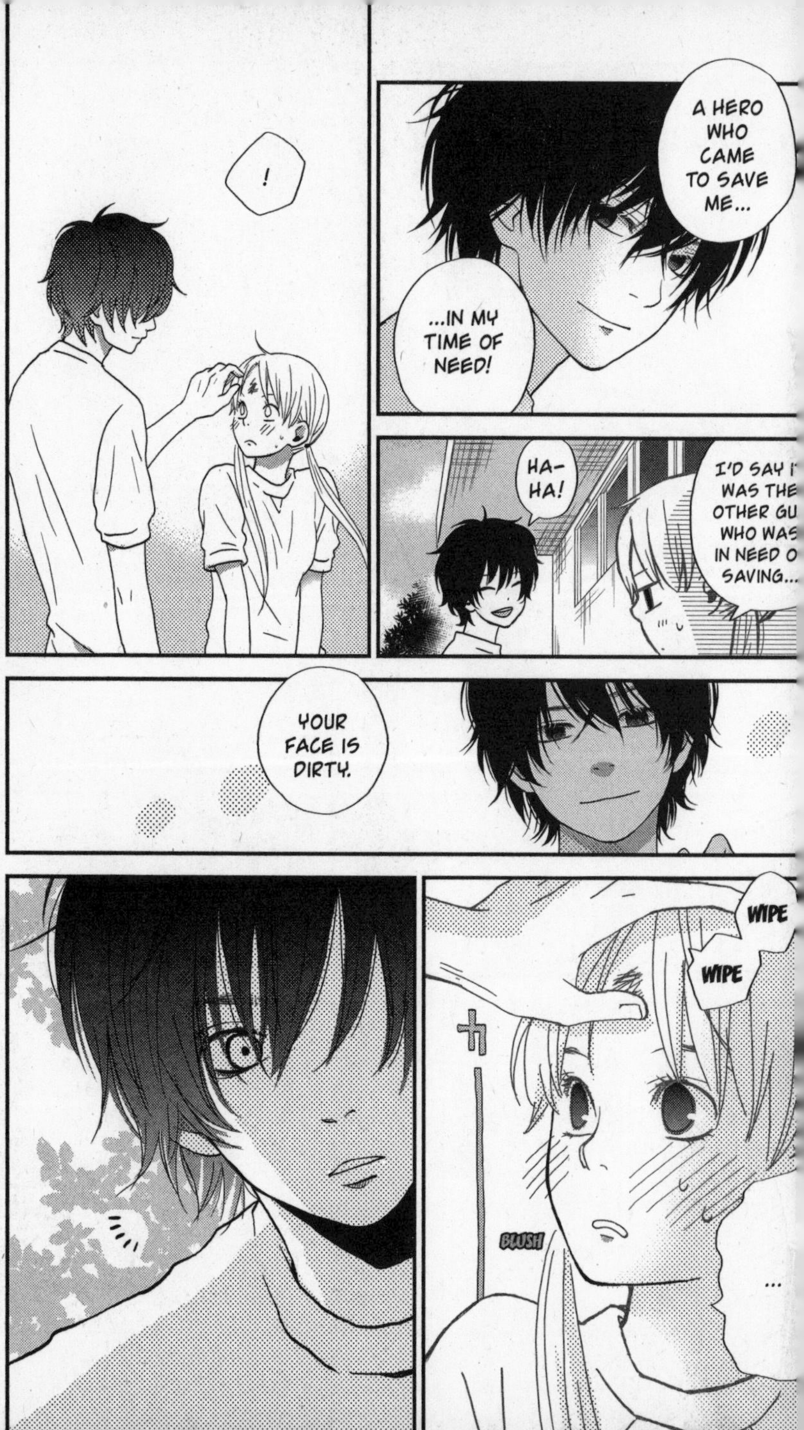
A HERO WHO CAME TO SAVE ME...
...IN MY TIME OF NEED!
I'D SAY I WAS THE OTHER GU WHO WAS IN NEED O SAVING...
HA-HA!
!
YOUR FACE IS DIRTY.
WIPE
WIPE
BLUSH
...

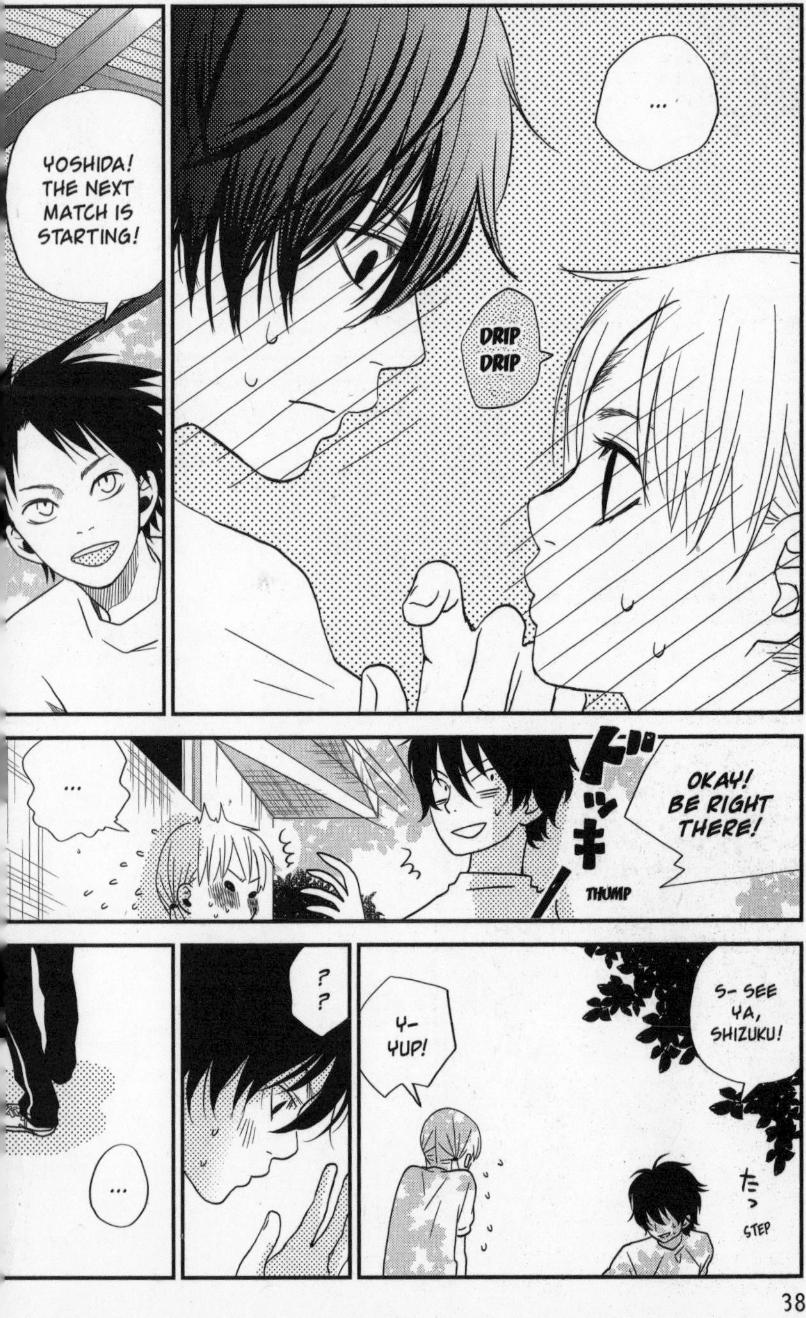
...
DRIP DRIP
YOSHIDA! THE NEXT MATCH IS STARTING!
OKAY! BE RIGHT THERE!
THUMP
...
S- SEE YA, SHIZUKU!
STEP
Y- YUP!
??
...

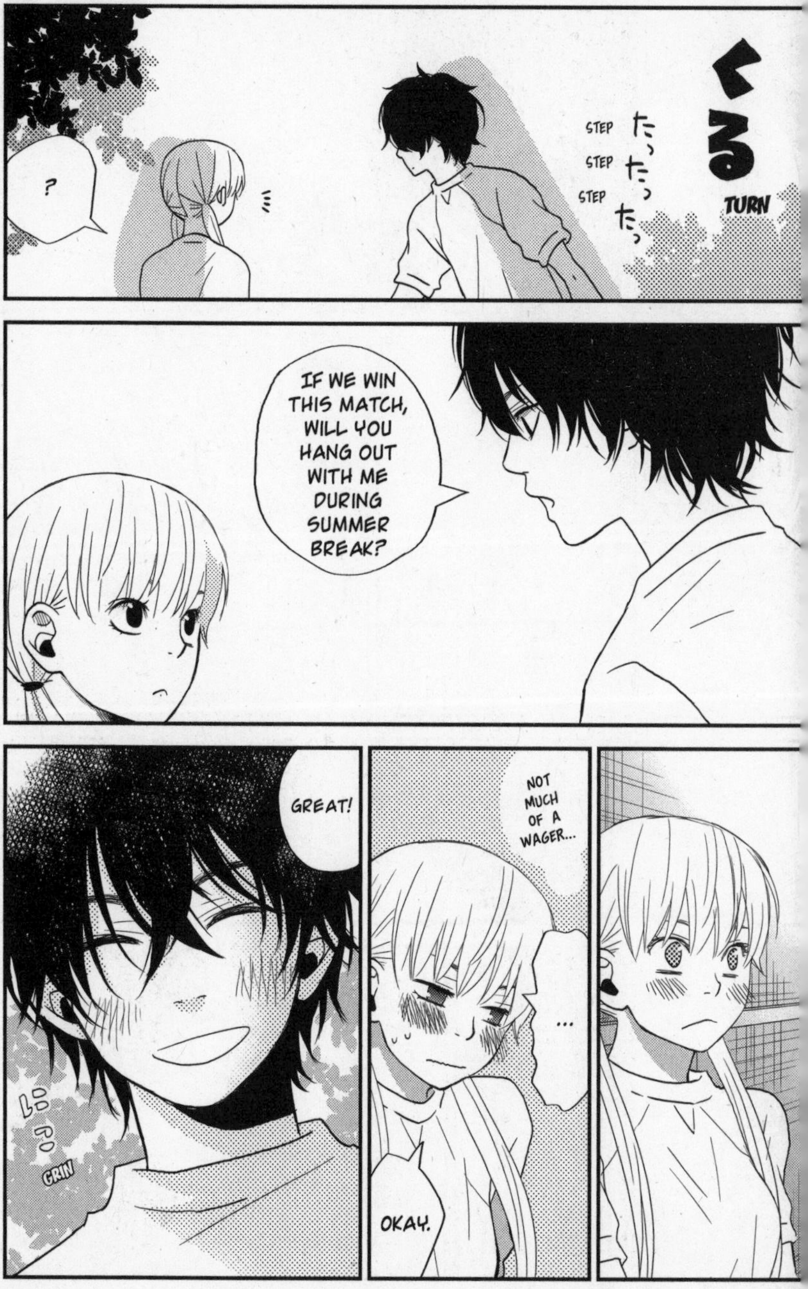
くる
TURN
たっ たっ たっ
STEP STEP STEP
?
IF WE WIN THIS MATCH, WILL YOU HANG OUT WITH ME DURING SUMMER BREAK?
NOT MUCH OF A WAGER...
...
OKAY.
GREAT!
にっ
GRIN

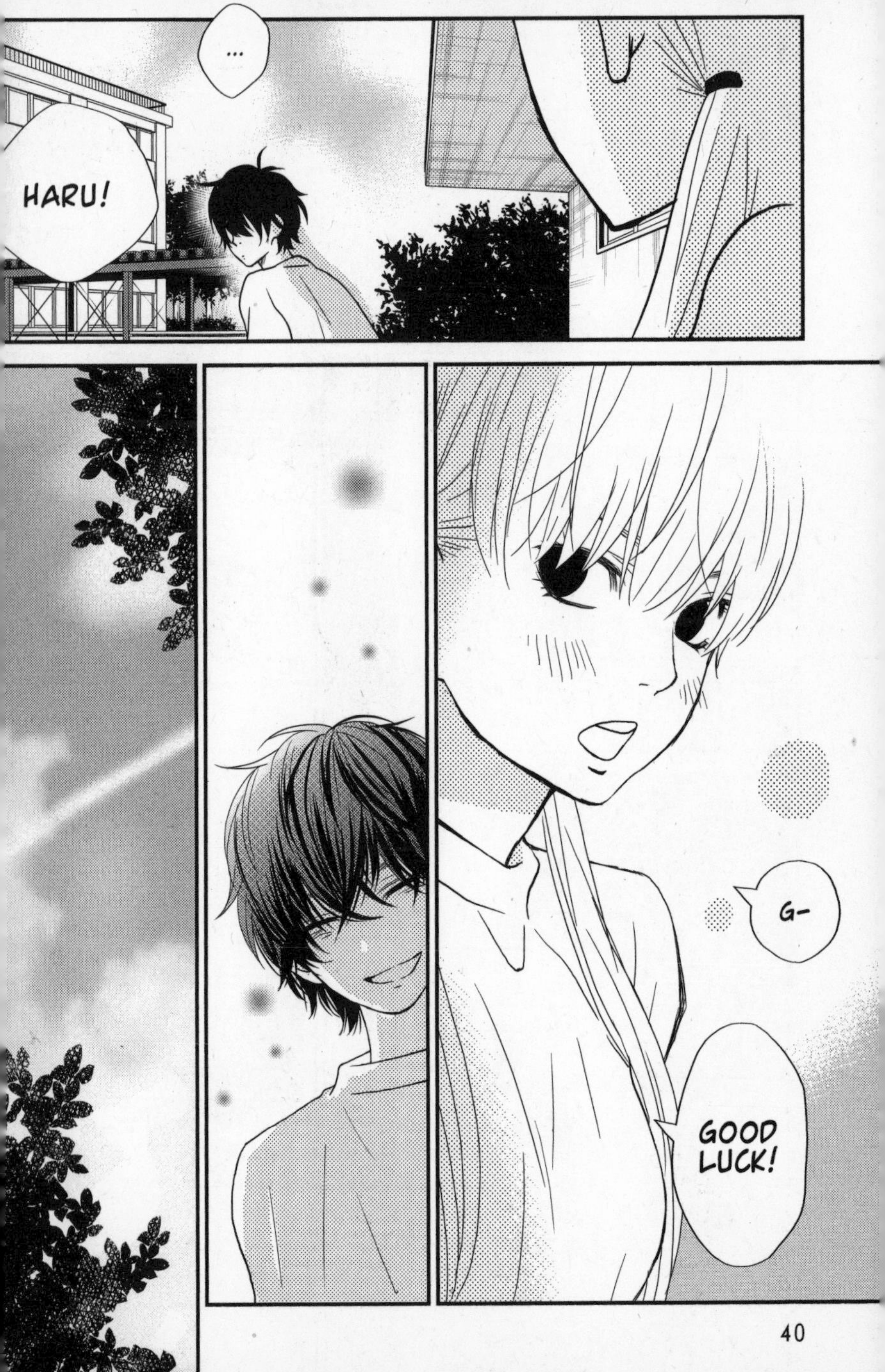
...
HARU!
G-
GOOD LUCK!

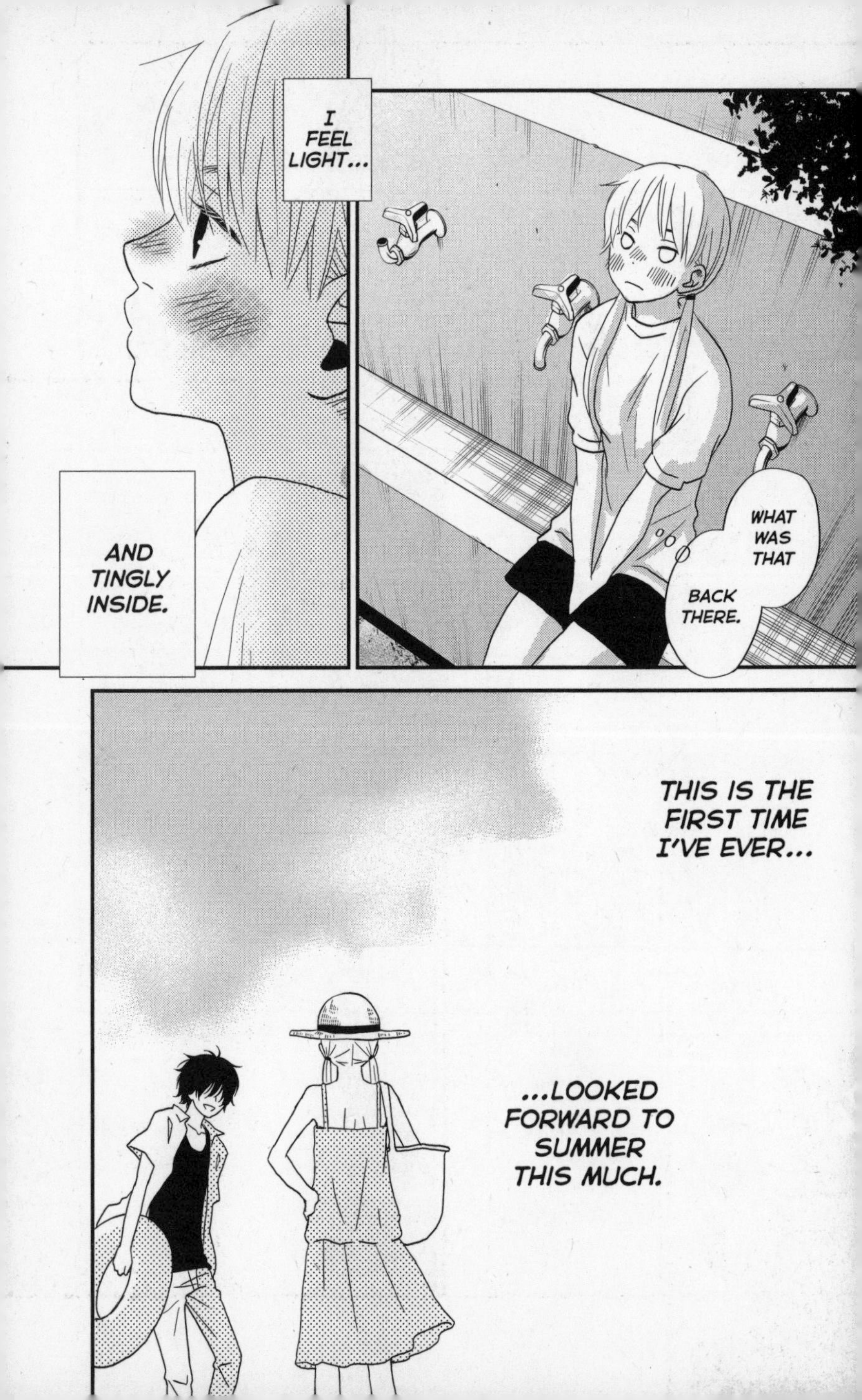
WHAT WAS THAT BACK THERE.
I FEEL LIGHT...
AND TINGLY INSIDE.
THIS IS THE FIRST TIME I'VE EVER...
...LOOKED FORWARD TO SUMMER THIS MUCH.

A NATURAL GUY

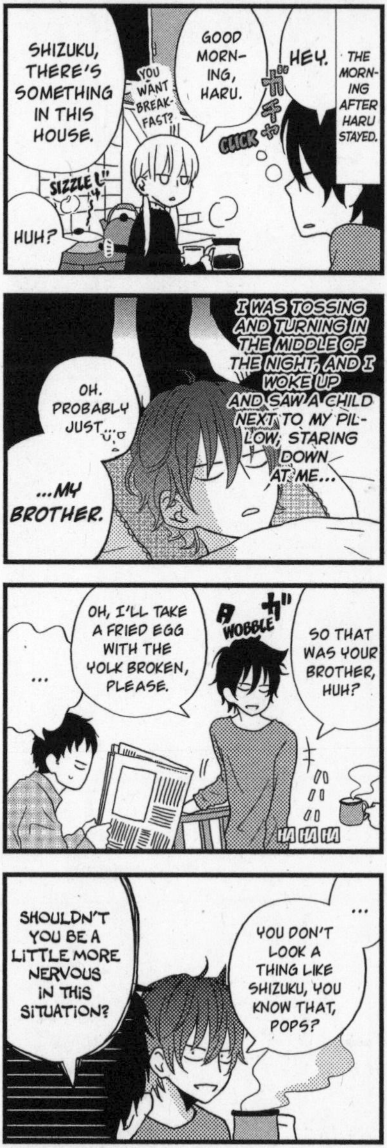
THE MORNING AFTER HARU STAYED.
HEY.
ガチャ
CLICK
GOOD MORNING, HARU.
YOU WANT BREAKFAST?
SHIZUKU, THERE'S SOMETHING IN THIS HOUSE.
SIZZLE
HUH?
I WAS TOSSING AND TURNING IN THE MIDDLE OF THE NIGHT, AND I WOKE UP AND SAW A CHILD NEXT TO MY PILLOW, STARING DOWN AT ME...
OH. PROBABLY JUST...
...MY BROTHER.
SO THAT WAS YOUR BROTHER, HUH?
ガタ
WOBBLE
OH, I'LL TAKE A FRIED EGG WITH THE YOLK BROKEN, PLEASE.
...
HA HA HA
...
YOU DON'T LOOK A THING LIKE SHIZUKU, YOU KNOW THAT, POPS?
SHOULDN'T YOU BE A LITTLE MORE NERVOUS IN THIS SITUATION?

AN ANNOYING GUY

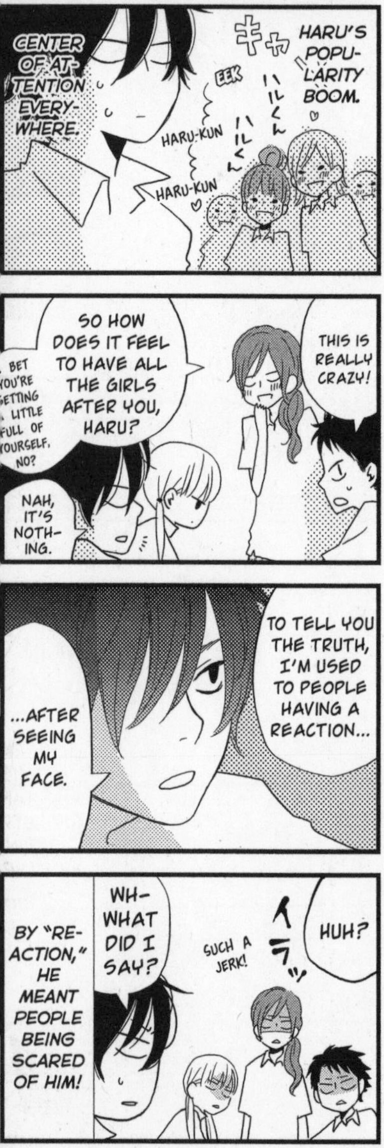
HARU'S POPULARITY BOOM.
キャ
EEK
ハルくん
ハルくん
HARU-KUN
HARU-KUN
CENTER OF ATTENTION EVERYWHERE.
THIS IS REALLY CRAZY!
SO HOW DOES IT FEEL TO HAVE ALL THE GIRLS AFTER YOU, HARU?
BET YOU'RE ETTING LITTLE FULL OF OURSELF, NO?
NAH, IT'S NOTHING.
TO TELL YOU THE TRUTH, I'M USED TO PEOPLE HAVING A REACTION...
...AFTER SEEING MY FACE.
HUH?
ヘラッ
SUCH A JERK!
WH-WHAT DID I SAY?
BY "REACTION," HE MEANT PEOPLE BEING SCARED OF HIM!

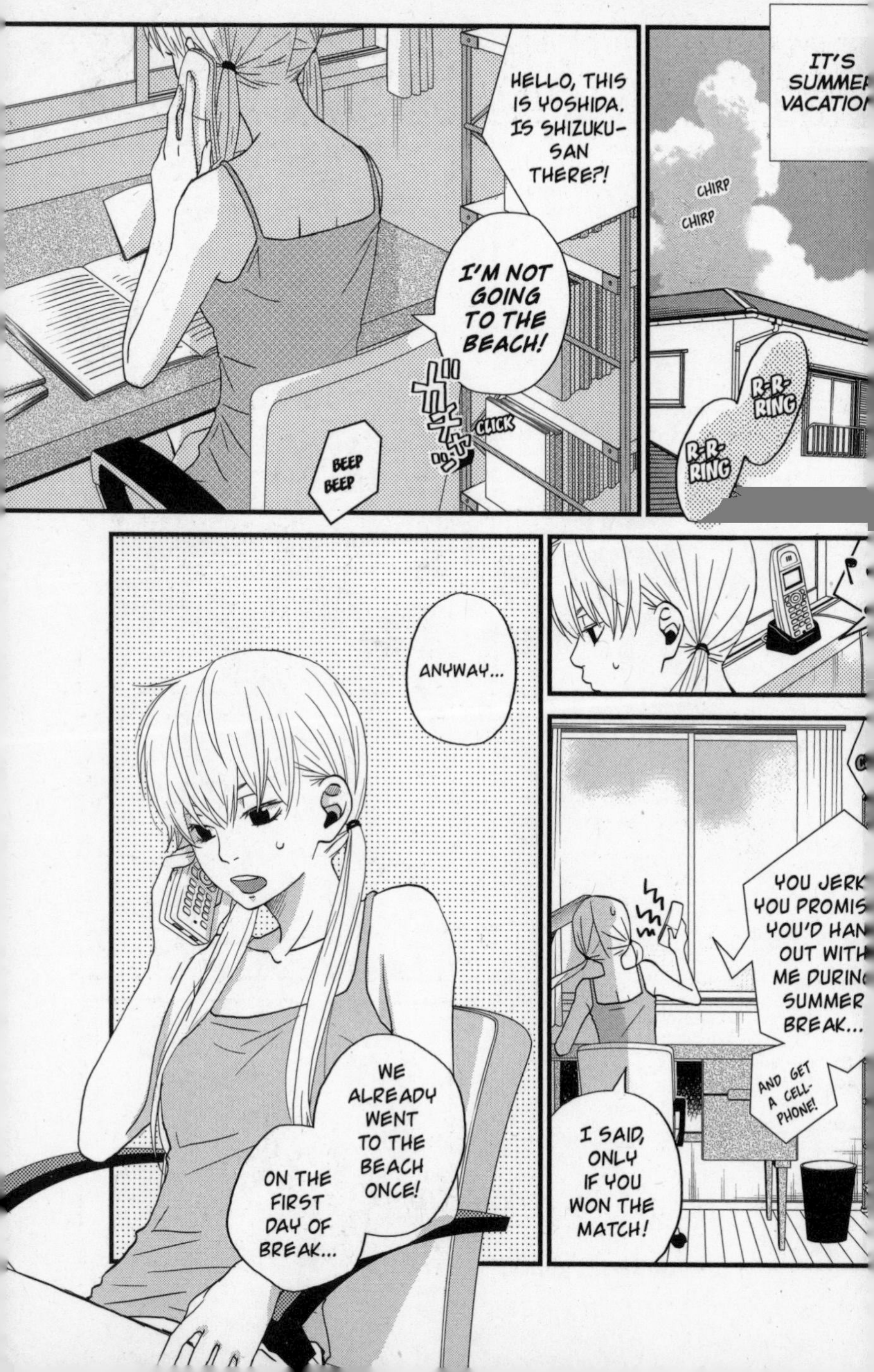
IT'S SUMME VACATIO
CHIRP
CHIRP
R-R-RING
R-R-RING
HELLO, THIS IS YOSHIDA. IS SHIZUKU-SAN THERE?!
I'M NOT GOING TO THE BEACH!
ガチャッ
CLICK
BEEP BEEP
YOU JERK YOU PROMIS YOU'D HAN OUT WITH ME DURIN SUMMER BREAK...
AND GET A CELL-PHONE!
I SAID, ONLY IF YOU WON THE MATCH!
ANYWAY...
WE ALREADY WENT TO THE BEACH ONCE!
ON THE FIRST DAY OF BREAK...

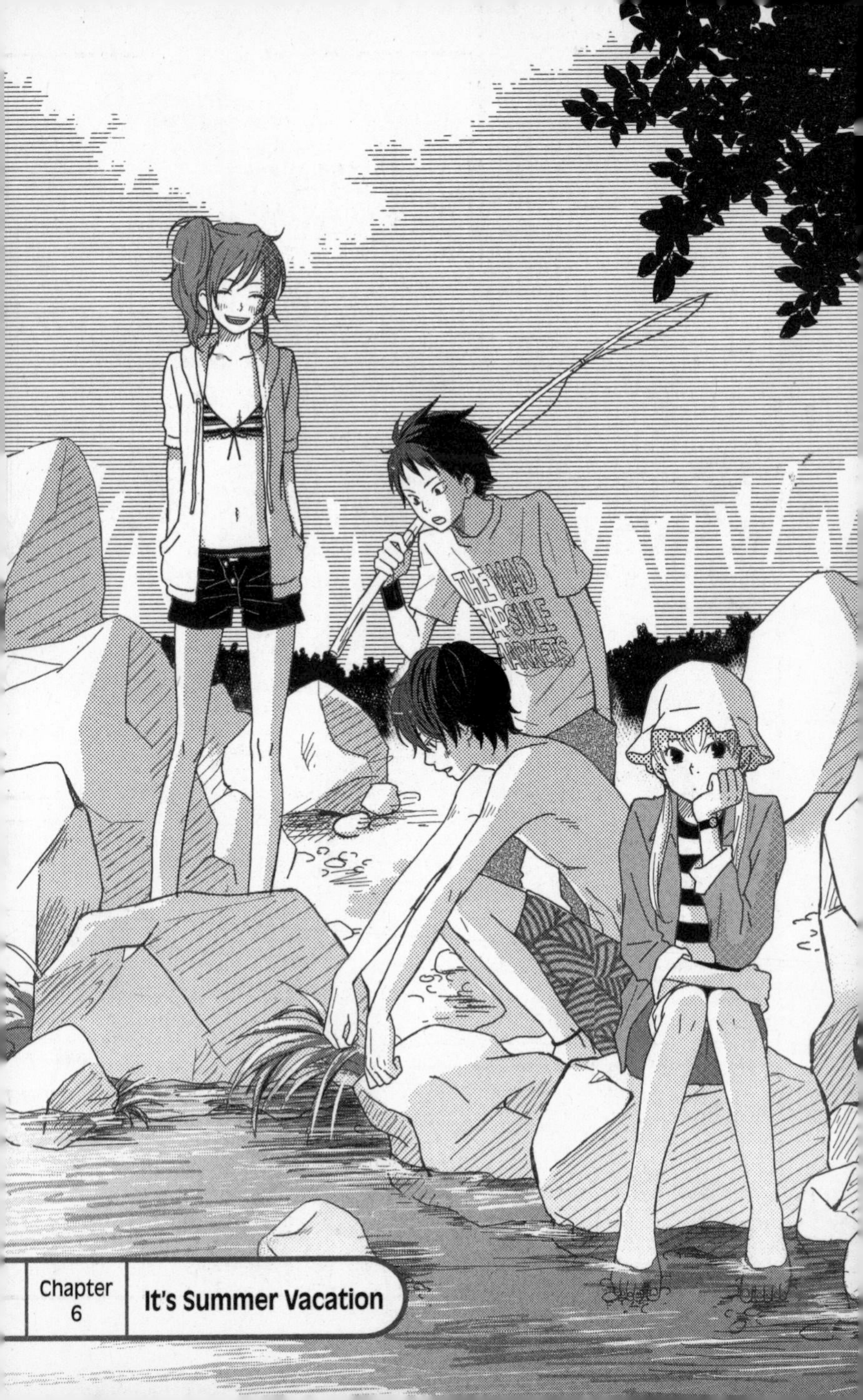
THE MAD CAPSULE MARKETS

Chapter 6 It's Summer Vacation

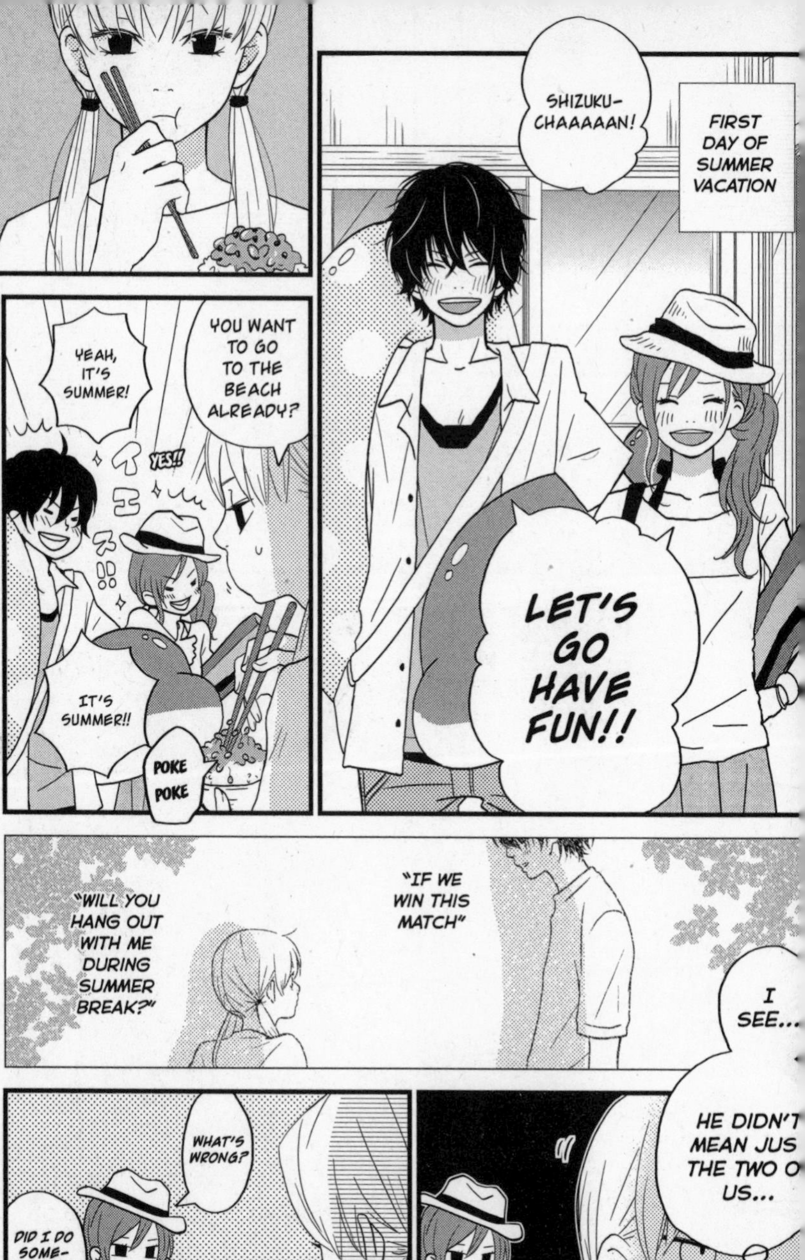
FIRST DAY OF SUMMER VACATION
SHIZUKU-CHAAAAAN!
LET'S GO HAVE FUN!!
YOU WANT TO GO TO THE BEACH ALREADY?
YEAH, IT'S SUMMER!
イエス!!
YES!!
IT'S SUMMER!!
POKE POKE
I SEE...
"IF WE WIN THIS MATCH"
"WILL YOU HANG OUT WITH ME DURING SUMMER BREAK?"
HE DIDN'T MEAN JUS THE TWO O US...
WHAT'S WRONG?
DID I DO SOME-THING WRONG?

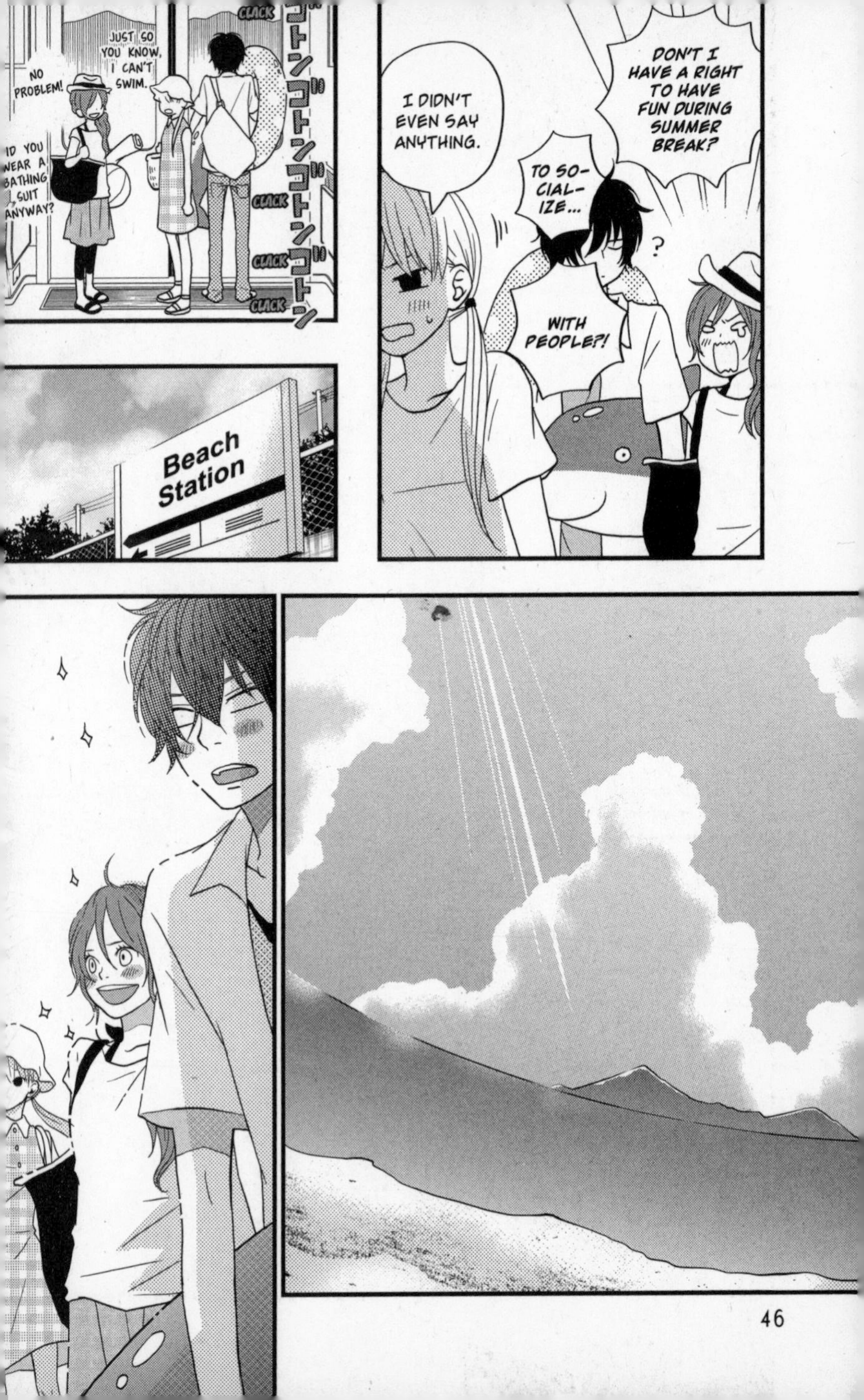
DON'T I HAVE A RIGHT TO HAVE FUN DURING SUMMER BREAK?
TO SO-CIAL-IZE...
WITH PEOPLE?!
?
I DIDN'T EVEN SAY ANYTHING.
CLACK
ゴトンゴトンゴトンゴトン
JUST SO YOU KNOW, I CAN'T SWIM.
NO PROBLEM!
CLACK
ID YOU WEAR A BATHING SUIT ANYWAY?
CLACK
CLACK
Beach Station

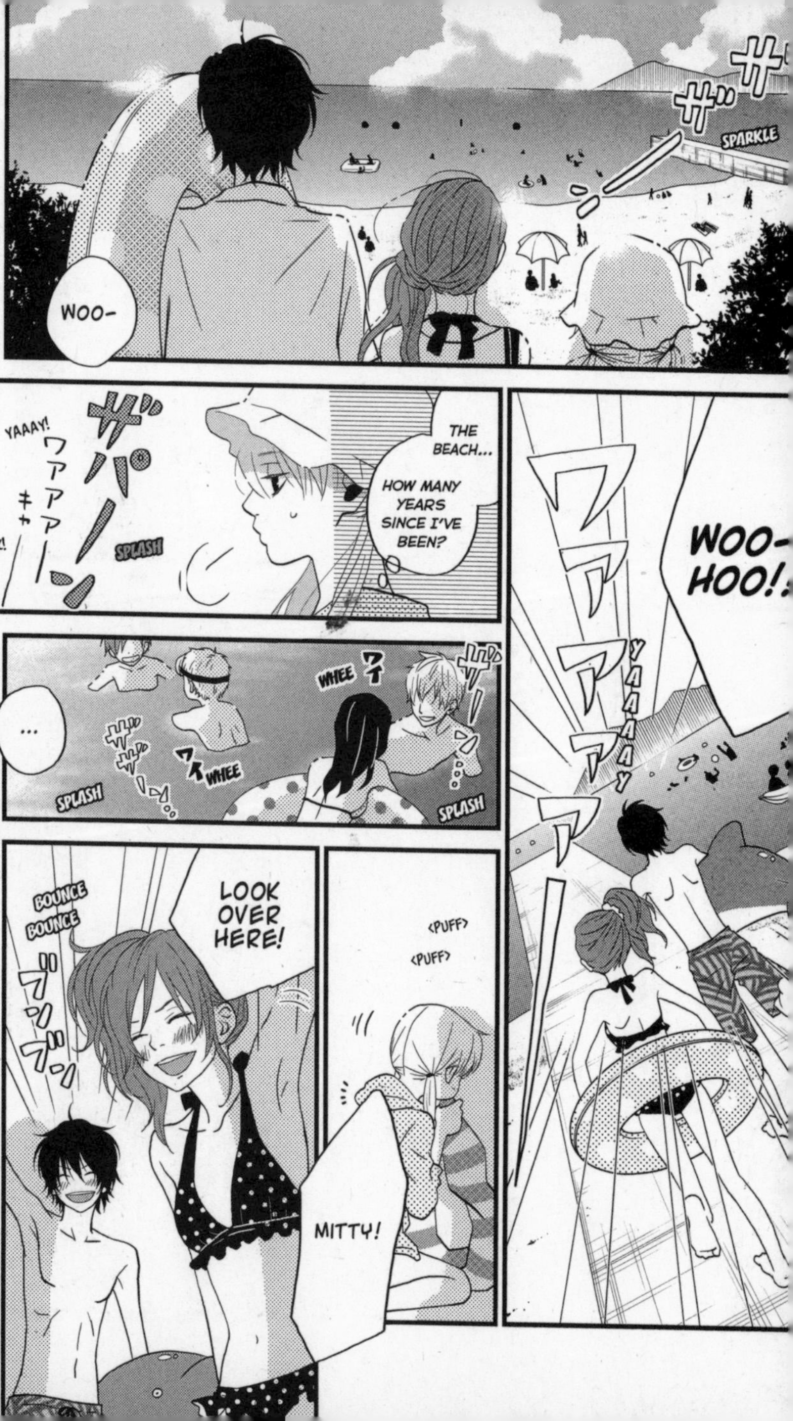
SPARKLE
WOO-
WOO-HOO!!
YAAAAAY
THE BEACH...
HOW MANY YEARS SINCE I'VE BEEN?
YAAAY!
EEK!
SPLASH
...
WHEE
WHEE
SPLASH
SPLASH
<PUFF>
<PUFF>
LOOK OVER HERE!
BOUNCE BOUNCE
MITTY!

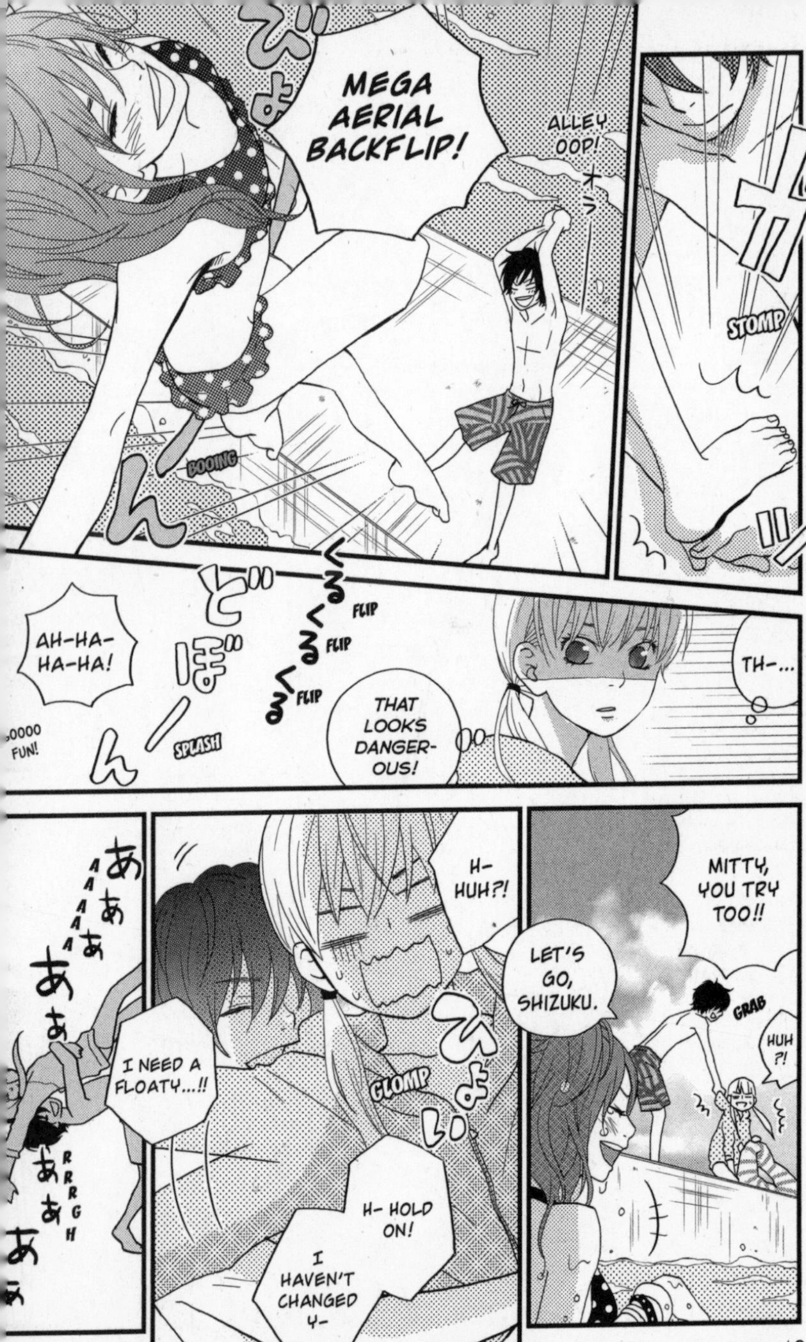
STOMP
MEGA AERIAL BACKFLIP!
ALLEY OOP!
オラ
BOOING
びよん
TH-...
THAT LOOKS DANGEROUS!
くるくるくる
FLIP
FLIP
FLIP
どぼーん
SPLASH
AH-HA-HA-HA!
OOOO FUN!
MITTY, YOU TRY TOO!!
GRAB
HUH ?!
H- HUH?!
LET'S GO, SHIZUKU.
ひょい
GLOMP
H- HOLD ON!
I HAVEN'T CHANGED Y-
AAAAAA
I NEED A FLOATY...!!
RRRGH

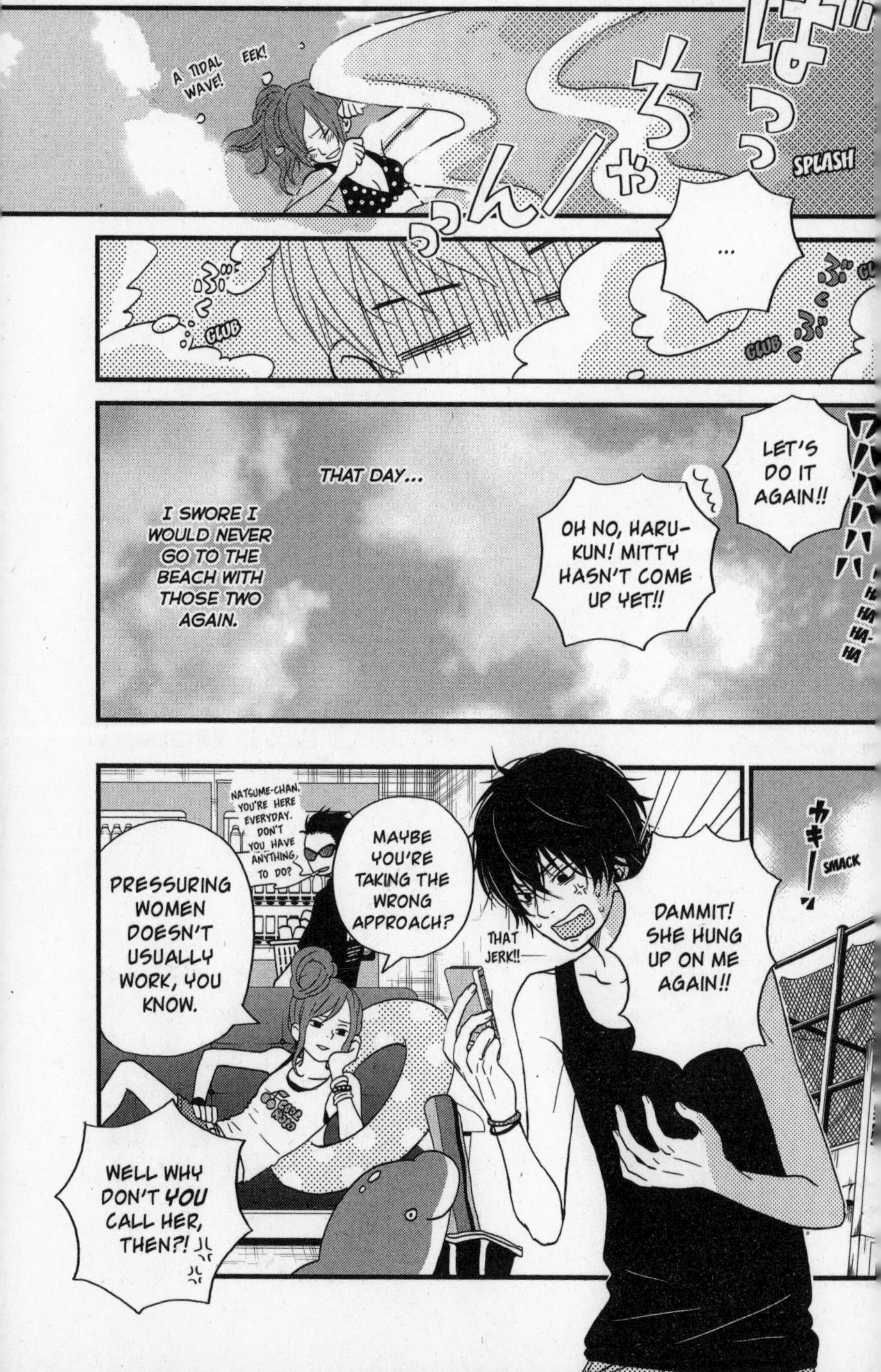
SPLASH
EEK!
A TIDAL WAVE!
...
GLUB
GLUB
HA HA HA-HA
LET'S DO IT AGAIN!!
OH NO, HARU-KUN! MITTY HASN'T COME UP YET!!
THAT DAY...
I SWORE I WOULD NEVER GO TO THE BEACH WITH THOSE TWO AGAIN.
SMACK
DAMMIT! SHE HUNG UP ON ME AGAIN!!
THAT JERK!!
MAYBE YOU'RE TAKING THE WRONG APPROACH?
NATSUME-CHAN, YOU'RE HERE EVERYDAY. DON'T YOU HAVE ANYTHING TO DO?
PRESSURING WOMEN DOESN'T USUALLY WORK, YOU KNOW.
WELL WHY DON'T YOU CALL HER, THEN?!

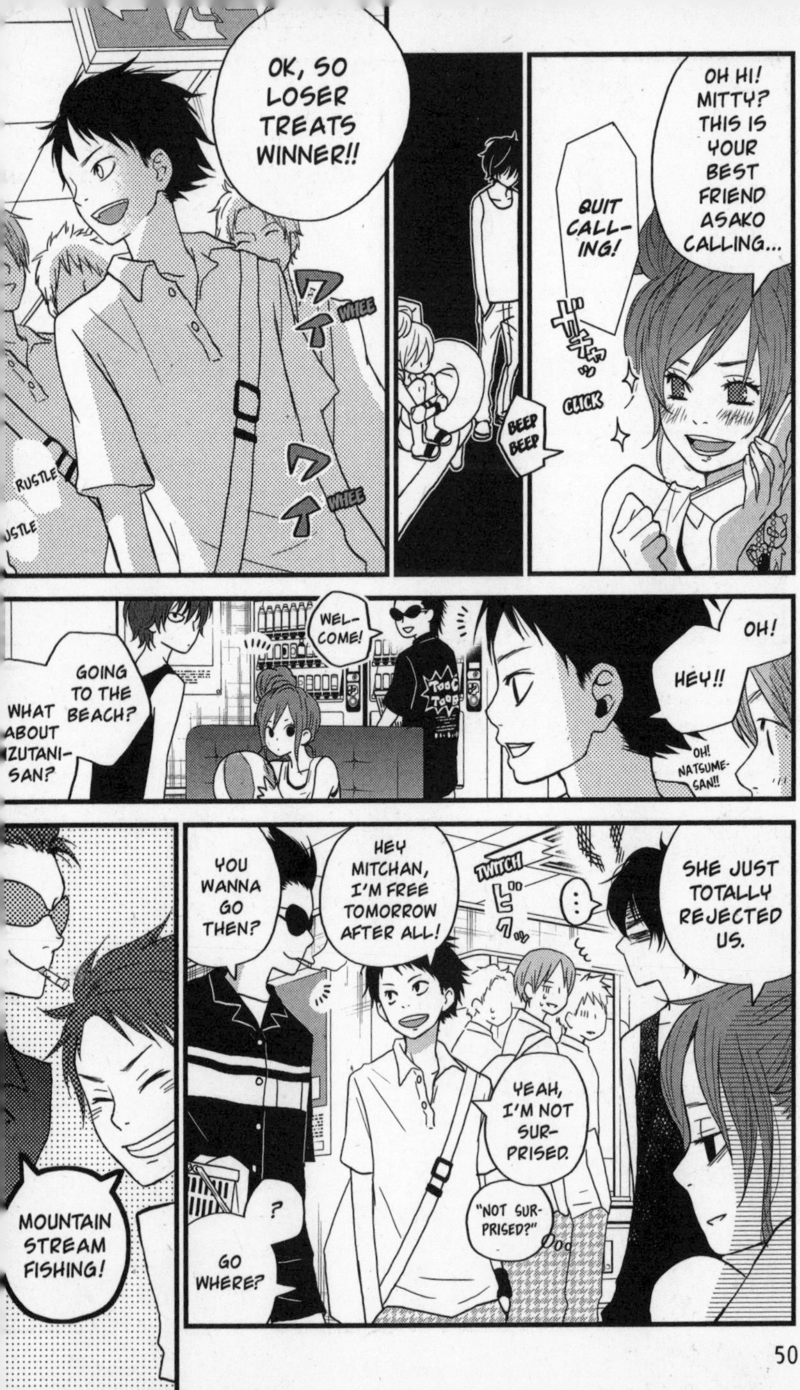
OH HI! MITTY? THIS IS YOUR BEST FRIEND ASAKO CALLING...
QUIT CALLING!
CLICK
BEEP BEEP
OK, SO LOSER TREATS WINNER!!
WHEE
WHEE
RUSTLE
USTLE
OH!
HEY!!
OH! NATSUME-SAN!!
WEL-COME!
GOING TO THE BEACH?
WHAT ABOUT ZUTANI-SAN?
SHE JUST TOTALLY REJECTED US.
...
TWITCH
HEY MITCHAN, I'M FREE TOMORROW AFTER ALL!
YOU WANNA GO THEN?
YEAH, I'M NOT SURPRISED.
"NOT SURPRISED?"
?
GO WHERE?
MOUNTAIN STREAM FISHING!

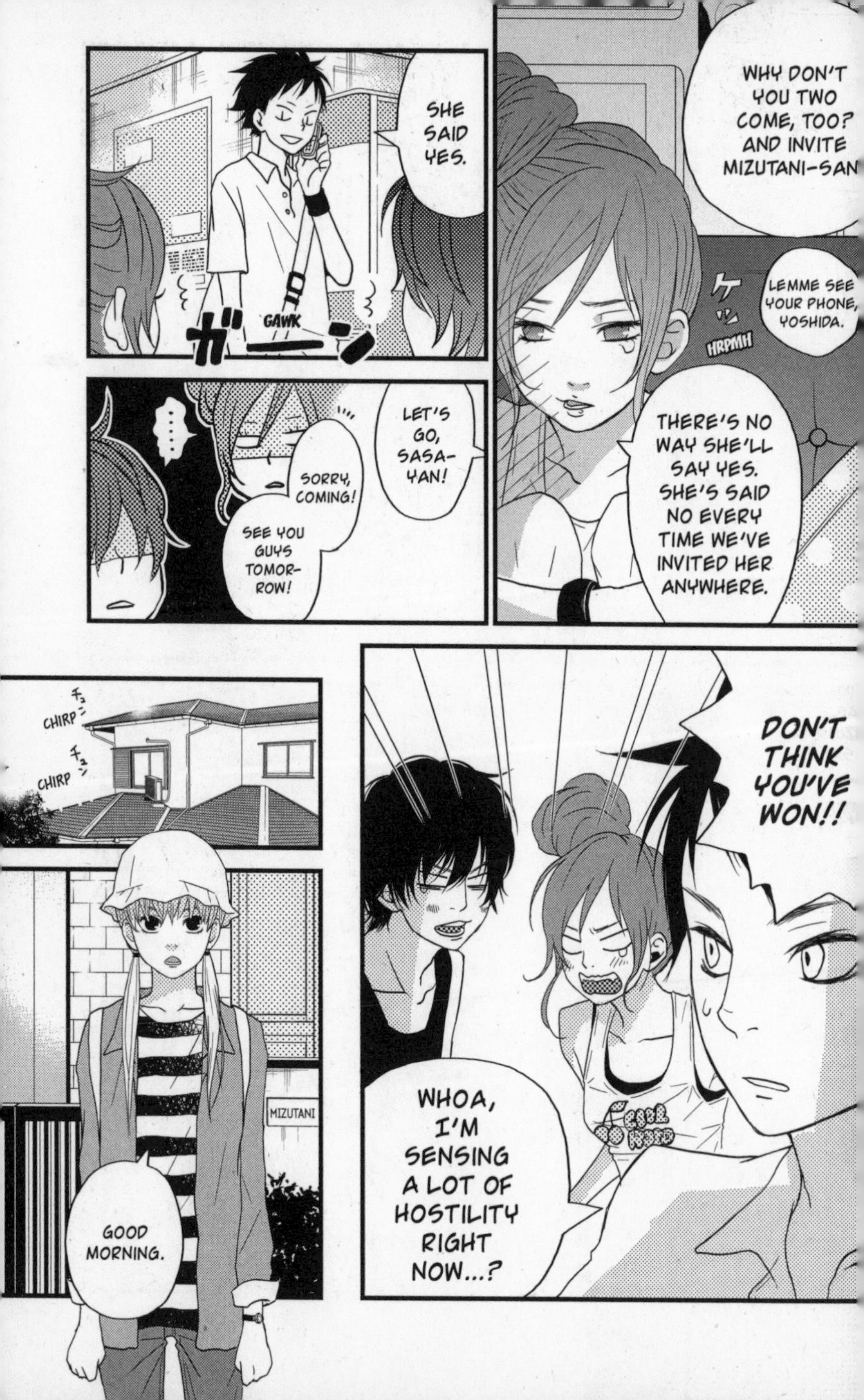
WHY DON'T YOU TWO COME, TOO? AND INVITE MIZUTANI-SAN
LEMME SEE YOUR PHONE, YOSHIDA.
HRPMH
THERE'S NO WAY SHE'LL SAY YES. SHE'S SAID NO EVERY TIME WE'VE INVITED HER ANYWHERE.
SHE SAID YES.
GAWK
LET'S GO, SASA-YAN!
SORRY, COMING!
SEE YOU GUYS TOMORROW!
......
DON'T THINK YOU'VE WON!!
WHOA, I'M SENSING A LOT OF HOSTILITY RIGHT NOW...?
CHIRP
CHIRP
MIZUTANI
GOOD MORNING.

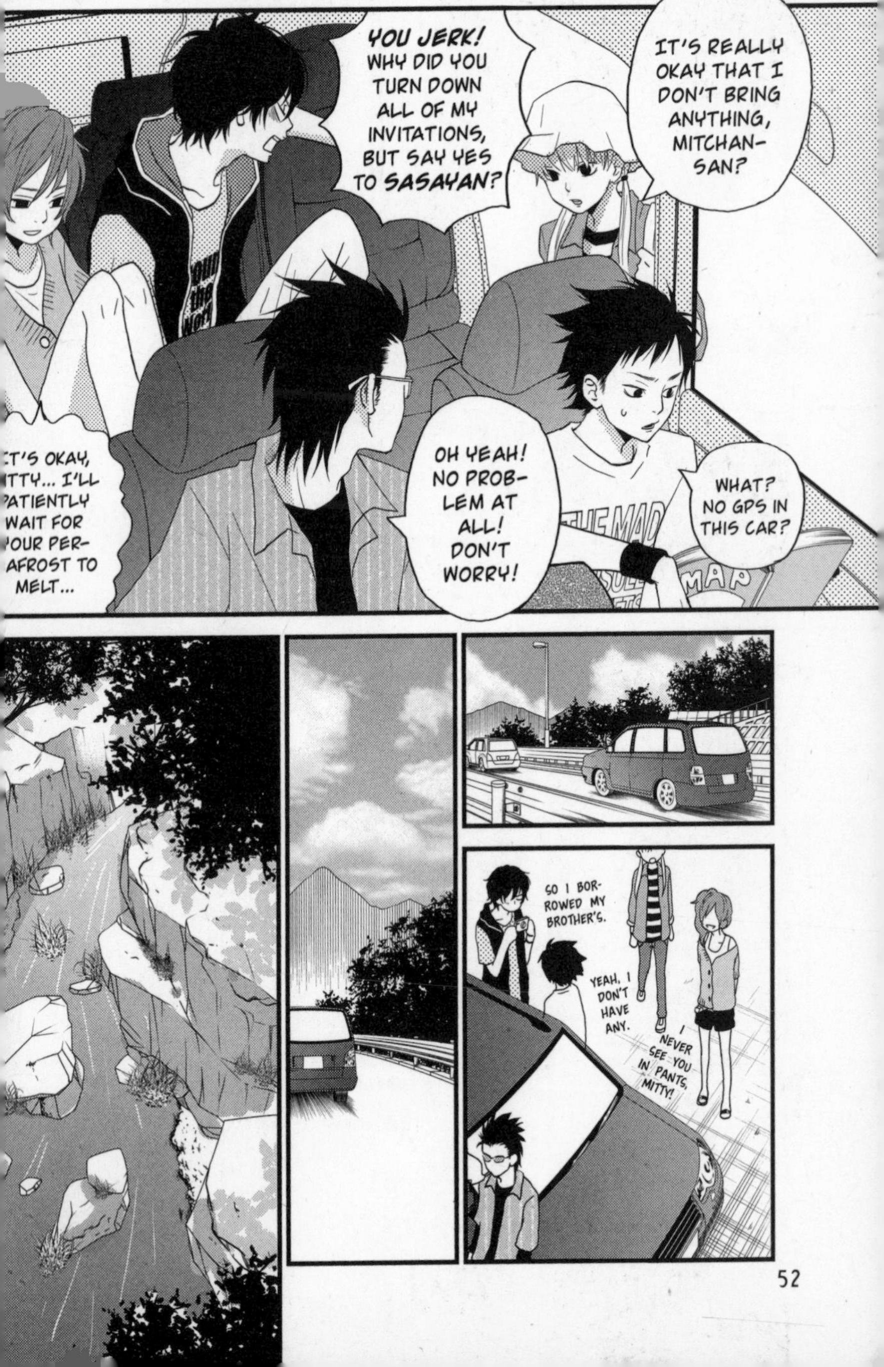
IT'S REALLY OKAY THAT I DON'T BRING ANYTHING, MITCHAN-SAN?
YOU JERK! WHY DID YOU TURN DOWN ALL OF MY INVITATIONS, BUT SAY YES TO SASAYAN?
WHAT? NO GPS IN THIS CAR?
OH YEAH! NO PROB-LEM AT ALL! DON'T WORRY!
'T'S OKAY, ITTY... I'LL ATIENTLY WAIT FOR OUR PER- AFROST TO MELT...
SO I BOR-ROWED MY BROTHER'S.
YEAH, I DON'T HAVE ANY.
I NEVER SEE YOU IN PANTS, MITTY!

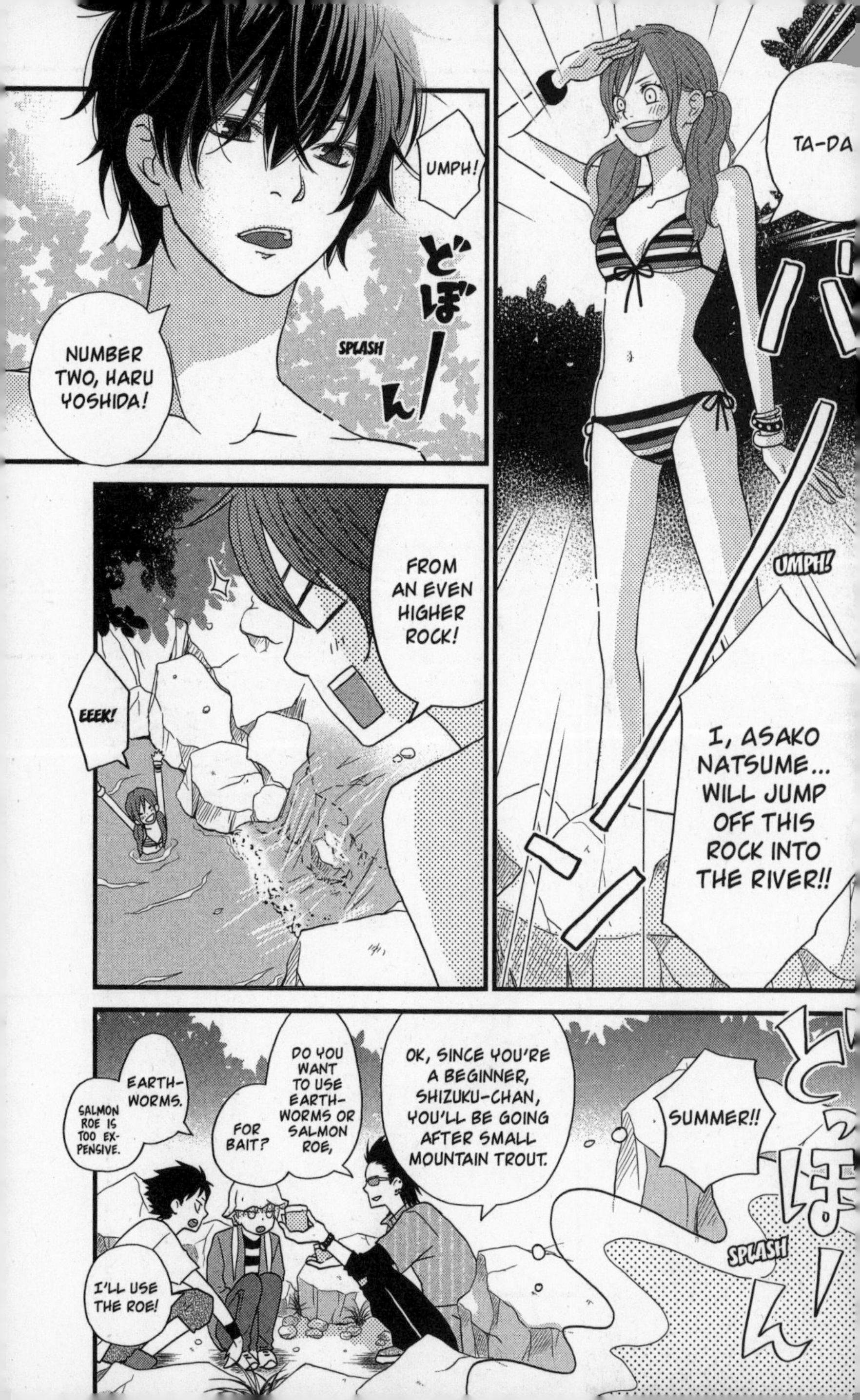

TA-DA
I, ASAKO NATSUME... WILL JUMP OFF THIS ROCK INTO THE RIVER!!
UMPH!
UMPH!
どぼーん
SPLASH
NUMBER TWO, HARU YOSHIDA!
FROM AN EVEN HIGHER ROCK!
EEEK!
どっぽーん
SPLASH
SUMMER!!
OK, SINCE YOU'RE A BEGINNER, SHIZUKU-CHAN, YOU'LL BE GOING AFTER SMALL MOUNTAIN TROUT.
DO YOU WANT TO USE EARTHWORMS OR SALMON ROE,
FOR BAIT?
EARTHWORMS.
SALMON ROE IS TOO EXPENSIVE.
I'LL USE THE ROE!

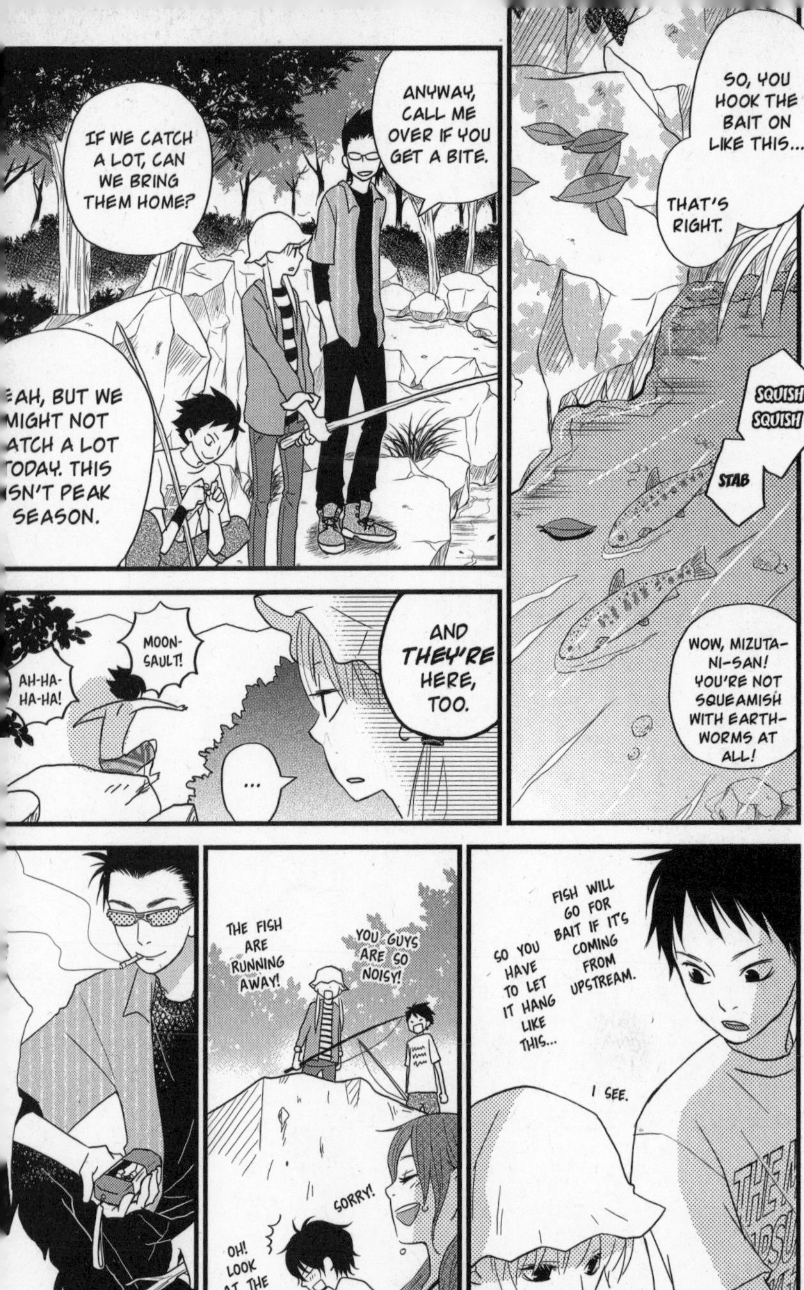
SO, YOU HOOK THE BAIT ON LIKE THIS...
THAT'S RIGHT.
SQUISH SQUISH
STAB
WOW, MIZUTANI-SAN! YOU'RE NOT SQUEAMISH WITH EARTHWORMS AT ALL!
ANYWAY, CALL ME OVER IF YOU GET A BITE.
IF WE CATCH A LOT, CAN WE BRING THEM HOME?
EAH, BUT WE MIGHT NOT ATCH A LOT ODAY. THIS SN'T PEAK SEASON.
AND THEY'RE HERE, TOO.
MOON-SAULT!
AH-HA-HA-HA!
...
FISH WILL GO FOR BAIT IF IT'S COMING FROM UPSTREAM.
SO YOU HAVE TO LET IT HANG LIKE THIS...
I SEE.
YOU GUYS ARE SO NOISY!
THE FISH ARE RUNNING AWAY!
SORRY!
OH! LOOK AT THE FISH!!

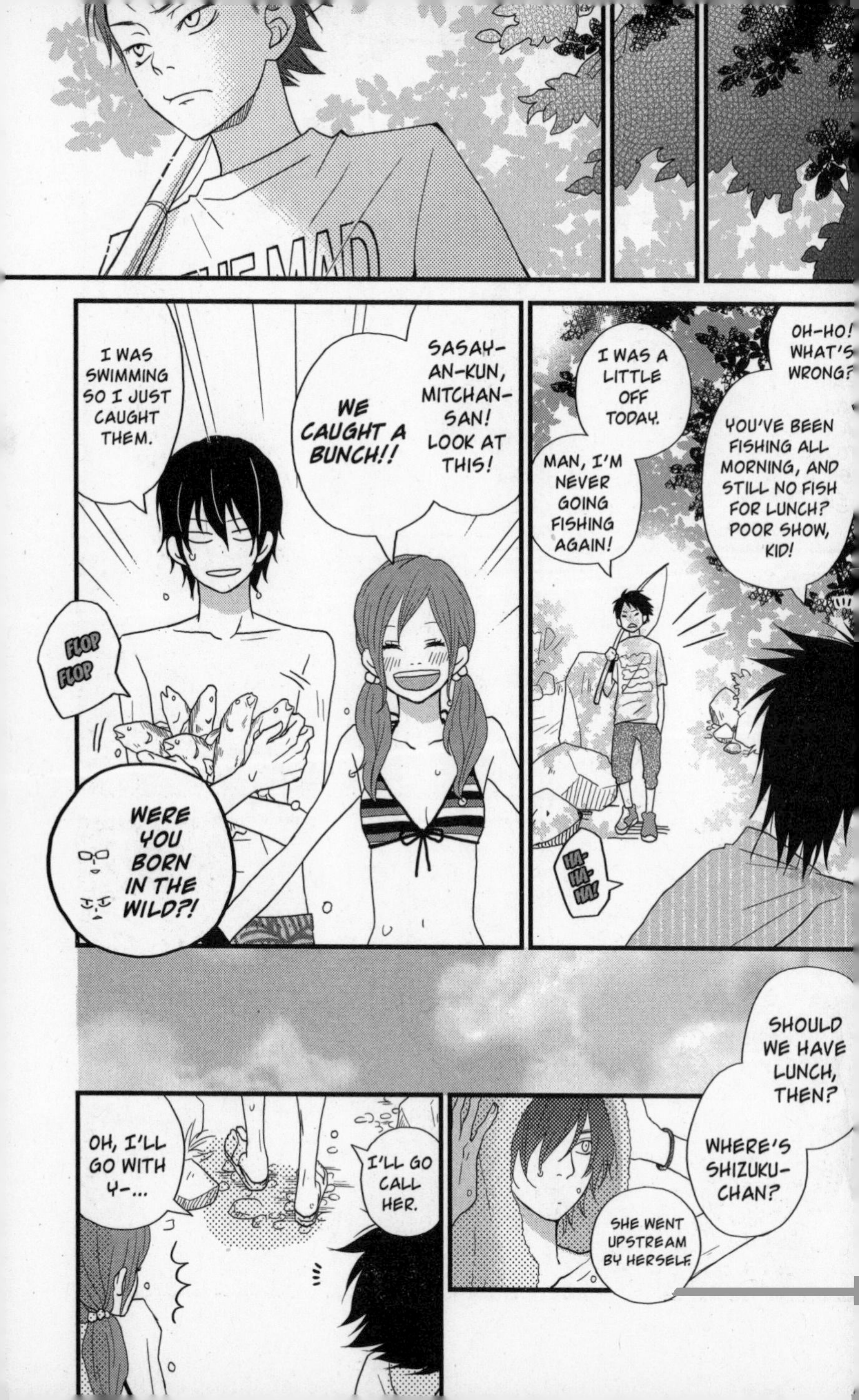
OH-HO! WHAT'S WRONG?
YOU'VE BEEN FISHING ALL MORNING, AND STILL NO FISH FOR LUNCH? POOR SHOW, KID!
I WAS A LITTLE OFF TODAY.
MAN, I'M NEVER GOING FISHING AGAIN!
HA-HA-HA!
SASAY-AN-KUN, MITCHAN-SAN! LOOK AT THIS!
WE CAUGHT A BUNCH!!
I WAS SWIMMING SO I JUST CAUGHT THEM.
FLOP FLOP
WERE YOU BORN IN THE WILD?!
SHOULD WE HAVE LUNCH, THEN?
WHERE'S SHIZUKU-CHAN?
SHE WENT UPSTREAM BY HERSELF.
I'LL GO CALL HER.
OH, I'LL GO WITH Y-...

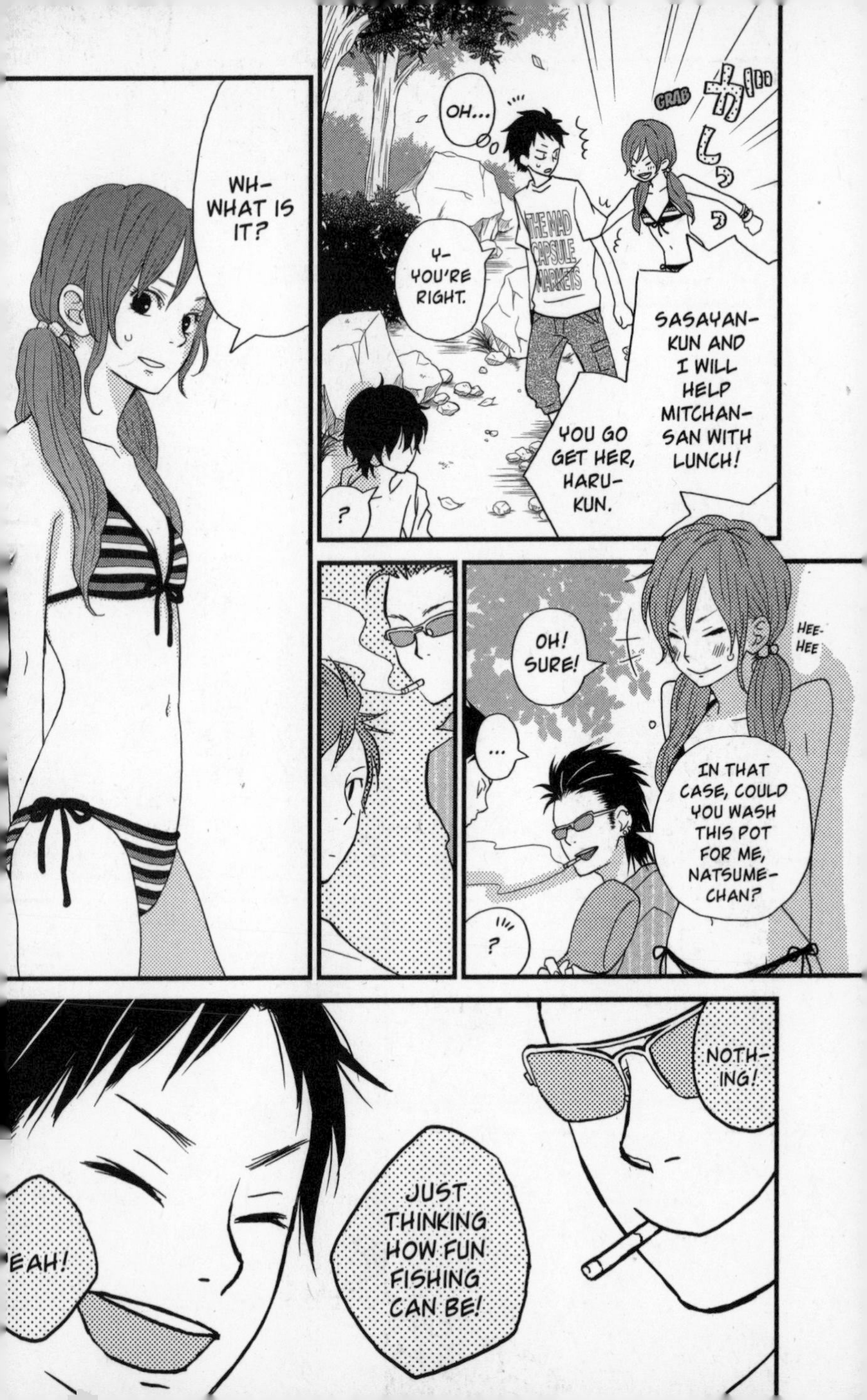
GRAB
SASAYAN-KUN AND I WILL HELP MITCHAN-SAN WITH LUNCH!
YOU GO GET HER, HARU-KUN.
THE MAD CAPSULE MARKETS
OH...
Y-YOU'RE RIGHT.
?
HEE-HEE
IN THAT CASE, COULD YOU WASH THIS POT FOR ME, NATSUME-CHAN?
OH! SURE!
...
?
WH-WHAT IS IT?
NOTH-ING!
JUST THINKING HOW FUN FISHING CAN BE!
EAH!

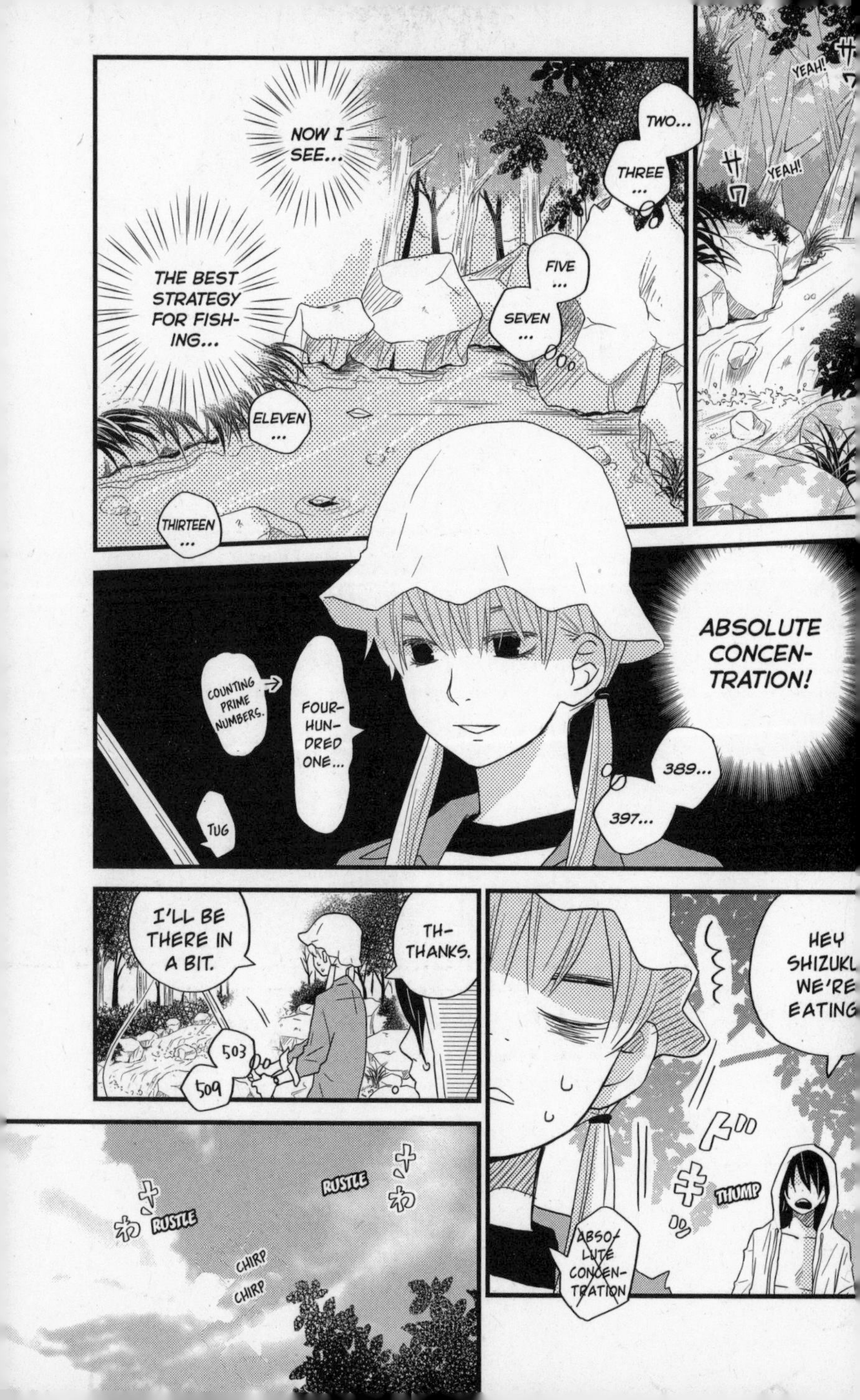
YEAH!
YEAH!
TWO...
THREE...
FIVE...
SEVEN...
NOW I SEE...
THE BEST STRATEGY FOR FISHING...
ELEVEN...
THIRTEEN...
ABSOLUTE CONCENTRATION!
389...
397...
FOUR-HUNDRED ONE...
COUNTING PRIME NUMBERS.
TUG
HEY SHIZUK WE'RE EATING
THUMP
ABSOLUTE CONCENTRATION
TH-THANKS.
I'LL BE THERE IN A BIT.
503
509
RUSTLE
RUSTLE
CHIRP
CHIRP

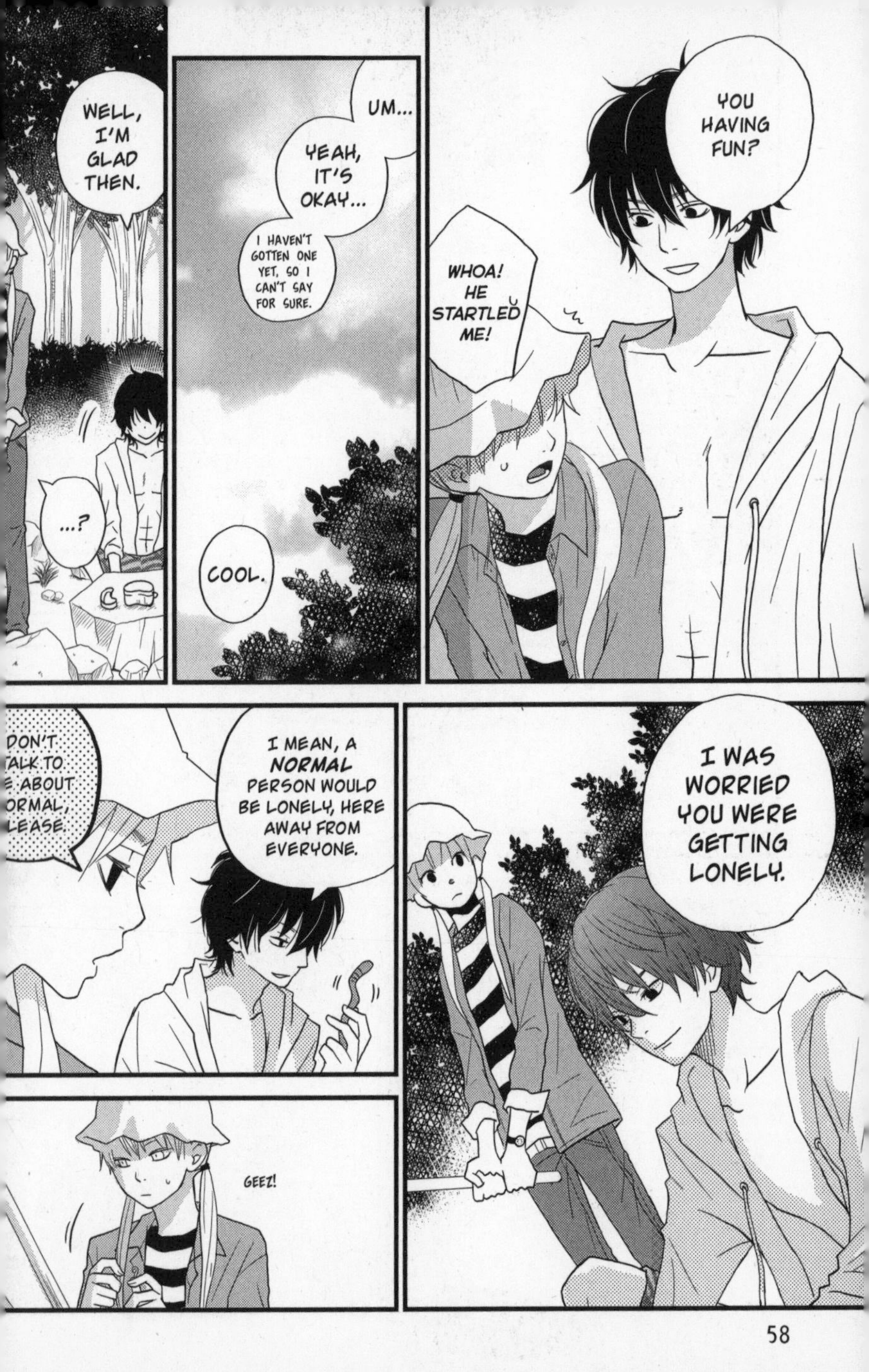
YOU HAVING FUN?
WHOA! HE STARTLED ME!
UM...
YEAH, IT'S OKAY...
I HAVEN'T GOTTEN ONE YET, SO I CAN'T SAY FOR SURE.
COOL.
WELL, I'M GLAD THEN.
...?
I WAS WORRIED YOU WERE GETTING LONELY.
I MEAN, A NORMAL PERSON WOULD BE LONELY, HERE AWAY FROM EVERYONE.
DON'T TALK TO E ABOUT ORMAL, LEASE.
GEEZ!

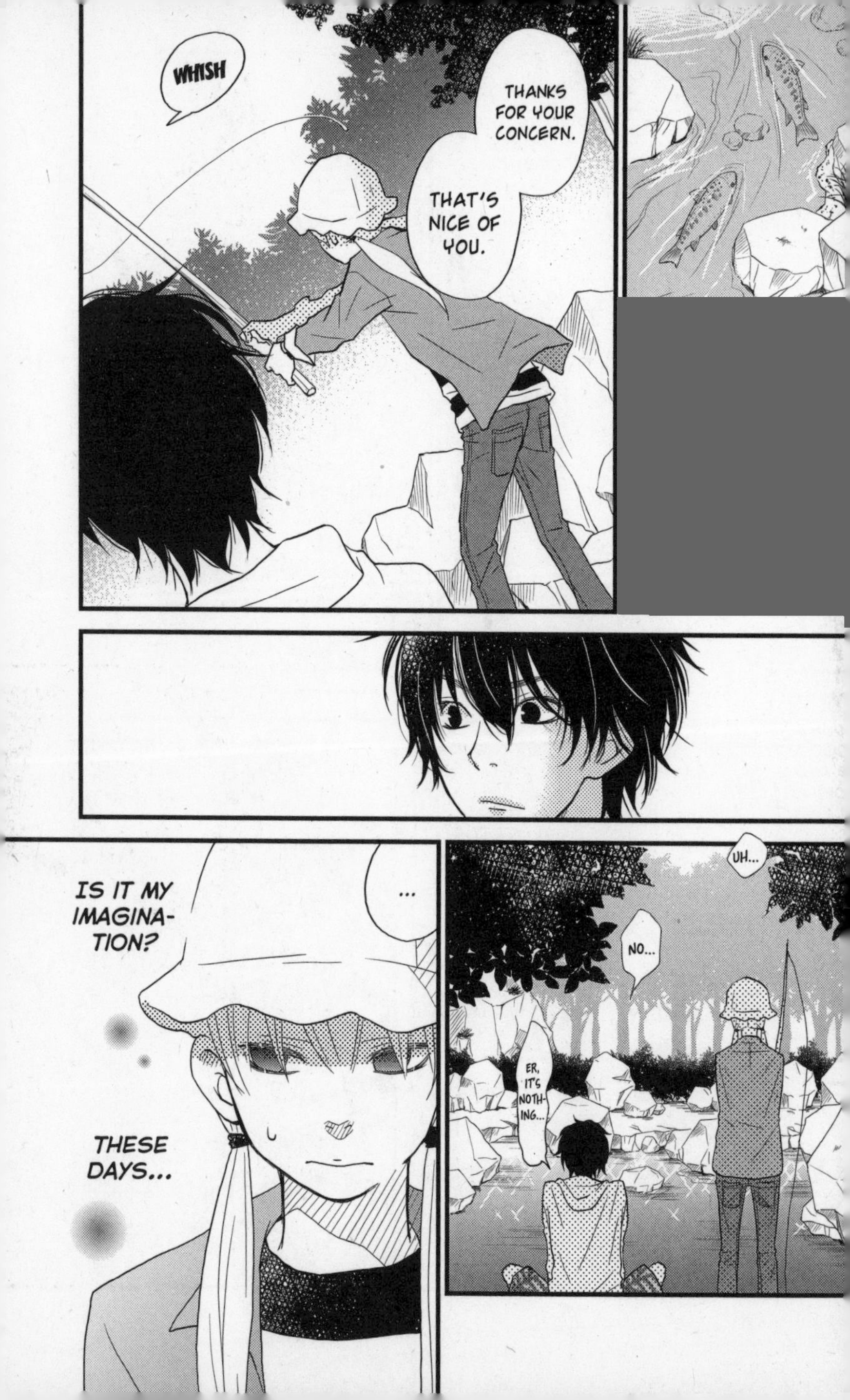
THANKS FOR YOUR CONCERN.
THAT'S NICE OF YOU.
WHISH
UH...
NO...
ER, IT'S NOTHING...
...
IS IT MY IMAGINATION?
THESE DAYS...

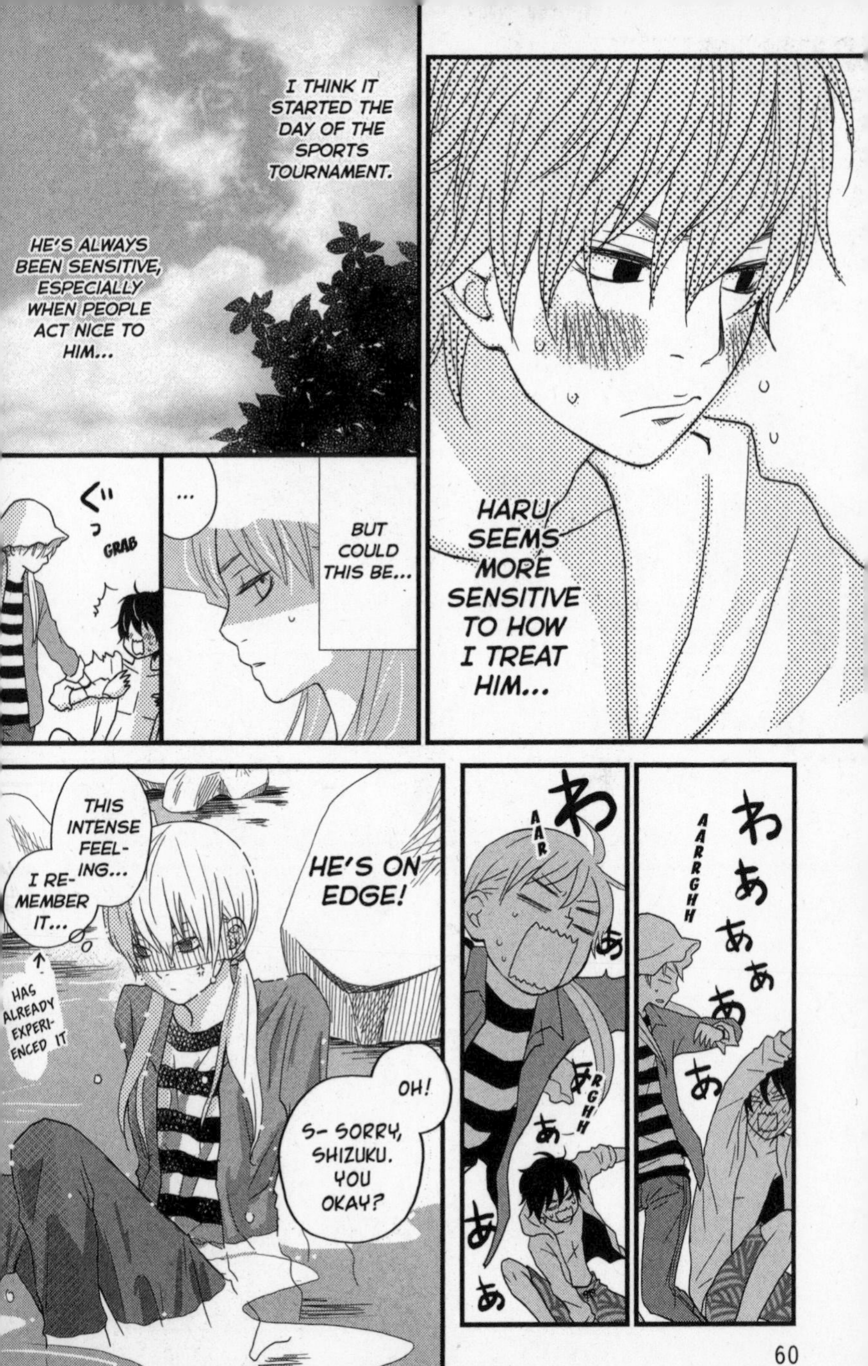
HARU SEEMS MORE SENSITIVE TO HOW I TREAT HIM...
I THINK IT STARTED THE DAY OF THE SPORTS TOURNAMENT.
HE'S ALWAYS BEEN SENSITIVE, ESPECIALLY WHEN PEOPLE ACT NICE TO HIM...
...
BUT COULD THIS BE...
ぐっ
GRAB
わあああああ
AARRGHH
わあああああ
AAR
RGHH
HE'S ON EDGE!
THIS INTENSE FEELING... I REMEMBER IT...
HAS ALREADY EXPERIENCED IT
OH!
S- SORRY, SHIZUKU. YOU OKAY?

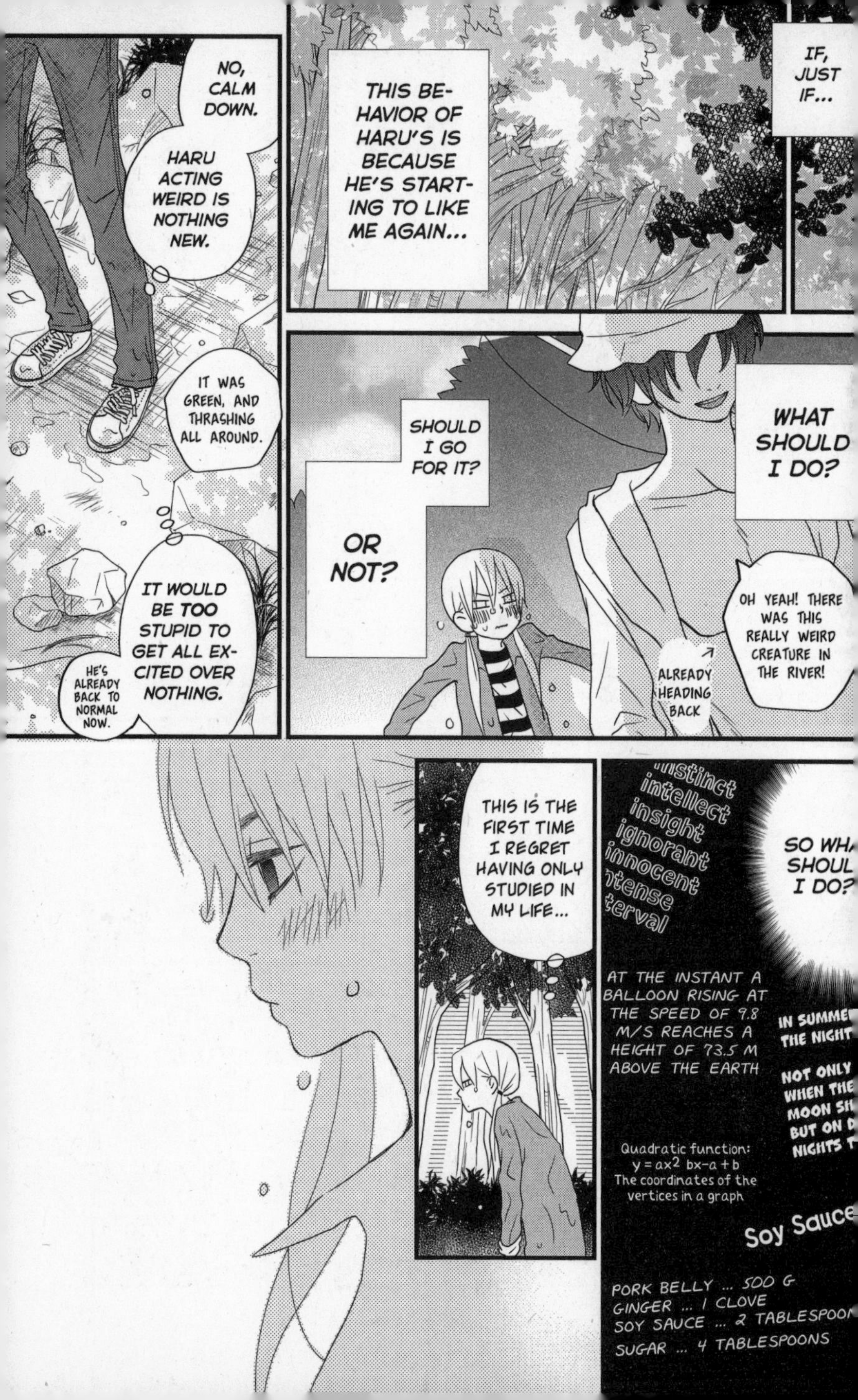
IF, JUST IF...
THIS BEHAVIOR OF HARU'S IS BECAUSE HE'S STARTING TO LIKE ME AGAIN...
WHAT SHOULD I DO?
SHOULD I GO FOR IT?
OR NOT?
OH YEAH! THERE WAS THIS REALLY WEIRD CREATURE IN THE RIVER!
ALREADY HEADING BACK
NO, CALM DOWN.
HARU ACTING WEIRD IS NOTHING NEW.
IT WAS GREEN, AND THRASHING ALL AROUND.
IT WOULD BE TOO STUPID TO GET ALL EXCITED OVER NOTHING.
HE'S ALREADY BACK TO NORMAL NOW.
SO WH SHOUL I DO?
nstinct
intellect
insight
ignorant
innocent
ntense
terval
AT THE INSTANT A BALLOON RISING AT THE SPEED OF 9.8 M/S REACHES A HEIGHT OF 73.5 M ABOVE THE EARTH
IN SUMME THE NIGHT
NOT ONLY WHEN THE MOON SH BUT ON D NIGHTS T
Quadratic function: y = ax2 bx-a + b The coordinates of the vertices in a graph
Soy Sauce
PORK BELLY ... 500 G
GINGER ... 1 CLOVE
SOY SAUCE ... 2 TABLESPOON
SUGAR ... 4 TABLESPOONS
THIS IS THE FIRST TIME I REGRET HAVING ONLY STUDIED IN MY LIFE...

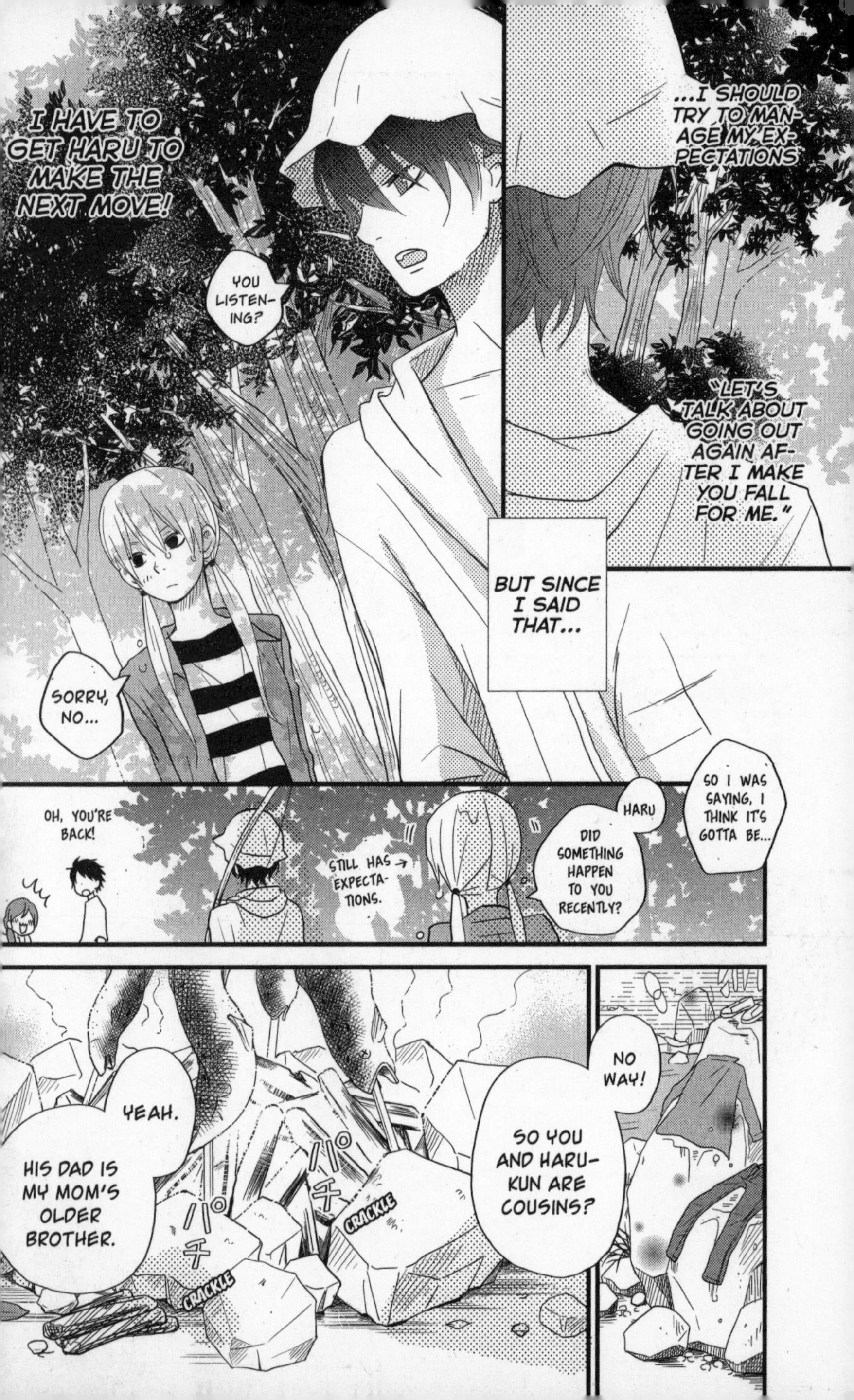
...I SHOULD TRY TO MANAGE MY EXPECTATIONS
"LET'S TALK ABOUT GOING OUT AGAIN AFTER I MAKE YOU FALL FOR ME."
BUT SINCE I SAID THAT...
I HAVE TO GET HARU TO MAKE THE NEXT MOVE!
YOU LISTENING?
SORRY, NO...
SO I WAS SAYING, I THINK IT'S GOTTA BE...
HARU
DID SOMETHING HAPPEN TO YOU RECENTLY?
STILL HAS EXPECTATIONS.
OH, YOU'RE BACK!
NO WAY!
SO YOU AND HARU-KUN ARE COUSINS?
パチ
CRACKLE
YEAH.
HIS DAD IS MY MOM'S OLDER BROTHER.
パチ
CRACKLE

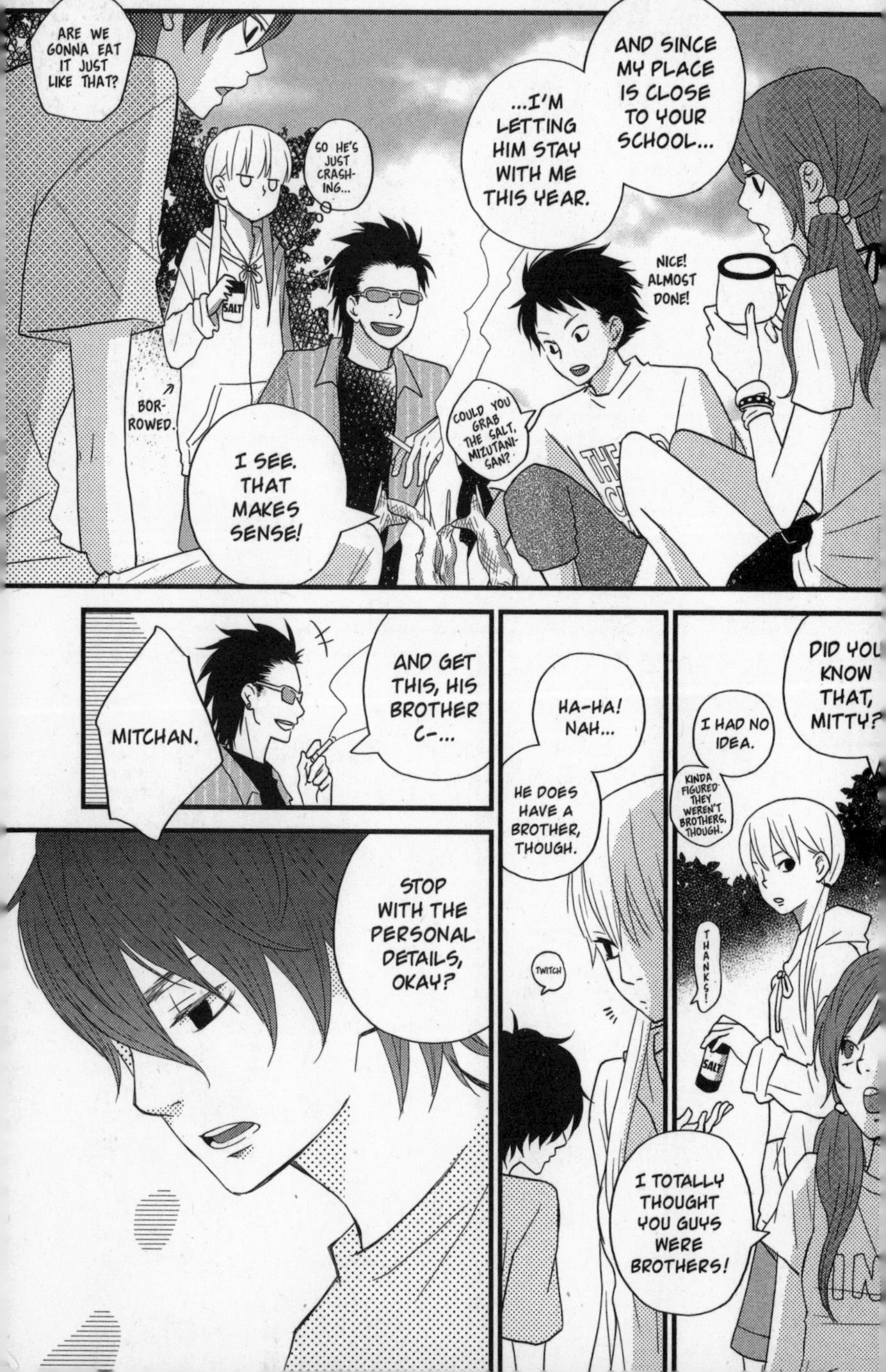
AND SINCE MY PLACE IS CLOSE TO YOUR SCHOOL...
...I'M LETTING HIM STAY WITH ME THIS YEAR.
NICE! ALMOST DONE!
SO HE'S JUST CRASHING...
ARE WE GONNA EAT IT JUST LIKE THAT?
SALT
COULD YOU GRAB THE SALT, MIZUTANI-SAN?
I SEE. THAT MAKES SENSE!
BOR-ROWED.
DID YOU KNOW THAT, MITTY?
I HAD NO IDEA.
KINDA FIGURED THEY WEREN'T BROTHERS, THOUGH.
HA-HA! NAH...
HE DOES HAVE A BROTHER, THOUGH.
THANKS!
SALT
TWITCH
I TOTALLY THOUGHT YOU GUYS WERE BROTHERS!
AND GET THIS, HIS BROTHER C-...
MITCHAN.
STOP WITH THE PERSONAL DETAILS, OKAY?

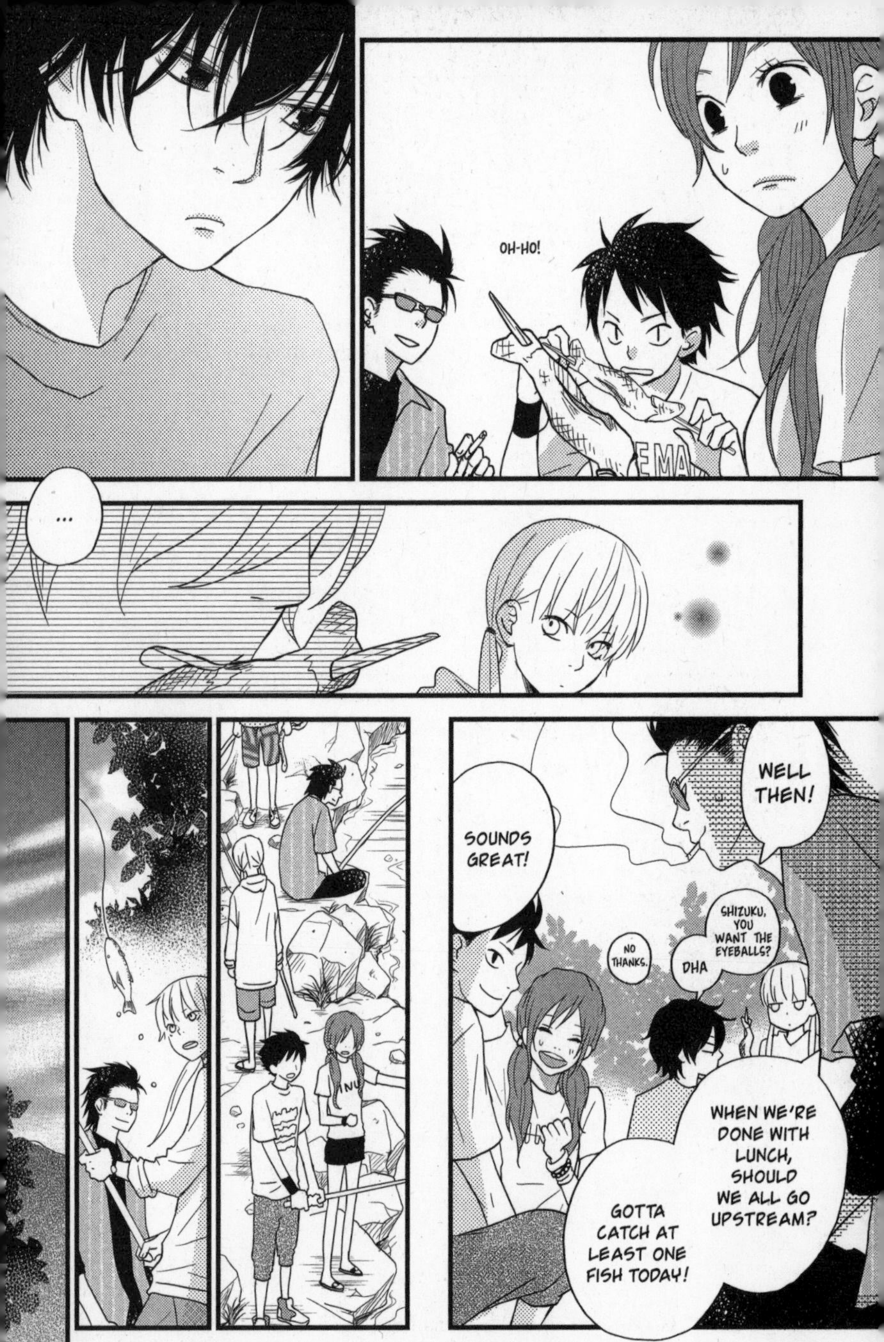
OH-HO!
...
WELL THEN!
SOUNDS GREAT!
SHIZUKU, YOU WANT THE EYEBALLS?
DHA
NO THANKS.
WHEN WE'RE DONE WITH LUNCH, SHOULD WE ALL GO UPSTREAM?
GOTTA CATCH AT LEAST ONE FISH TODAY!

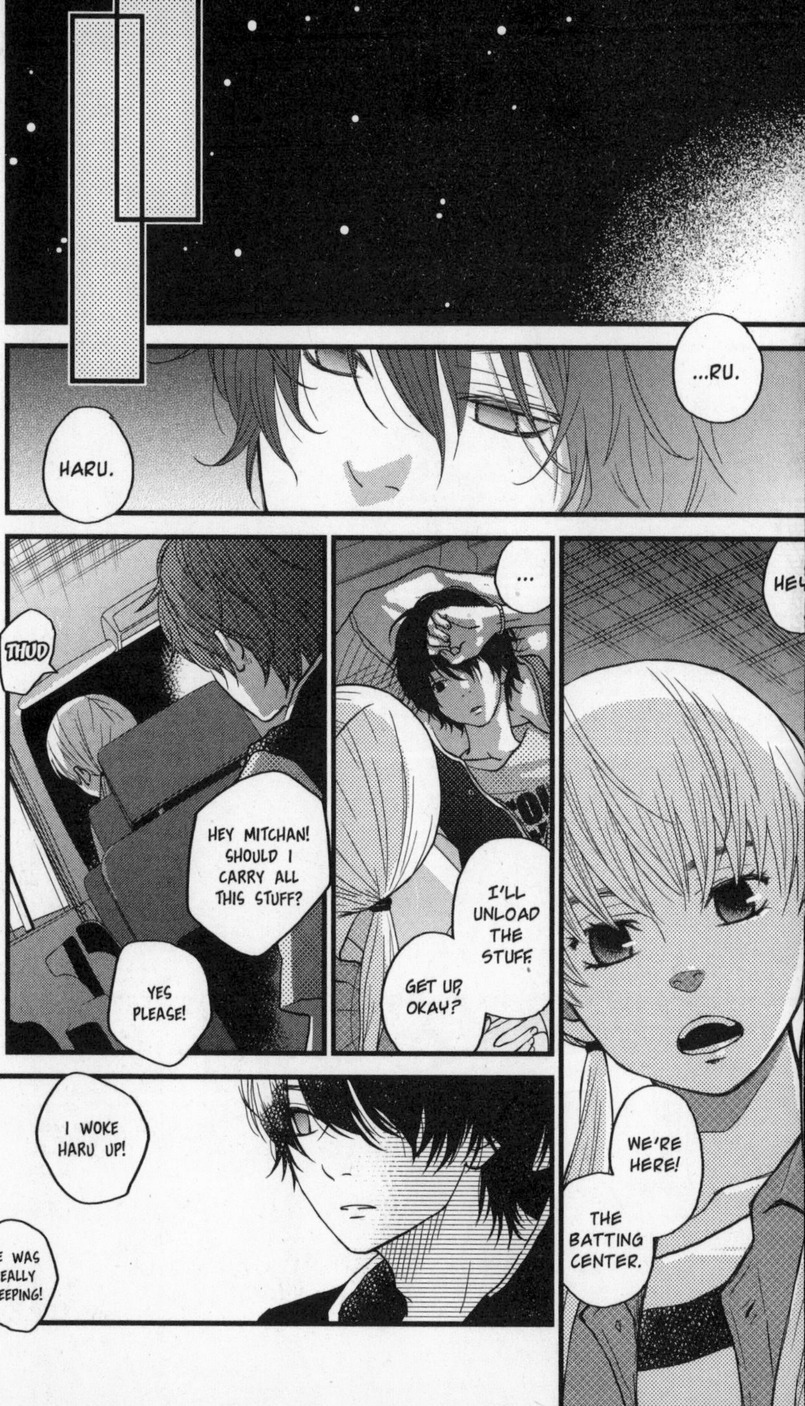
...RU.
HARU.
HE
WE'RE HERE!
THE BATTING CENTER.
...
I'LL UNLOAD THE STUFF.
GET UP, OKAY?
THUD
HEY MITCHAN! SHOULD I CARRY ALL THIS STUFF?
YES PLEASE!
I WOKE HARU UP!
HE WAS REALLY SLEEPING!

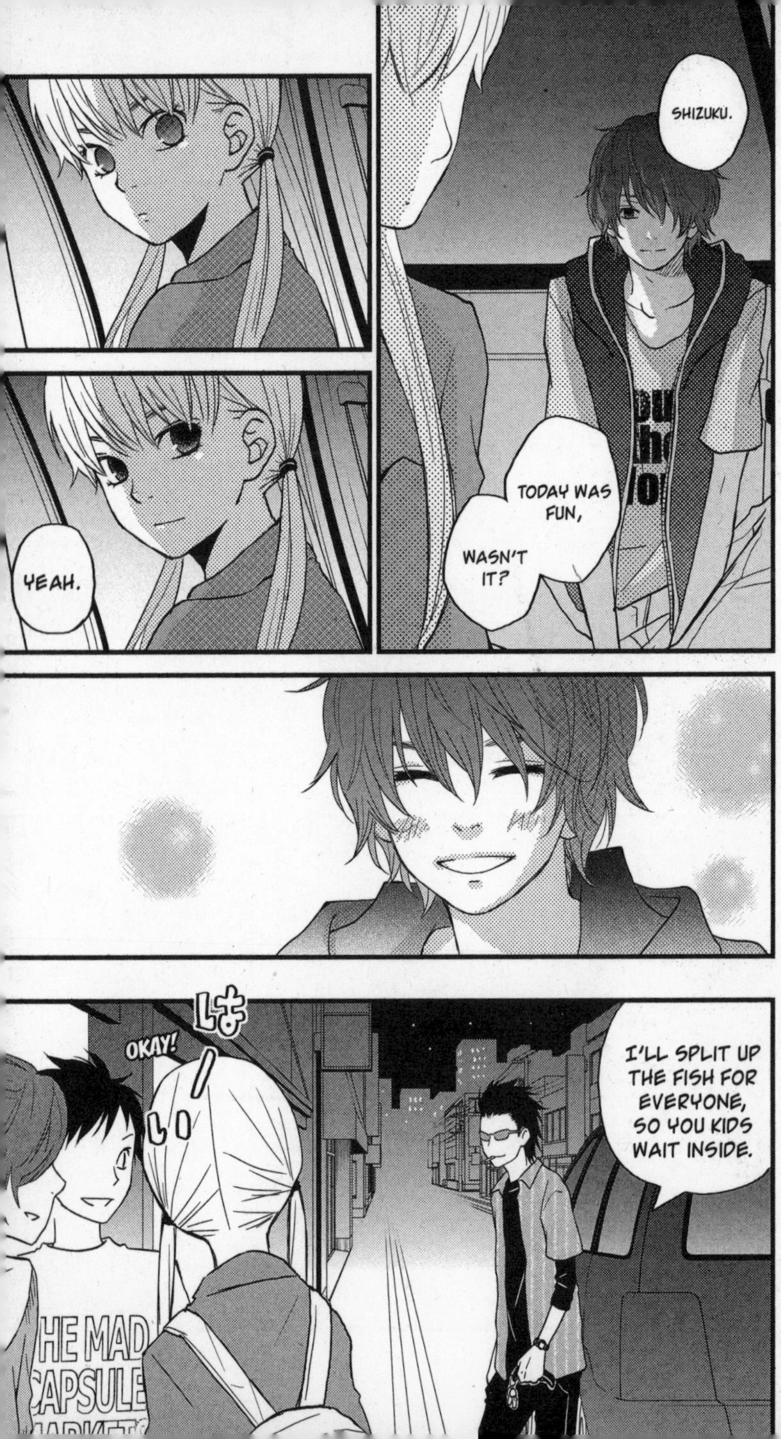
SHIZUKU.
TODAY WAS FUN,
WASN'T IT?
YEAH.
I'LL SPLIT UP THE FISH FOR EVERYONE, SO YOU KIDS WAIT INSIDE.
OKAY!

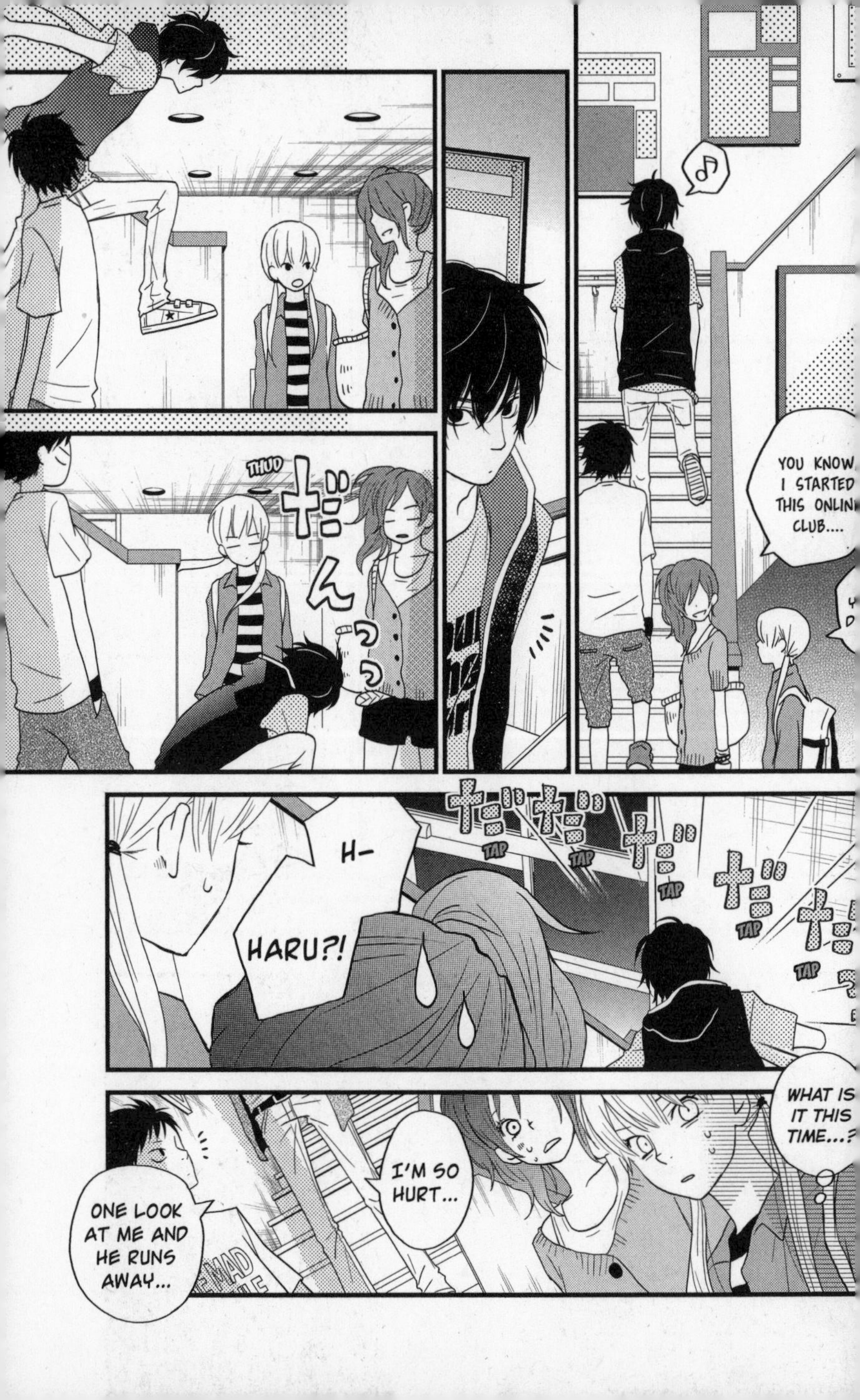
YOU KNOW, I STARTED THIS ONLIN CLUB....
THUD
TAP
TAP
TAP
TAP
TAP
H-
HARU?!
WHAT IS IT THIS TIME...?
I'M SO HURT...
ONE LOOK AT ME AND HE RUNS AWAY...

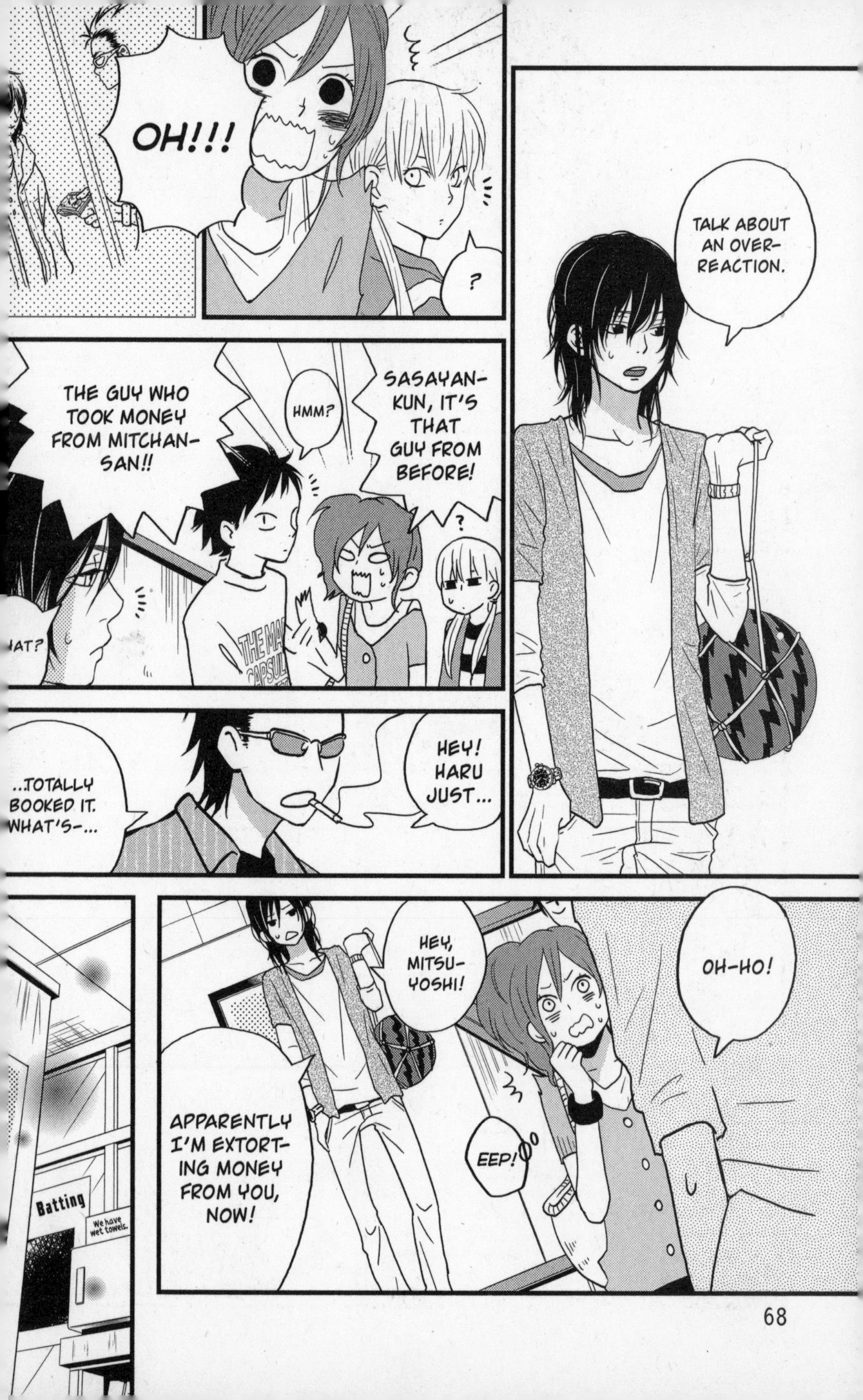
OH!!!
?
SASAYAN-KUN, IT'S THAT GUY FROM BEFORE!
HMM?
THE GUY WHO TOOK MONEY FROM MITCHAN-SAN!!
?
HAT?
HEY! HARU JUST...
...TOTALLY BOOKED IT. WHAT'S-...
TALK ABOUT AN OVER-REACTION.
OH-HO!
HEY, MITSU-YOSHI!
EEP!
APPARENTLY I'M EXTORT-ING MONEY FROM YOU, NOW!
Batting
We have wet towels.

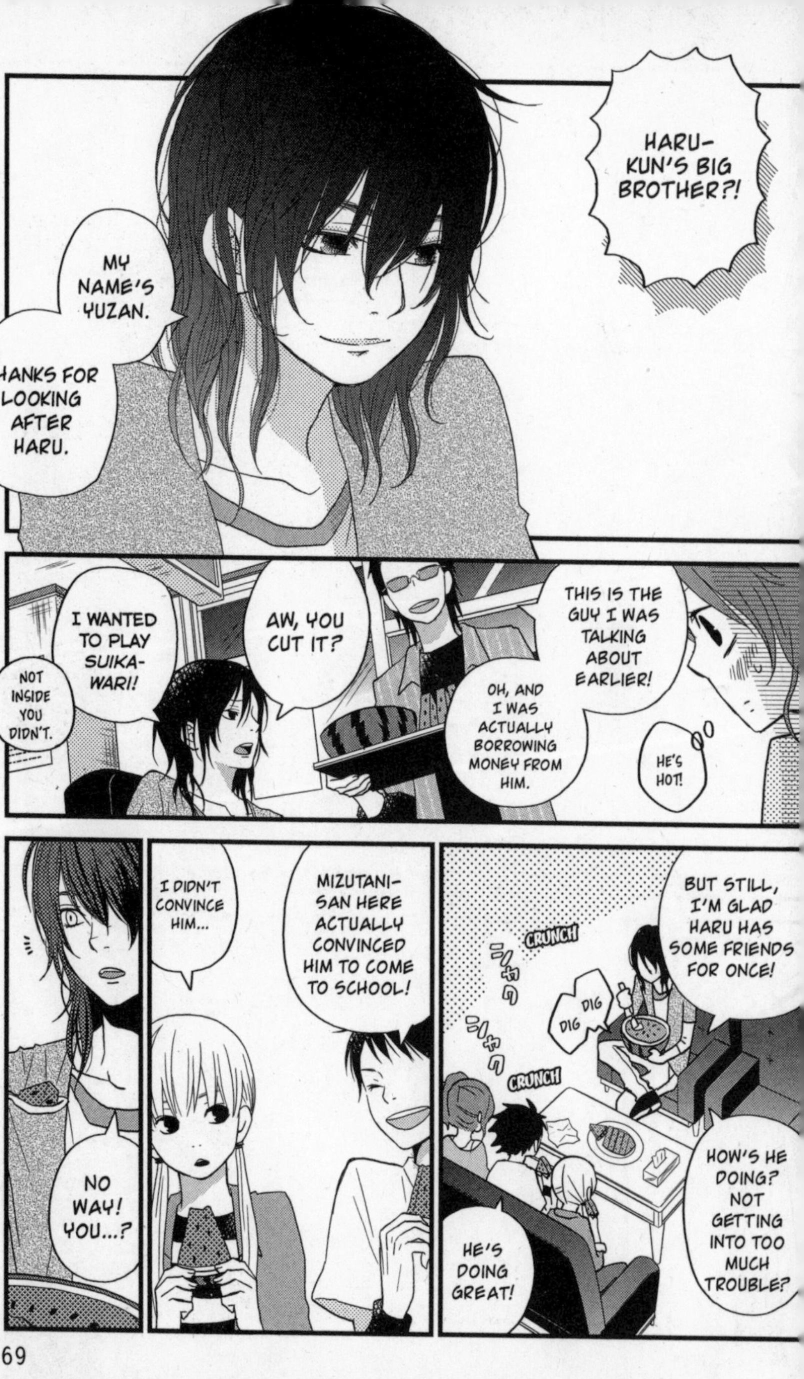
HARU-KUN'S BIG BROTHER?!
MY NAME'S YUZAN.
THANKS FOR LOOKING AFTER HARU.
THIS IS THE GUY I WAS TALKING ABOUT EARLIER!
HE'S HOT!
OH, AND I WAS ACTUALLY BORROWING MONEY FROM HIM.
AW, YOU CUT IT?
I WANTED TO PLAY SUIKA-WARI!
NOT INSIDE YOU DIDN'T.
BUT STILL, I'M GLAD HARU HAS SOME FRIENDS FOR ONCE!
CRUNCH
DIG DIG
CRUNCH
HOW'S HE DOING? NOT GETTING INTO TOO MUCH TROUBLE?
HE'S DOING GREAT!
MIZUTANI-SAN HERE ACTUALLY CONVINCED HIM TO COME TO SCHOOL!
I DIDN'T CONVINCE HIM...
NO WAY! YOU...?

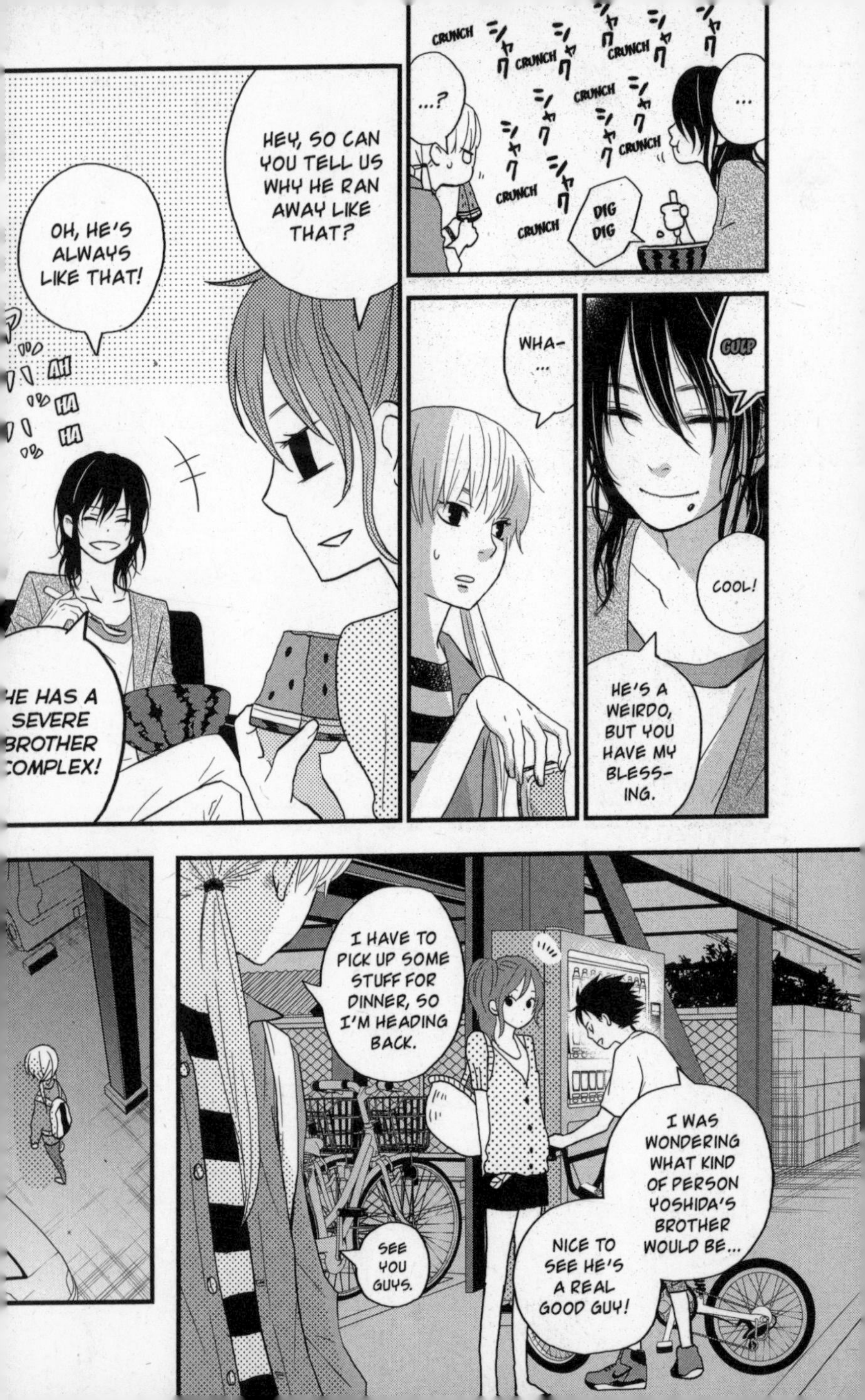
...
シャク CRUNCH シャク CRUNCH シャク CRUNCH シャク CRUNCH
シャク CRUNCH シャク CRUNCH シャク CRUNCH
DIG DIG
...?
GULP
COOL!
HE'S A WEIRDO, BUT YOU HAVE MY BLESS-ING.
WHA-...
HEY, SO CAN YOU TELL US WHY HE RAN AWAY LIKE THAT?
OH, HE'S ALWAYS LIKE THAT!
AH HA HA
HE HAS A SEVERE BROTHER COMPLEX!
I WAS WONDERING WHAT KIND OF PERSON YOSHIDA'S BROTHER WOULD BE...
NICE TO SEE HE'S A REAL GOOD GUY!
I HAVE TO PICK UP SOME STUFF FOR DINNER, SO I'M HEADING BACK.
SEE YOU GUYS.

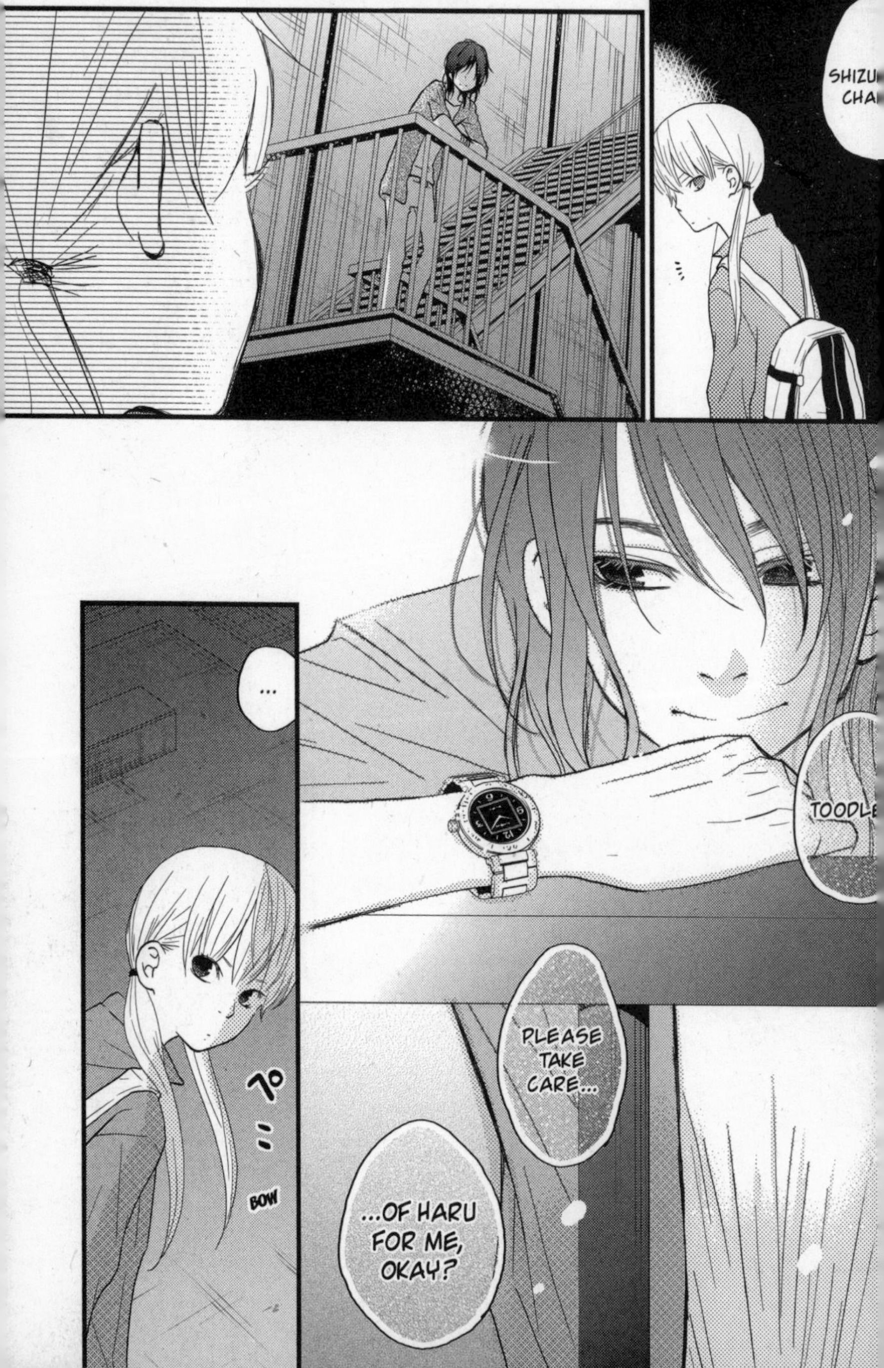
SHIZU... CHA...
...
TOODLE...
...
PLEASE TAKE CARE...
...OF HARU FOR ME, OKAY?
BOW

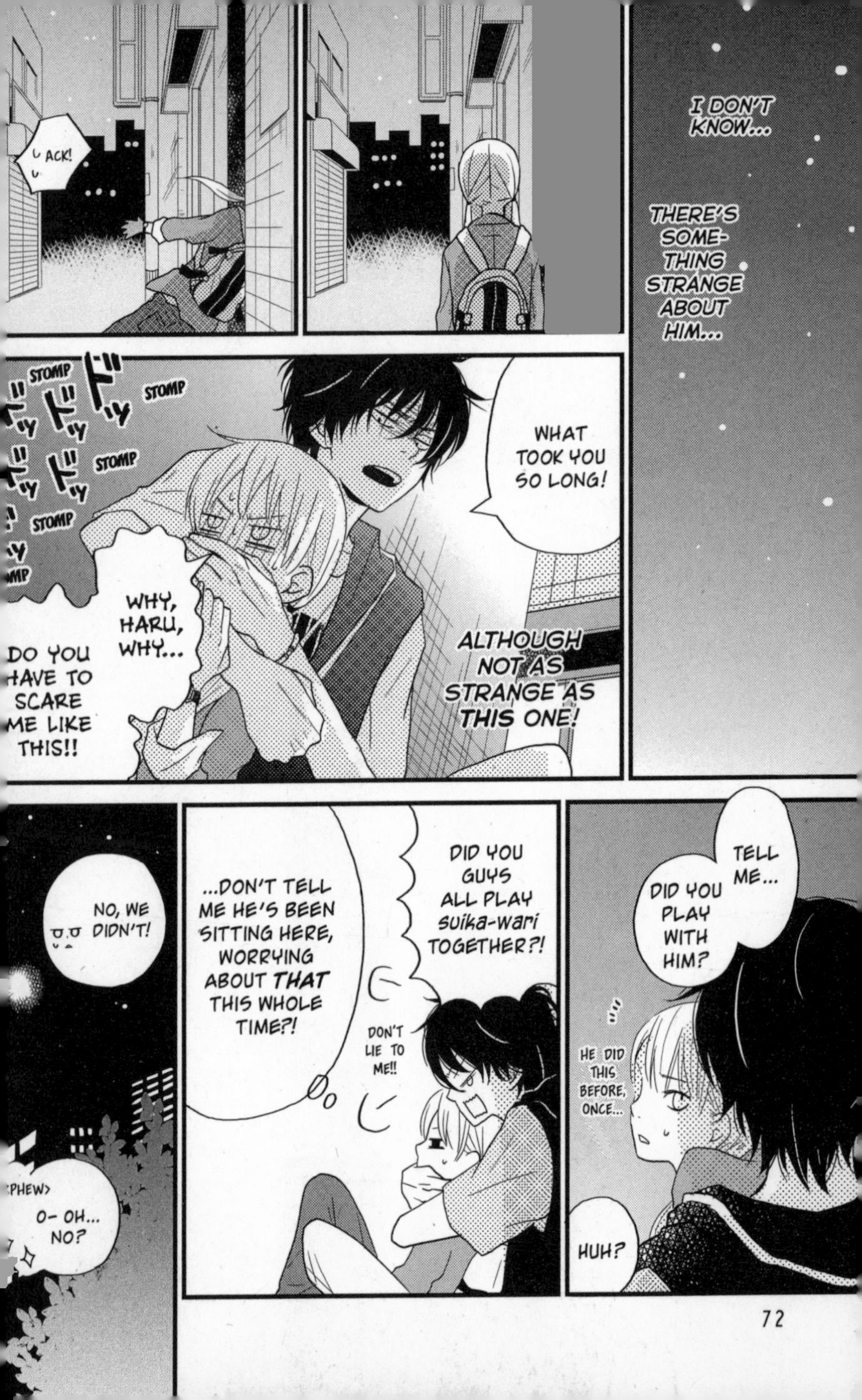

I DON'T KNOW...
THERE'S SOME-THING STRANGE ABOUT HIM...
ACK!
STOMP STOMP STOMP STOMP
WHAT TOOK YOU SO LONG!
ALTHOUGH NOT AS STRANGE AS THIS ONE!
WHY, HARU, WHY...
DO YOU HAVE TO SCARE ME LIKE THIS!!
TELL ME...
DID YOU PLAY WITH HIM?
...
HE DID THIS BEFORE, ONCE...
HUH?
DID YOU GUYS ALL PLAY suika-wari TOGETHER?!
...DON'T TELL ME HE'S BEEN SITTING HERE, WORRYING ABOUT THAT THIS WHOLE TIME?!
DON'T LIE TO ME!!
NO, WE DIDN'T!
PHEW>
O- OH... NO?

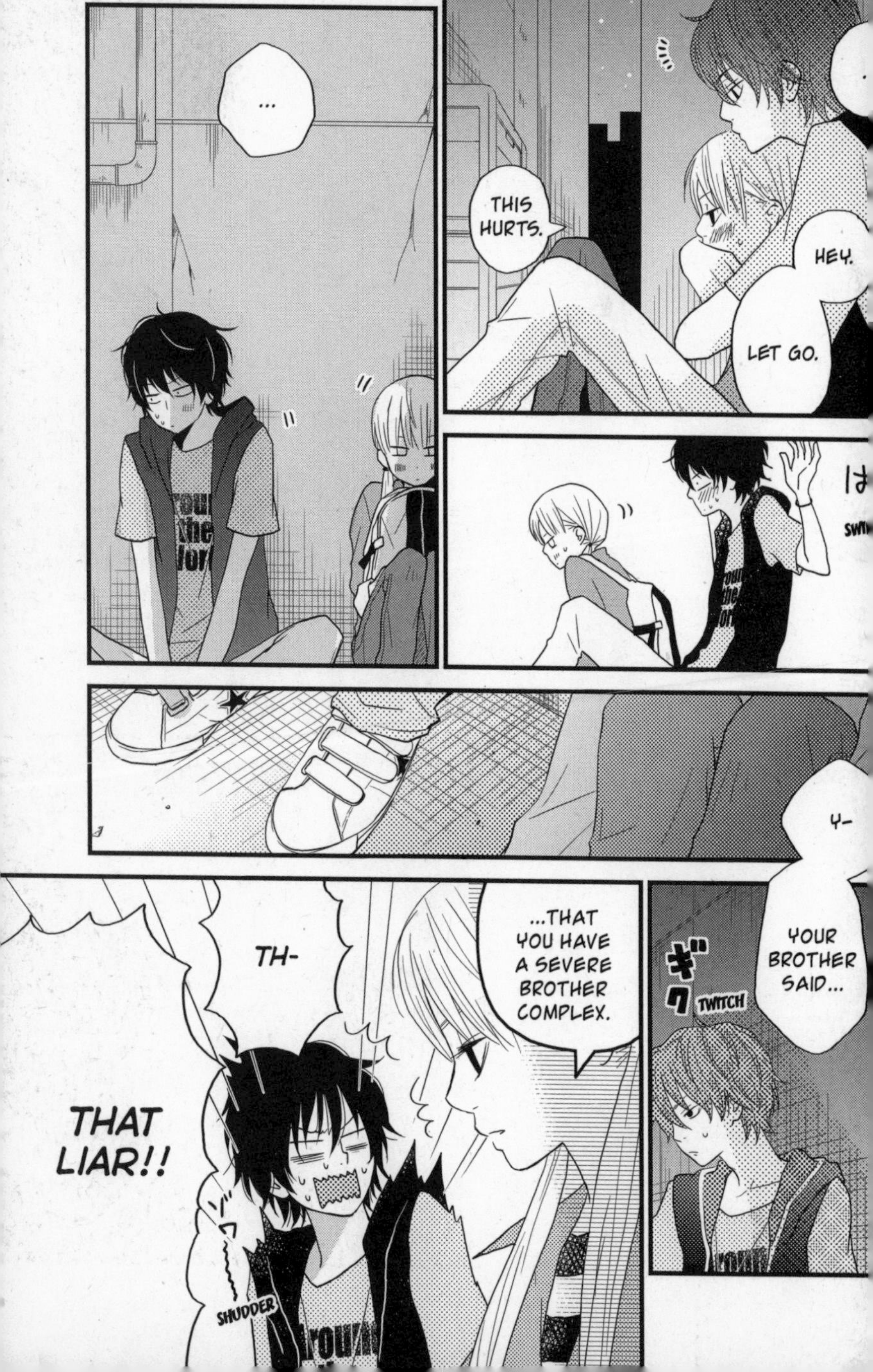
HEY.
LET GO.
THIS HURTS.
は
SWI
...
Y-
YOUR BROTHER SAID...
ギク
TWITCH
...THAT YOU HAVE A SEVERE BROTHER COMPLEX.
TH-
THAT LIAR!!
ゾワ〜
SHUDDER

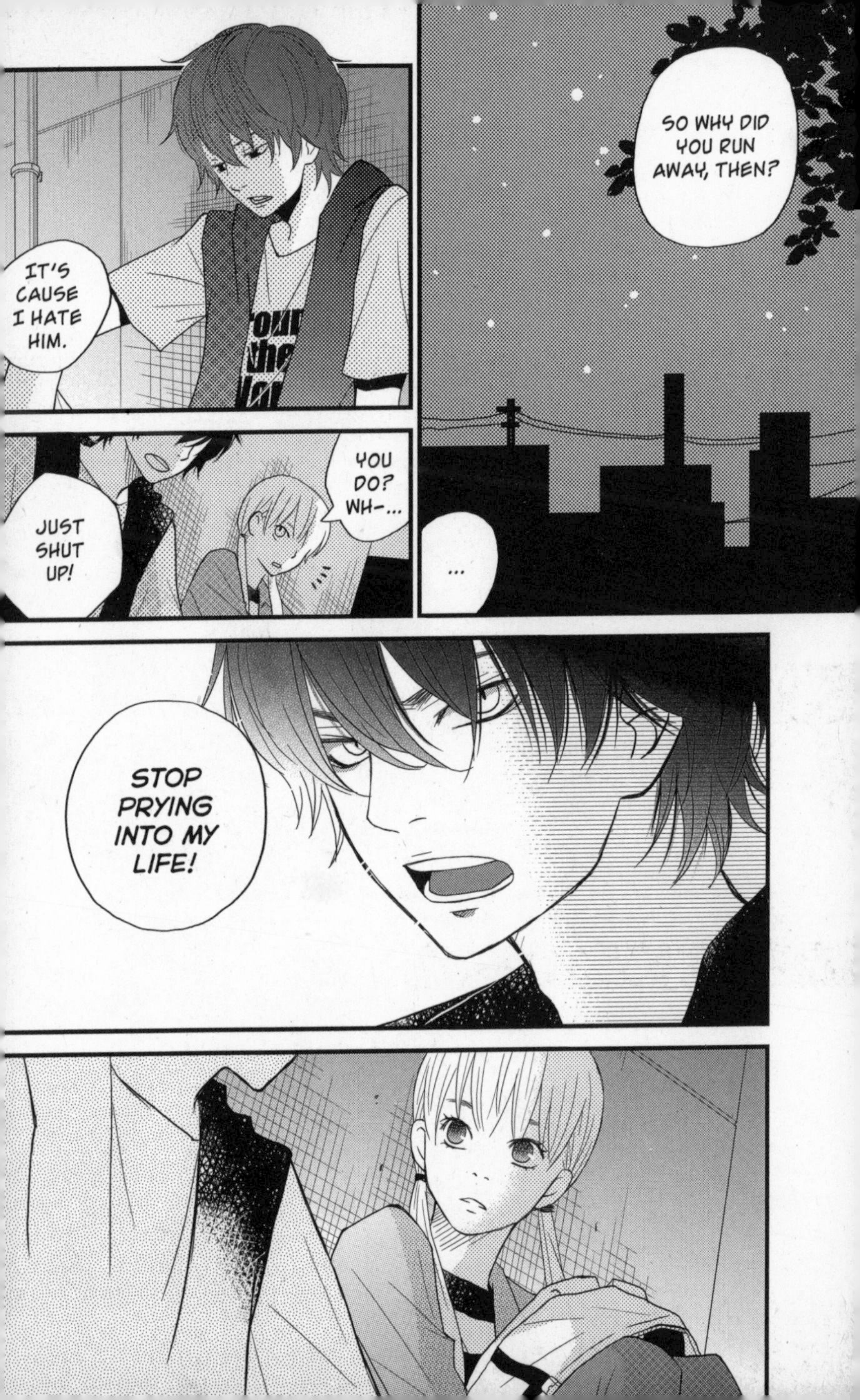
SO WHY DID YOU RUN AWAY, THEN?
...
IT'S CAUSE I HATE HIM.
YOU DO? WH-...
JUST SHUT UP!
STOP PRYING INTO MY LIFE!

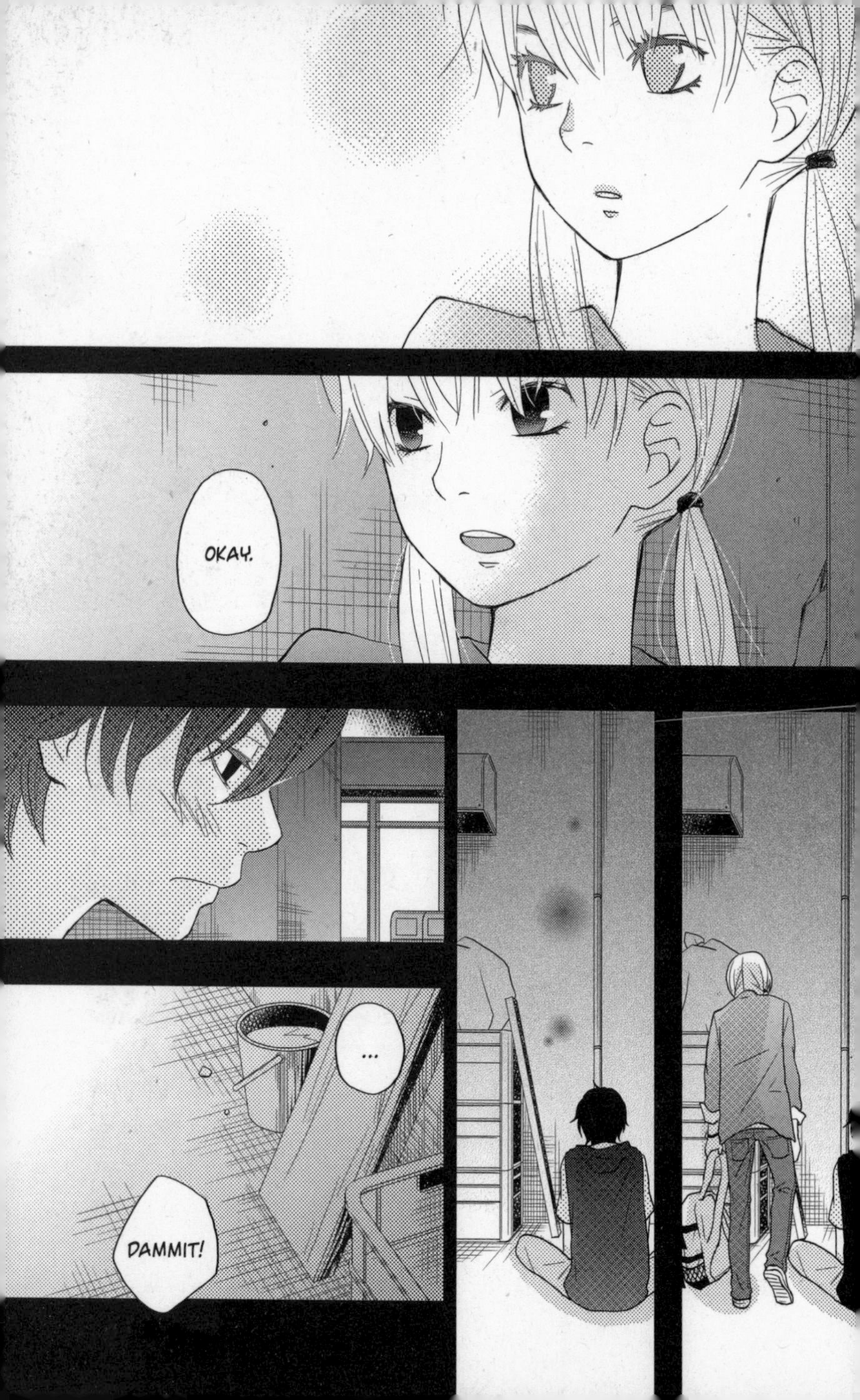
OKAY.
...
DAMMIT!

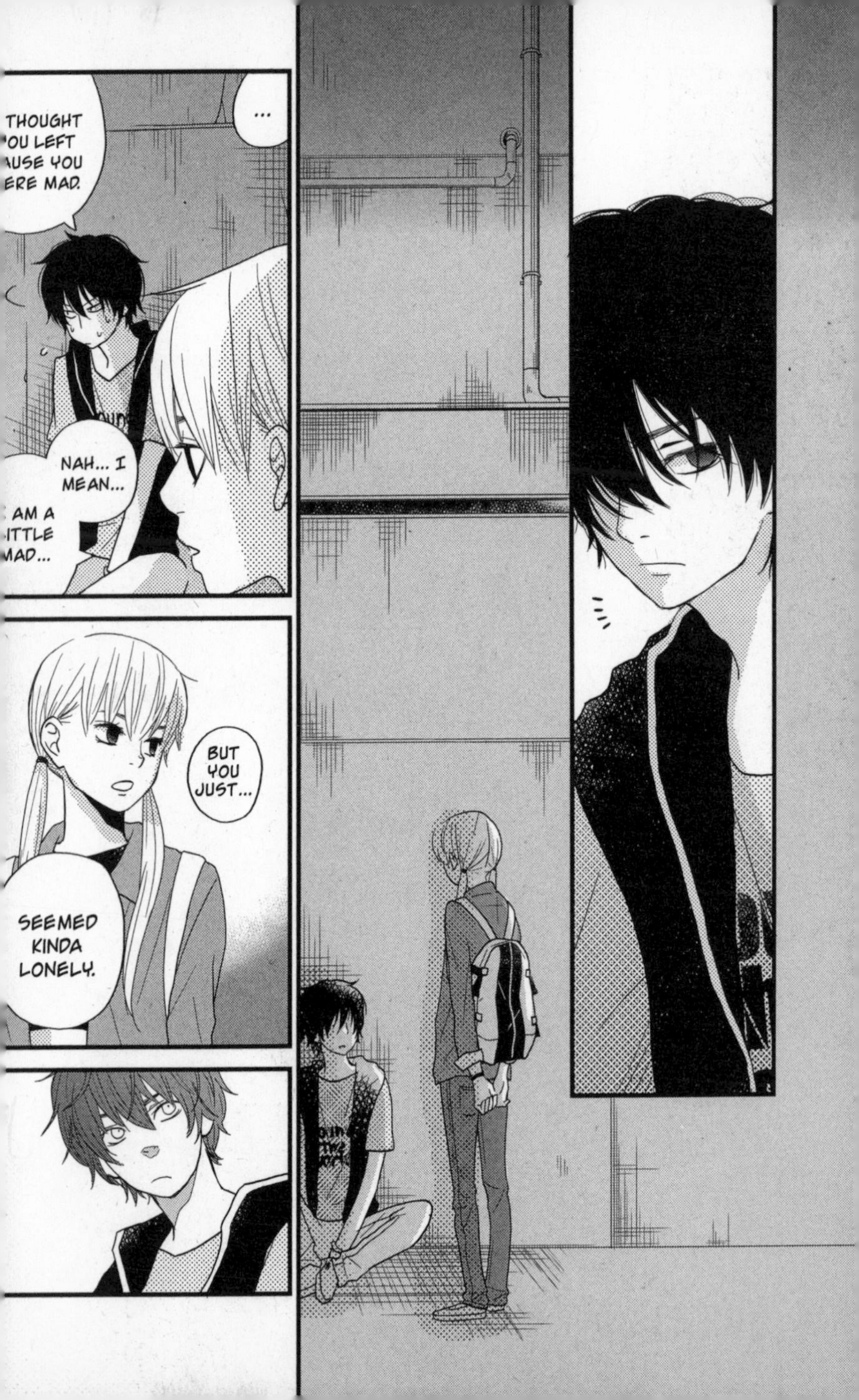
...
THOUGHT OU LEFT AUSE YOU ERE MAD.
NAH... I MEAN...
AM A ITTLE MAD...
BUT YOU JUST...
SEEMED KINDA LONELY.

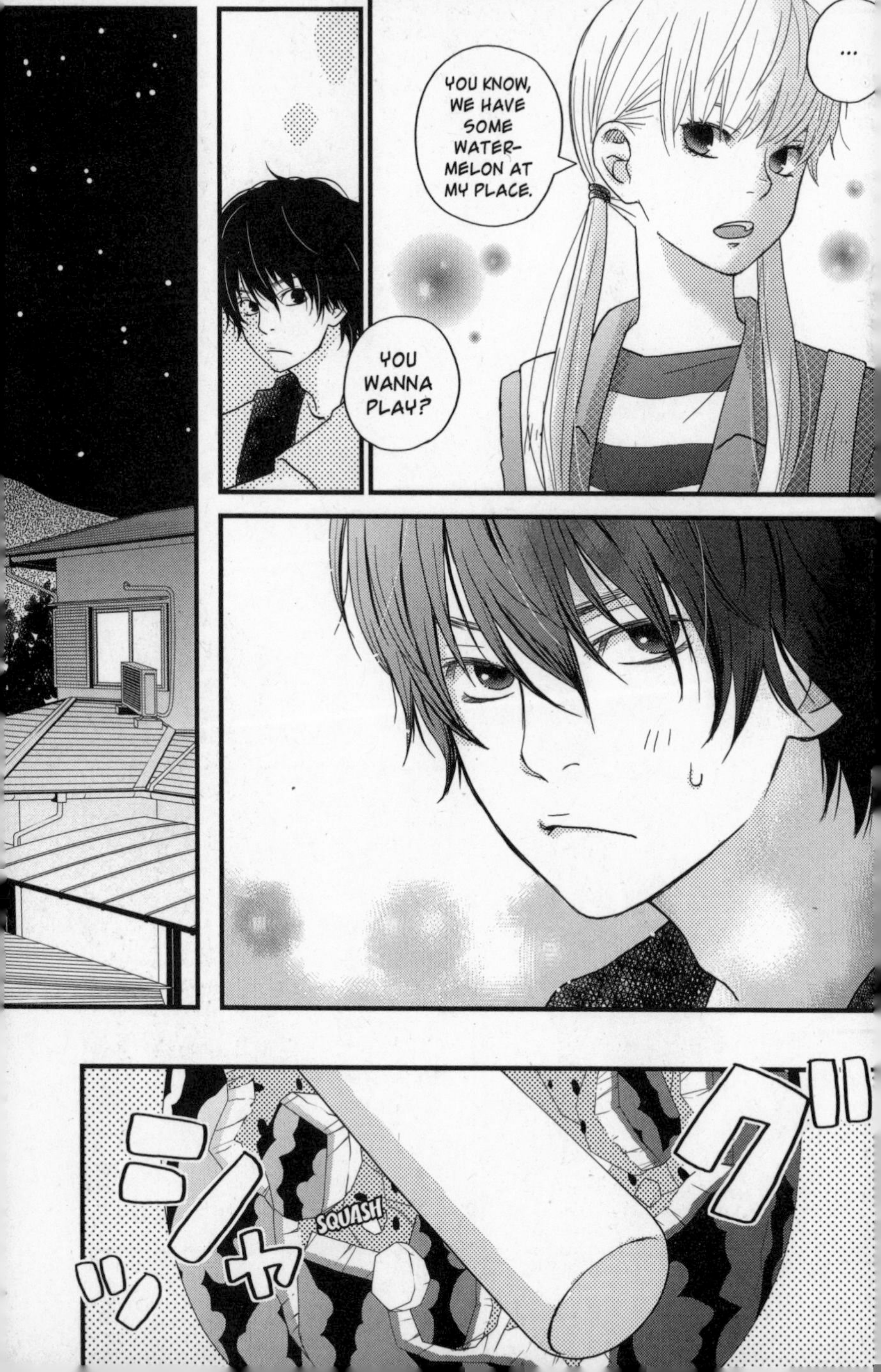
...
YOU KNOW, WE HAVE SOME WATER-MELON AT MY PLACE.
YOU WANNA PLAY?
SQUASH

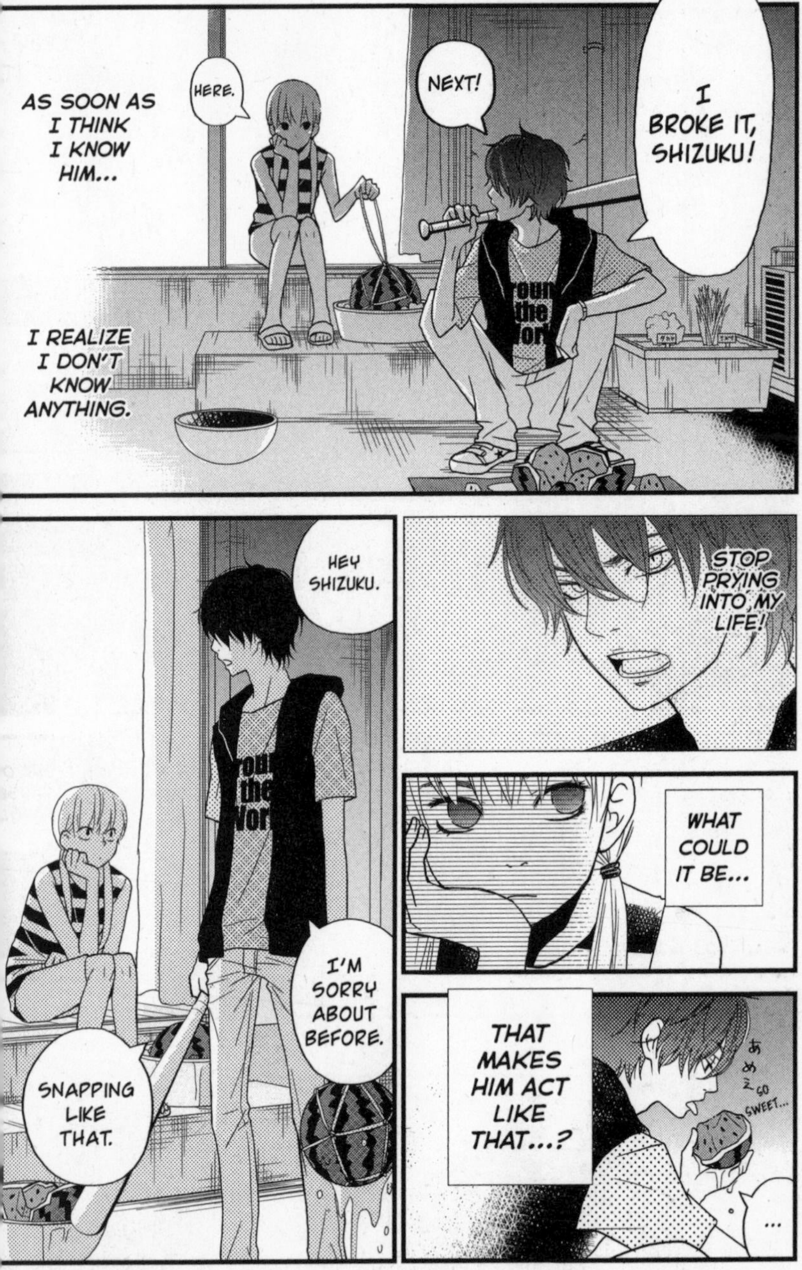
I BROKE IT, SHIZUKU!
NEXT!
HERE.
AS SOON AS I THINK I KNOW HIM...
I REALIZE I DON'T KNOW ANYTHING.
STOP PRYING INTO MY LIFE!
WHAT COULD IT BE...
THAT MAKES HIM ACT LIKE THAT...?
あめえ SO SWEET...
...
HEY SHIZUKU.
I'M SORRY ABOUT BEFORE.
SNAPPING LIKE THAT.

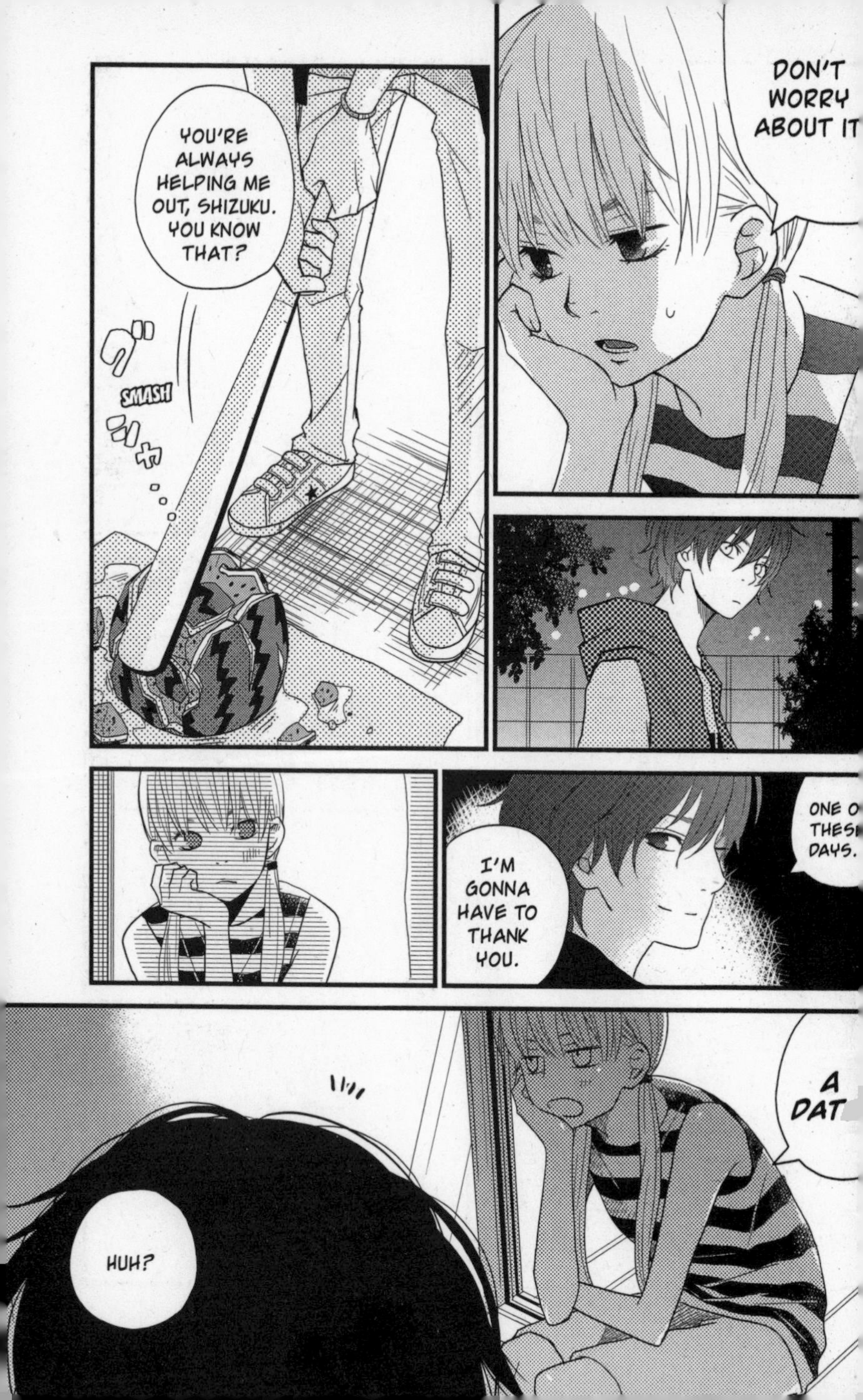
DON'T WORRY ABOUT IT
YOU'RE ALWAYS HELPING ME OUT, SHIZUKU. YOU KNOW THAT?
SMASH
ONE O THES DAYS.
I'M GONNA HAVE TO THANK YOU.
A DAT
HUH?

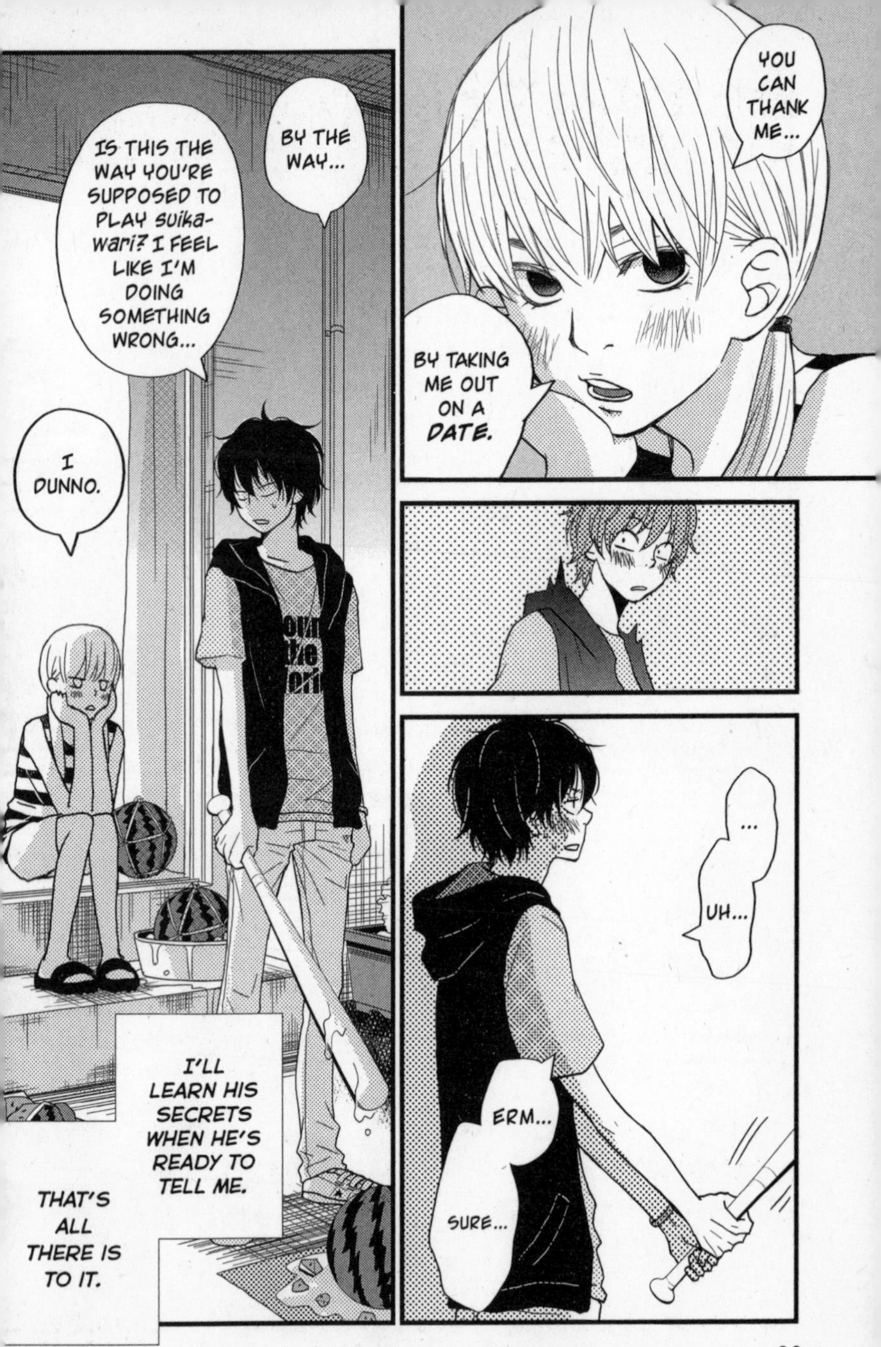
YOU CAN THANK ME...
BY TAKING ME OUT ON A DATE.
...
UH...
ERM...
SURE...
BY THE WAY...
IS THIS THE WAY YOU'RE SUPPOSED TO PLAY suika-wari? I FEEL LIKE I'M DOING SOMETHING WRONG...
I DUNNO.
I'LL LEARN HIS SECRETS WHEN HE'S READY TO TELL ME.
THAT'S ALL THERE IS TO IT.

Hates Losing

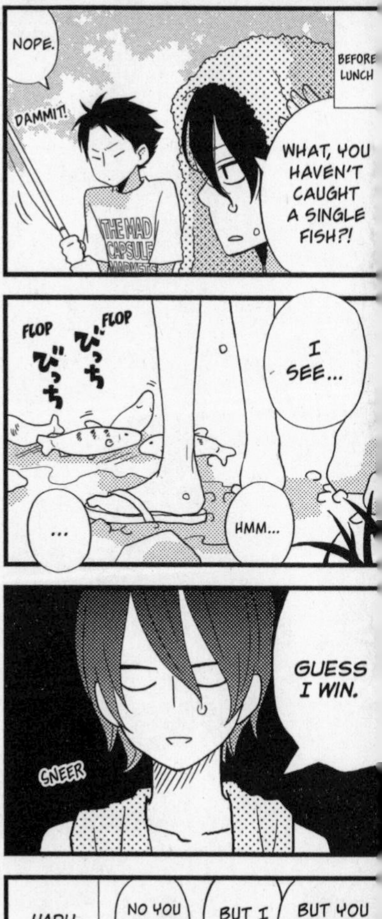
BEFORE LUNCH
WHAT, YOU HAVEN'T CAUGHT A SINGLE FISH?!
NOPE.
DAMMIT!
I SEE...
HMM...
FLOP
びっち
FLOP
びっち
...
GUESS I WIN.
SNEER
BUT YOU DIDN'T FISH THEM.
BUT I WON.
NO YOU DIDN'T.
YES I DID.
FLOP
FLOP
HARU WAS STILL MAD THAT SASAY-AN GOT SHIZUKU TO COME.

Nerves

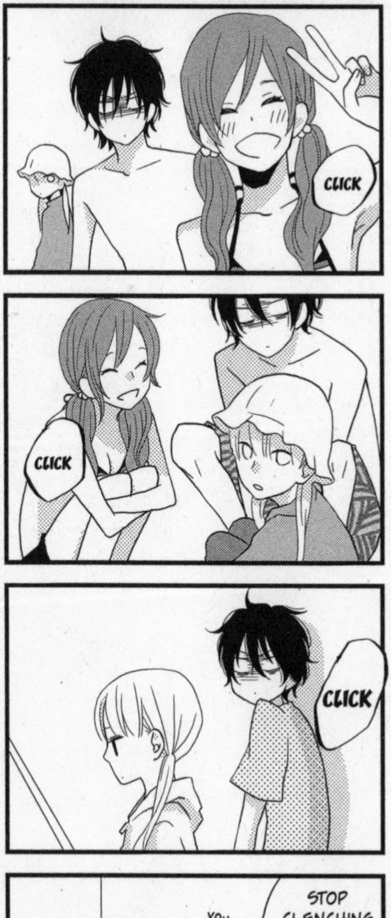
CLICK
CLICK
CLICK
STOP CLENCHING UP IN FRONT OF THE CAMERA, YOSHIDA.
YOU LOOK CREEPY!
CLENCH
HIS FIRST TIME HANGING OUT WITH FRIENDS AND TAKING PICTURES.

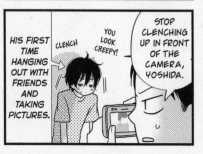

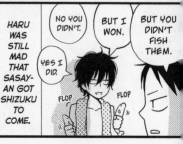

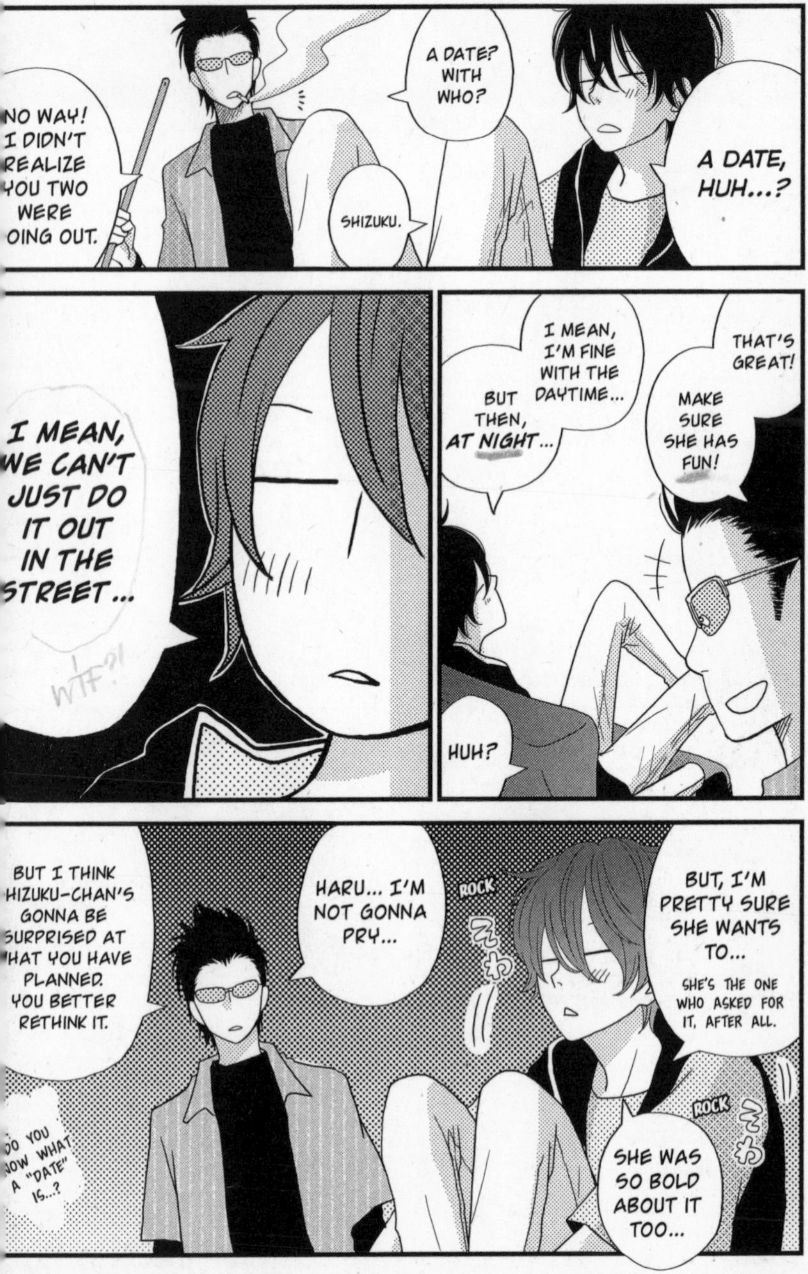
A DATE, HUH...?
A DATE? WITH WHO?
SHIZUKU.
NO WAY! I DIDN'T REALIZE YOU TWO WERE OING OUT.
THAT'S GREAT!
MAKE SURE SHE HAS FUN!
I MEAN, I'M FINE WITH THE DAYTIME...
BUT THEN, AT NIGHT...
HUH?
I MEAN, WE CAN'T JUST DO IT OUT IN THE STREET...
WTF?!
BUT, I'M PRETTY SURE SHE WANTS TO...
SHE'S THE ONE WHO ASKED FOR IT, AFTER ALL.
ROCK
ROCK
SHE WAS SO BOLD ABOUT IT TOO...
HARU... I'M NOT GONNA PRY...
BUT I THINK HIZUKU-CHAN'S GONNA BE SURPRISED AT HAT YOU HAVE PLANNED. YOU BETTER RETHINK IT.
O YOU NOW WHAT A "DATE" IS...?

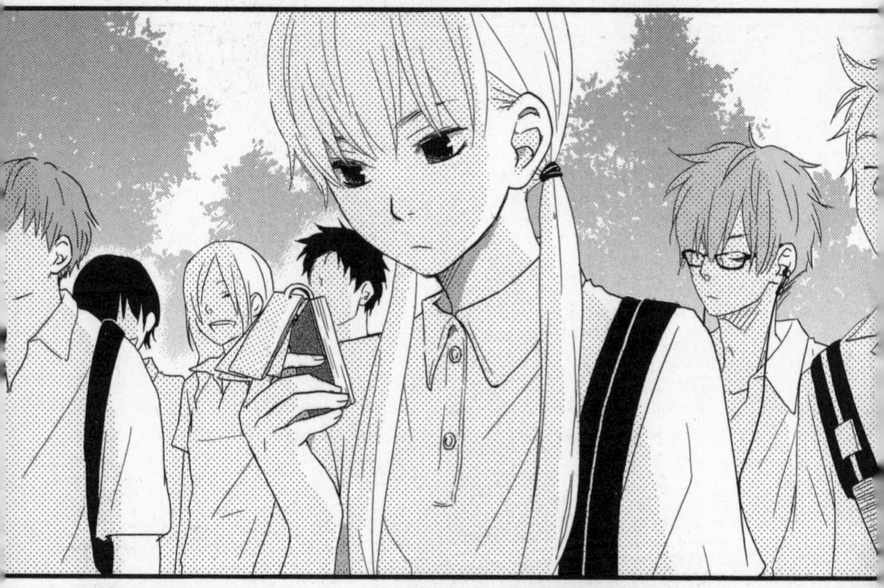

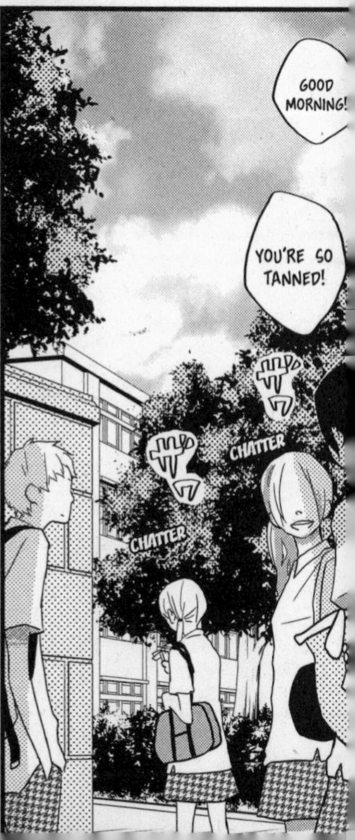
GOOD MORNING!
YOU'RE SO TANNED!
ザワ
ザワ
CHATTER
CHATTER

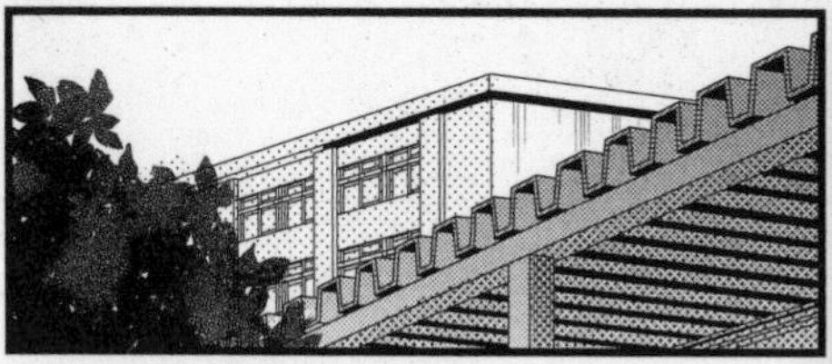

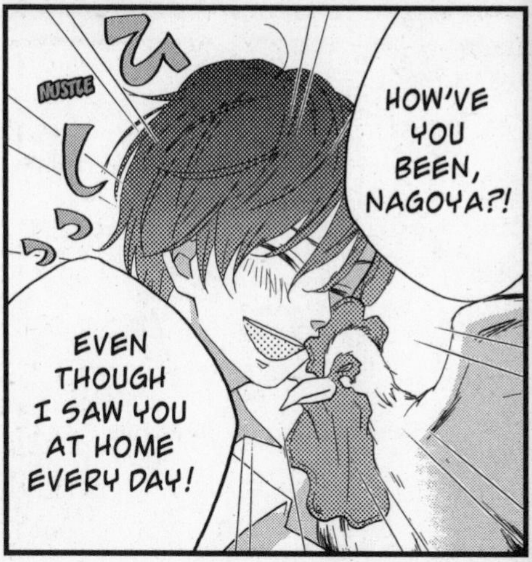
ひしっ
HUSTLE
HOW'VE YOU BEEN, NAGOYA?!
EVEN THOUGH I SAW YOU AT HOME EVERY DAY!

*Haru took Nagoya home for summer vacation.

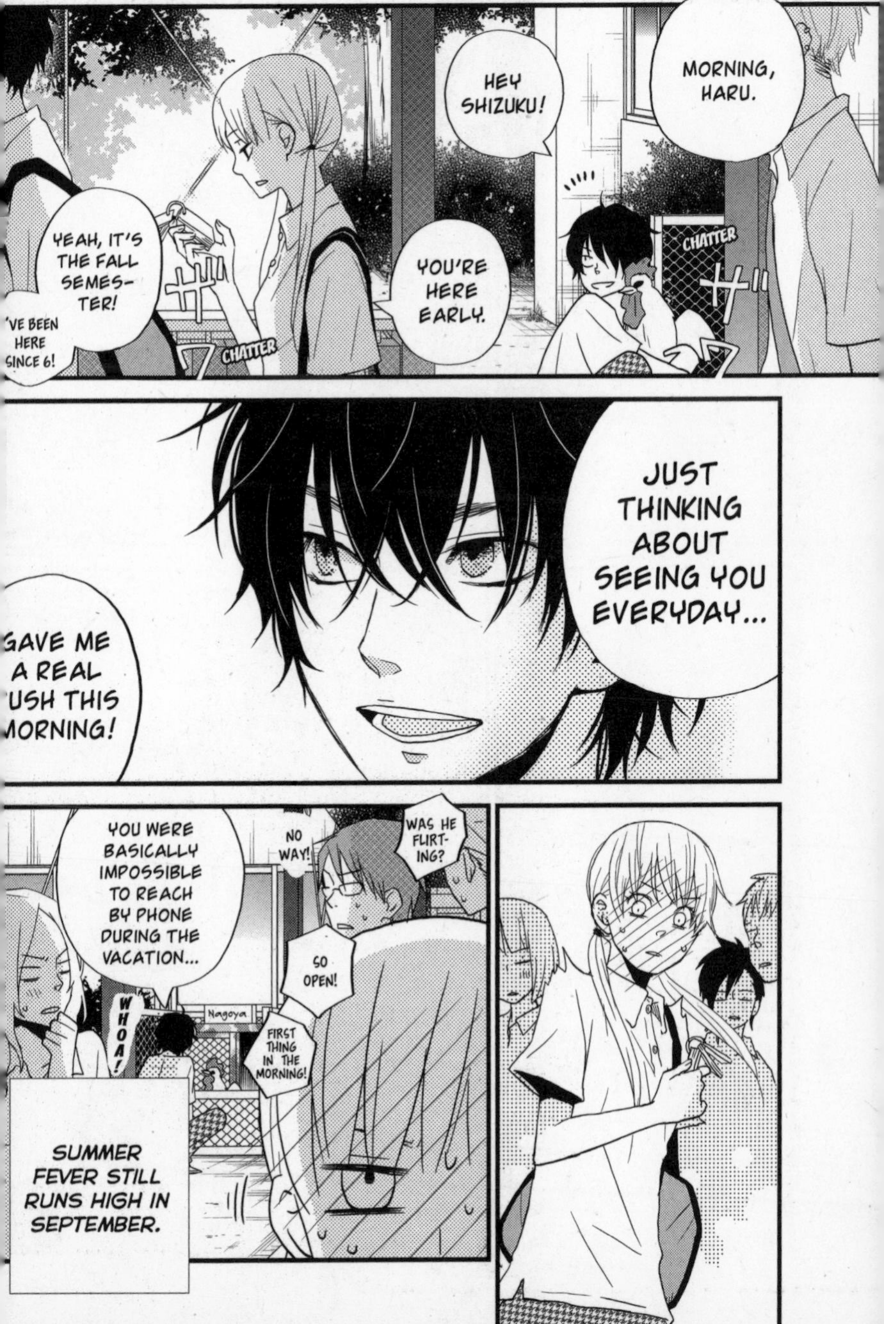
MORNING, HARU.
HEY SHIZUKU!
YOU'RE HERE EARLY.
CHATTER
CHATTER
YEAH, IT'S THE FALL SEMES-TER!
'VE BEEN HERE SINCE 6!
JUST THINKING ABOUT SEEING YOU EVERYDAY...
GAVE ME A REAL USH THIS ORNING!
WAS HE FLIRT-ING?
NO WAY!
YOU WERE BASICALLY IMPOSSIBLE TO REACH BY PHONE DURING THE VACATION...
SO OPEN!
FIRST THING IN THE MORNING!
WHOA!
Nagoya
SUMMER FEVER STILL RUNS HIGH IN SEPTEMBER.

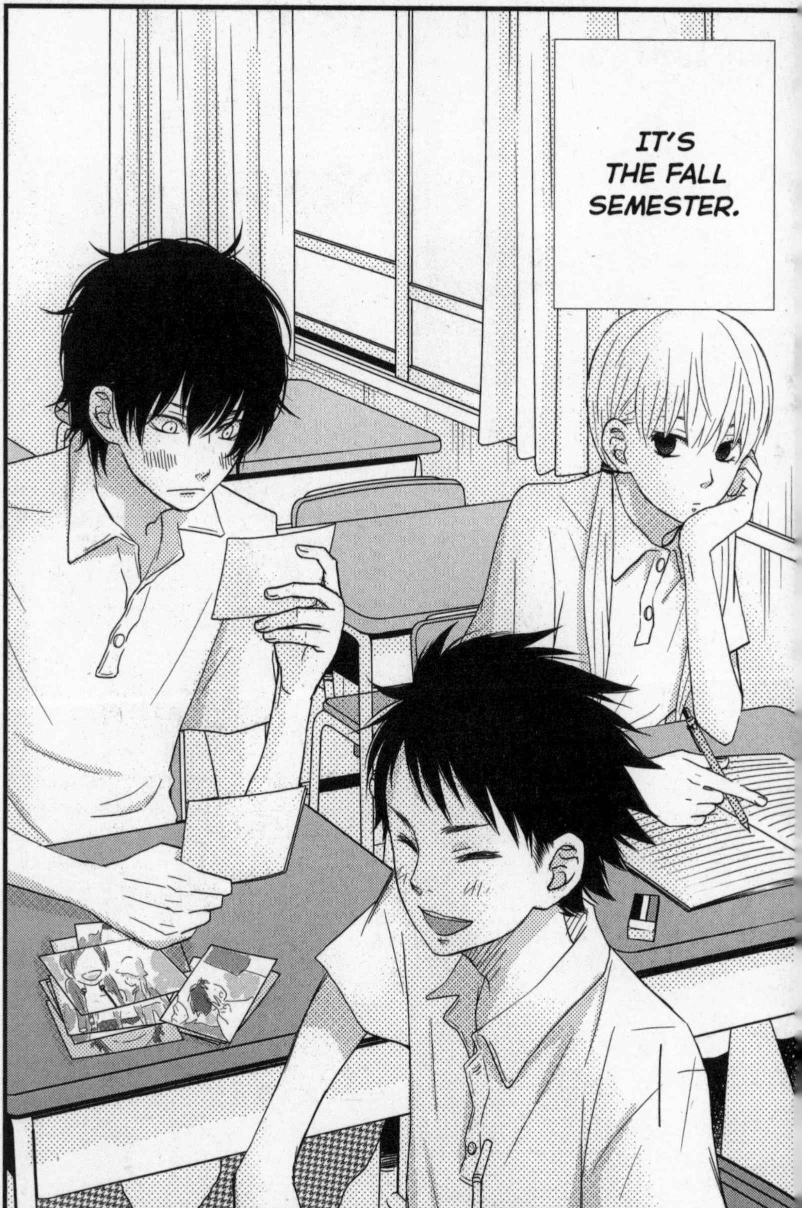
IT'S THE FALL SEMESTER.

Chapter 7 Yoshida-kun's Family Situation

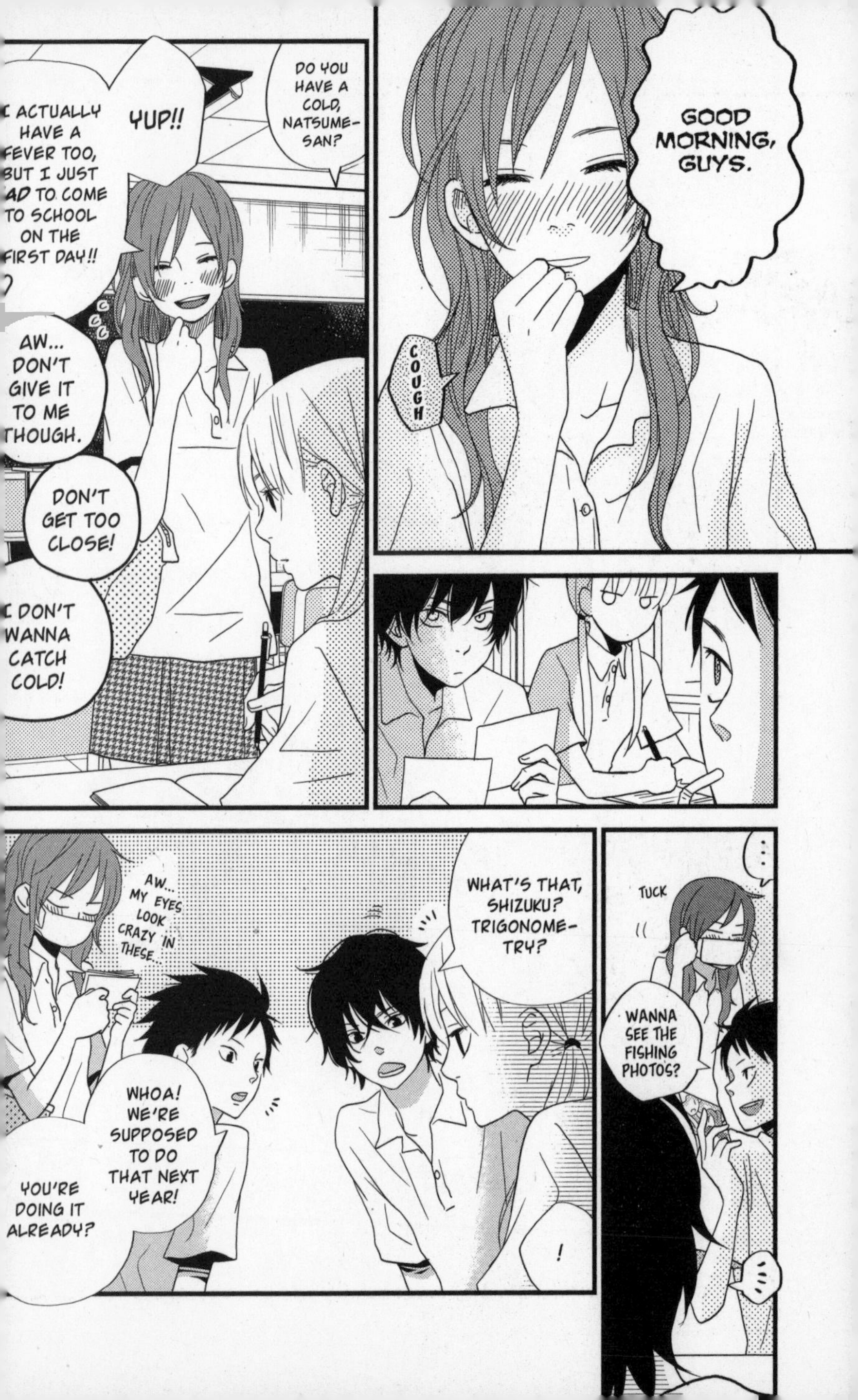

GOOD MORNING, GUYS.
COUGH
DO YOU HAVE A COLD, NATSUME-SAN?
YUP!!
I ACTUALLY HAVE A FEVER TOO, BUT I JUST HAD TO COME TO SCHOOL ON THE FIRST DAY!!
AW... DON'T GIVE IT TO ME THOUGH.
DON'T GET TOO CLOSE!
I DON'T WANNA CATCH COLD!
...
TUCK
WANNA SEE THE FISHING PHOTOS?
...
WHAT'S THAT, SHIZUKU? TRIGONOMETRY?
AW... MY EYES LOOK CRAZY IN THESE.
WHOA! WE'RE SUPPOSED TO DO THAT NEXT YEAR!
YOU'RE DOING IT ALREADY?
!

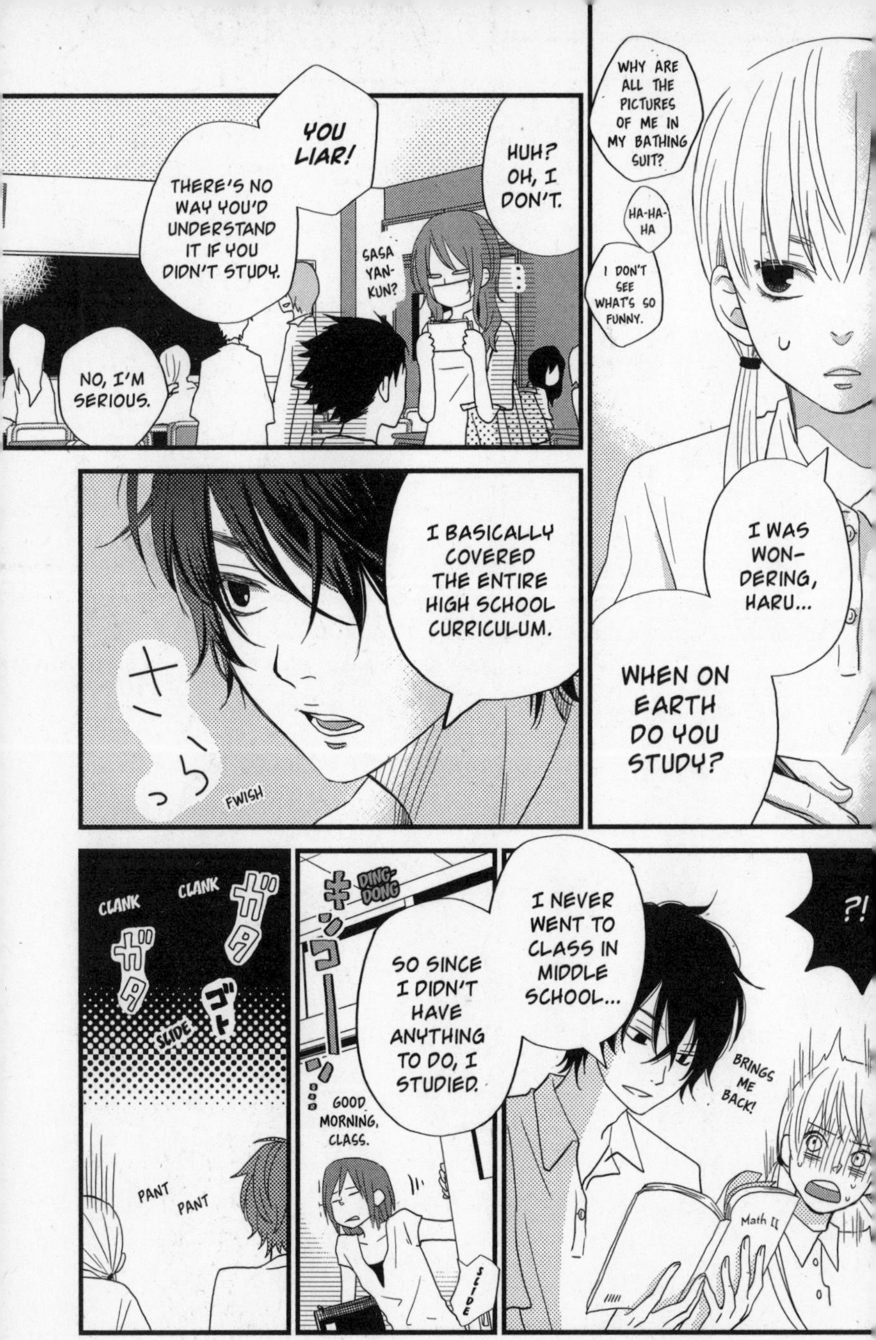
WHY ARE ALL THE PICTURES OF ME IN MY BATHING SUIT?
HA-HA-HA
I DON'T SEE WHAT'S SO FUNNY.
I WAS WONDERING, HARU...
WHEN ON EARTH DO YOU STUDY?
HUH? OH, I DON'T.
SASA YAN-KUN?
YOU LIAR!
THERE'S NO WAY YOU'D UNDERSTAND IT IF YOU DIDN'T STUDY.
NO, I'M SERIOUS.
I BASICALLY COVERED THE ENTIRE HIGH SCHOOL CURRICULUM.
FWISH
?!
I NEVER WENT TO CLASS IN MIDDLE SCHOOL...
SO SINCE I DIDN'T HAVE ANYTHING TO DO, I STUDIED.
BRINGS ME BACK!
Math II
DING-DONG
GOOD MORNING, CLASS.
SLIDE
CLANK
CLANK
SLIDE
PANT
PANT

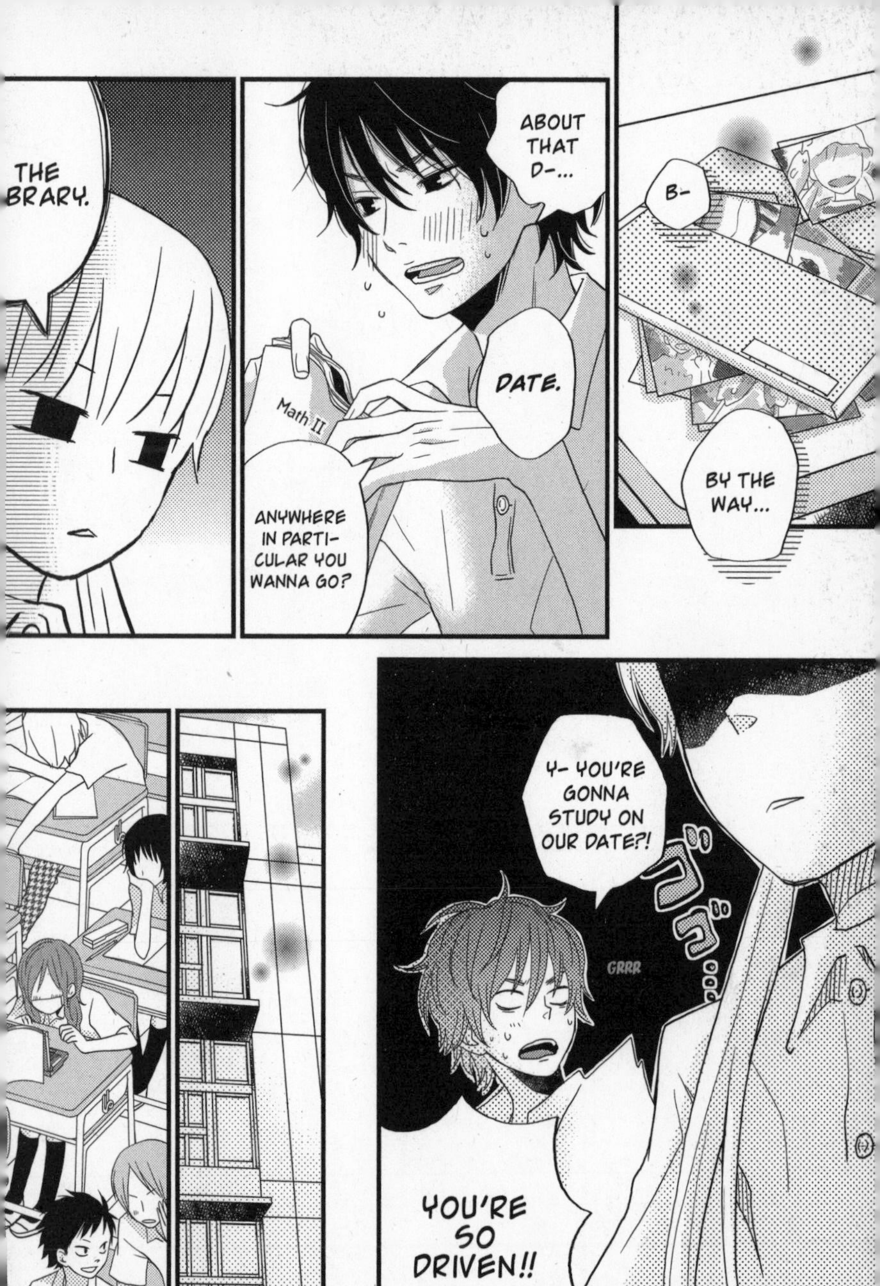
B-
BY THE WAY...
ABOUT THAT D-...
DATE.
Math II
ANYWHERE IN PARTICULAR YOU WANNA GO?
THE BRARY.
Y- YOU'RE GONNA STUDY ON OUR DATE?!
GRRR
YOU'RE SO DRIVEN!!

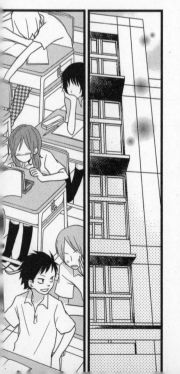

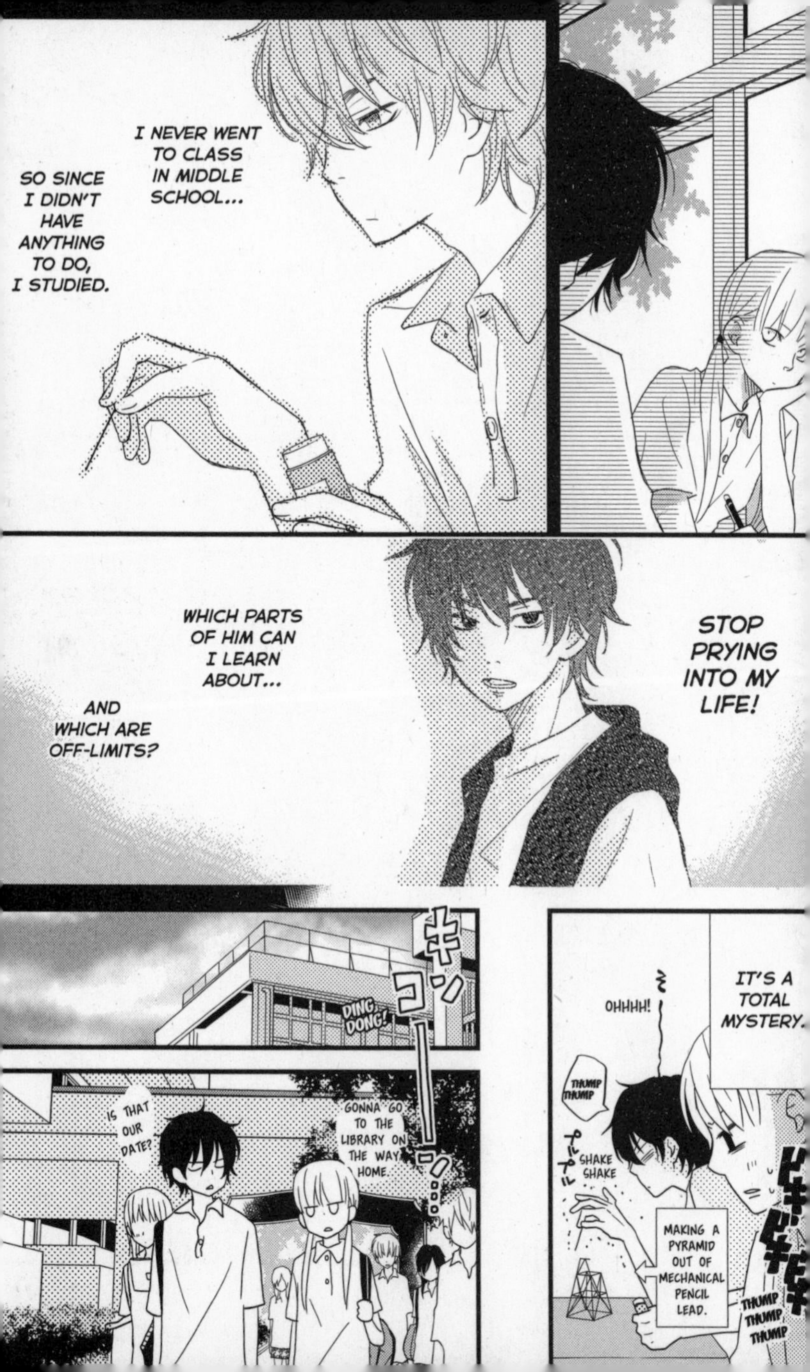
I NEVER WENT TO CLASS IN MIDDLE SCHOOL...
SO SINCE I DIDN'T HAVE ANYTHING TO DO, I STUDIED.
STOP PRYING INTO MY LIFE!
WHICH PARTS OF HIM CAN I LEARN ABOUT...
AND WHICH ARE OFF-LIMITS?
IT'S A TOTAL MYSTERY.
OHHHH!
THUMP THUMP
SHAKE SHAKE
MAKING A PYRAMID OUT OF MECHANICAL PENCIL LEAD.
THUMP THUMP THUMP
DING DONG!
GONNA GO TO THE LIBRARY ON THE WAY HOME.
IS THAT OUR DATE?

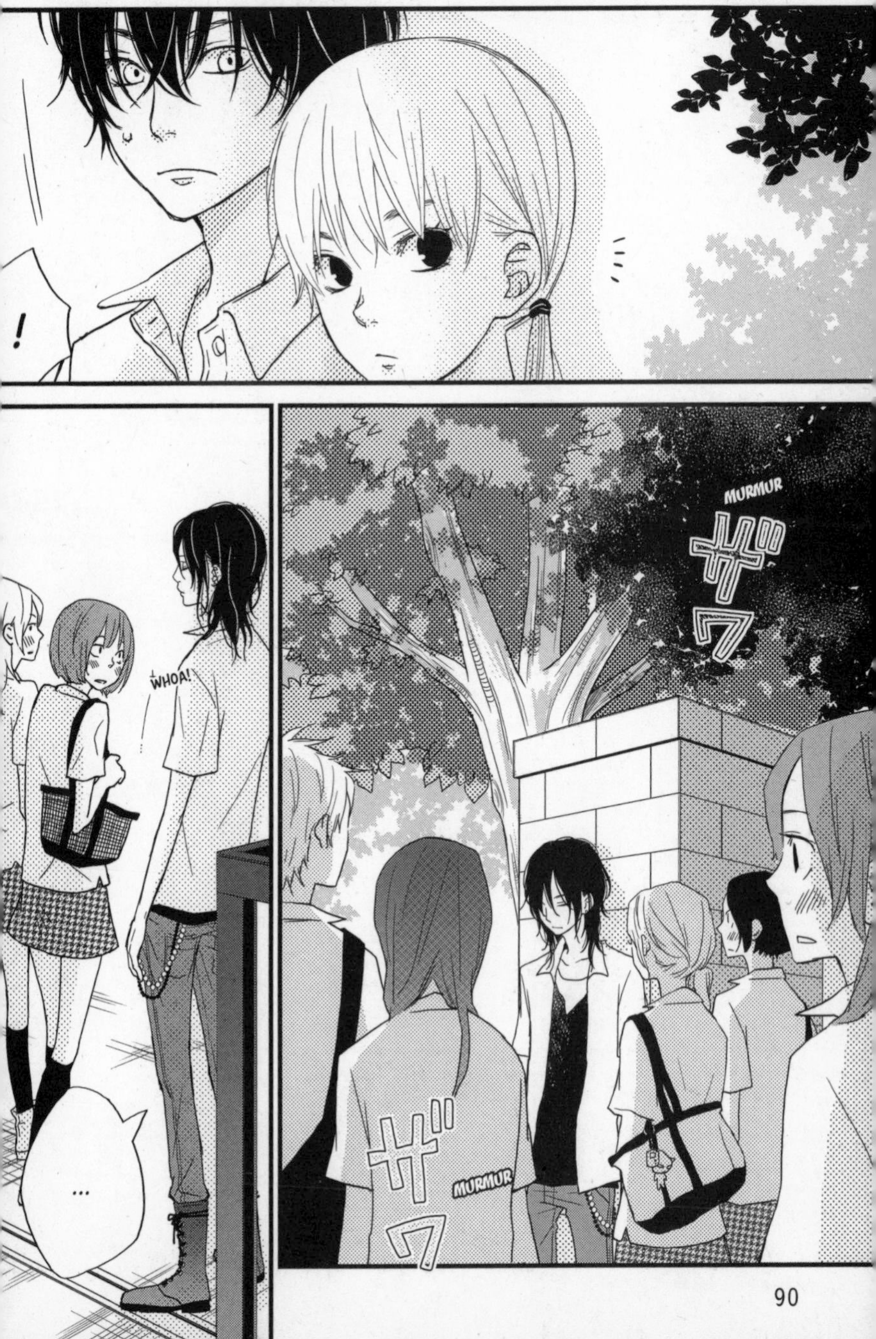
!
MURMUR
ザワ
ザワ
MURMUR
WHOA!
...

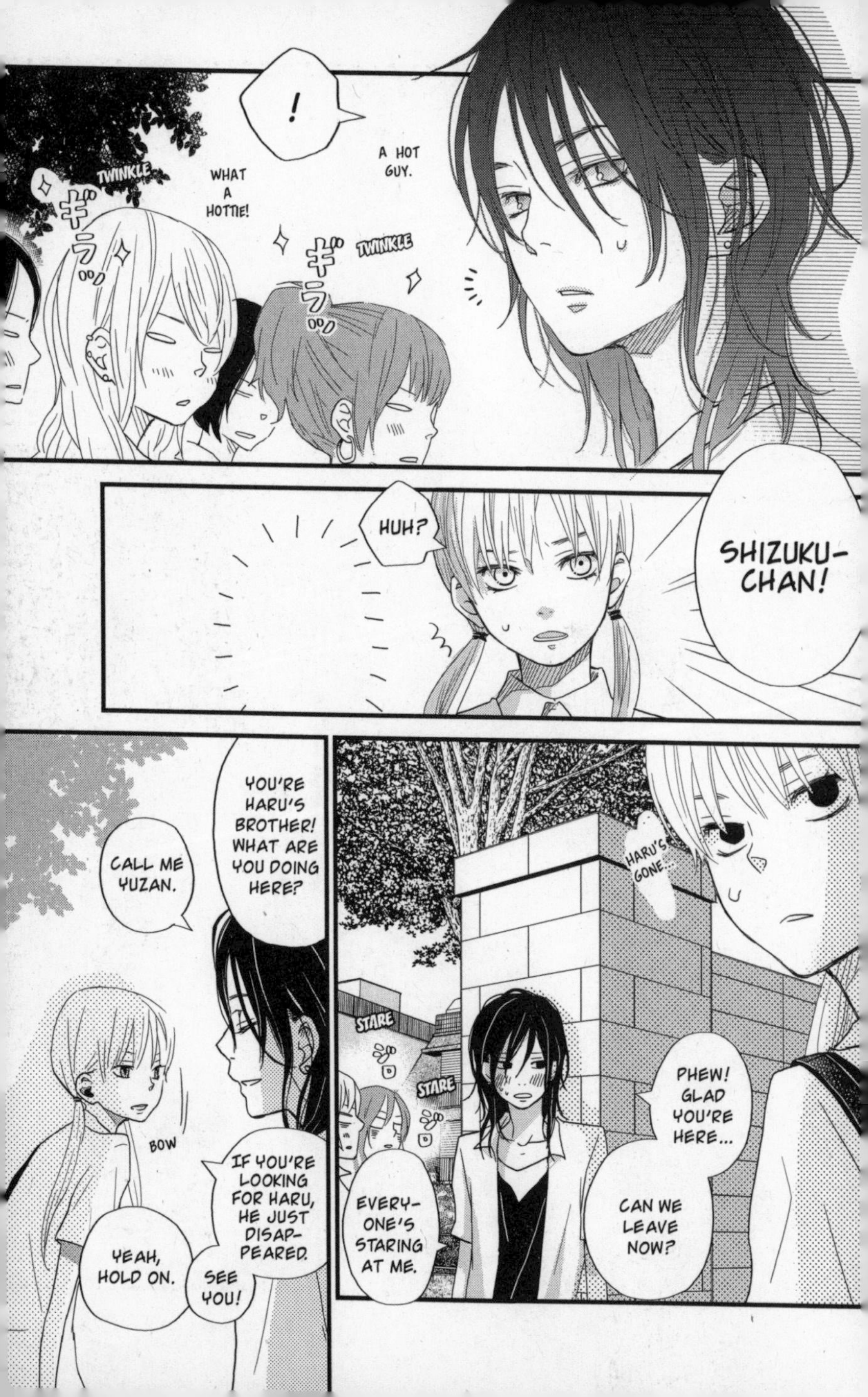
!
A HOT GUY.
TWINKLE
ギラッ
WHAT A HOTTIE!
TWINKLE
ギラッ
SHIZUKU-CHAN!
HUH?
HARU'S GONE...
PHEW! GLAD YOU'RE HERE...
CAN WE LEAVE NOW?
STARE
STARE
EVERY-ONE'S STARING AT ME.
YOU'RE HARU'S BROTHER! WHAT ARE YOU DOING HERE?
CALL ME YUZAN.
IF YOU'RE LOOKING FOR HARU, HE JUST DISAP-PEARED.
BOW
SEE YOU!
YEAH, HOLD ON.

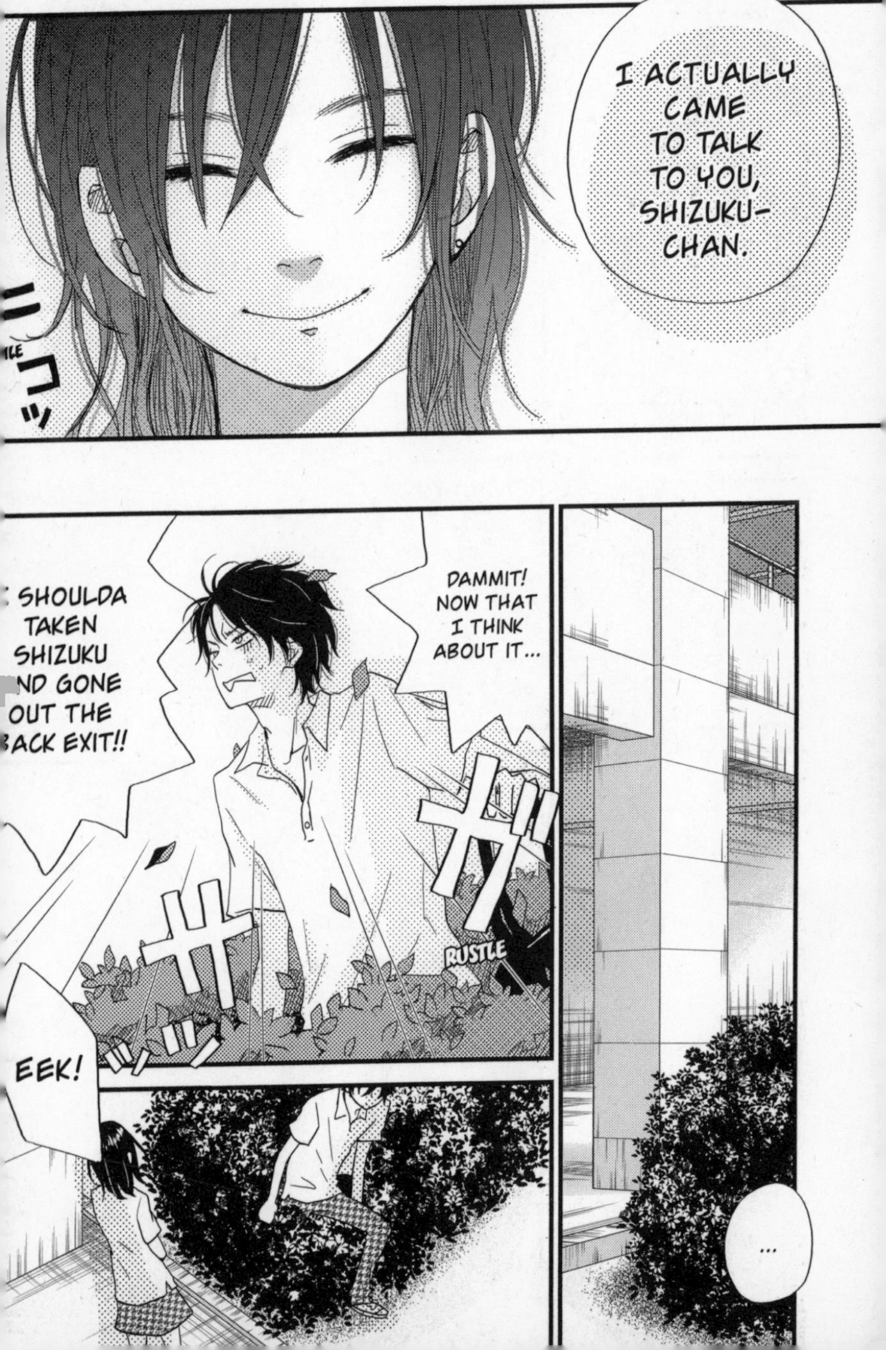
I ACTUALLY CAME TO TALK TO YOU, SHIZUKU-CHAN.
ニコッ
...
DAMMIT! NOW THAT I THINK ABOUT IT...
SHOULDA TAKEN SHIZUKU ND GONE OUT THE ACK EXIT!!
ガサ
RUSTLE
EEK!

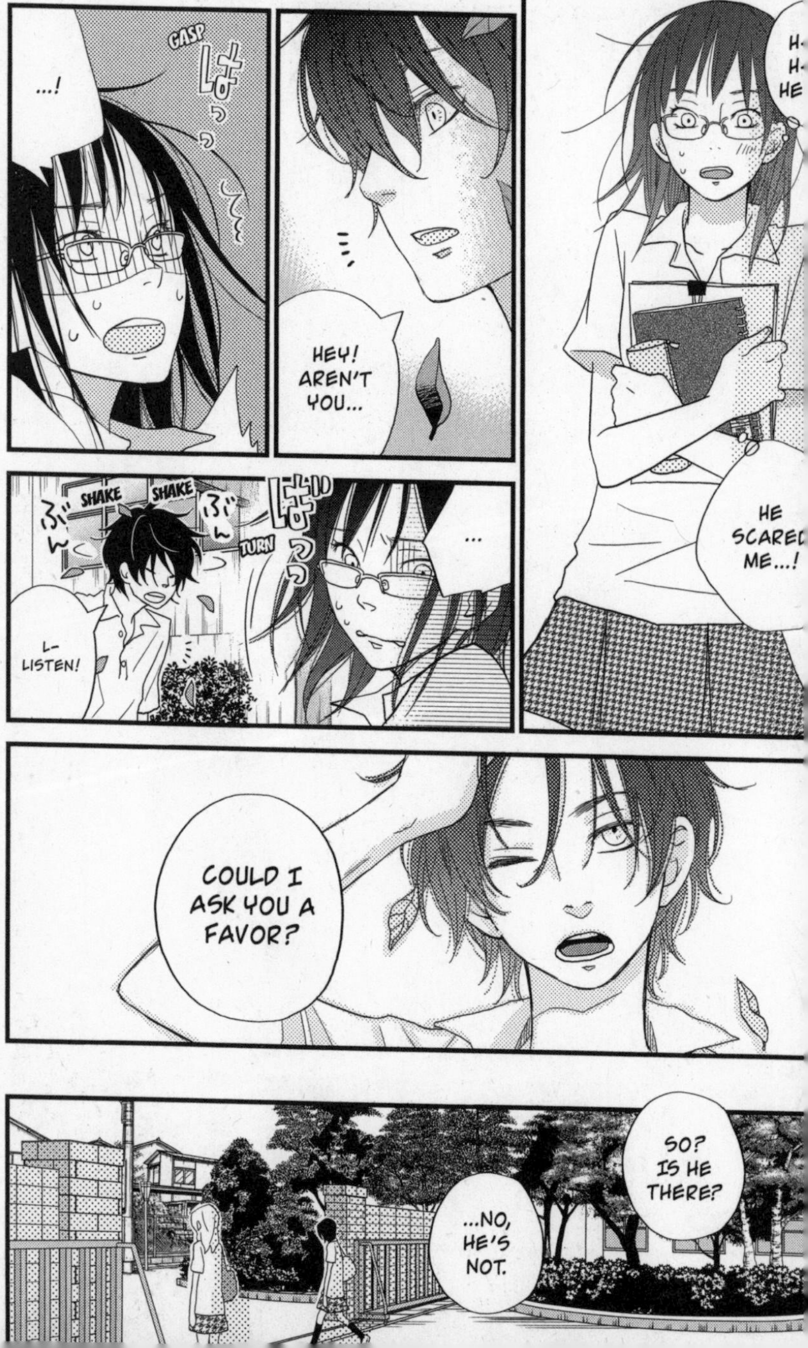

H-H-HE
HE SCARED ME...!
HEY! AREN'T YOU...
...!
GASP
はっ
...
ばっ
TURN
SHAKE
SHAKE
ぶん
ぶん
L-LISTEN!
COULD I ASK YOU A FAVOR?
SO? IS HE THERE?
...NO, HE'S NOT.

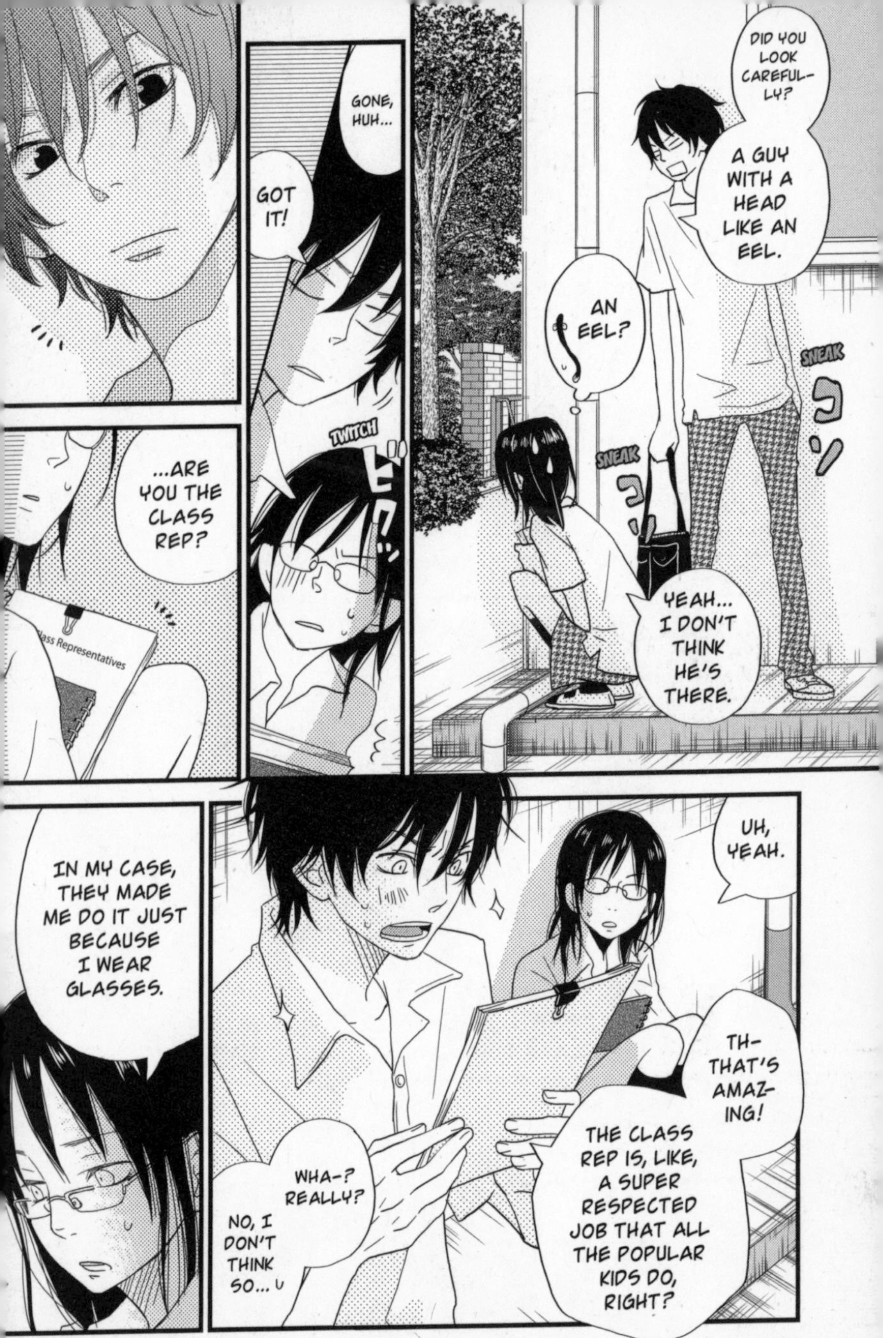
DID YOU LOOK CAREFUL-LY?
A GUY WITH A HEAD LIKE AN EEL.
AN EEL?
SNEAK
SNEAK
YEAH... I DON'T THINK HE'S THERE.
GONE, HUH...
GOT IT!
TWITCH
...ARE YOU THE CLASS REP?
UH, YEAH.
TH-THAT'S AMAZ-ING!
THE CLASS REP IS, LIKE, A SUPER RESPECTED JOB THAT ALL THE POPULAR KIDS DO, RIGHT?
WHA-? REALLY?
NO, I DON'T THINK SO...
IN MY CASE, THEY MADE ME DO IT JUST BECAUSE I WEAR GLASSES.

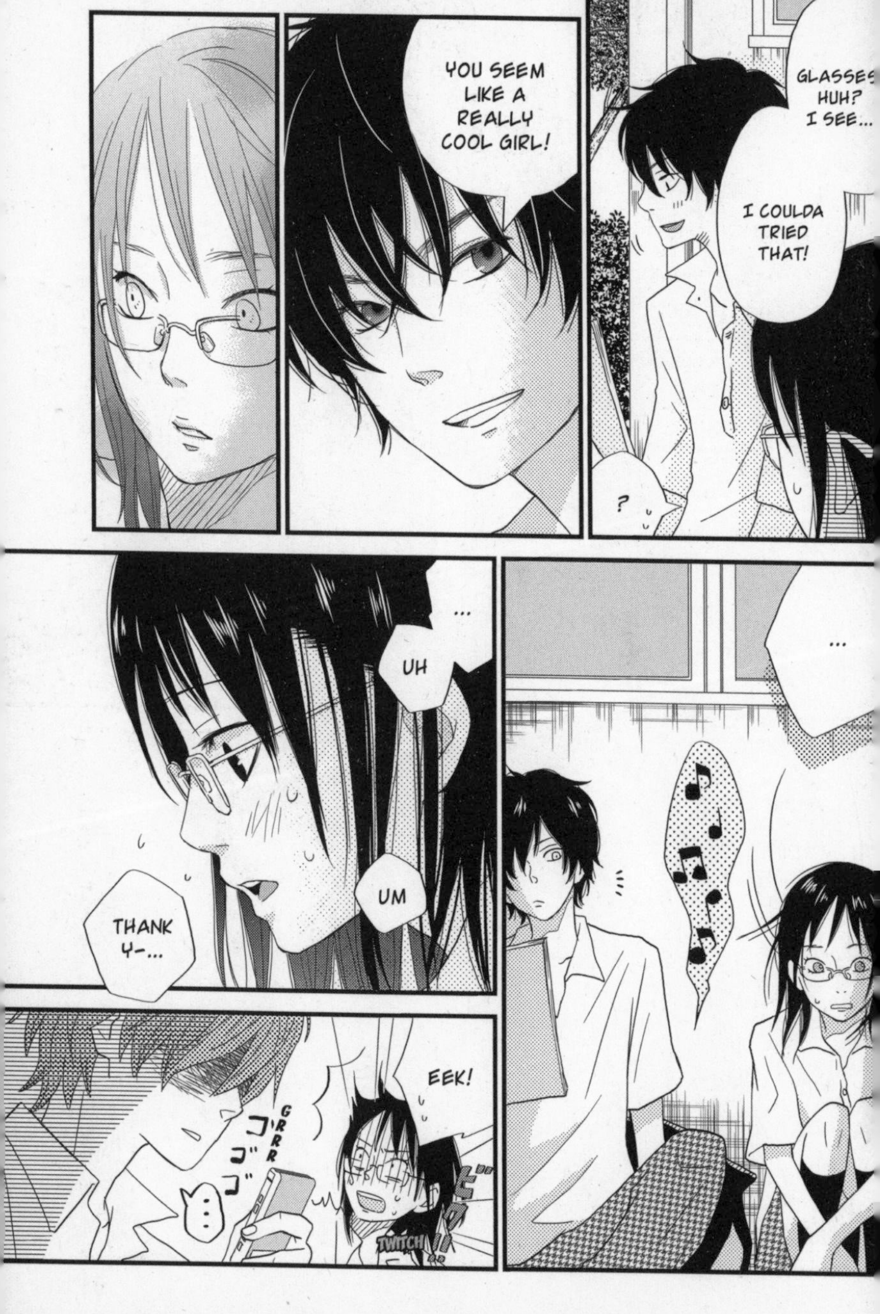
GLASSES HUH? I SEE...
I COULDA TRIED THAT!
?
YOU SEEM LIKE A REALLY COOL GIRL!
...
...
UH
UM
THANK Y-...
EEK!
GRRR
...
TWITCH

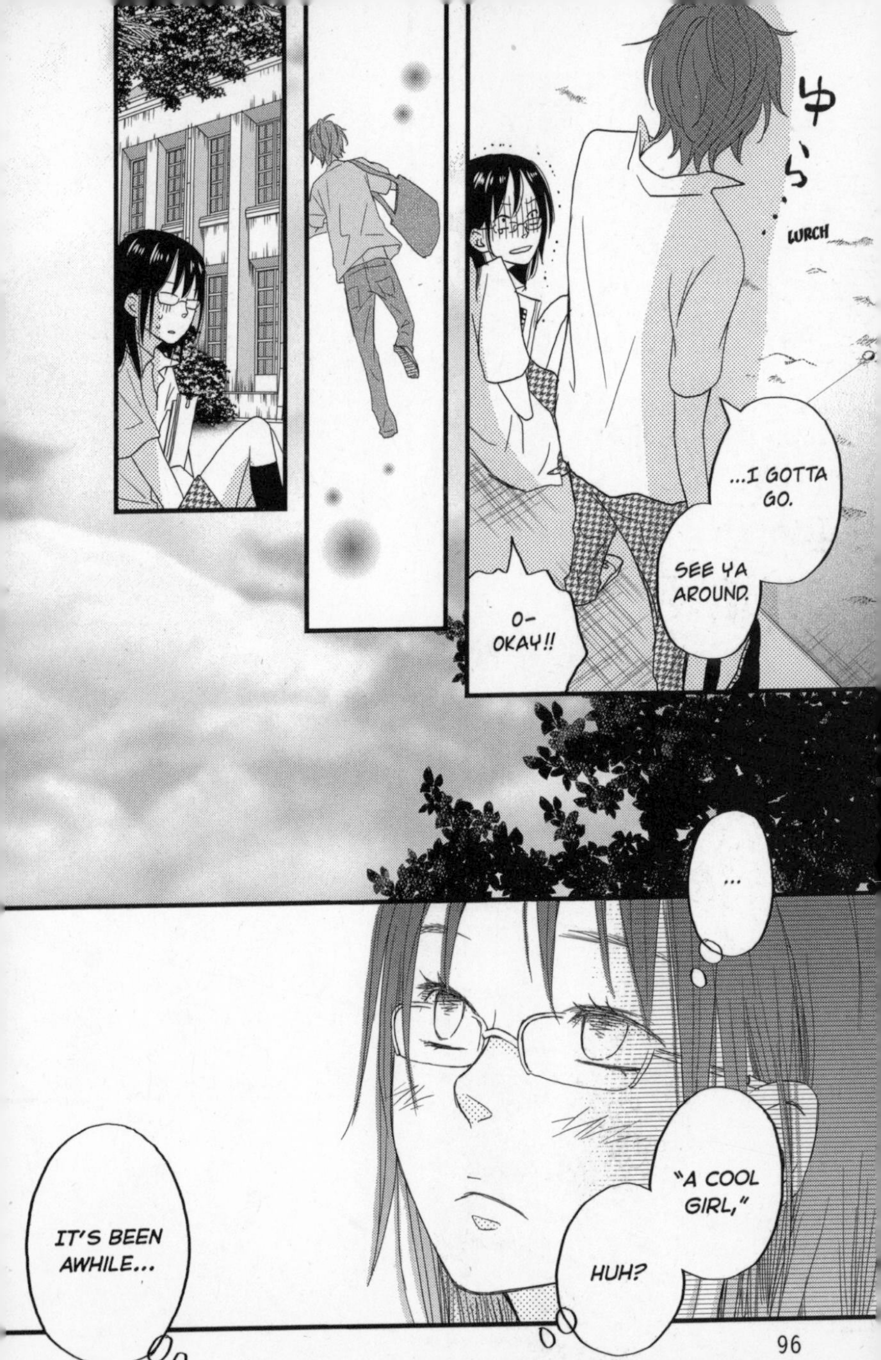

ゆら
LURCH
...I GOTTA GO.
SEE YA AROUND.
O-OKAY!!
...
"A COOL GIRL,"
HUH?
IT'S BEEN AWHILE...

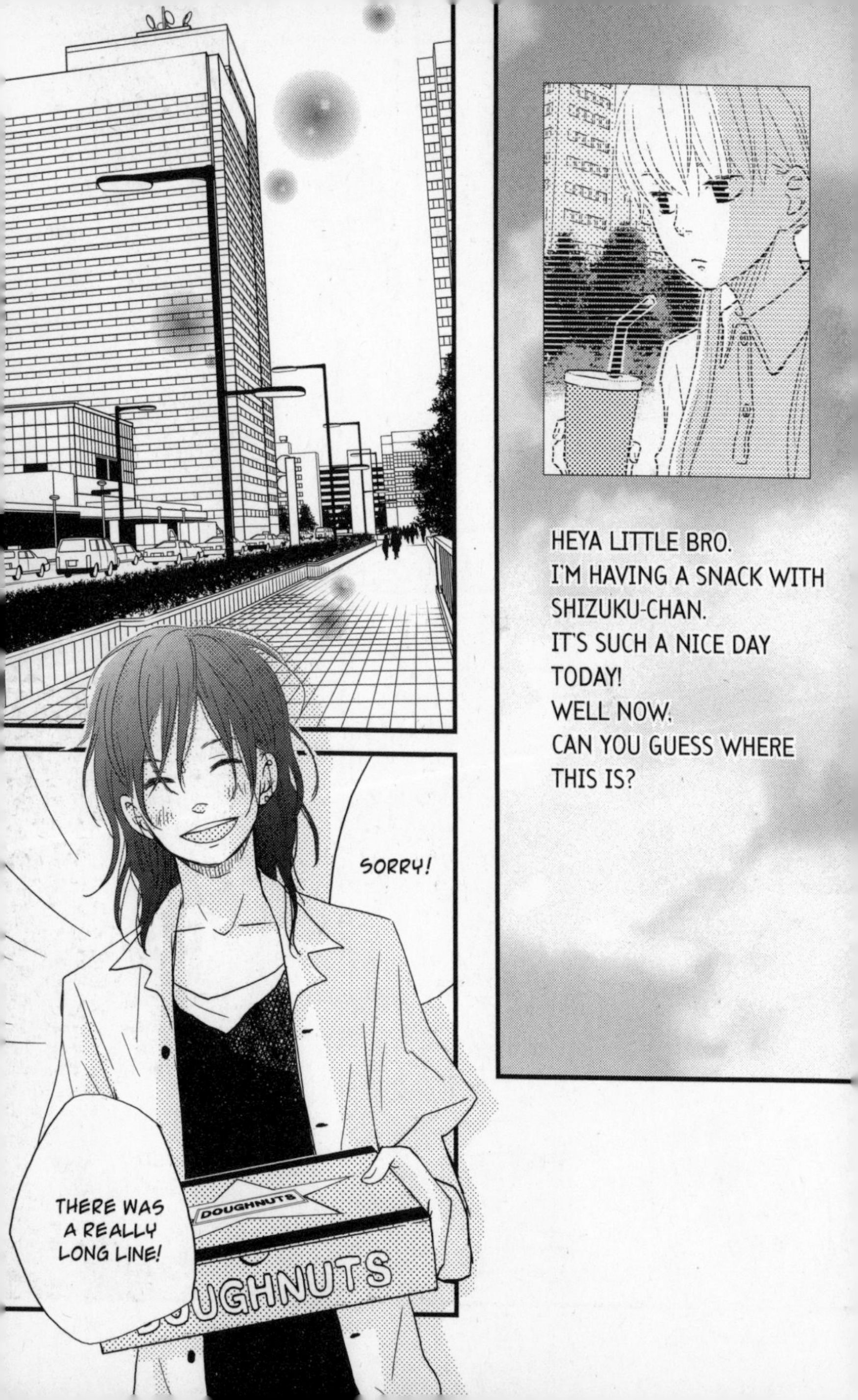
HEYA LITTLE BRO.
I'M HAVING A SNACK WITH
SHIZUKU-CHAN.
IT'S SUCH A NICE DAY
TODAY!
WELL NOW.
CAN YOU GUESS WHERE
THIS IS?
SORRY!
DOUGHNUTS
THERE WAS A REALLY LONG LINE!
DOUGHNUTS

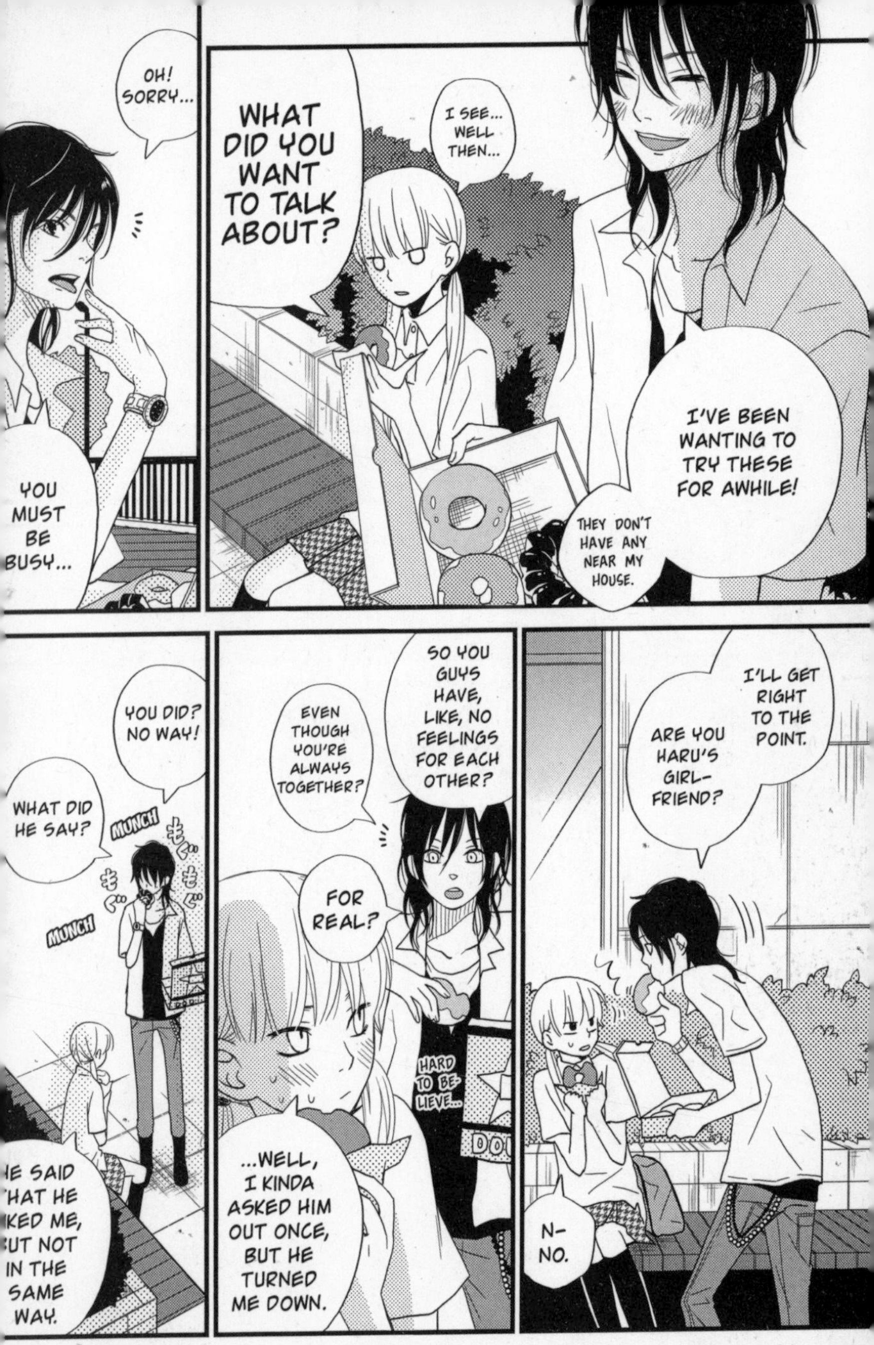
I'VE BEEN WANTING TO TRY THESE FOR AWHILE!
THEY DON'T HAVE ANY NEAR MY HOUSE.
I SEE... WELL THEN...
WHAT DID YOU WANT TO TALK ABOUT?
OH! SORRY...
YOU MUST BE BUSY...
I'LL GET RIGHT TO THE POINT.
ARE YOU HARU'S GIRL-FRIEND?
N-NO.
SO YOU GUYS HAVE, LIKE, NO FEELINGS FOR EACH OTHER?
EVEN THOUGH YOU'RE ALWAYS TOGETHER?
FOR REAL?
HARD TO BE-LIEVE...
...WELL, I KINDA ASKED HIM OUT ONCE, BUT HE TURNED ME DOWN.
YOU DID? NO WAY!
WHAT DID HE SAY?
MUNCH
もぐもぐ
MUNCH
E SAID HAT HE IKED ME, UT NOT IN THE SAME WAY.

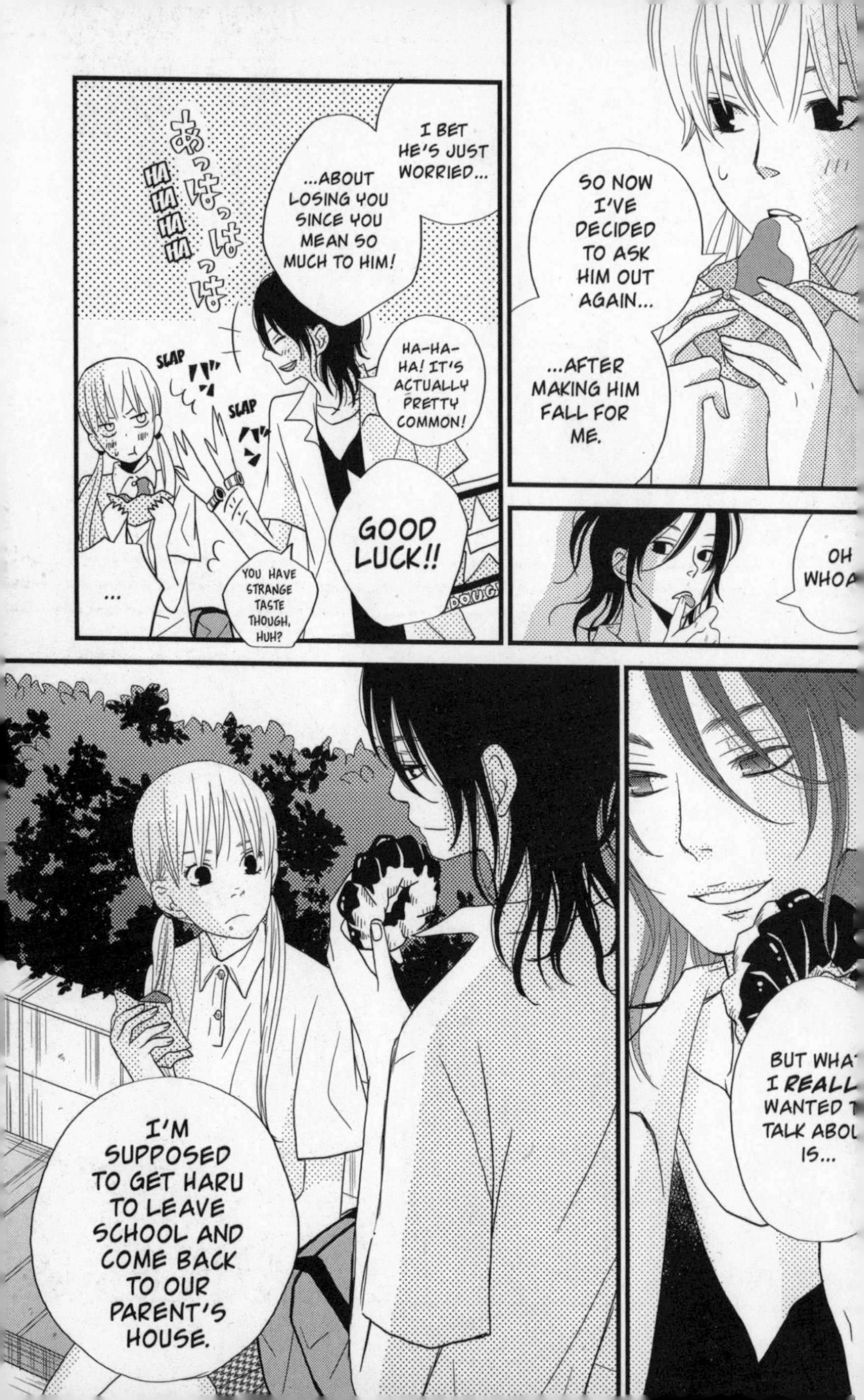
SO NOW I'VE DECIDED TO ASK HIM OUT AGAIN...
...AFTER MAKING HIM FALL FOR ME.
OH WHOA
I BET HE'S JUST WORRIED...
...ABOUT LOSING YOU SINCE YOU MEAN SO MUCH TO HIM!
あっはっはっは
HA HA HA HA
HA-HA-HA! IT'S ACTUALLY PRETTY COMMON!
SLAP
SLAP
GOOD LUCK!!
YOU HAVE STRANGE TASTE THOUGH, HUH?
...
BUT WHAT I REALL WANTED T TALK ABOU IS...
I'M SUPPOSED TO GET HARU TO LEAVE SCHOOL AND COME BACK TO OUR PARENT'S HOUSE.

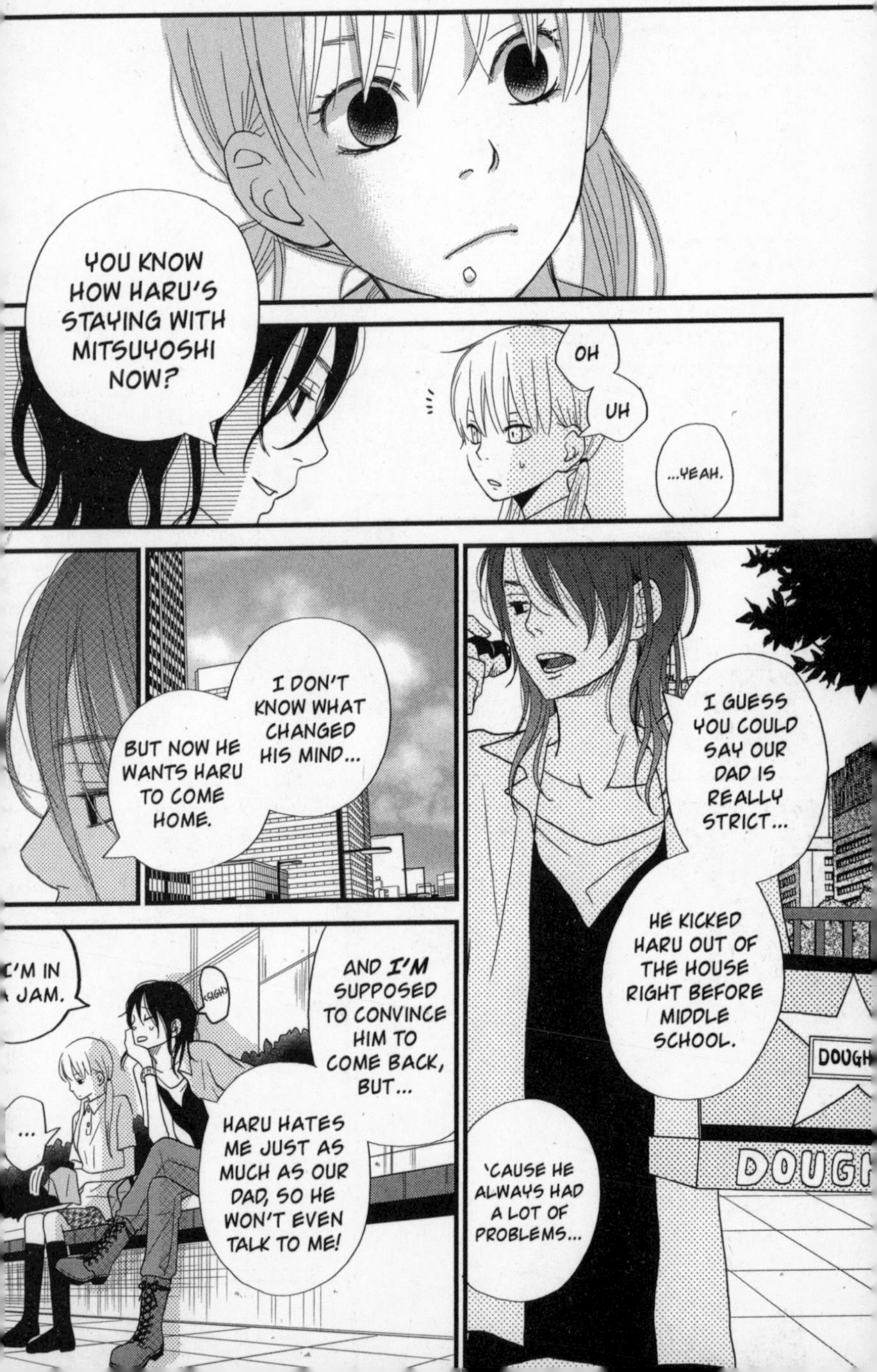
YOU KNOW HOW HARU'S STAYING WITH MITSUYOSHI NOW?
OH
UH
...YEAH.
I GUESS YOU COULD SAY OUR DAD IS REALLY STRICT...
HE KICKED HARU OUT OF THE HOUSE RIGHT BEFORE MIDDLE SCHOOL.
DOUGH
DOUGH
'CAUSE HE ALWAYS HAD A LOT OF PROBLEMS...
I DON'T KNOW WHAT CHANGED HIS MIND...
BUT NOW HE WANTS HARU TO COME HOME.
AND I'M SUPPOSED TO CONVINCE HIM TO COME BACK, BUT...
HARU HATES ME JUST AS MUCH AS OUR DAD, SO HE WON'T EVEN TALK TO ME!
SIGH
'M IN JAM.
...

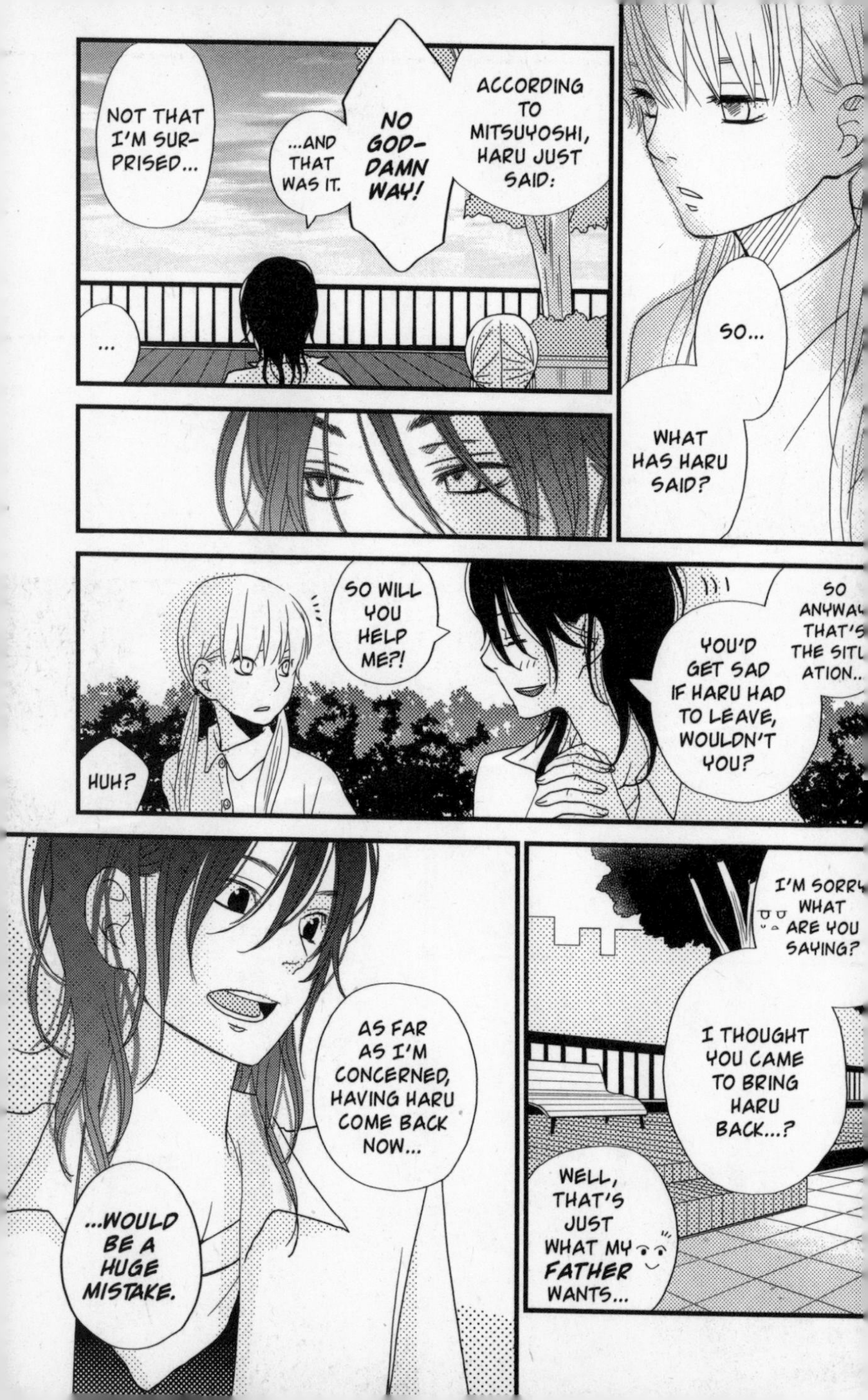
SO...
WHAT HAS HARU SAID?
ACCORDING TO MITSUYOSHI, HARU JUST SAID:
NO GOD-DAMN WAY!
...AND THAT WAS IT.
NOT THAT I'M SUR-PRISED...
...
SO ANYWA THAT'S THE SITU ATION..
YOU'D GET SAD IF HARU HAD TO LEAVE, WOULDN'T YOU?
SO WILL YOU HELP ME?!
HUH?
I'M SORR WHAT ARE YOU SAYING?
I THOUGHT YOU CAME TO BRING HARU BACK...?
WELL, THAT'S JUST WHAT MY FATHER WANTS...
AS FAR AS I'M CONCERNED, HAVING HARU COME BACK NOW...
...WOULD BE A HUGE MISTAKE.

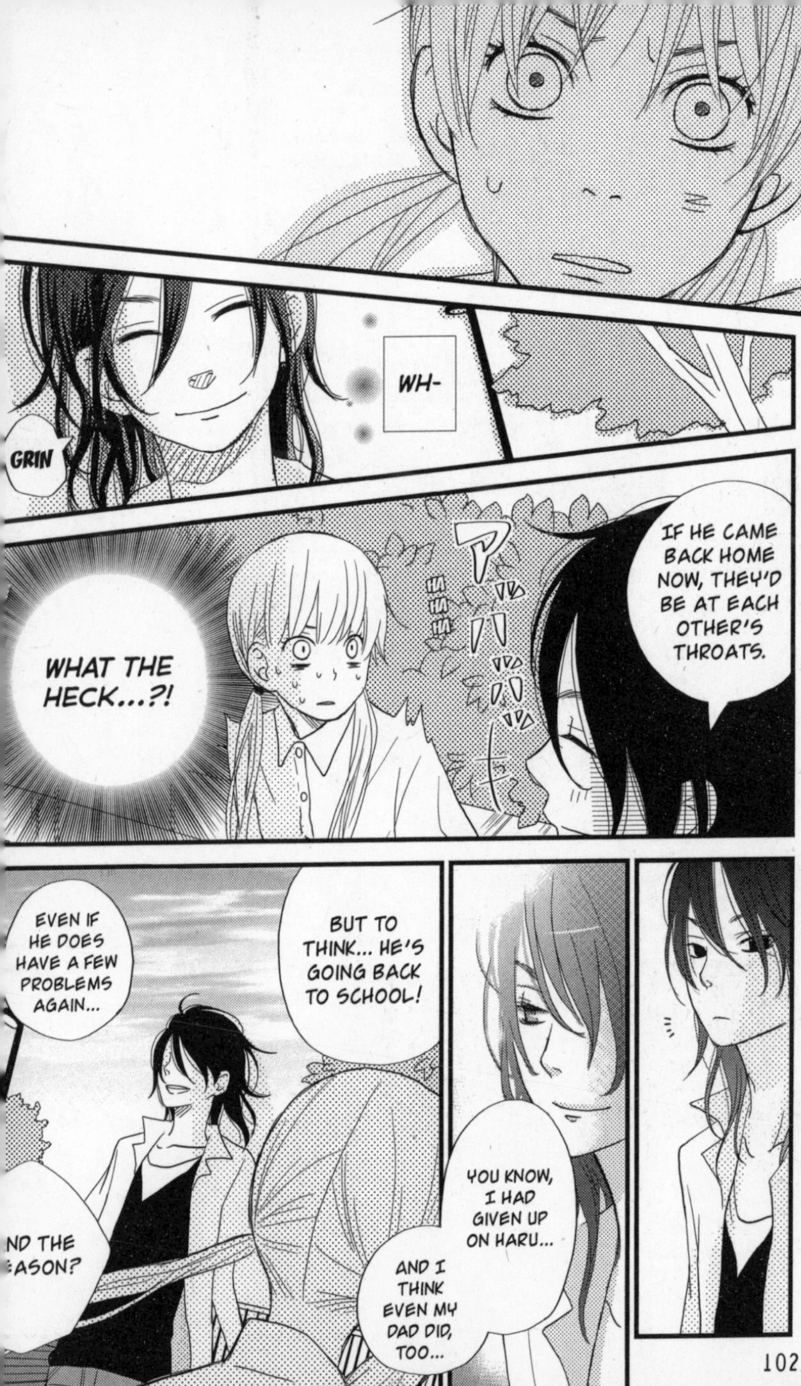
WH-
GRIN
IF HE CAME BACK HOME NOW, THEY'D BE AT EACH OTHER'S THROATS.
HA HA HA
WHAT THE HECK...?!
YOU KNOW, I HAD GIVEN UP ON HARU...
AND I THINK EVEN MY DAD DID, TOO...
BUT TO THINK... HE'S GOING BACK TO SCHOOL!
EVEN IF HE DOES HAVE A FEW PROBLEMS AGAIN...
ND THE EASON?

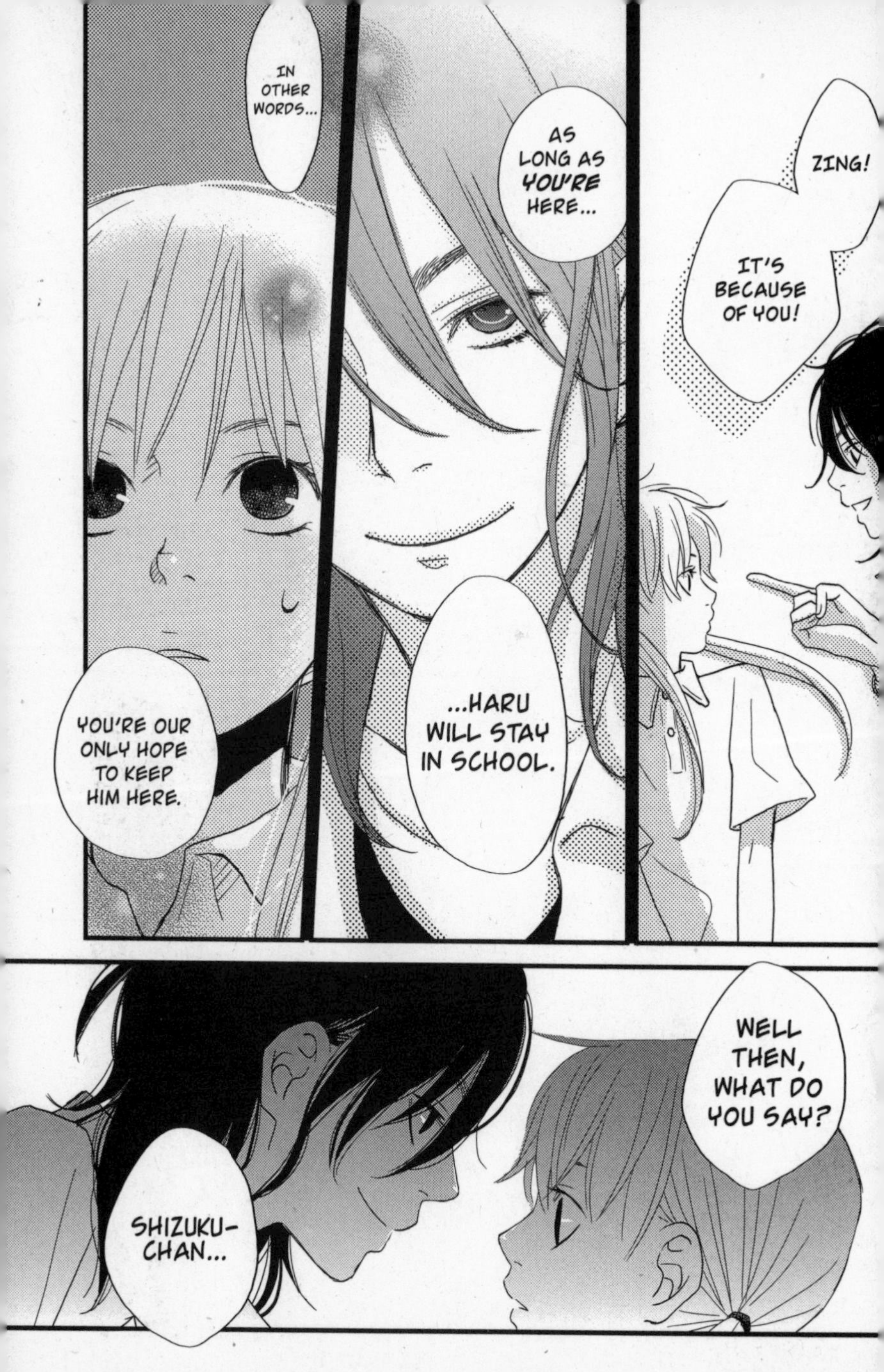
ZING!
IT'S BECAUSE OF YOU!
AS LONG AS *YOU'RE* HERE...
...HARU WILL STAY IN SCHOOL.
IN OTHER WORDS...
YOU'RE OUR ONLY HOPE TO KEEP HIM HERE.
WELL THEN, WHAT DO YOU SAY?
SHIZUKU-CHAN...

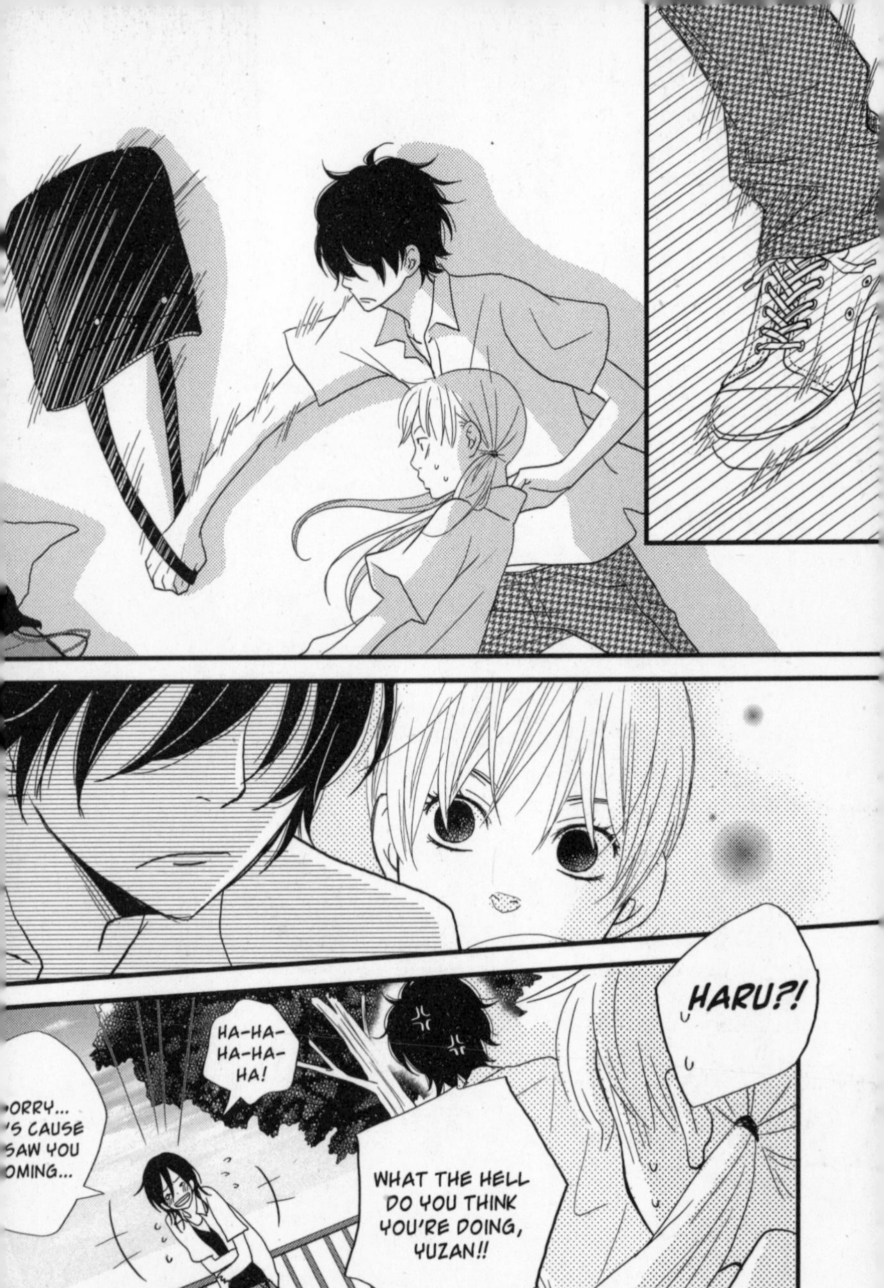
HARU?!
WHAT THE HELL DO YOU THINK YOU'RE DOING, YUZAN!!
HA-HA-HA-HA-HA!
ORRY... 'S CAUSE SAW YOU OMING...

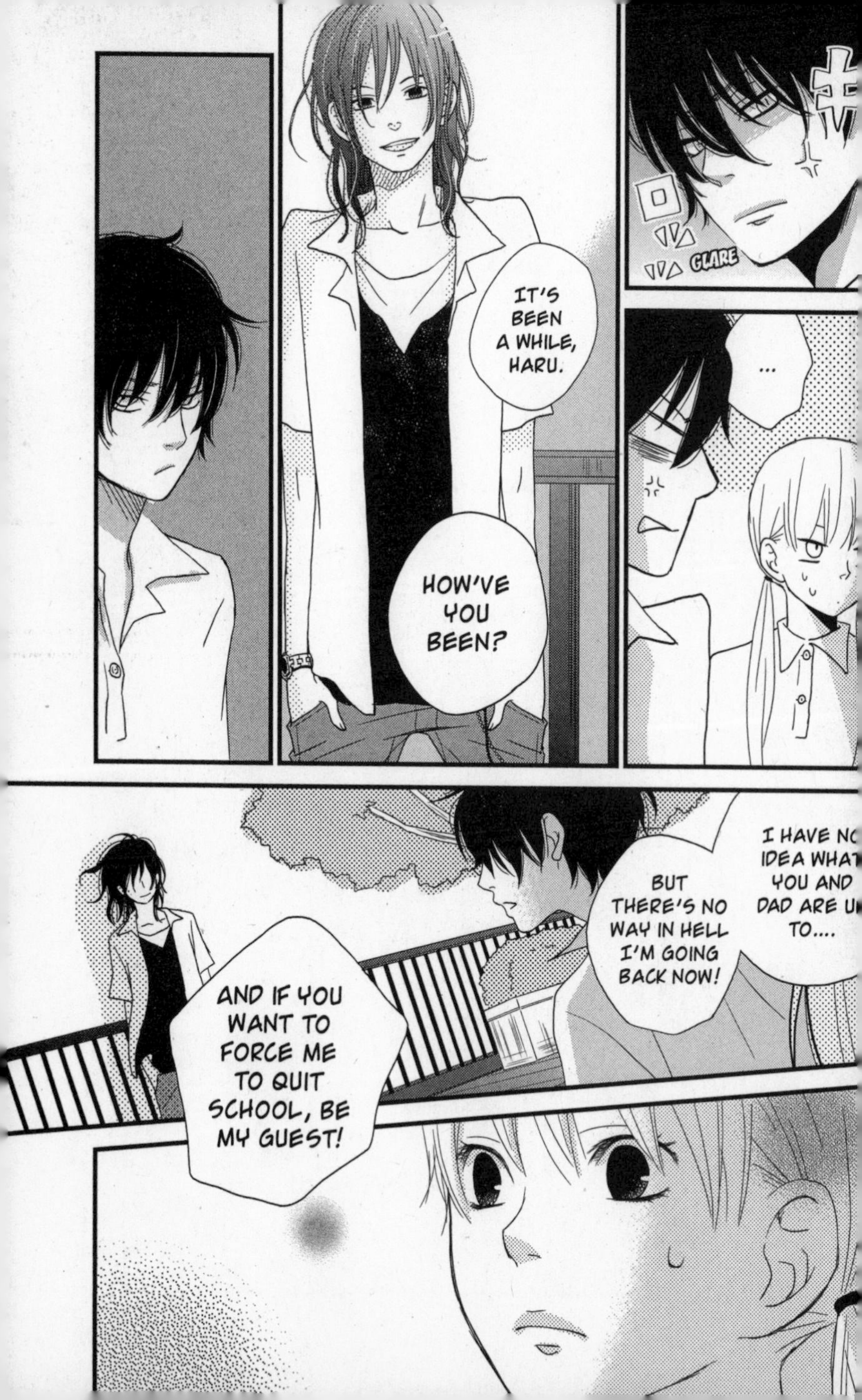
GLARE
...
IT'S BEEN A WHILE, HARU.
HOW'VE YOU BEEN?
I HAVE NO IDEA WHAT YOU AND DAD ARE UP TO....
BUT THERE'S NO WAY IN HELL I'M GOING BACK NOW!
AND IF YOU WANT TO FORCE ME TO QUIT SCHOOL, BE MY GUEST!

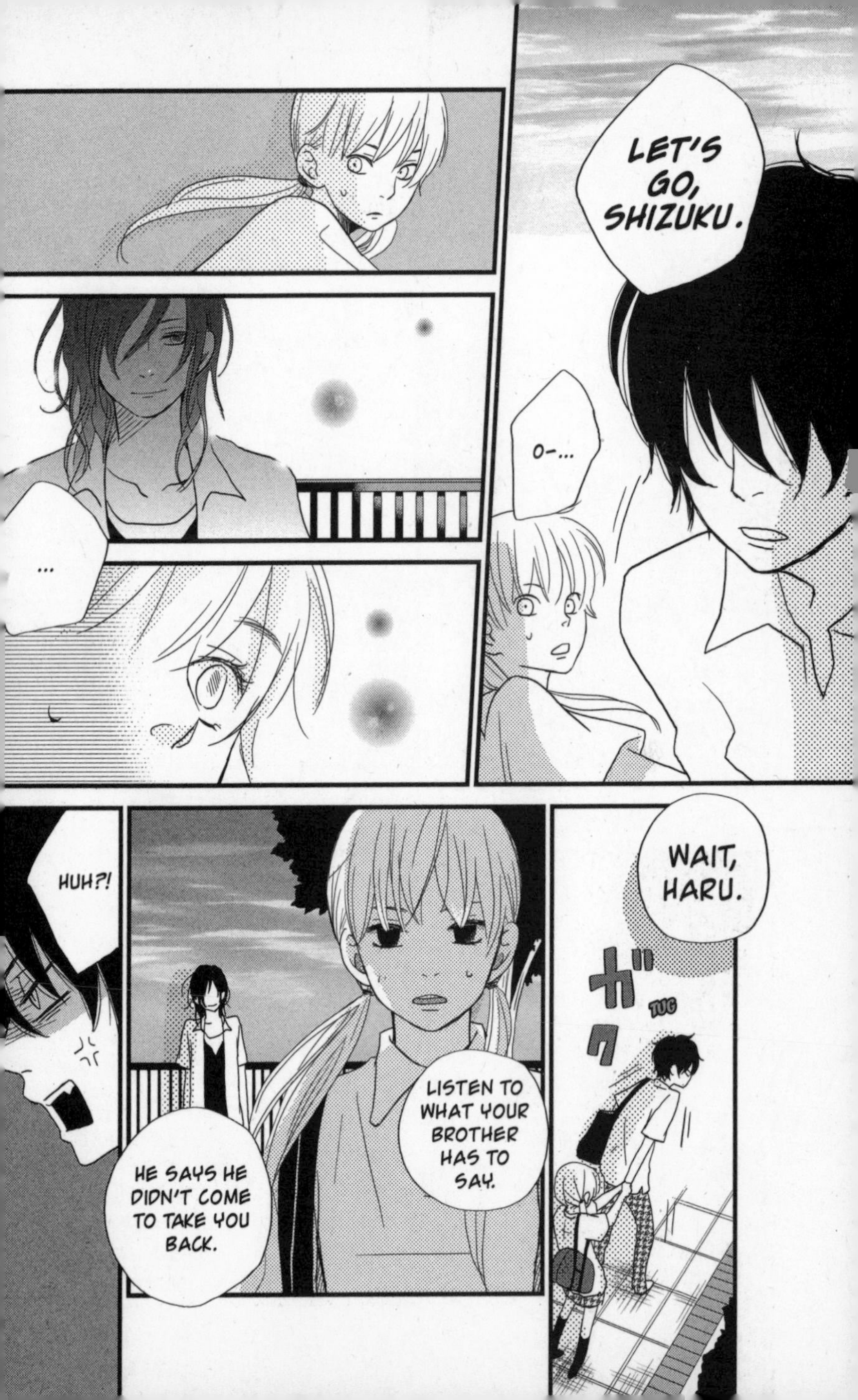
LET'S GO, SHIZUKU.
O-...
...
WAIT, HARU.
ガク
TUG
LISTEN TO WHAT YOUR BROTHER HAS TO SAY.
HE SAYS HE DIDN'T COME TO TAKE YOU BACK.
HUH?!

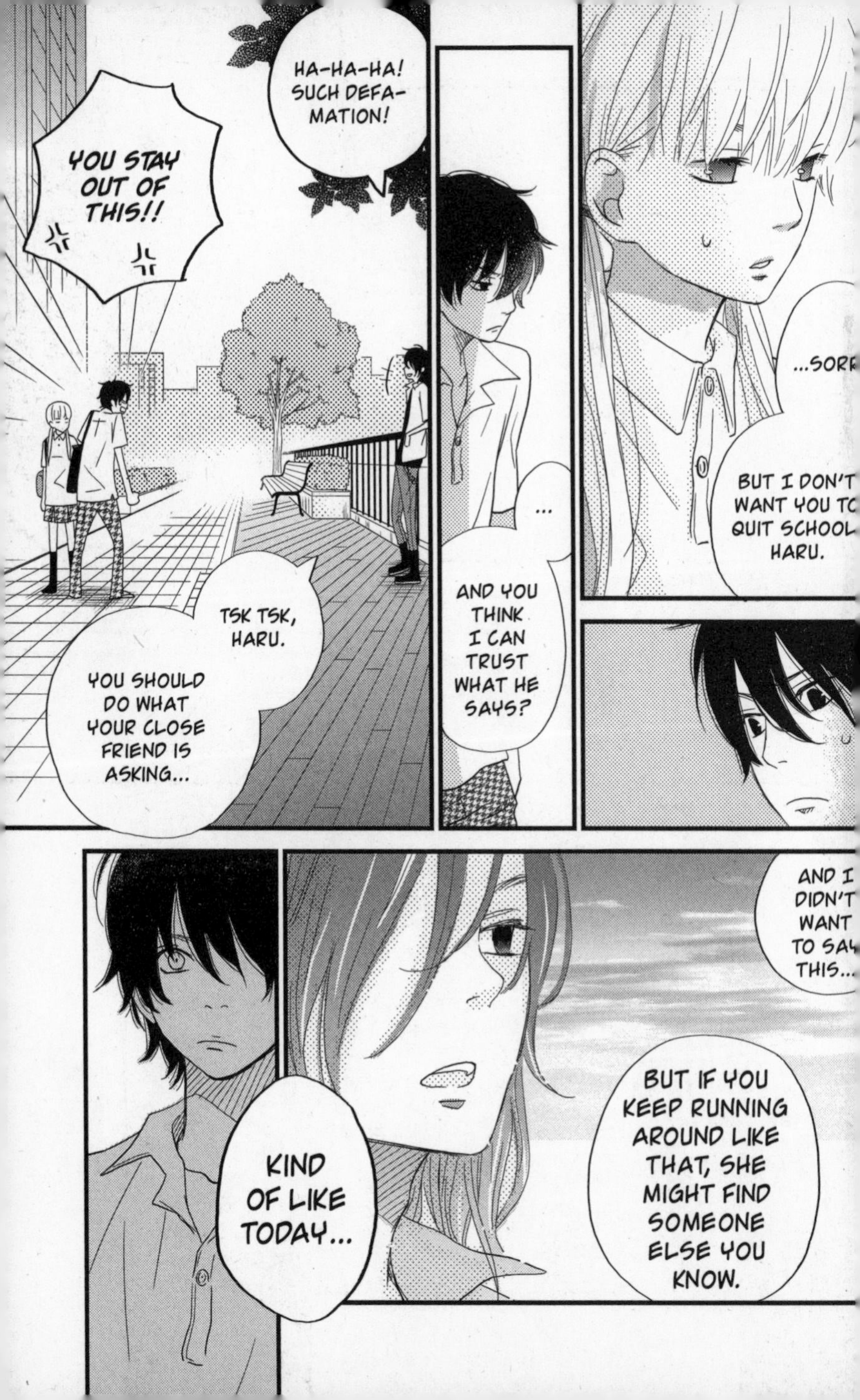
...SORR
BUT I DON'T WANT YOU TO QUIT SCHOOL HARU.
...
AND YOU THINK I CAN TRUST WHAT HE SAYS?
HA-HA-HA! SUCH DEFA-MATION!
YOU STAY OUT OF THIS!!
TSK TSK, HARU.
YOU SHOULD DO WHAT YOUR CLOSE FRIEND IS ASKING...
AND I DIDN'T WANT TO SAY THIS...
BUT IF YOU KEEP RUNNING AROUND LIKE THAT, SHE MIGHT FIND SOMEONE ELSE YOU KNOW.
KIND OF LIKE TODAY...

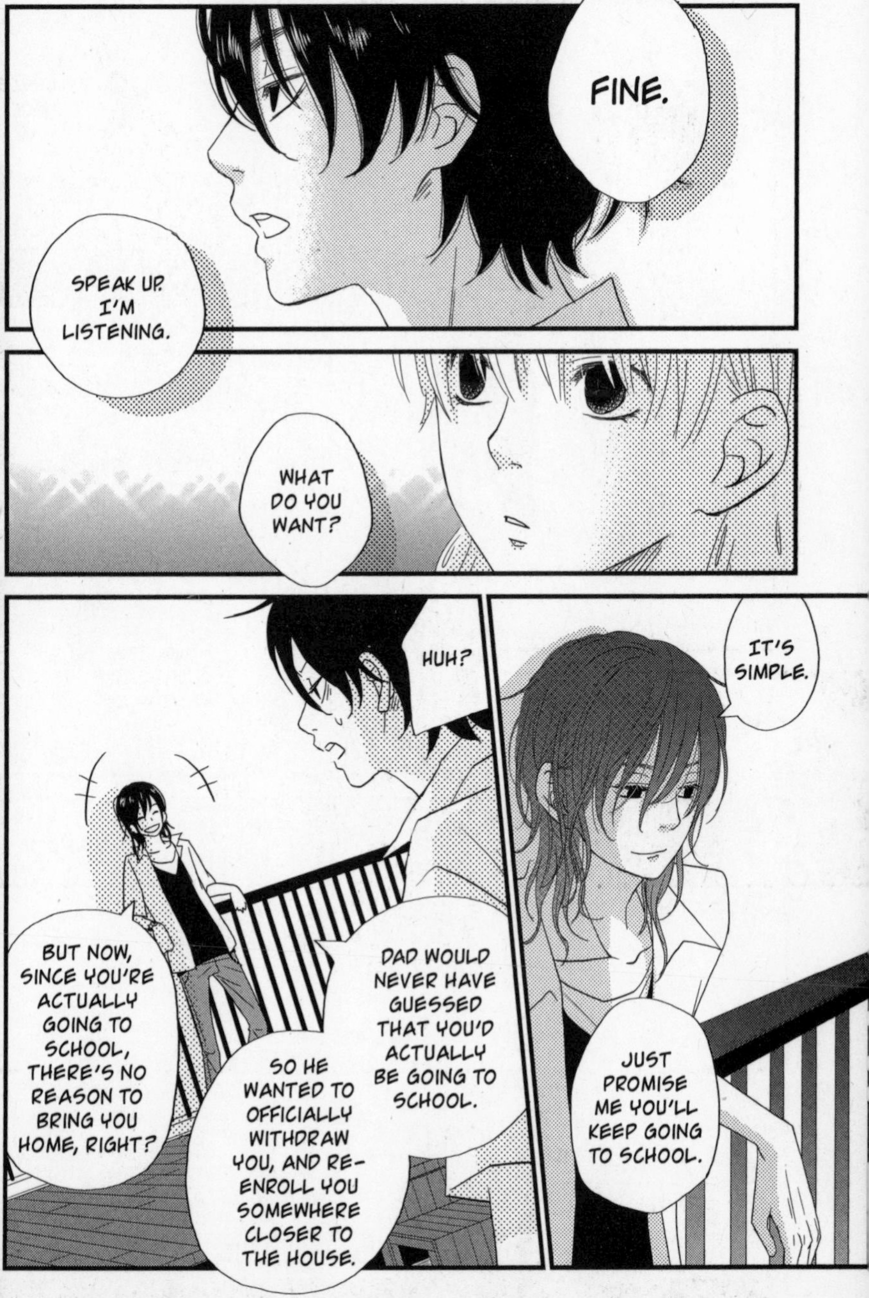
FINE.
SPEAK UP. I'M LISTENING.
WHAT DO YOU WANT?
IT'S SIMPLE.
JUST PROMISE ME YOU'LL KEEP GOING TO SCHOOL.
HUH?
DAD WOULD NEVER HAVE GUESSED THAT YOU'D ACTUALLY BE GOING TO SCHOOL.
SO HE WANTED TO OFFICIALLY WITHDRAW YOU, AND RE-ENROLL YOU SOMEWHERE CLOSER TO THE HOUSE.
BUT NOW, SINCE YOU'RE ACTUALLY GOING TO SCHOOL, THERE'S NO REASON TO BRING YOU HOME, RIGHT?

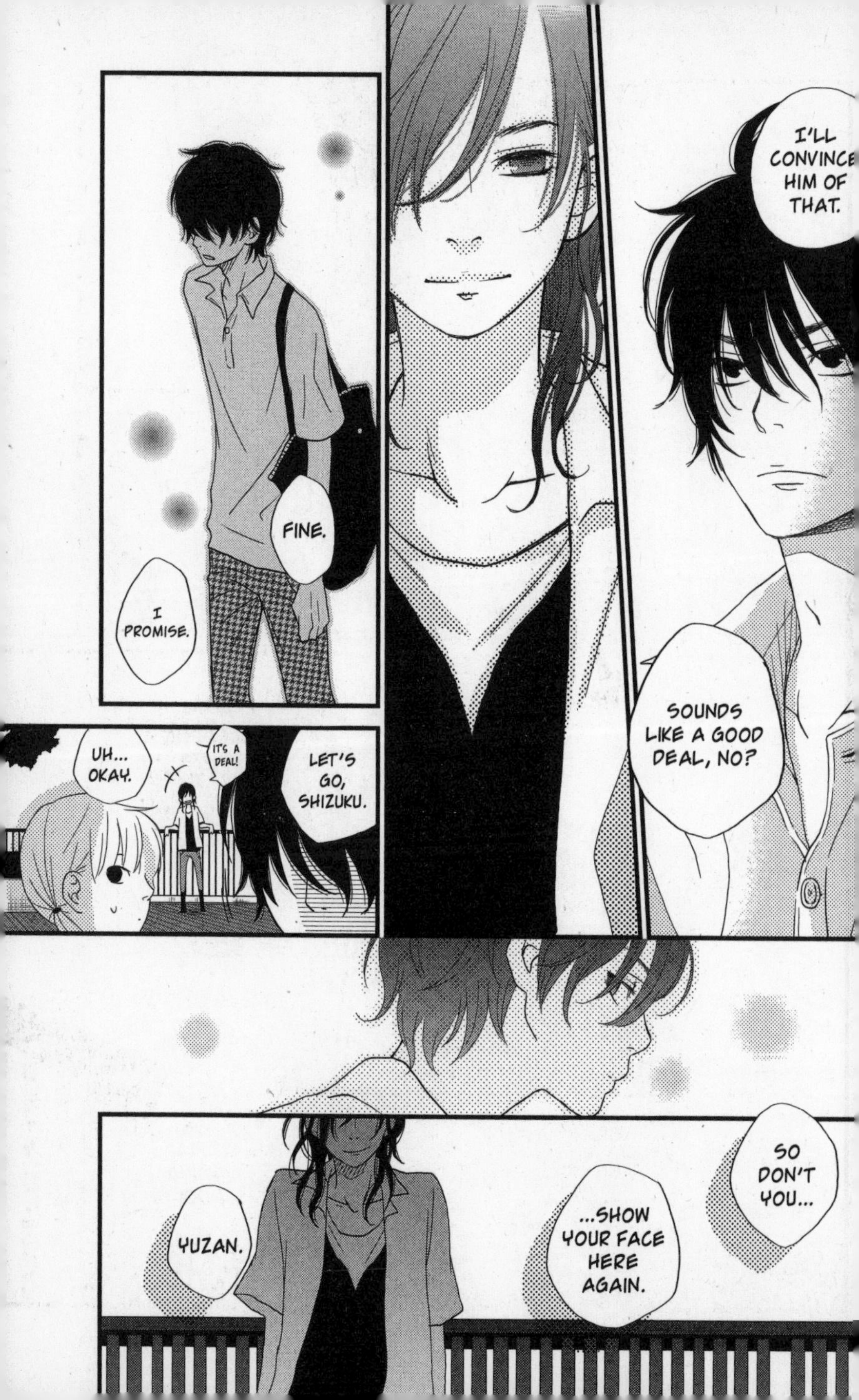
I'LL CONVINCE HIM OF THAT.
SOUNDS LIKE A GOOD DEAL, NO?
FINE.
I PROMISE.
LET'S GO, SHIZUKU.
IT'S A DEAL!
UH... OKAY.
SO DON'T YOU...
...SHOW YOUR FACE HERE AGAIN.
YUZAN.

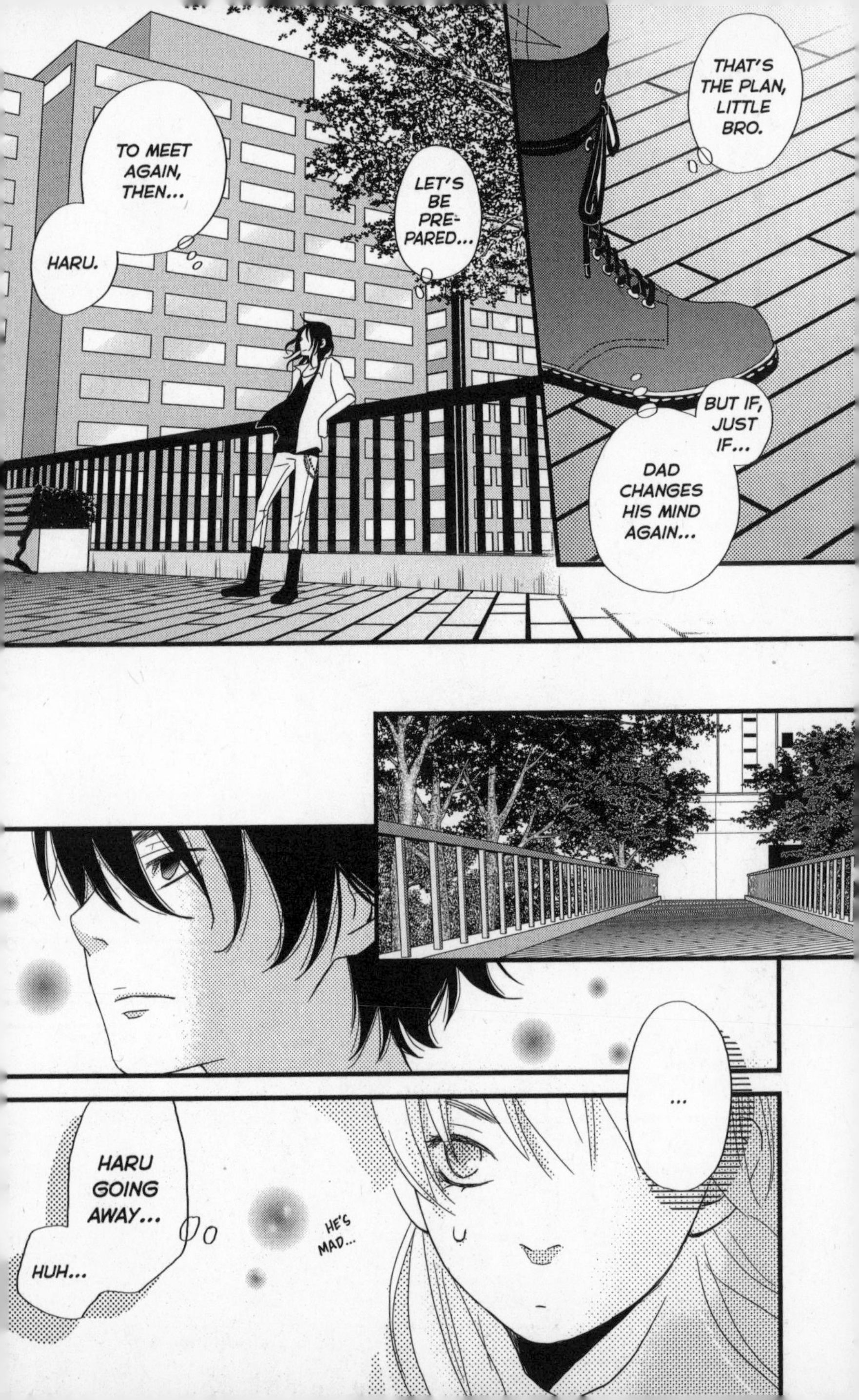
THAT'S THE PLAN, LITTLE BRO.
BUT IF, JUST IF...
DAD CHANGES HIS MIND AGAIN...
LET'S BE PRE-PARED...
TO MEET AGAIN, THEN...
HARU.
...
HE'S MAD...
HARU GOING AWAY...
HUH...

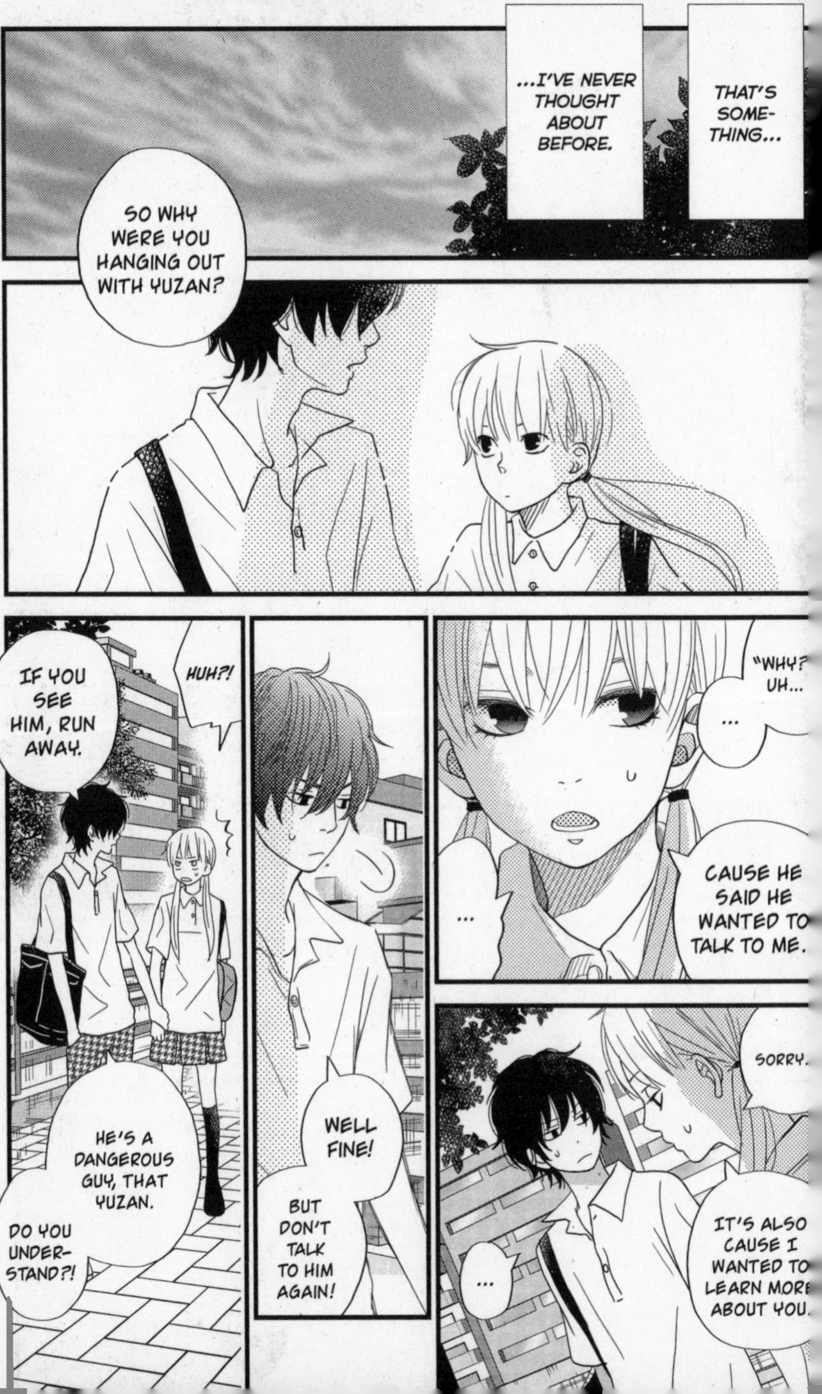
THAT'S SOMETHING...
...I'VE NEVER THOUGHT ABOUT BEFORE.
SO WHY WERE YOU HANGING OUT WITH YUZAN?
"WHY? UH... ...
...
CAUSE HE SAID HE WANTED TO TALK TO ME.
SORRY.
IT'S ALSO CAUSE I WANTED TO LEARN MORE ABOUT YOU.
...
WELL FINE!
BUT DON'T TALK TO HIM AGAIN!
HUH?!
IF YOU SEE HIM, RUN AWAY.
HE'S A DANGEROUS GUY, THAT YUZAN.
DO YOU UNDERSTAND?!

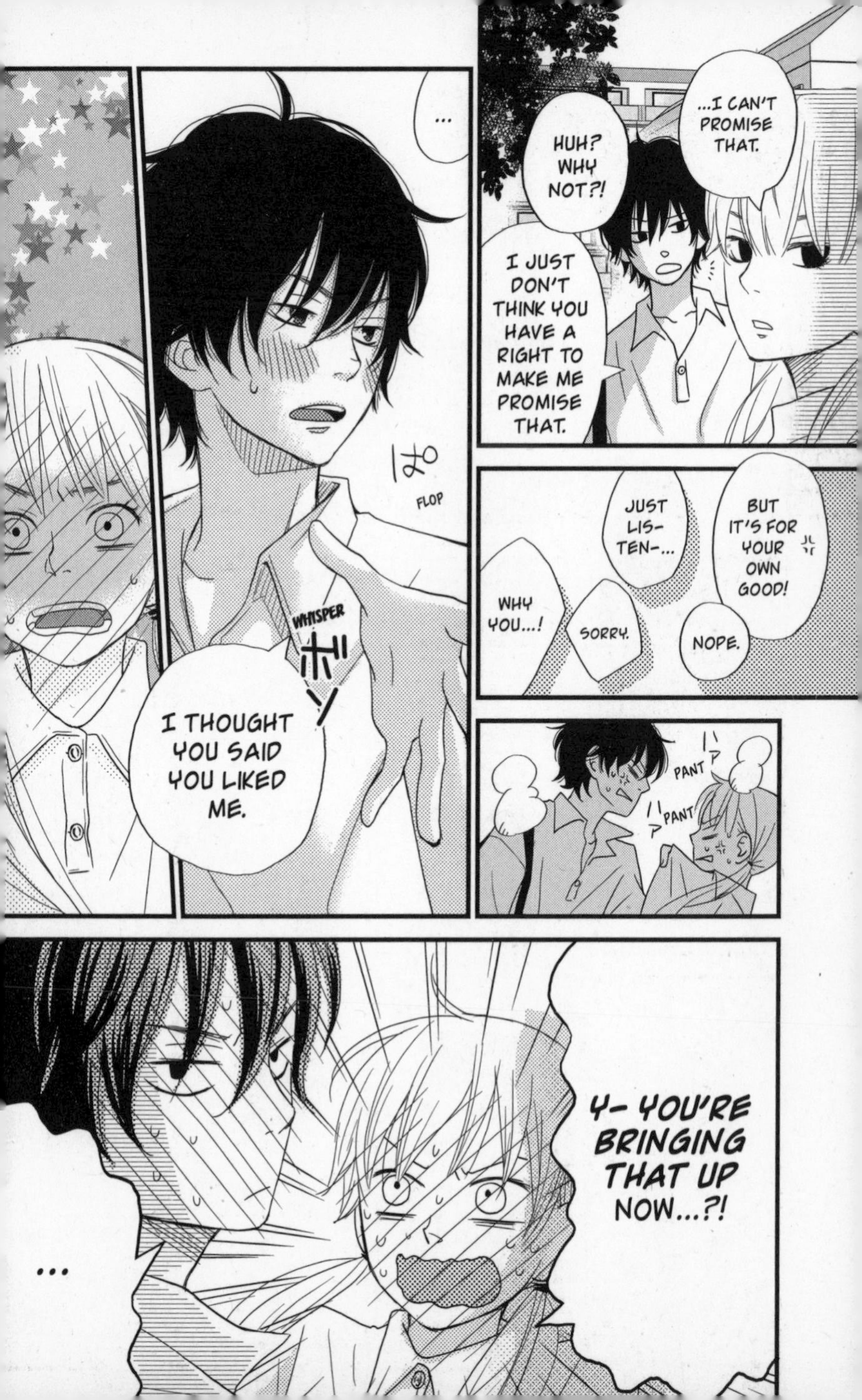
...I CAN'T PROMISE THAT.
HUH? WHY NOT?!
I JUST DON'T THINK YOU HAVE A RIGHT TO MAKE ME PROMISE THAT.
BUT IT'S FOR YOUR OWN GOOD!
JUST LIS- TEN-...
NOPE.
SORRY.
WHY YOU...!
PANT
PANT
...
FLOP
WHISPER
I THOUGHT YOU SAID YOU LIKED ME.
Y- YOU'RE BRINGING THAT UP NOW...?!
...

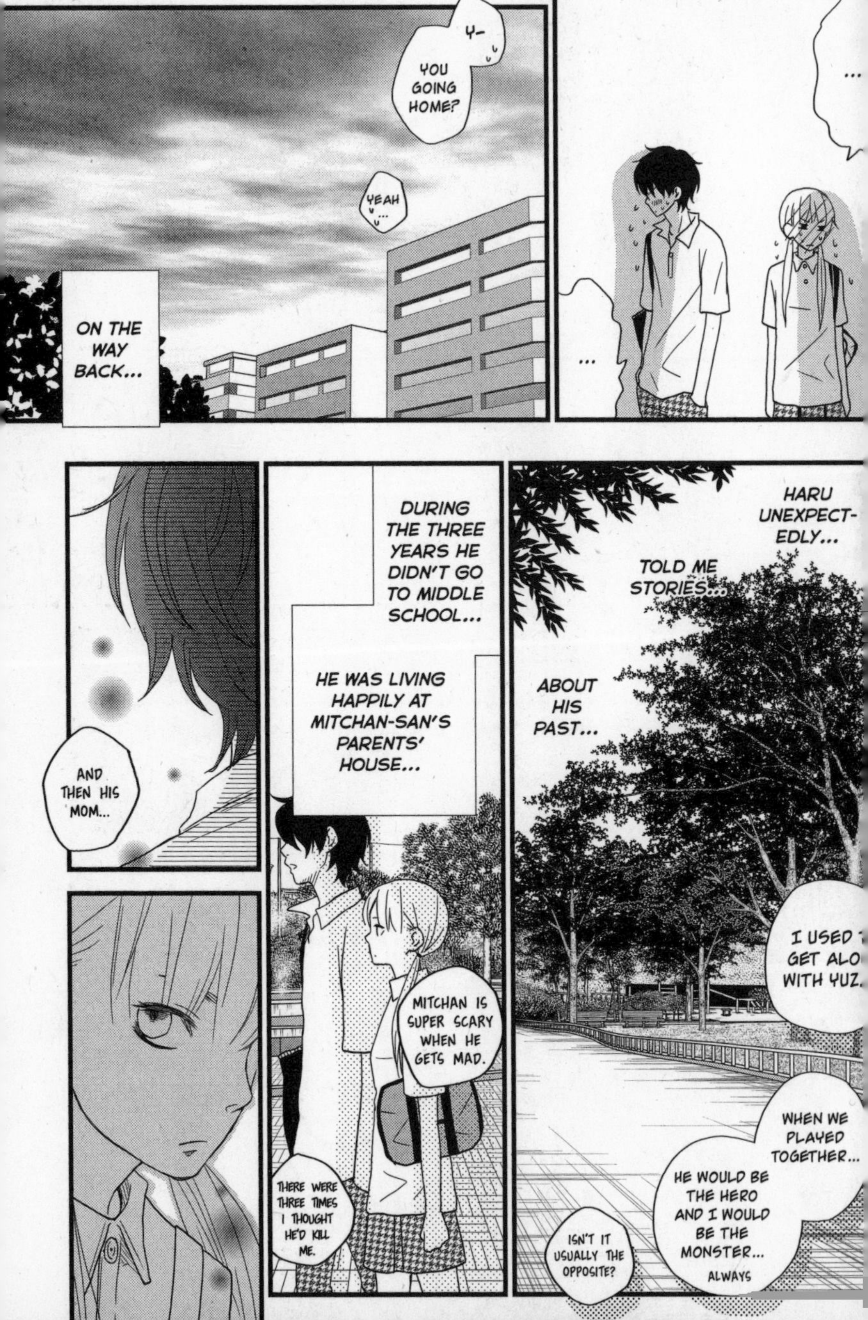
...
...
Y-
YOU GOING HOME?
YEAH...
ON THE WAY BACK...
HARU UNEXPECT-EDLY...
TOLD ME STORIES...
ABOUT HIS PAST...
I USED T
GET ALO
WITH YUZ.
WHEN WE PLAYED TOGETHER...
HE WOULD BE THE HERO AND I WOULD BE THE MONSTER...
ALWAYS
ISN'T IT USUALLY THE OPPOSITE?
DURING THE THREE YEARS HE DIDN'T GO TO MIDDLE SCHOOL...
HE WAS LIVING HAPPILY AT MITCHAN-SAN'S PARENTS' HOUSE...
MITCHAN IS SUPER SCARY WHEN HE GETS MAD.
THERE WERE THREE TIMES I THOUGHT HE'D KILL ME.
AND THEN HIS MOM...

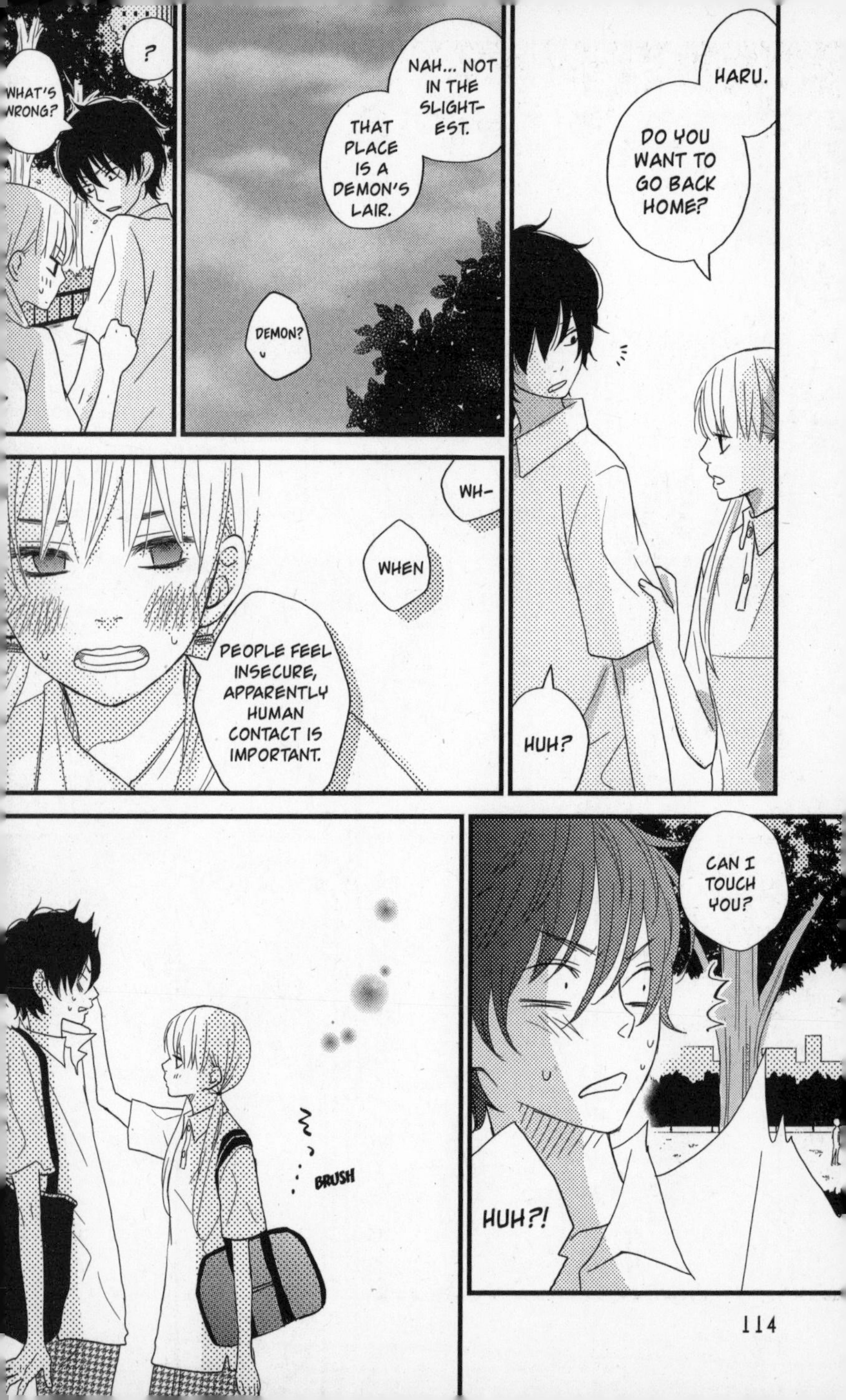
HARU.
DO YOU WANT TO GO BACK HOME?
HUH?
NAH... NOT IN THE SLIGHT-EST.
THAT PLACE IS A DEMON'S LAIR.
DEMON?
?
WHAT'S WRONG?
WH-
WHEN
PEOPLE FEEL INSECURE, APPARENTLY HUMAN CONTACT IS IMPORTANT.
CAN I TOUCH YOU?
HUH?!
BRUSH

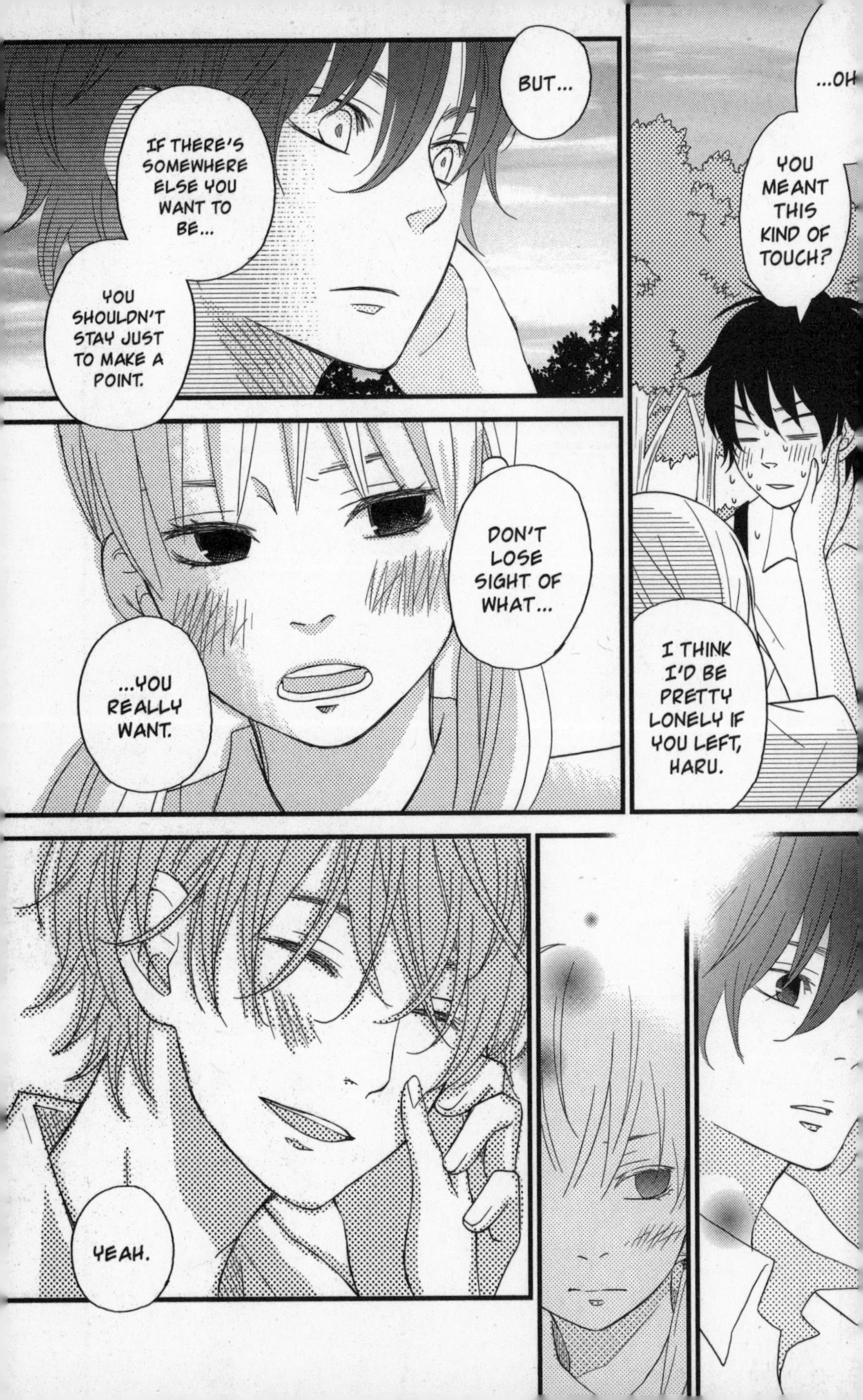
...OH
YOU MEANT THIS KIND OF TOUCH?
I THINK I'D BE PRETTY LONELY IF YOU LEFT, HARU.
BUT...
IF THERE'S SOMEWHERE ELSE YOU WANT TO BE...
YOU SHOULDN'T STAY JUST TO MAKE A POINT.
DON'T LOSE SIGHT OF WHAT...
...YOU REALLY WANT.
YEAH.

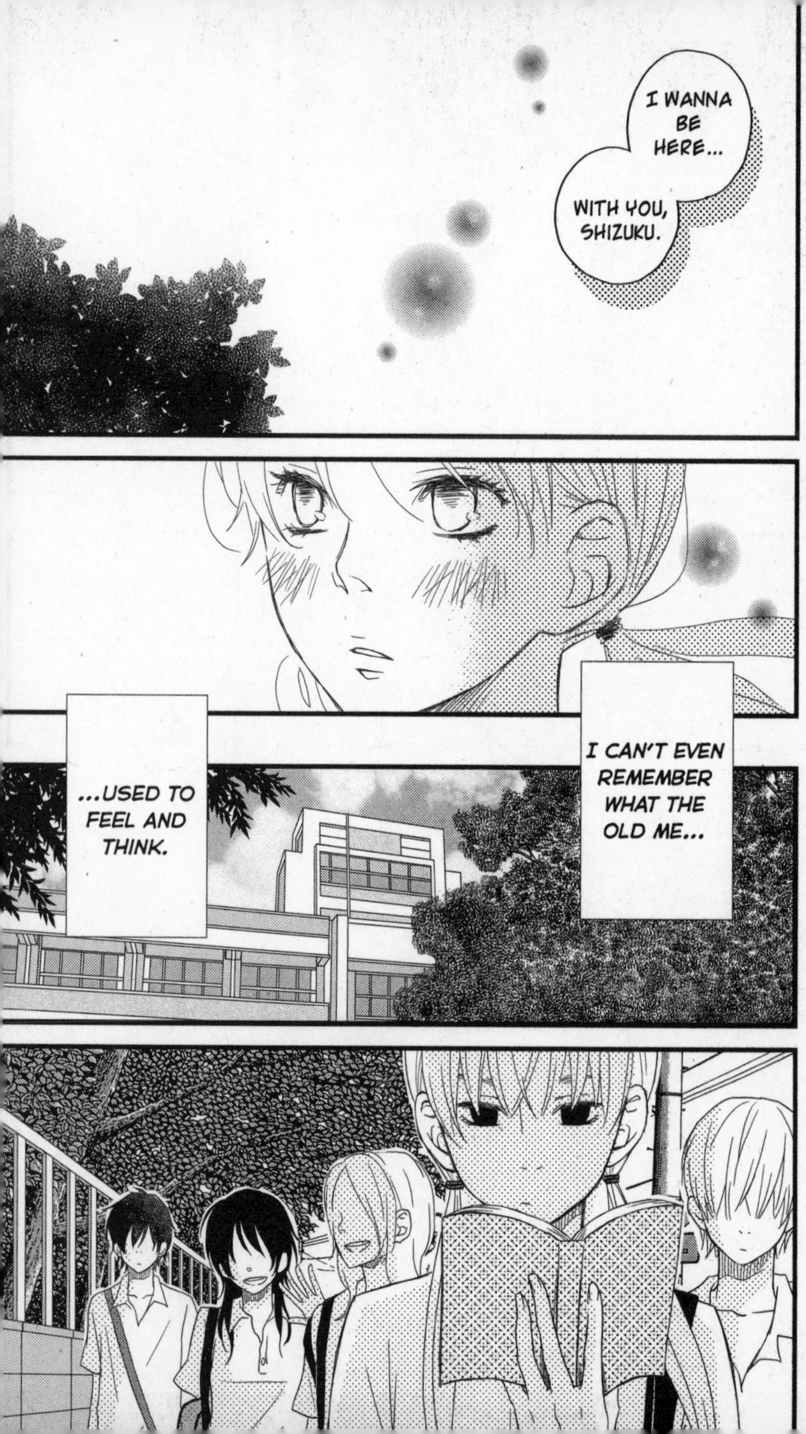
I WANNA BE HERE...
WITH YOU, SHIZUKU.
I CAN'T EVEN REMEMBER WHAT THE OLD ME...
...USED TO FEEL AND THINK.

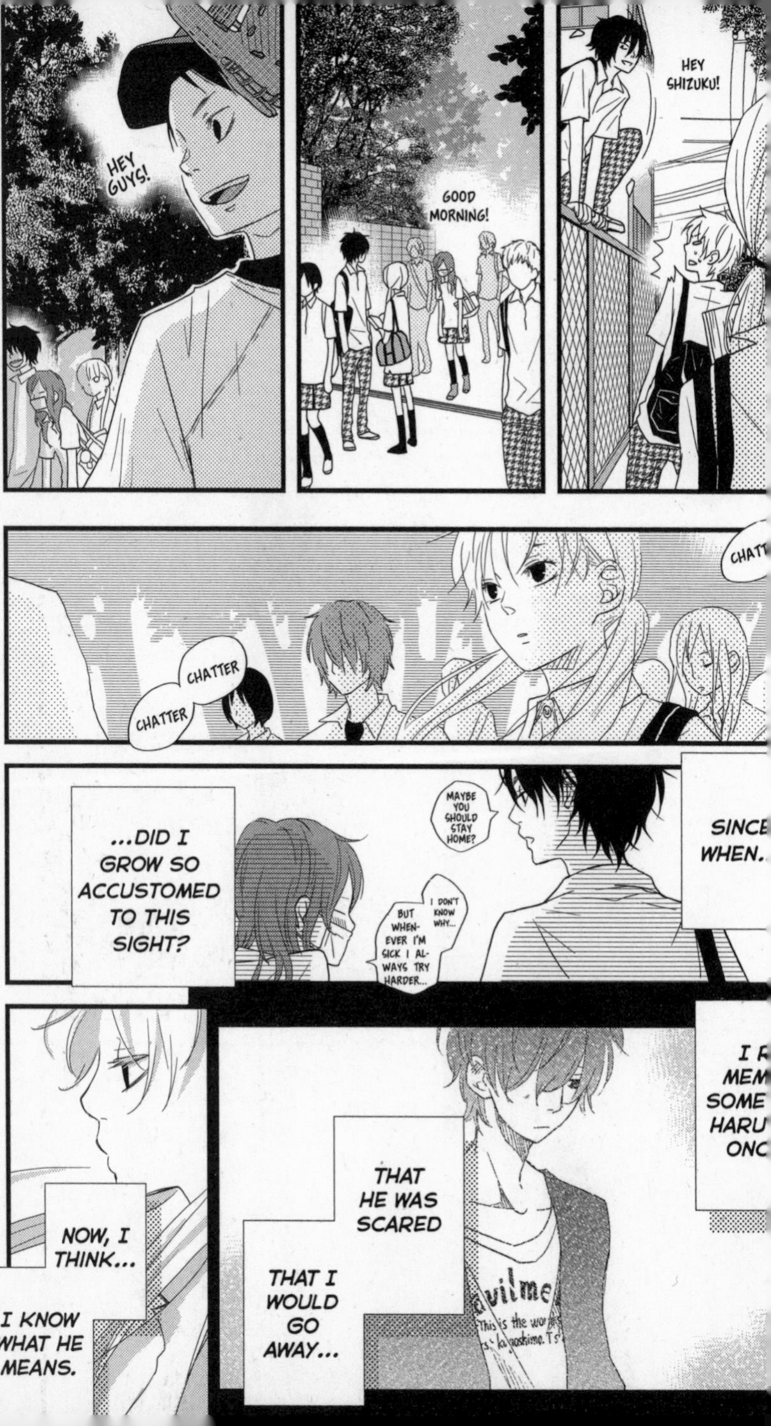
HEY SHIZUKU!
GOOD MORNING!
HEY GUYS!
CHATT
CHATTER
CHATTER
SINCE WHEN..
MAYBE YOU SHOULD STAY HOME?
I DON'T KNOW WHY...
BUT WHENEVER I'M SICK I ALWAYS TRY HARDER...
...DID I GROW SO ACCUSTOMED TO THIS SIGHT?
I R MEM SOME HARU ONC
THAT HE WAS SCARED
THAT I WOULD GO AWAY...
NOW, I THINK...
I KNOW WHAT HE MEANS.

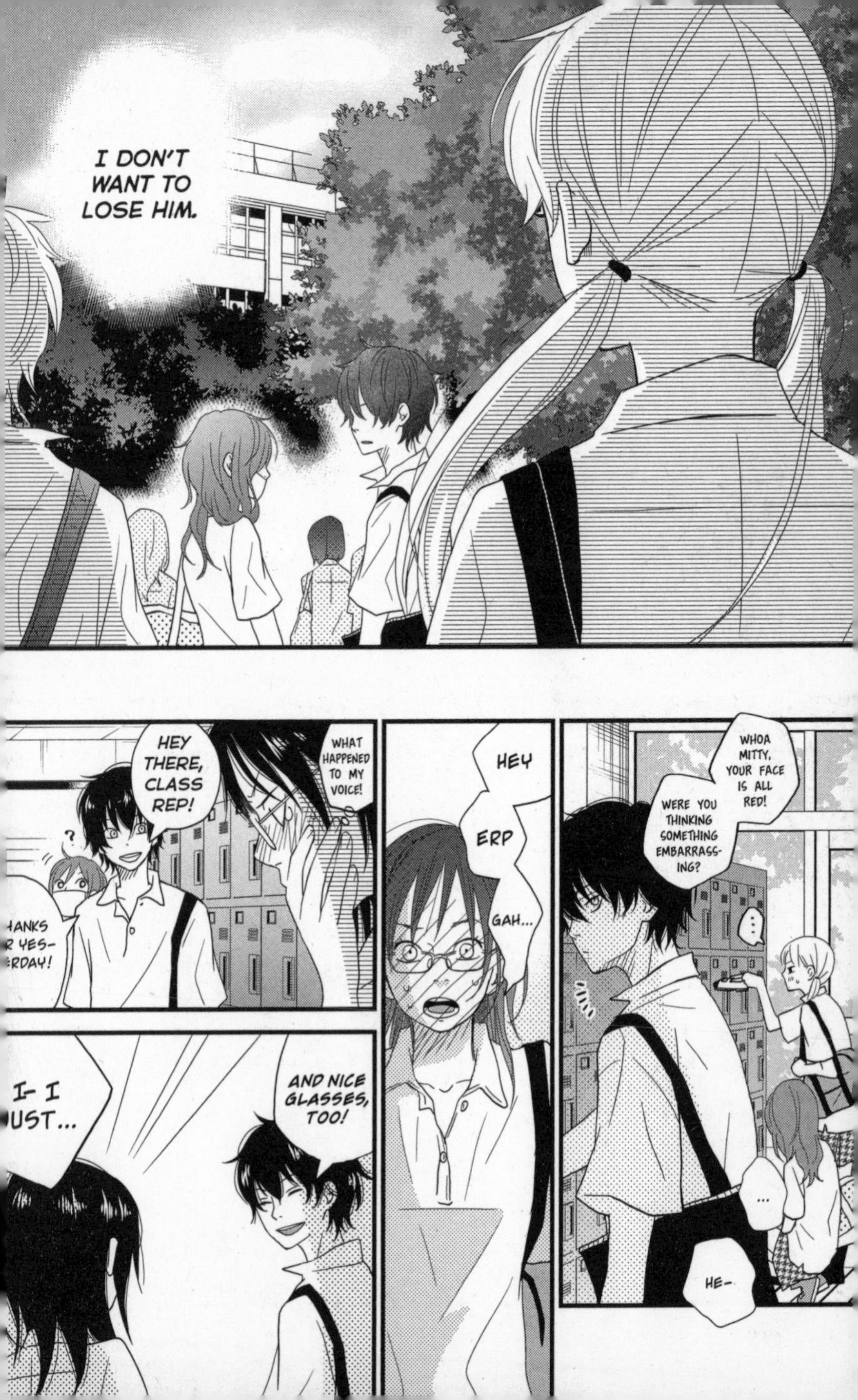

I DON'T WANT TO LOSE HIM.
WHOA MITTY, YOUR FACE IS ALL RED!
WERE YOU THINKING SOMETHING EMBARRASS-ING?
...
...
HE-
HEY
ERP
GAH...
HEY THERE, CLASS REP!
WHAT HAPPENED TO MY VOICE!
?
HANKS
R YES-
ERDAY!
AND NICE GLASSES, TOO!
I- I
UST...

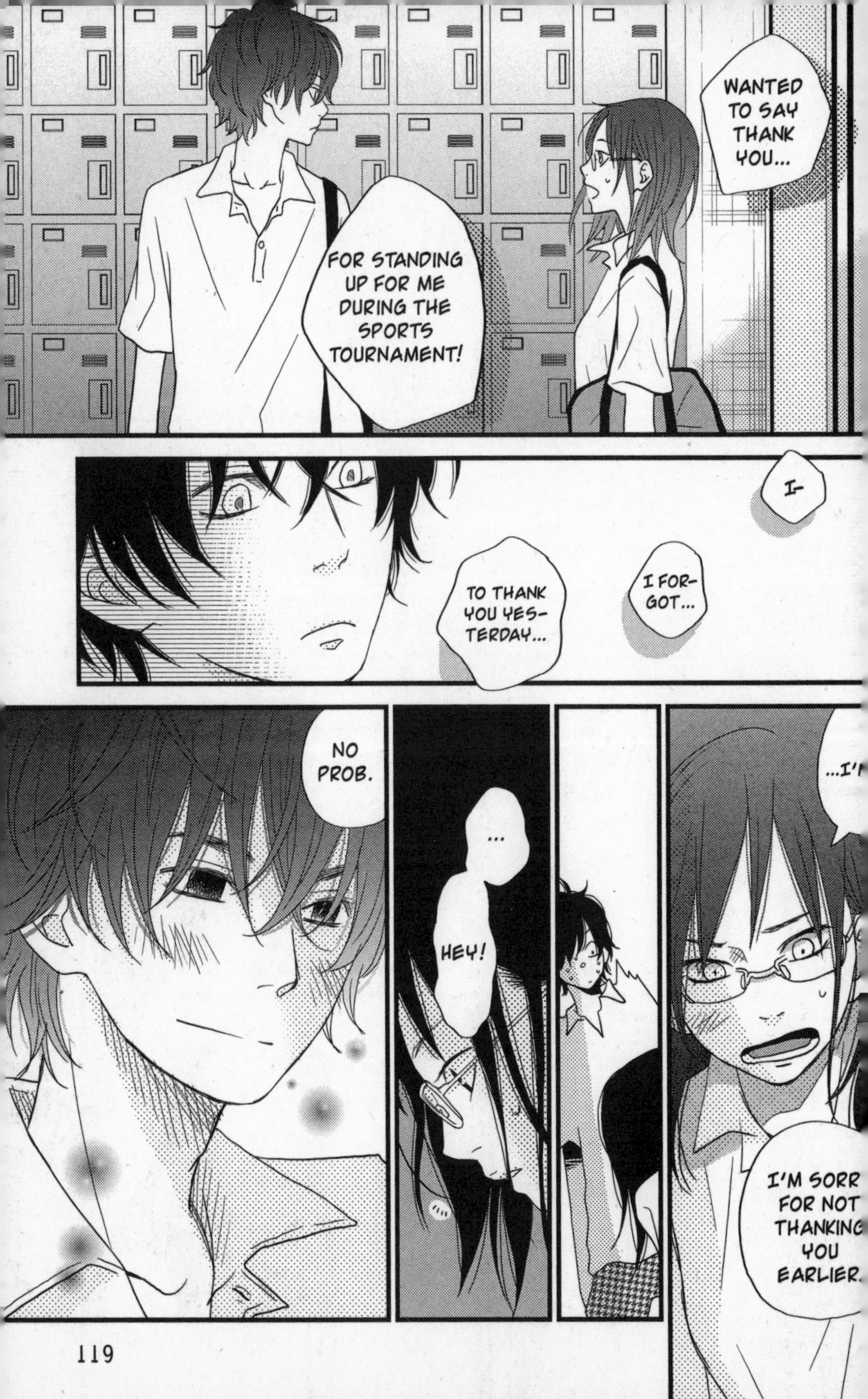
WANTED TO SAY THANK YOU...
FOR STANDING UP FOR ME DURING THE SPORTS TOURNAMENT!
I-
I FOR-GOT...
TO THANK YOU YES-TERDAY...
...I'
I'M SORR FOR NOT THANKING YOU EARLIER.
...
HEY!
NO PROB.

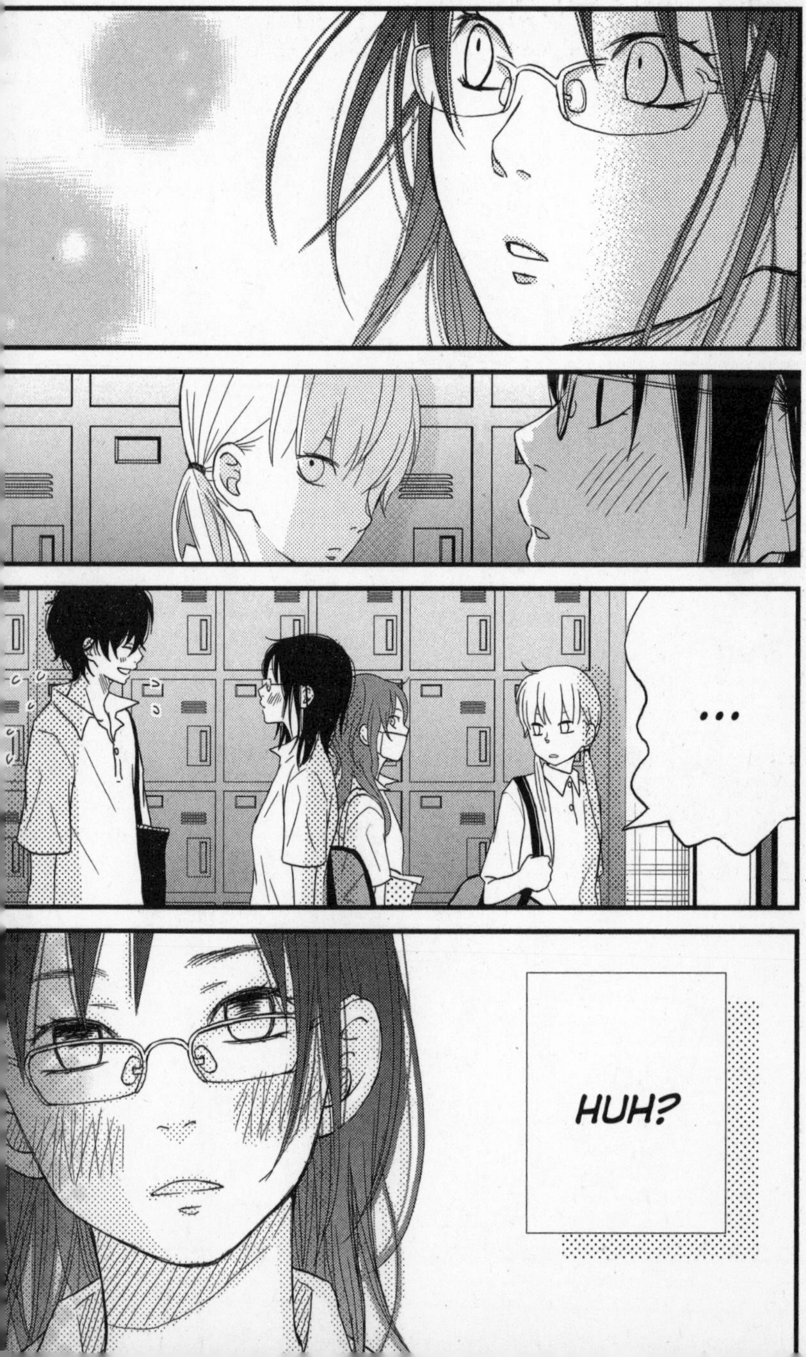
...
HUH?

Haru's Big Brother's Urgent Matter

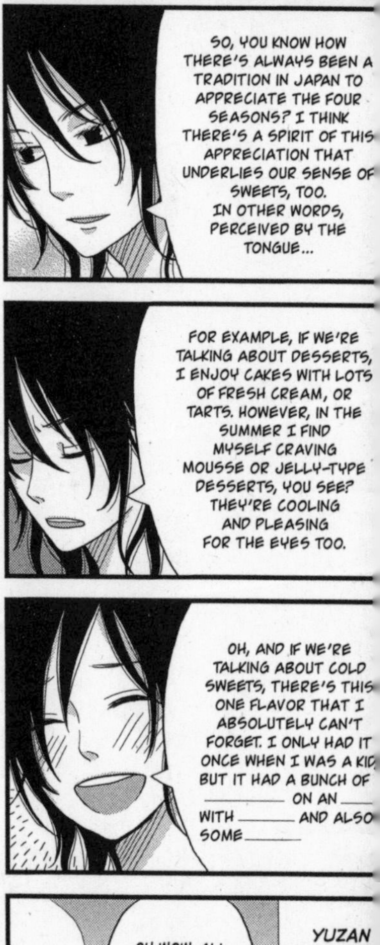
SO, YOU KNOW HOW THERE'S ALWAYS BEEN A TRADITION IN JAPAN TO APPRECIATE THE FOUR SEASONS? I THINK THERE'S A SPIRIT OF THIS APPRECIATION THAT UNDERLIES OUR SENSE OF SWEETS, TOO. IN OTHER WORDS, PERCEIVED BY THE TONGUE...
FOR EXAMPLE, IF WE'RE TALKING ABOUT DESSERTS, I ENJOY CAKES WITH LOTS OF FRESH CREAM, OR TARTS. HOWEVER, IN THE SUMMER I FIND MYSELF CRAVING MOUSSE OR JELLY-TYPE DESSERTS, YOU SEE? THEY'RE COOLING AND PLEASING FOR THE EYES TOO.
OH, AND IF WE'RE TALKING ABOUT COLD SWEETS, THERE'S THIS ONE FLAVOR THAT I ABSOLUTELY CAN'T FORGET. I ONLY HAD IT ONCE WHEN I WAS A KID BUT IT HAD A BUNCH OF ______ ON AN ____ WITH ______ AND ALSO SOME ______
YUZAN ACTUALL TALKED ABOUT SWEETS 80% O THE TIM
OH WOW, ALL THIS TALK REALLY MADE ME CRAVE SOMETHING SWEET.
AND IT MADE ME WANT TO THROW UP.

Glasses

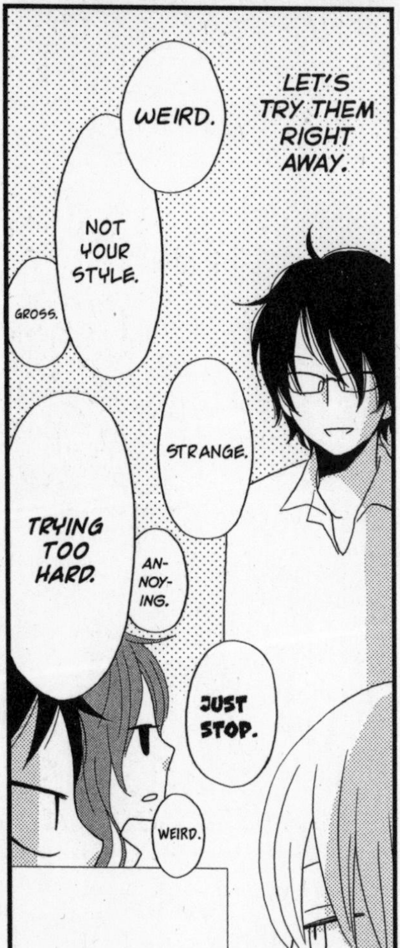
LET'S TRY THEM RIGHT AWAY.
WEIRD.
NOT YOUR STYLE.
GROSS.
STRANGE.
TRYING TOO HARD.
AN-NOY-ING.
JUST STOP.
WEIRD.
NOT FOR HARU.

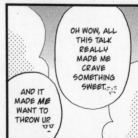

Day of the sports tournament

What 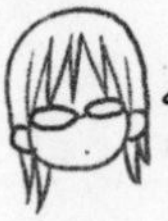 dropped on the older student's head.

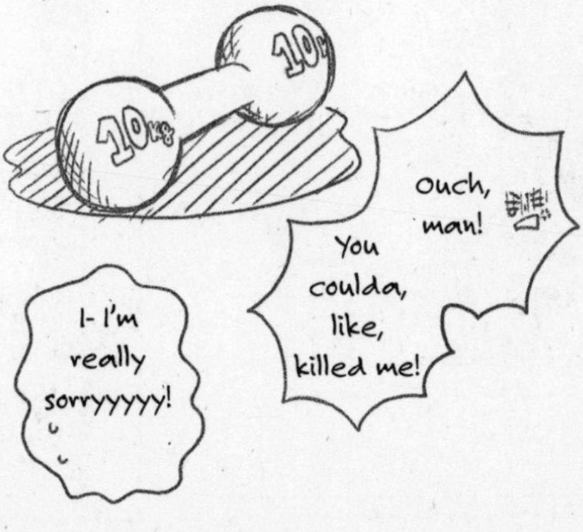
Ouch, man!
You coulda, like, killed me!
I- I'm really sorryyyyy!

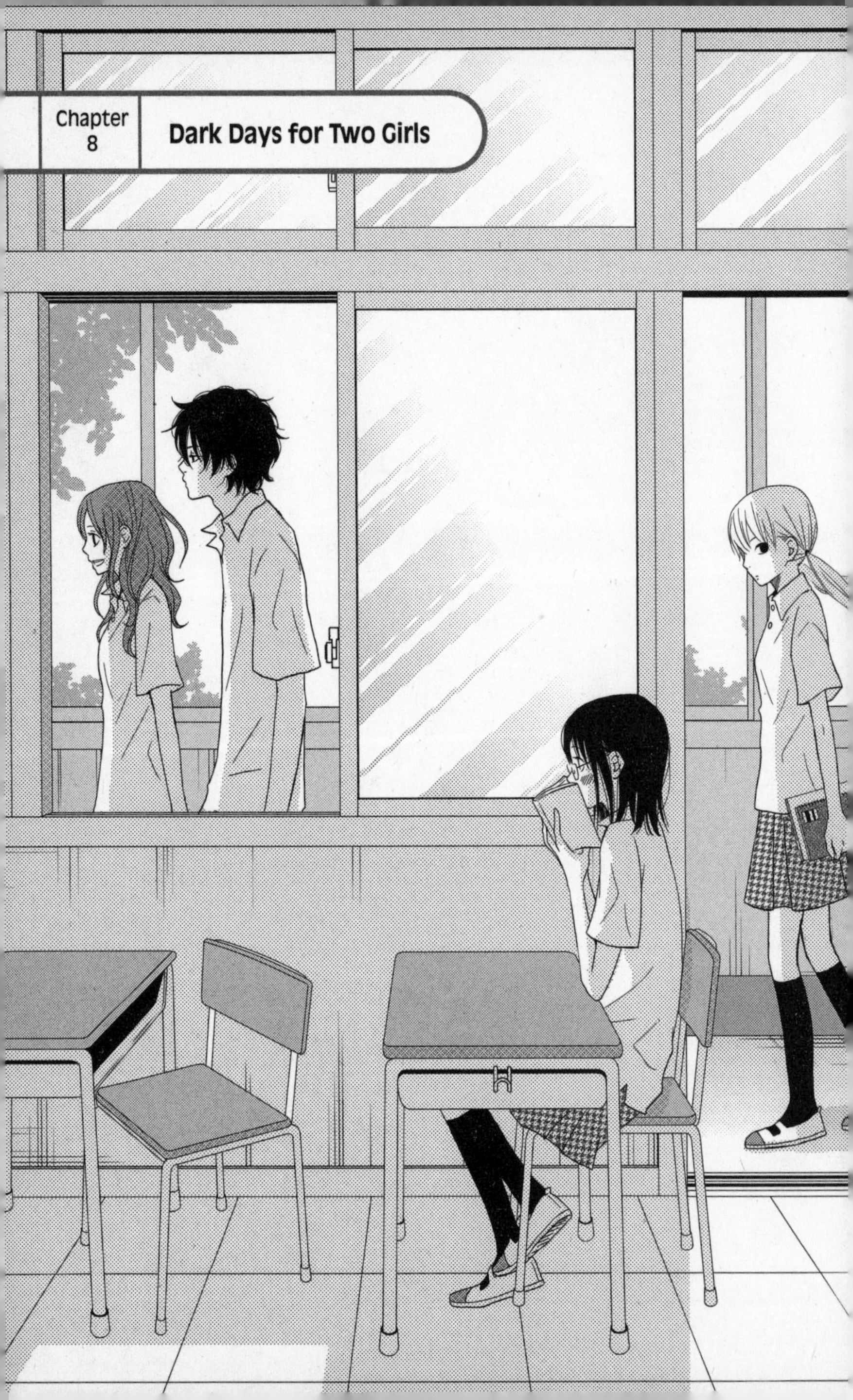
Chapter 8
Dark Days for Two Girls

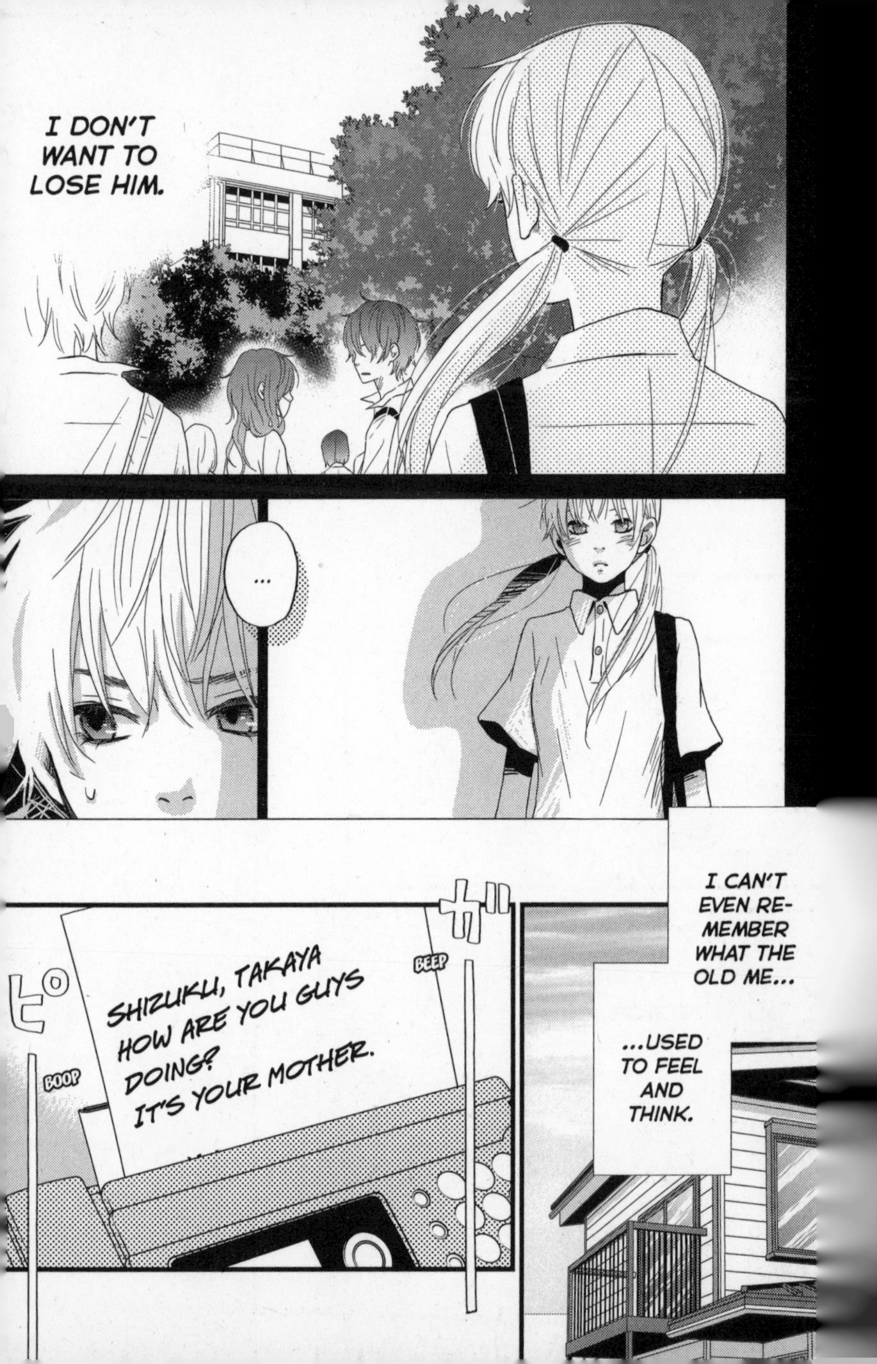
I DON'T WANT TO LOSE HIM.
...
I CAN'T EVEN RE-MEMBER WHAT THE OLD ME...
...USED TO FEEL AND THINK.
ガッ
BEEP
ピ
BOOP
SHIZUKU, TAKAYA HOW ARE YOU GUYS DOING? IT'S YOUR MOTHER.

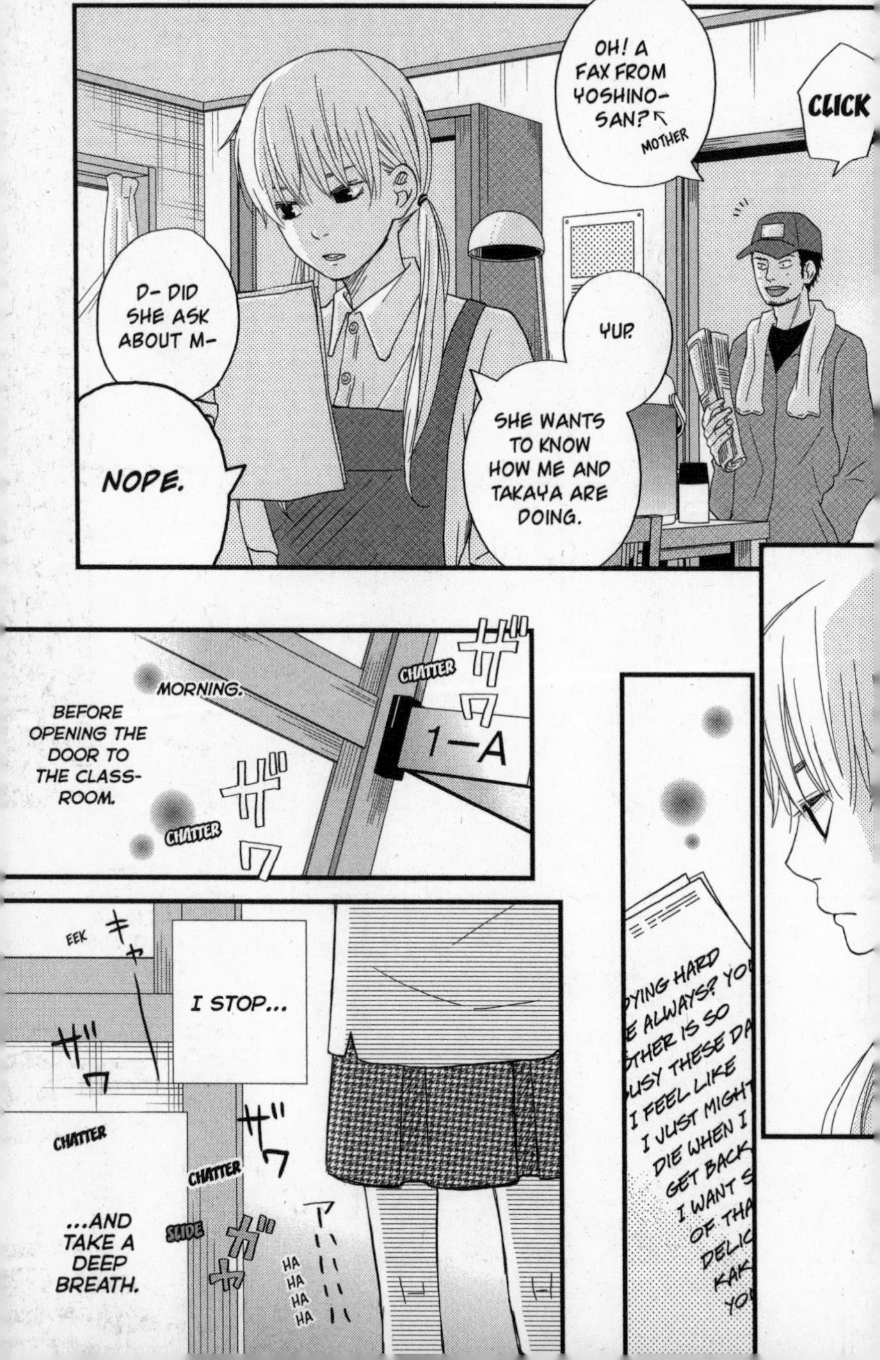
CLICK
OH! A FAX FROM YOSHINO-SAN?
MOTHER
YUP.
SHE WANTS TO KNOW HOW ME AND TAKAYA ARE DOING.
D- DID SHE ASK ABOUT M-
NOPE.
YING HARD
E ALWAYS? YOU
OTHER IS SO
USY THESE DA
I FEEL LIKE
I JUST MIGHT
DIE WHEN I
GET BACK
I WANT S
OF THA
DELIC
KAK
YO
CHATTER
ザワ
1-A
MORNING.
BEFORE OPENING THE DOOR TO THE CLASSROOM.
CHATTER
ザワ
I STOP...
EEK
キャー
ザワ
CHATTER
ザワ
CHATTER
アハハハ
HA HA HA HA
SLIDE
ガッ
...AND TAKE A DEEP BREATH.

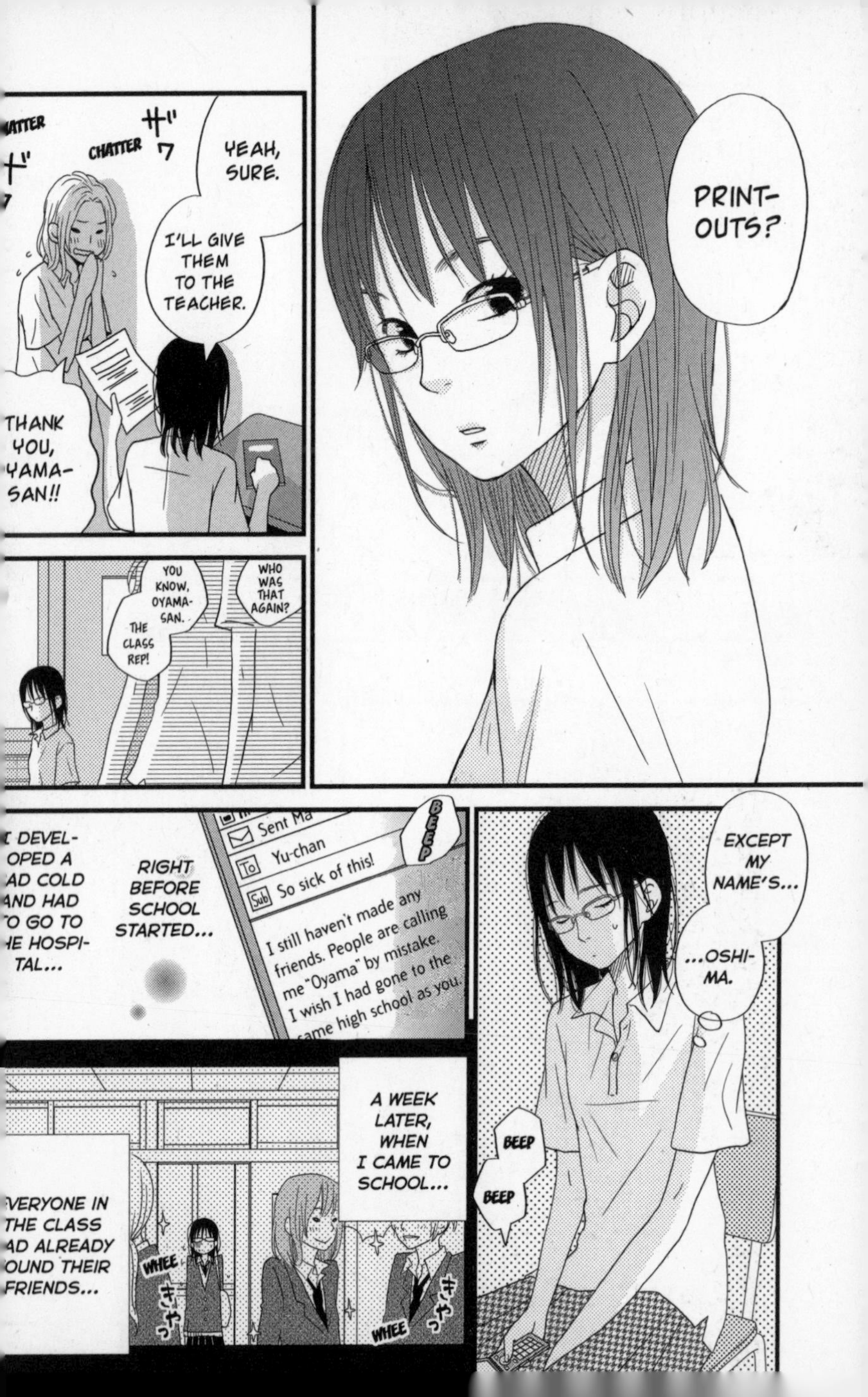

PRINT-OUTS?
ATTER
CHATTER
ザワ
YEAH, SURE.
I'LL GIVE THEM TO THE TEACHER.
THANK YOU, YAMA-SAN!!
WHO WAS THAT AGAIN?
YOU KNOW, OYAMA-SAN.
THE CLASS REP!
EXCEPT MY NAME'S...
...OSHI-MA.
BEEP
BEEP
BEEP
Sent Ma
To Yu-chan
Sub So sick of this!
I still haven't made any friends. People are calling me "Oyama" by mistake. I wish I had gone to the same high school as you.
RIGHT BEFORE SCHOOL STARTED...
DEVEL-OPED A AD COLD AND HAD TO GO TO O GO TO E HOSPI-TAL...
A WEEK LATER, WHEN I CAME TO SCHOOL...
VERYONE IN THE CLASS AD ALREADY OUND THEIR FRIENDS...
WHEE
WHEE

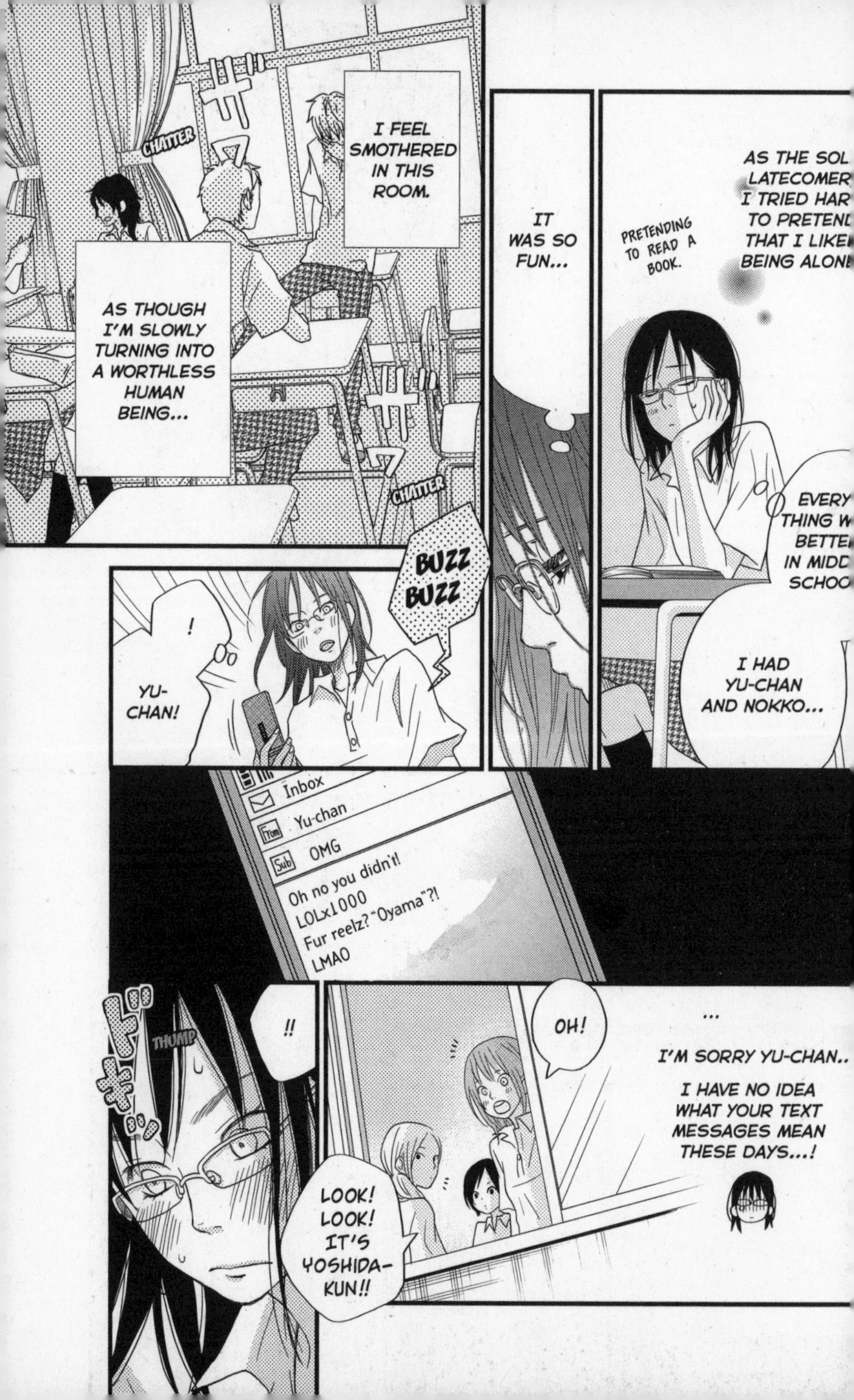
AS THE SOL
LATECOMER
I TRIED HAR
TO PRETEND
THAT I LIKE
BEING ALON
PRETENDING TO READ A BOOK.
EVERY THING W BETTE IN MIDD SCHOO
I HAD YU-CHAN AND NOKKO...
IT WAS SO FUN...
I FEEL SMOTHERED IN THIS ROOM.
CHATTER
AS THOUGH I'M SLOWLY TURNING INTO A WORTHLESS HUMAN BEING...
CHATTER
BUZZ BUZZ
!
YU-CHAN!
Inbox
Yu-chan
OMG
Oh no you didn't!
LOLx1000
Fur reelz? "Oyama"?!
LMAO
OH!
...
I'M SORRY YU-CHAN..
I HAVE NO IDEA WHAT YOUR TEXT MESSAGES MEAN THESE DAYS...!
LOOK! LOOK! IT'S YOSHIDA-KUN!!
!!
THUMP

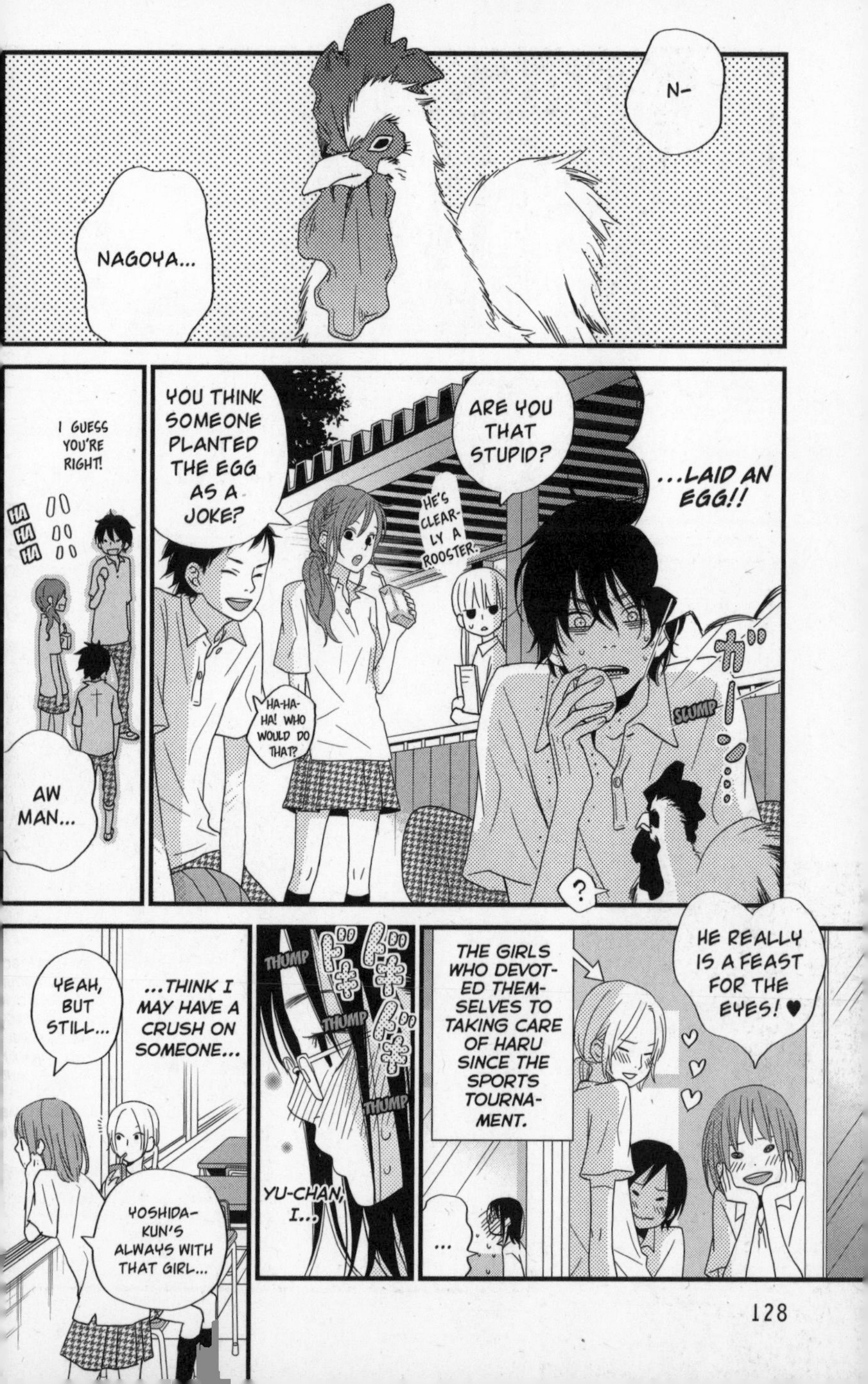
N-
NAGOYA...
...LAID AN EGG!!
ARE YOU THAT STUPID?
HE'S CLEARLY A ROOSTER.
YOU THINK SOMEONE PLANTED THE EGG AS A JOKE?
HA-HA-HA! WHO WOULD DO THAT?
SLUMP
?
I GUESS YOU'RE RIGHT!
HA HA HA
AW MAN...
HE REALLY IS A FEAST FOR THE EYES! ♥
THE GIRLS WHO DEVOTED THEMSELVES TO TAKING CARE OF HARU SINCE THE SPORTS TOURNAMENT.
...
THUMP
THUMP
THUMP
YU-CHAN, I...
...THINK I MAY HAVE A CRUSH ON SOMEONE...
YEAH, BUT STILL...
YOSHIDA-KUN'S ALWAYS WITH THAT GIRL...

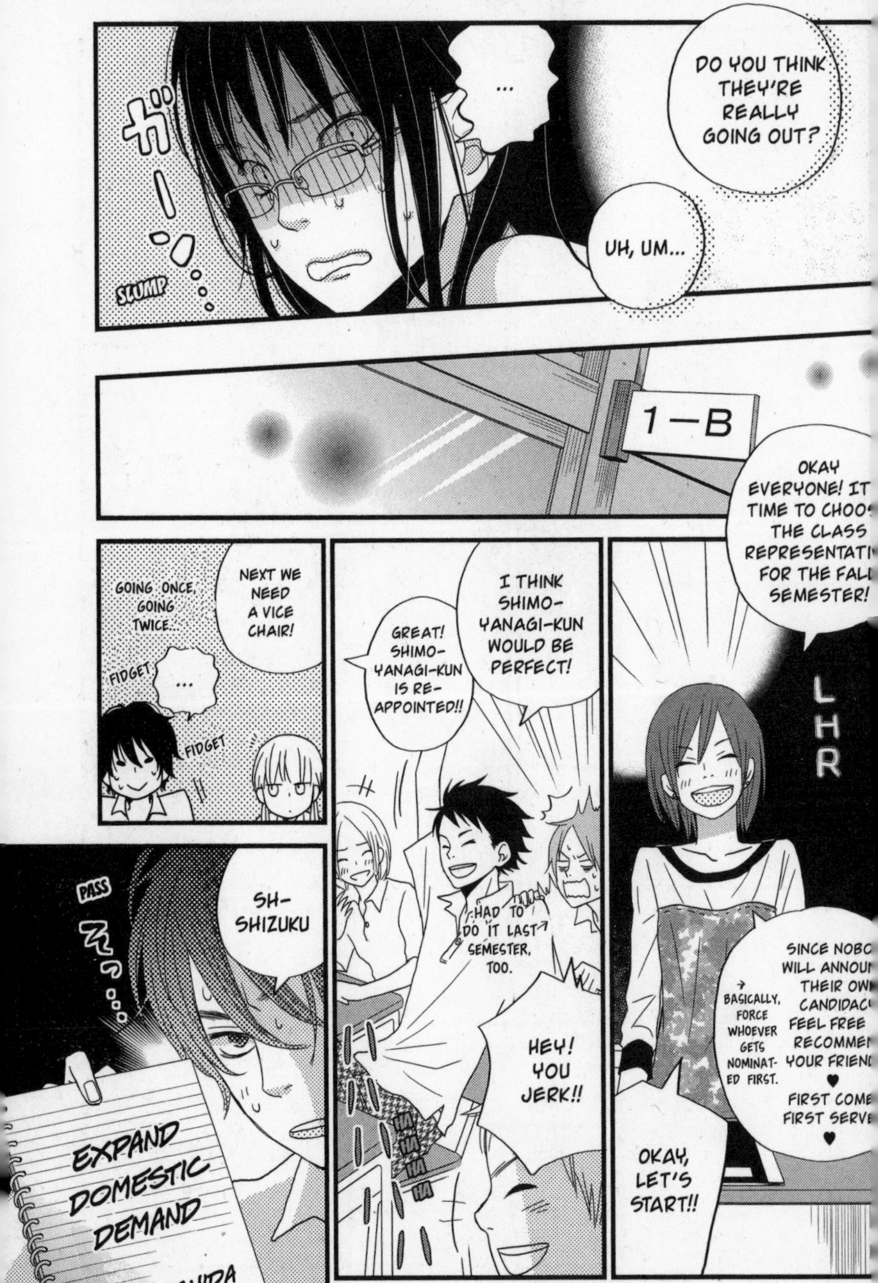
DO YOU THINK THEY'RE REALLY GOING OUT?
UH, UM...
...
SLUMP
1—B
OKAY EVERYONE! IT TIME TO CHOOS THE CLASS REPRESENTATI FOR THE FALL SEMESTER!
LHR
SINCE NOBO WILL ANNOU THEIR OWN CANDIDAC FEEL FREE RECOMME YOUR FRIEN ♥ FIRST COME FIRST SERVE ♥
→ BASICALLY, FORCE WHOEVER GETS NOMINATED FIRST.
OKAY, LET'S START!!
I THINK SHIMO-YANAGI-KUN WOULD BE PERFECT!
GREAT! SHIMO-YANAGI-KUN IS RE-APPOINTED!!
HAD TO DO IT LAST→ SEMESTER, TOO.
HEY! YOU JERK!!
HA HA HA HA
NEXT WE NEED A VICE CHAIR!
GOING ONCE, GOING TWICE...
FIDGET
...
FIDGET
SH-SHIZUKU
PASS
EXPAND DOMESTIC DEMAND
HARU YOSHIDA

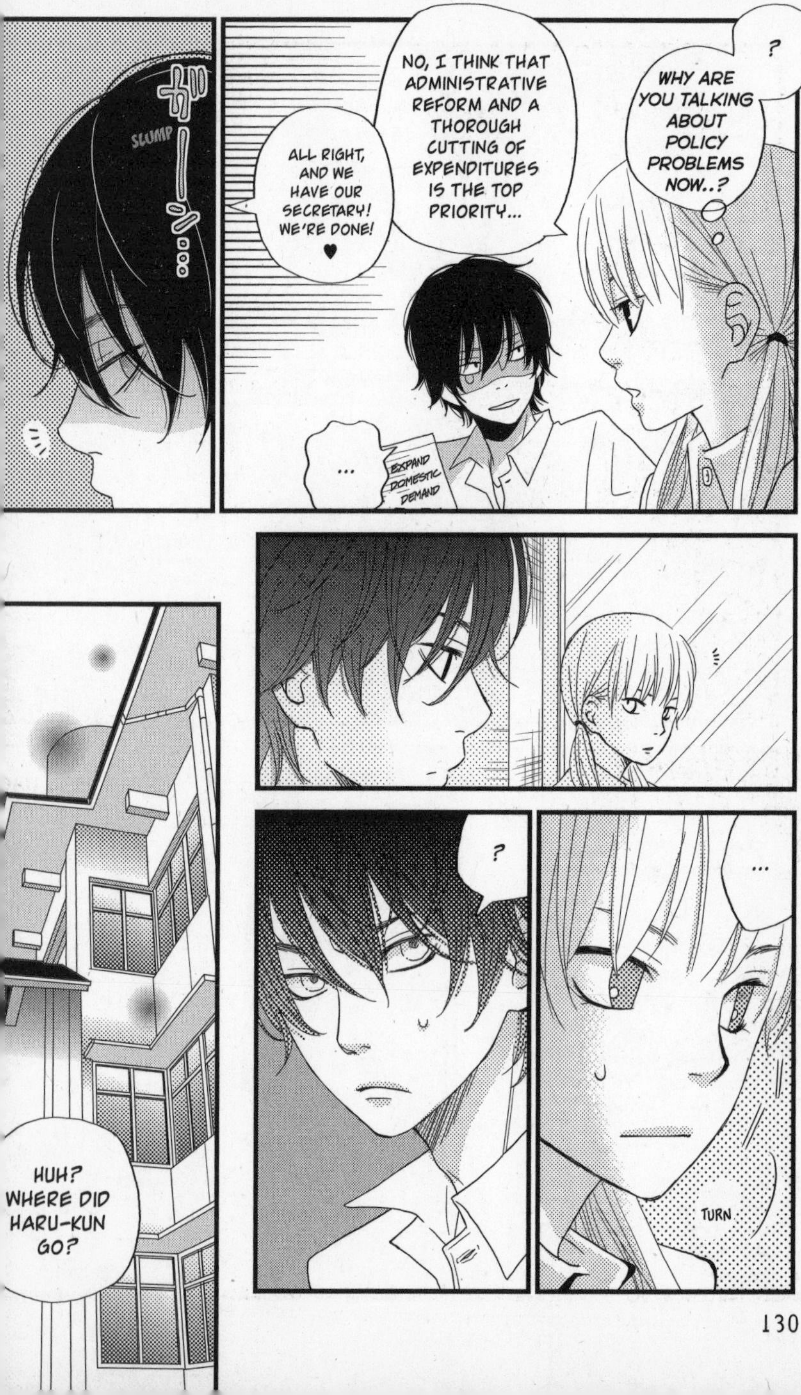
?
WHY ARE YOU TALKING ABOUT POLICY PROBLEMS NOW..?
NO, I THINK THAT ADMINISTRATIVE REFORM AND A THOROUGH CUTTING OF EXPENDITURES IS THE TOP PRIORITY...
ALL RIGHT, AND WE HAVE OUR SECRETARY! WE'RE DONE! ♥
EXPAND DOMESTIC DEMAND
...
SLUMP
...
TURN
?
HUH? WHERE DID HARU-KUN GO?

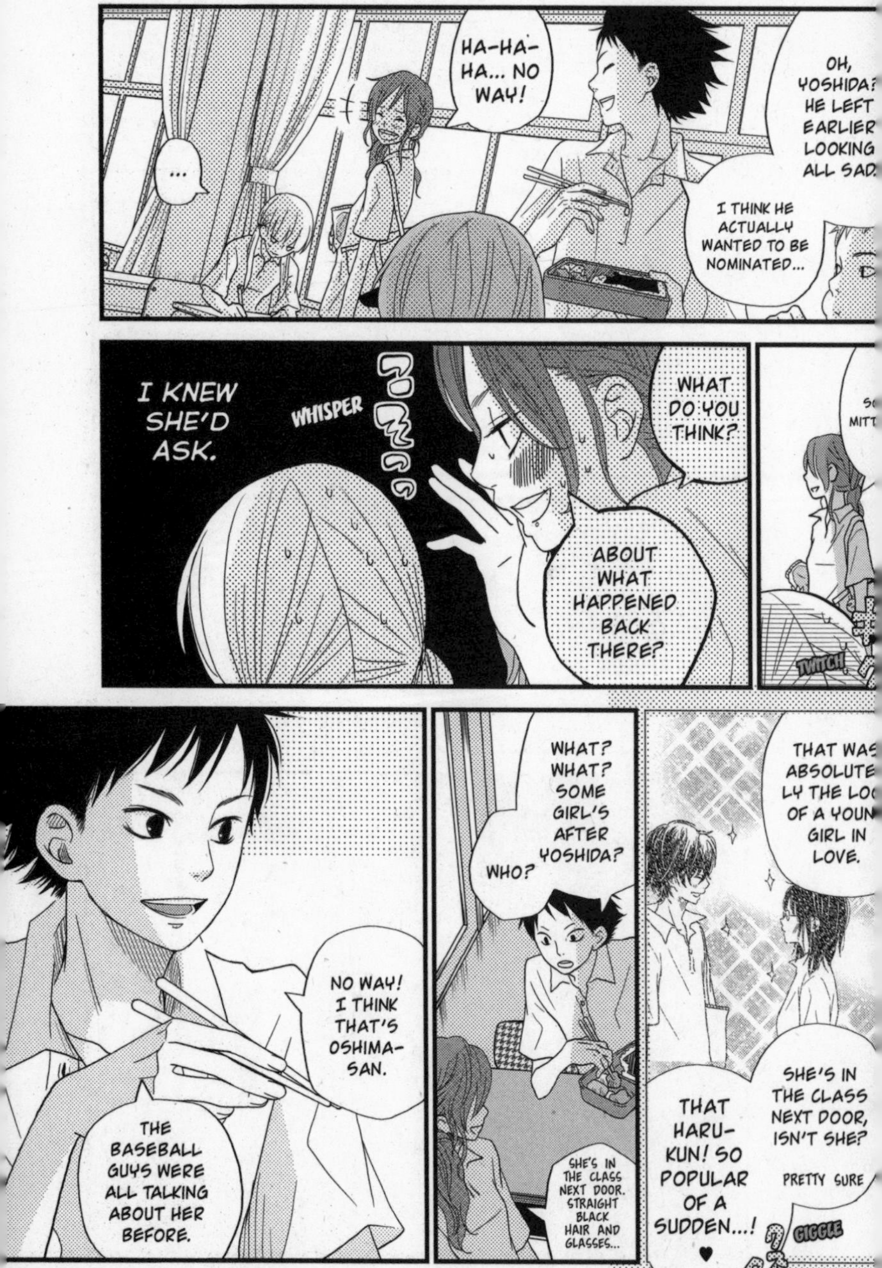
OH, YOSHIDA? HE LEFT EARLIER LOOKING ALL SAD.
I THINK HE ACTUALLY WANTED TO BE NOMINATED...
HA-HA-HA... NO WAY!
...
TWITCH
WHAT DO YOU THINK?
ABOUT WHAT HAPPENED BACK THERE?
WHISPER
I KNEW SHE'D ASK.
THAT WAS ABSOLUTE-LY THE LOO OF A YOUN GIRL IN LOVE.
SHE'S IN THE CLASS NEXT DOOR, ISN'T SHE?
PRETTY SURE
GIGGLE
THAT HARU-KUN! SO POPULAR OF A SUDDEN...! ♥
WHAT? WHAT? SOME GIRL'S AFTER YOSHIDA?
WHO?
SHE'S IN THE CLASS NEXT DOOR. STRAIGHT BLACK HAIR AND GLASSES...
NO WAY! I THINK THAT'S OSHIMA-SAN.
THE BASEBALL GUYS WERE ALL TALKING ABOUT HER BEFORE.

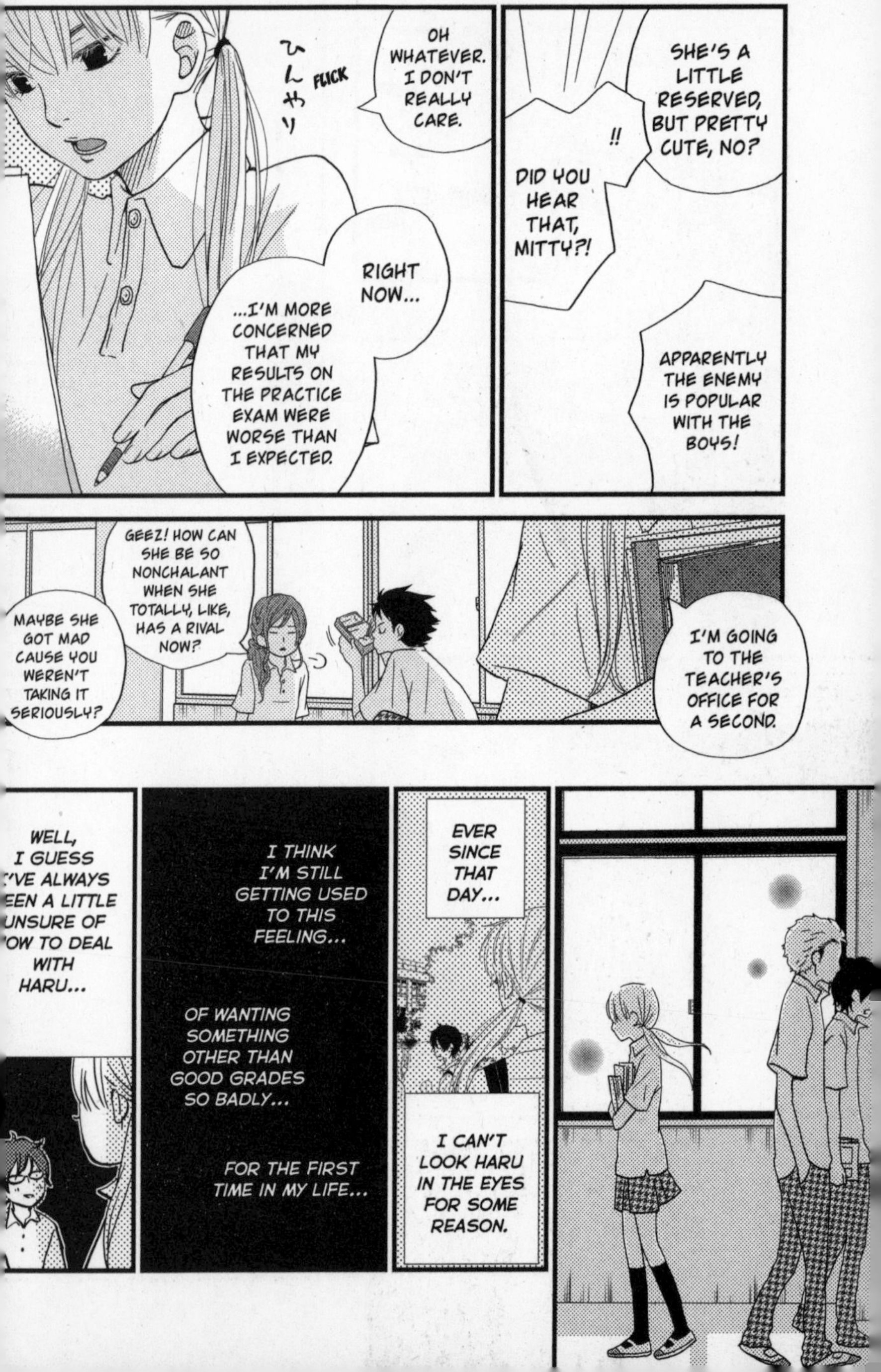
SHE'S A LITTLE RESERVED, BUT PRETTY CUTE, NO?
!!
DID YOU HEAR THAT, MITTY?!
APPARENTLY THE ENEMY IS POPULAR WITH THE BOYS!
ひんやり
FLICK
OH WHATEVER. I DON'T REALLY CARE.
RIGHT NOW...
...I'M MORE CONCERNED THAT MY RESULTS ON THE PRACTICE EXAM WERE WORSE THAN I EXPECTED.
I'M GOING TO THE TEACHER'S OFFICE FOR A SECOND.
GEEZ! HOW CAN SHE BE SO NONCHALANT WHEN SHE TOTALLY, LIKE, HAS A RIVAL NOW?
MAYBE SHE GOT MAD CAUSE YOU WEREN'T TAKING IT SERIOUSLY?
EVER SINCE THAT DAY...
I CAN'T LOOK HARU IN THE EYES FOR SOME REASON.
I THINK I'M STILL GETTING USED TO THIS FEELING...
OF WANTING SOMETHING OTHER THAN GOOD GRADES SO BADLY...
FOR THE FIRST TIME IN MY LIFE...
WELL, I GUESS 'VE ALWAYS EEN A LITTLE UNSURE OF OW TO DEAL WITH HARU...

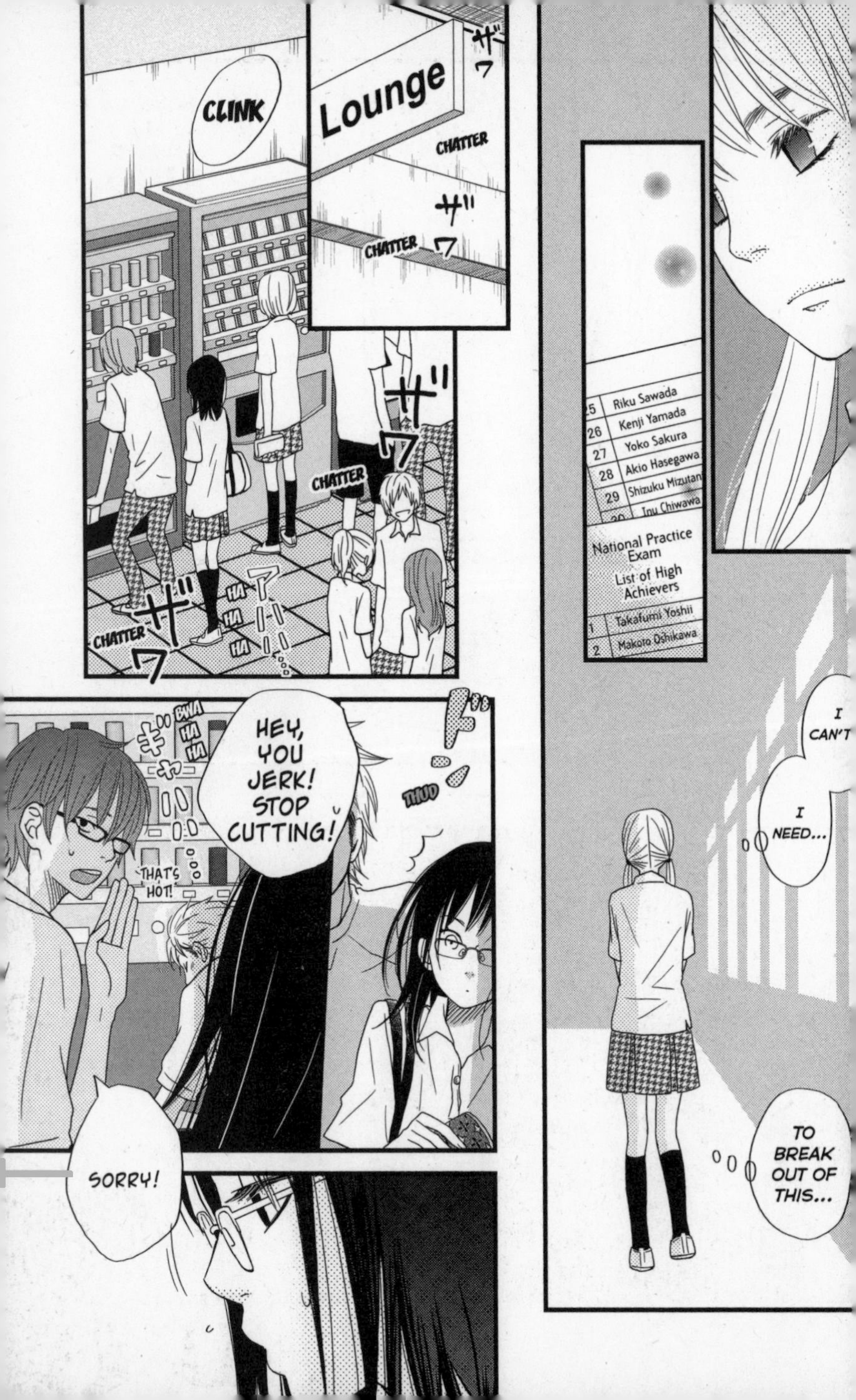
25 Riku Sawada
26 Kenji Yamada
27 Yoko Sakura
28 Akio Hasegawa
29 Shizuku Mizutani
Inu Chiwawa
National Practice Exam
List of High Achievers
1 Takafumi Yoshii
2 Makoto Oshikawa
I CAN'T
I NEED...
TO BREAK OUT OF THIS...
Lounge
ザワ
CHATTER
ザワ
CHATTER
CLINK
ザワ
CHATTER
CHATTER
ザワ
HA HA HA
THUD
HEY, YOU JERK! STOP CUTTING!
BWA HA HA
THAT'S HOT!
SORRY!

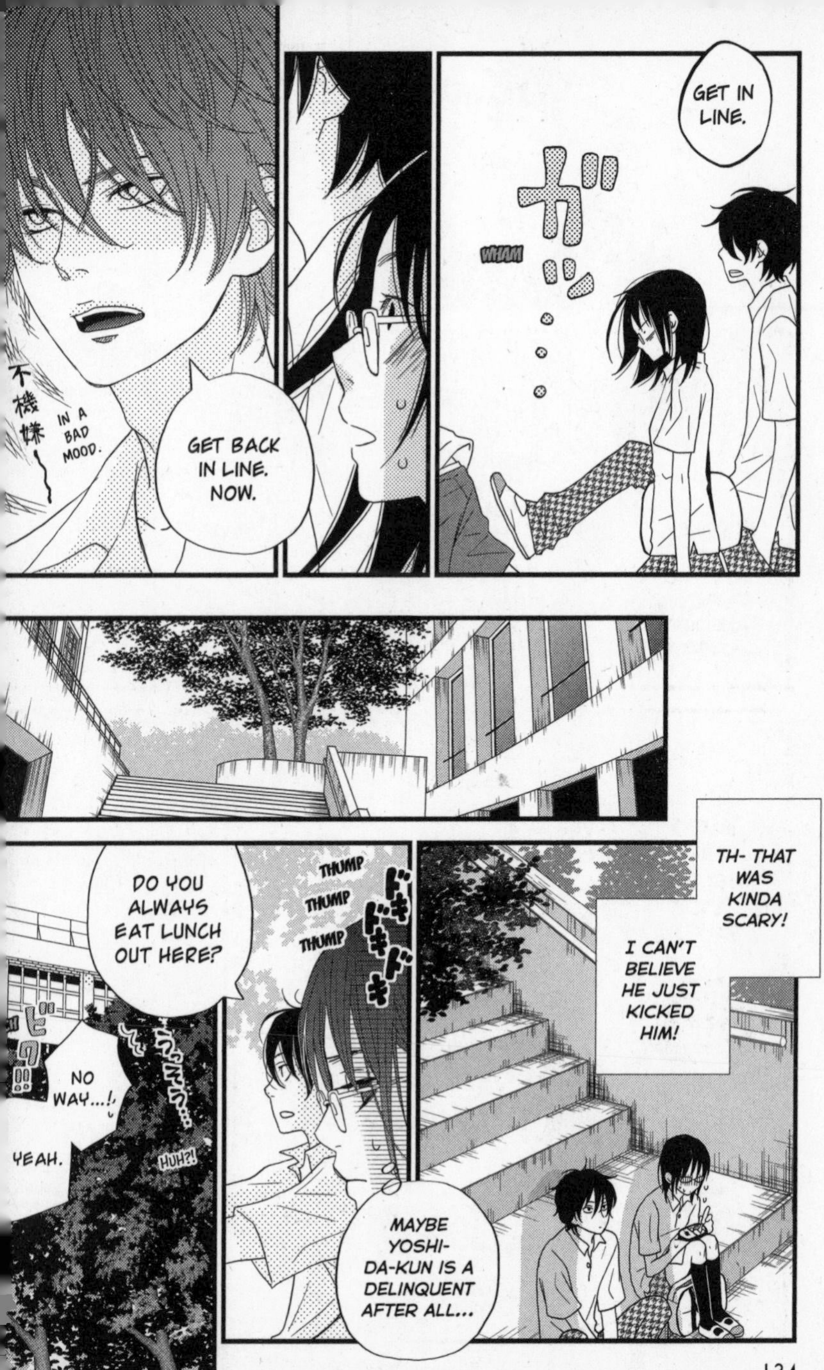
GET IN LINE.
ガッ
WHAM
GET BACK IN LINE. NOW.
不機嫌~
IN A BAD MOOD.
TH- THAT WAS KINDA SCARY!
I CAN'T BELIEVE HE JUST KICKED HIM!
DO YOU ALWAYS EAT LUNCH OUT HERE?
ドキドキ
THUMP THUMP THUMP
ビクッ!!
NO WAY...!,
YEAH.
HUH?!
MAYBE YOSHI-DA-KUN IS A DELINQUENT AFTER ALL...

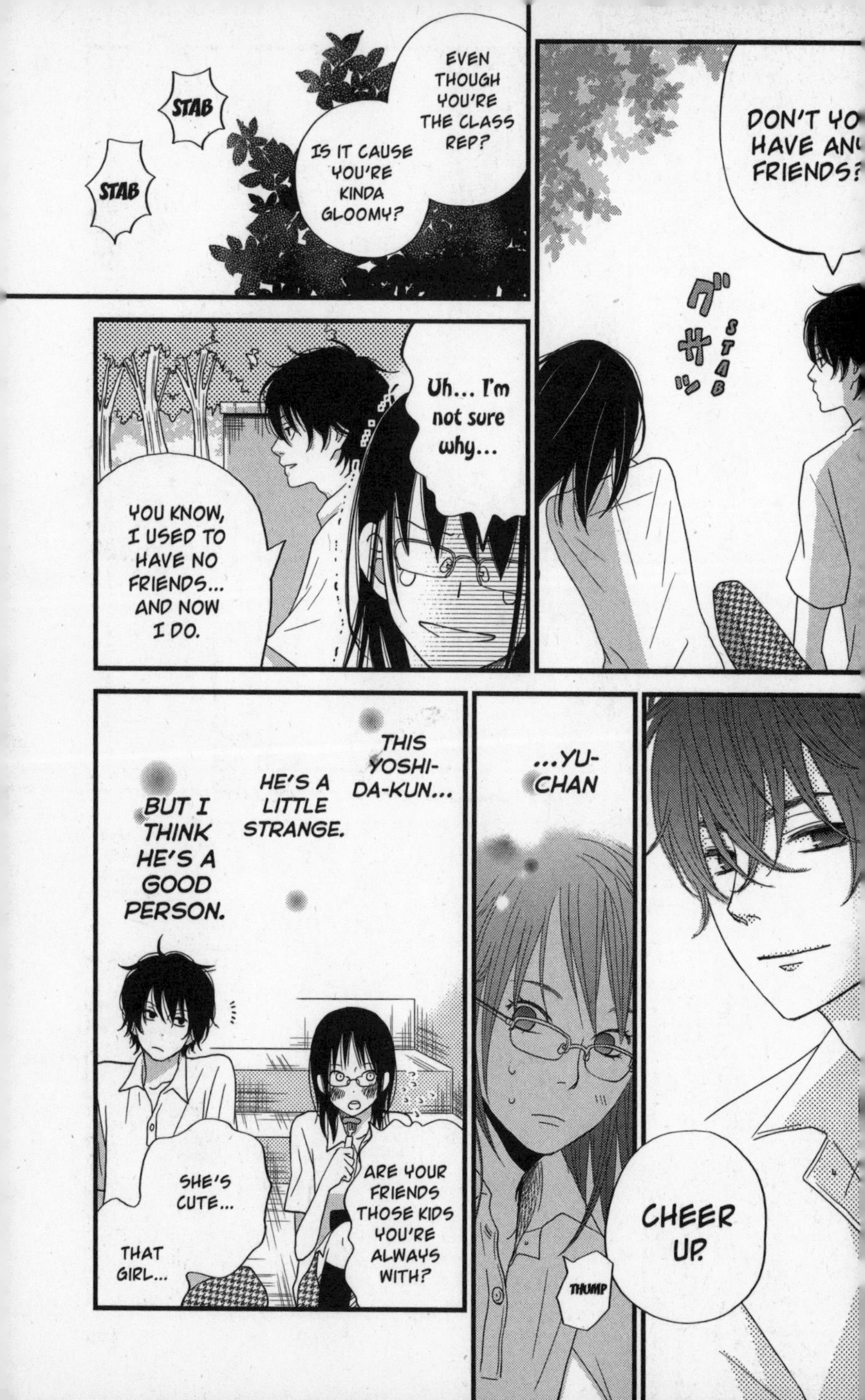
DON'T YO HAVE AN FRIENDS?
グサッ STAB
EVEN THOUGH YOU'RE THE CLASS REP?
IS IT CAUSE YOU'RE KINDA GLOOMY?
STAB
STAB
Uh... I'm not sure why...
YOU KNOW, I USED TO HAVE NO FRIENDS... AND NOW I DO.
CHEER UP.
THUMP
...YU-CHAN
THIS YOSHIDA-KUN...
HE'S A LITTLE STRANGE.
BUT I THINK HE'S A GOOD PERSON.
ARE YOUR FRIENDS THOSE KIDS YOU'RE ALWAYS WITH?
SHE'S CUTE...
THAT GIRL...

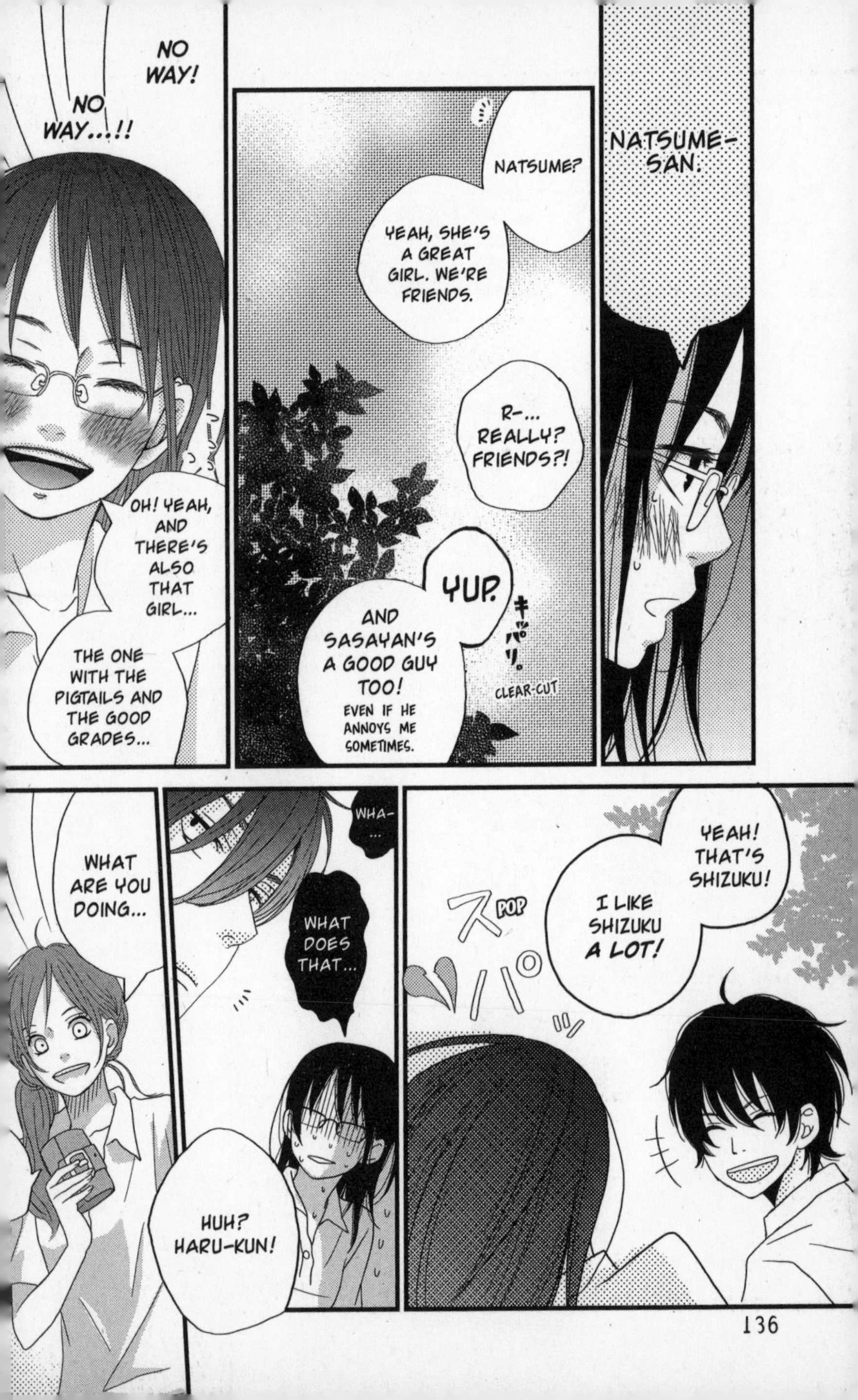
NATSUME-SAN...
...
NATSUME?
YEAH, SHE'S A GREAT GIRL. WE'RE FRIENDS.
R-... REALLY? FRIENDS?!
YUP.
キッパリ。
CLEAR-CUT
AND SASAYAN'S A GOOD GUY TOO!
EVEN IF HE ANNOYS ME SOMETIMES.
NO WAY!
NO WAY...!!
OH! YEAH, AND THERE'S ALSO THAT GIRL...
THE ONE WITH THE PIGTAILS AND THE GOOD GRADES...
YEAH! THAT'S SHIZUKU!
I LIKE SHIZUKU A LOT!
スパッ
POP
WHA-...
WHAT DOES THAT...
WHAT ARE YOU DOING...
HUH? HARU-KUN!

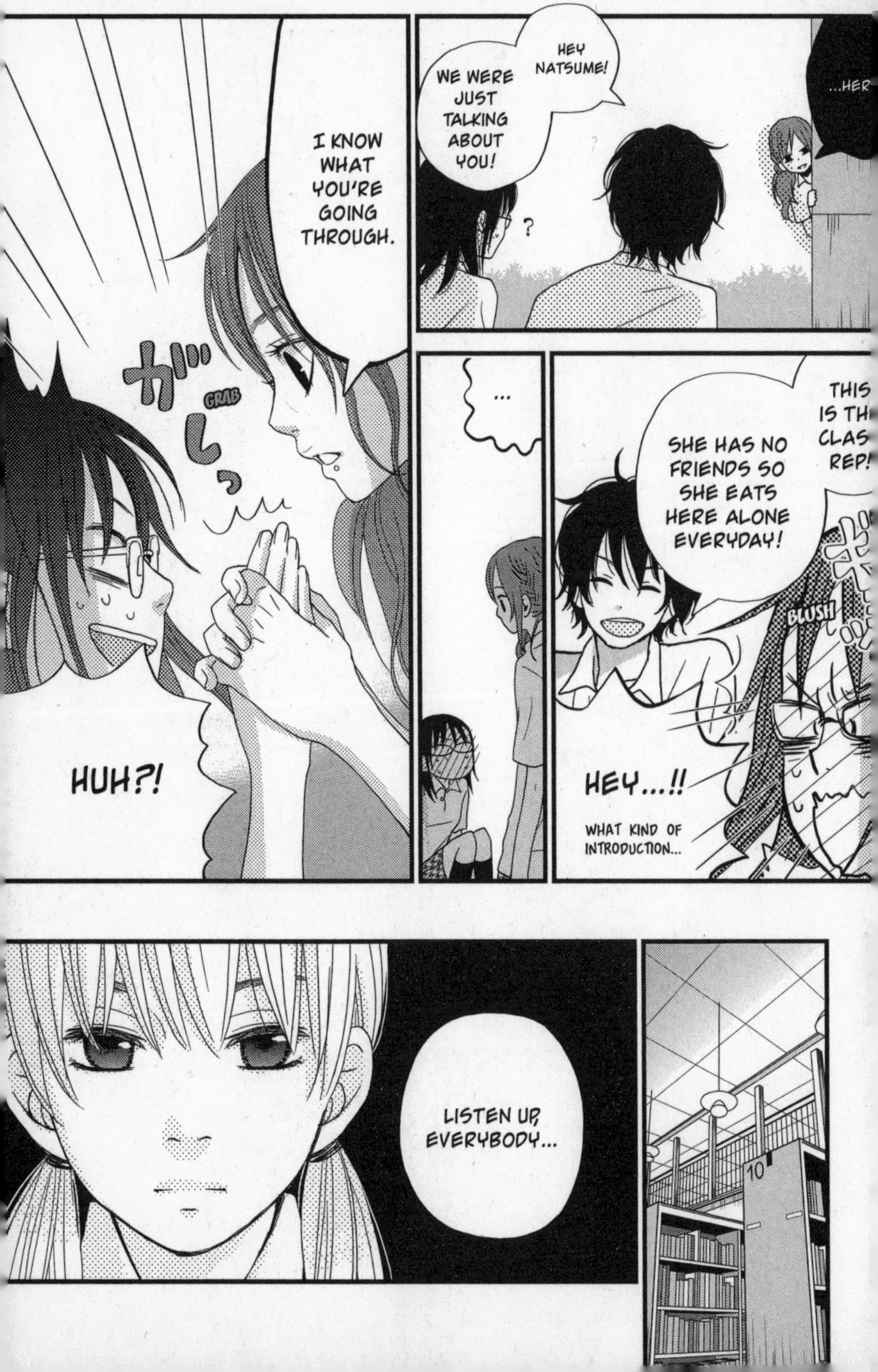
...HER
HEY NATSUME!
WE WERE JUST TALKING ABOUT YOU!
THIS IS TH CLAS REP!
SHE HAS NO FRIENDS SO SHE EATS HERE ALONE EVERYDAY!
BLUSH
HEY...!!
WHAT KIND OF INTRODUCTION...
...
I KNOW WHAT YOU'RE GOING THROUGH.
GRAB
HUH?!
LISTEN UP, EVERYBODY...

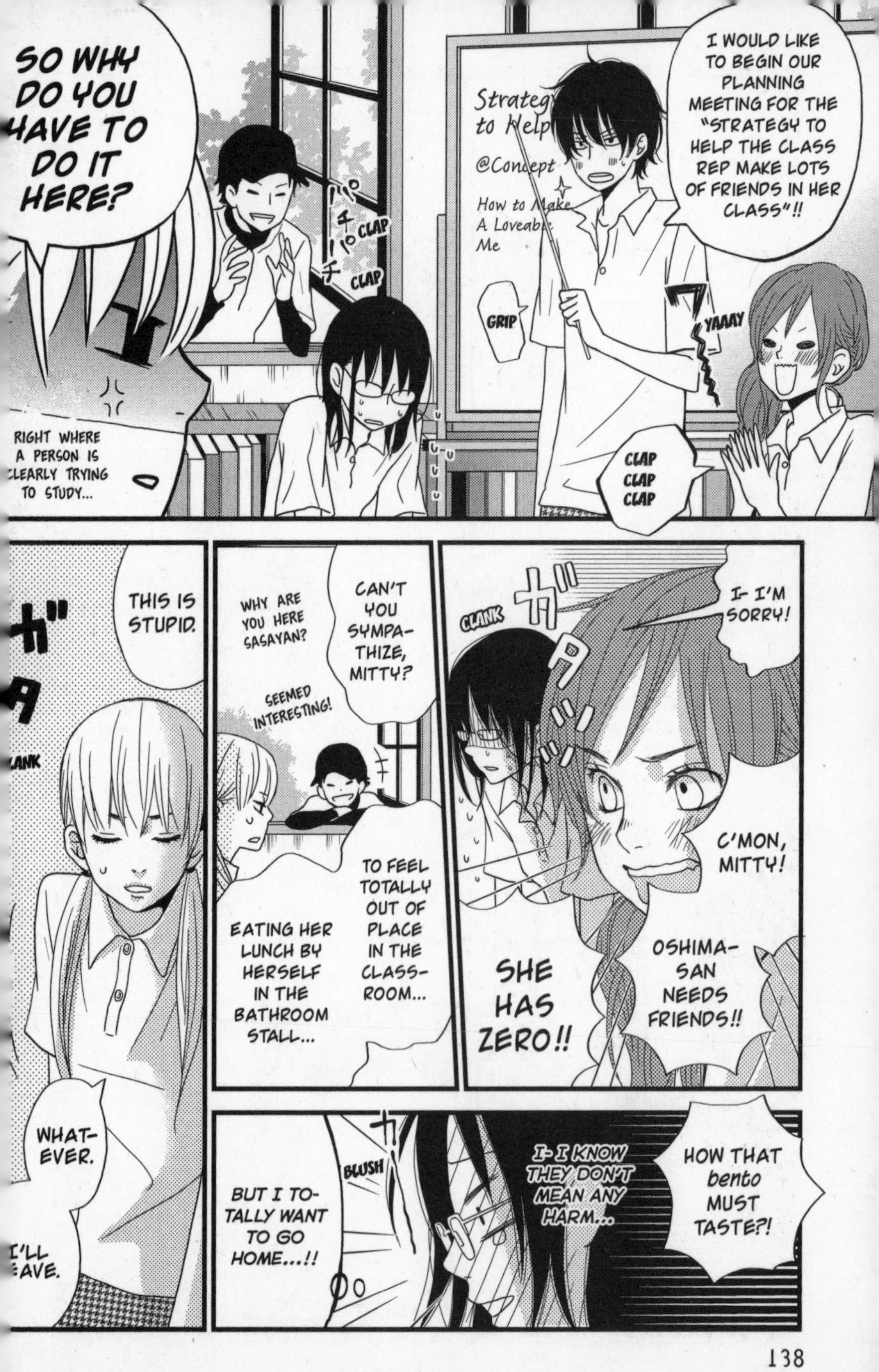
I WOULD LIKE TO BEGIN OUR PLANNING MEETING FOR THE "STRATEGY TO HELP THE CLASS REP MAKE LOTS OF FRIENDS IN HER CLASS"!!
Strateg
to Help
@Concept
How to Make A Loveab Me
GRIP
YAAAY
CLAP
CLAP
CLAP CLAP CLAP
SO WHY DO YOU HAVE TO DO IT HERE?
RIGHT WHERE A PERSON IS CLEARLY TRYING TO STUDY...
I- I'M SORRY!
CLANK
C'MON, MITTY!
OSHIMA-SAN NEEDS FRIENDS!!
SHE HAS ZERO!!
CAN'T YOU SYMPATHIZE, MITTY?
WHY ARE YOU HERE SASAYAN?
SEEMED INTERESTING!
TO FEEL TOTALLY OUT OF PLACE IN THE CLASSROOM...
EATING HER LUNCH BY HERSELF IN THE BATHROOM STALL...
HOW THAT bento MUST TASTE?!
I- I KNOW THEY DON'T MEAN ANY HARM...
BLUSH
BUT I TOTALLY WANT TO GO HOME...!!
THIS IS STUPID.
LANK
WHAT-EVER.
I'LL
EAVE.

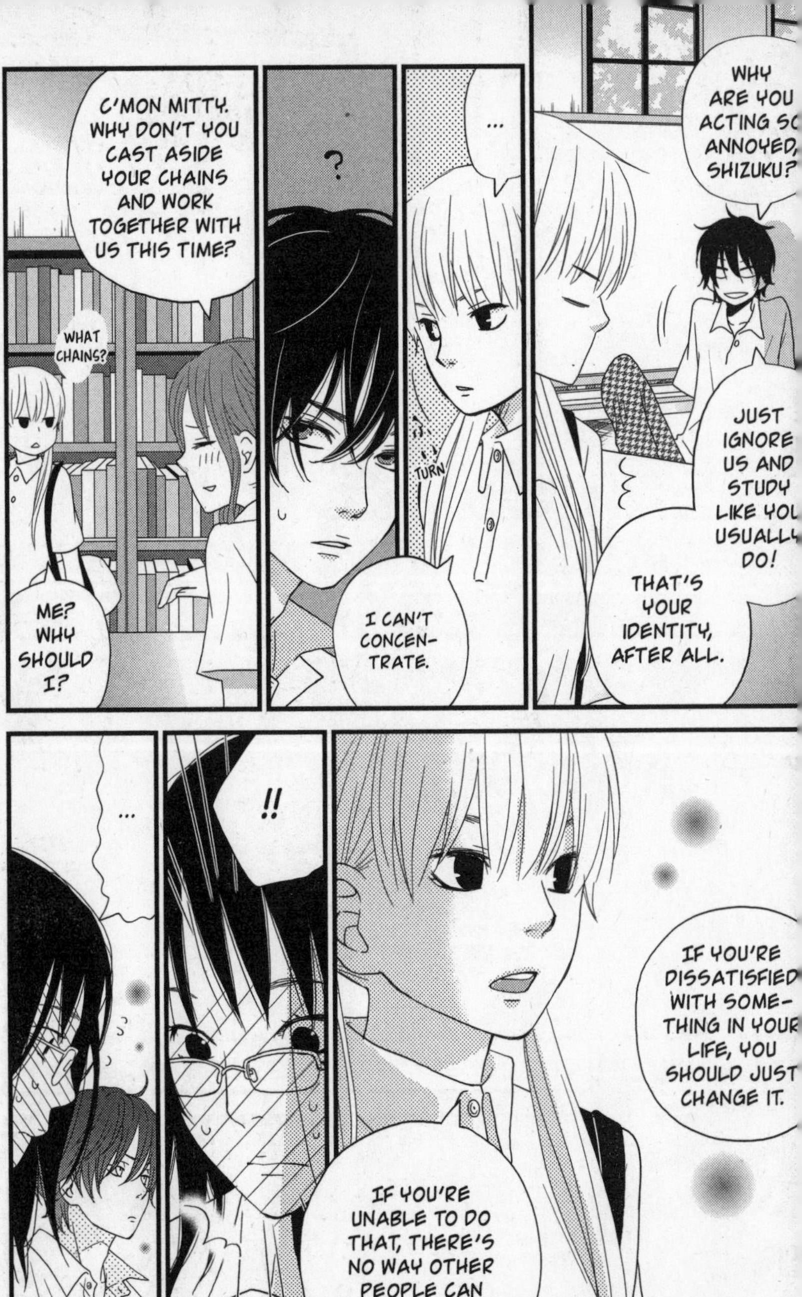
WHY ARE YOU ACTING SO ANNOYED, SHIZUKU?
JUST IGNORE US AND STUDY LIKE YOU USUALLY DO!
THAT'S YOUR IDENTITY, AFTER ALL.
...
TURN
I CAN'T CONCENTRATE.
?
C'MON MITTY. WHY DON'T YOU CAST ASIDE YOUR CHAINS AND WORK TOGETHER WITH US THIS TIME?
WHAT CHAINS?
ME? WHY SHOULD I?
IF YOU'RE DISSATISFIED WITH SOME-THING IN YOUR LIFE, YOU SHOULD JUST CHANGE IT.
IF YOU'RE UNABLE TO DO THAT, THERE'S NO WAY OTHER PEOPLE CAN HELP YOU.
!!
...

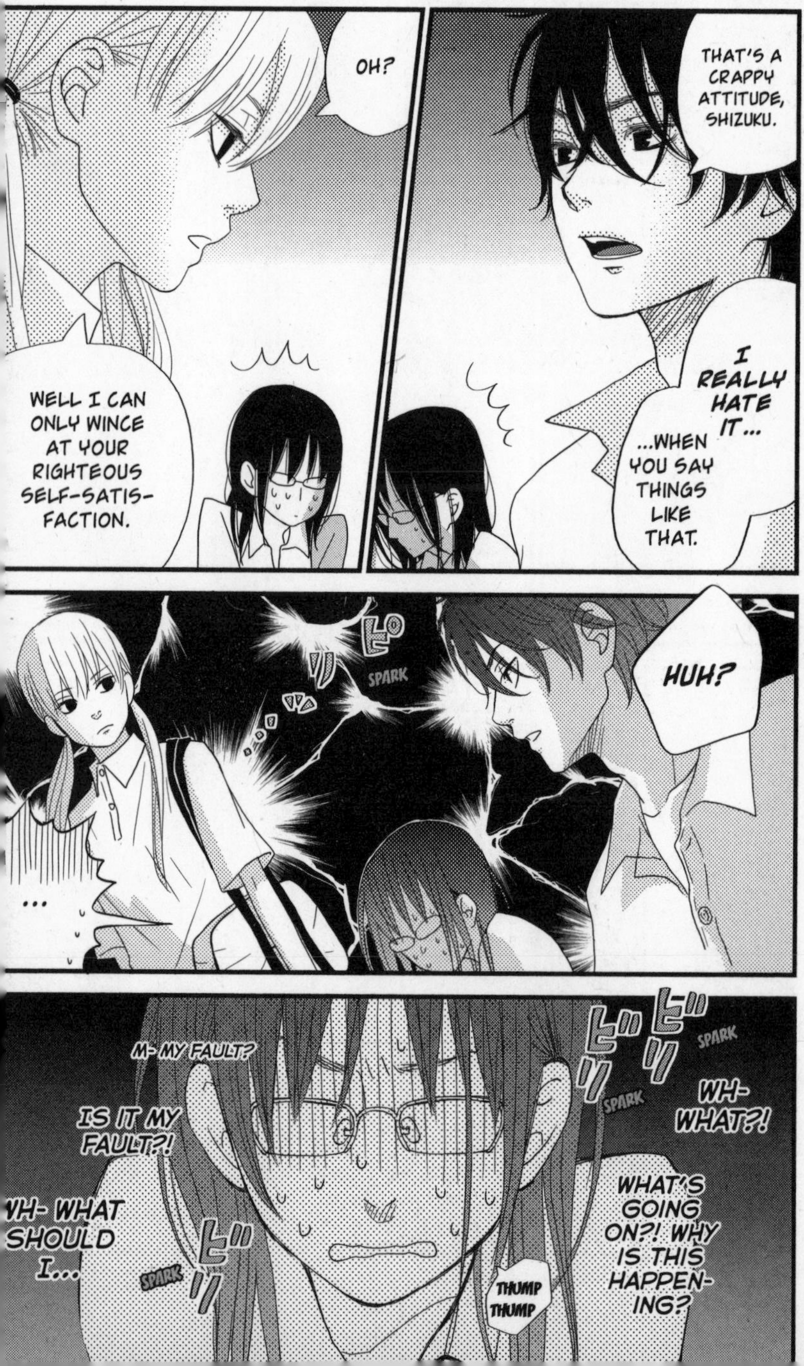
THAT'S A CRAPPY ATTITUDE, SHIZUKU.
I REALLY HATE IT...
...WHEN YOU SAY THINGS LIKE THAT.
OH?
WELL I CAN ONLY WINCE AT YOUR RIGHTEOUS SELF-SATIS-FACTION.
HUH?
SPARK
...
SPARK
WH- WHAT?!
SPARK
WHAT'S GOING ON?! WHY IS THIS HAPPEN-ING?
THUMP THUMP
M- MY FAULT?
IS IT MY FAULT?!
WH- WHAT SHOULD I...
SPARK

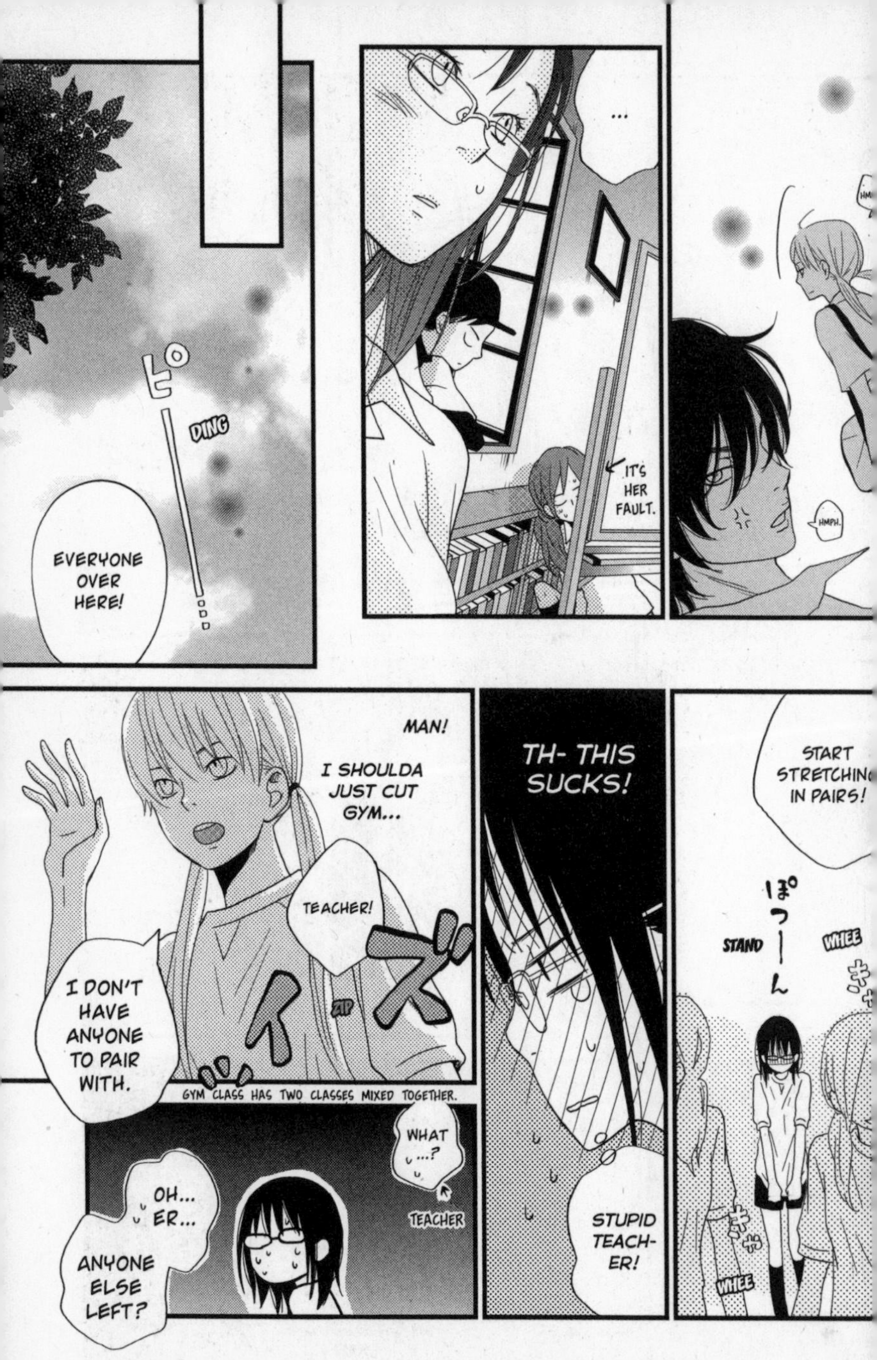
HM
HMPH.
...
IT'S HER FAULT.
ピ
DING
EVERYONE OVER HERE!
START STRETCHIN IN PAIRS!
ぽつーん
STAND
WHEE
キャ
WHEE
TH- THIS SUCKS!
STUPID TEACHER!
MAN!
I SHOULDA JUST CUT GYM...
TEACHER!
ズイ
ZIP
I DON'T HAVE ANYONE TO PAIR WITH.
GYM CLASS HAS TWO CLASSES MIXED TOGETHER.
WHAT ...?
TEACHER
OH... ER...
ANYONE ELSE LEFT?

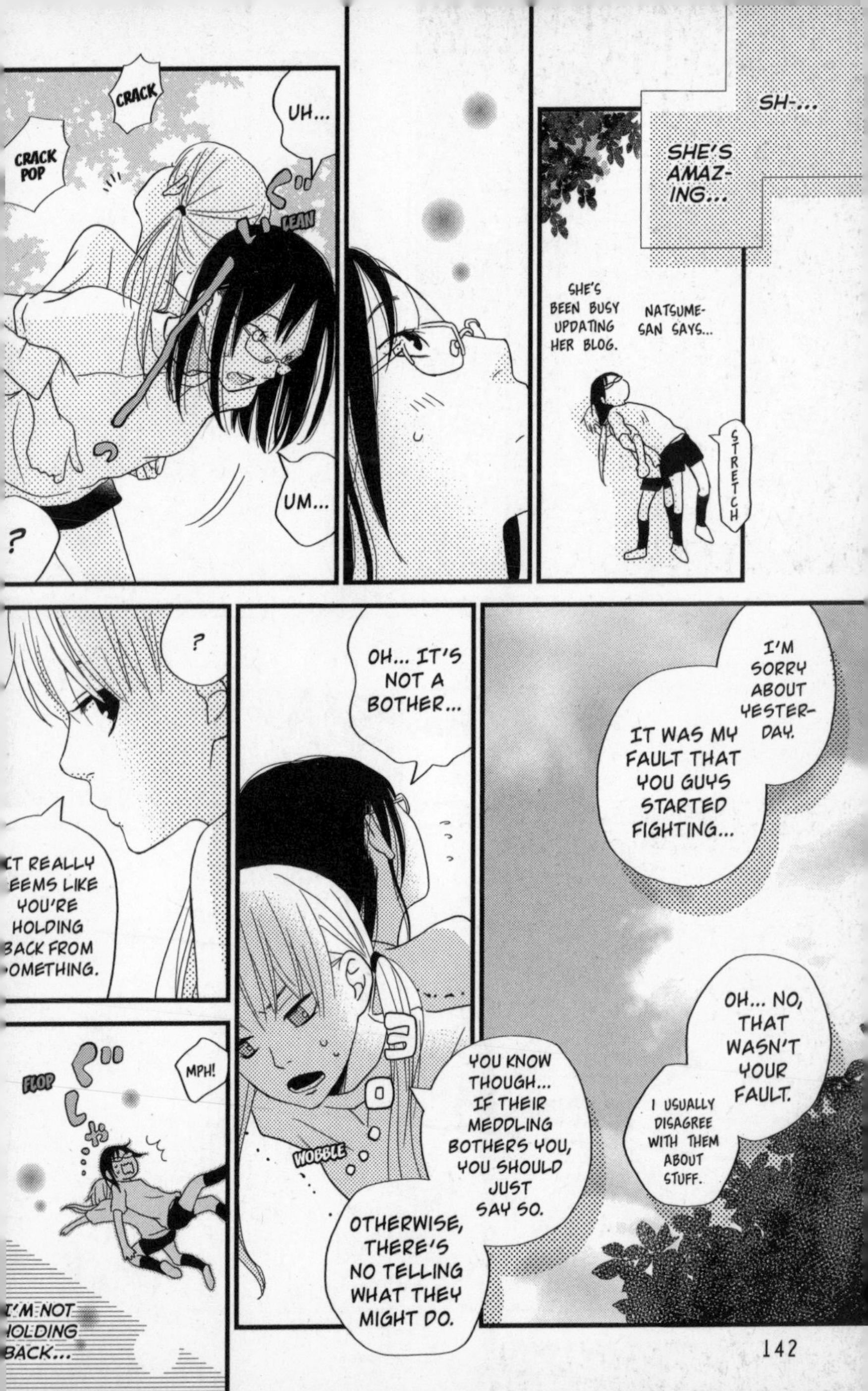
SH-...
SHE'S AMAZ- ING...
NATSUME-SAN SAYS...
SHE'S BEEN BUSY UPDATING HER BLOG.
STRETCH
UH...
CRACK
CRACK POP
LEAN
UM...
?
I'M SORRY ABOUT YESTER-DAY.
IT WAS MY FAULT THAT YOU GUYS STARTED FIGHTING...
OH... NO, THAT WASN'T YOUR FAULT.
I USUALLY DISAGREE WITH THEM ABOUT STUFF.
OH... IT'S NOT A BOTHER...
YOU KNOW THOUGH... IF THEIR MEDDLING BOTHERS YOU, YOU SHOULD JUST SAY SO.
OTHERWISE, THERE'S NO TELLING WHAT THEY MIGHT DO.
WOBBLE
?
T REALLY EEMS LIKE YOU'RE HOLDING ACK FROM OMETHING.
MPH!
FLOP
'M NOT OLDING BACK...

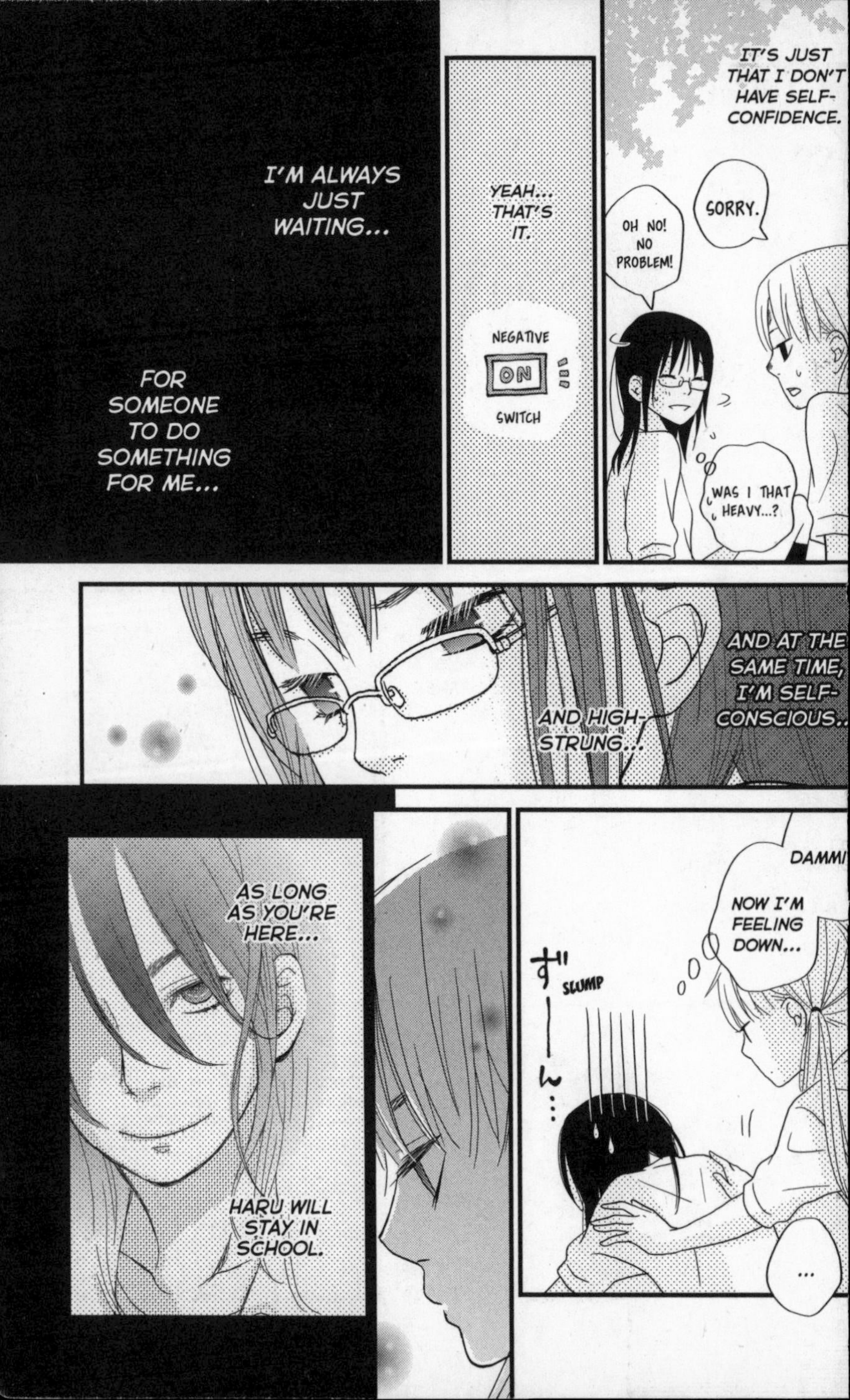
IT'S JUST THAT I DON'T HAVE SELF-CONFIDENCE.
SORRY.
OH NO! NO PROBLEM!
WAS I THAT HEAVY...?
YEAH... THAT'S IT.
NEGATIVE
ON
SWITCH
I'M ALWAYS JUST WAITING...
FOR SOMEONE TO DO SOMETHING FOR ME...
AND AT THE SAME TIME, I'M SELF-CONSCIOUS...
AND HIGH-STRUNG...
DAMMI
NOW I'M FEELING DOWN...
ずーん...
SLUMP
...
AS LONG AS YOU'RE HERE...
HARU WILL STAY IN SCHOOL.

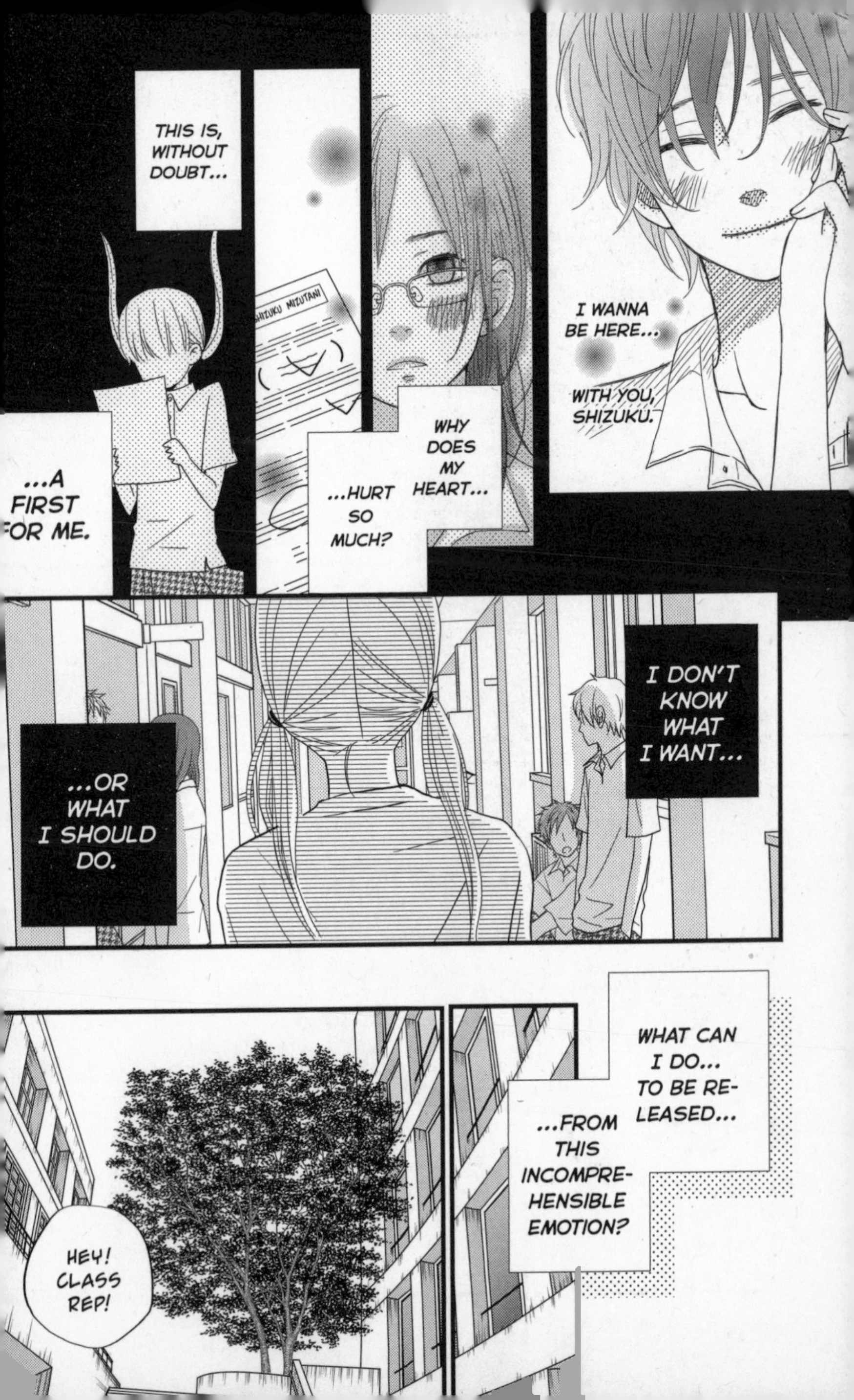
I WANNA BE HERE...
WITH YOU, SHIZUKU.
WHY DOES MY HEART...
...HURT SO MUCH?
SHIZUKU MIZUTANI
THIS IS, WITHOUT DOUBT...
...A FIRST FOR ME.
I DON'T KNOW WHAT I WANT...
...OR WHAT I SHOULD DO.
WHAT CAN I DO... TO BE RE-LEASED...
...FROM THIS INCOMPREHENSIBLE EMOTION?
HEY! CLASS REP!

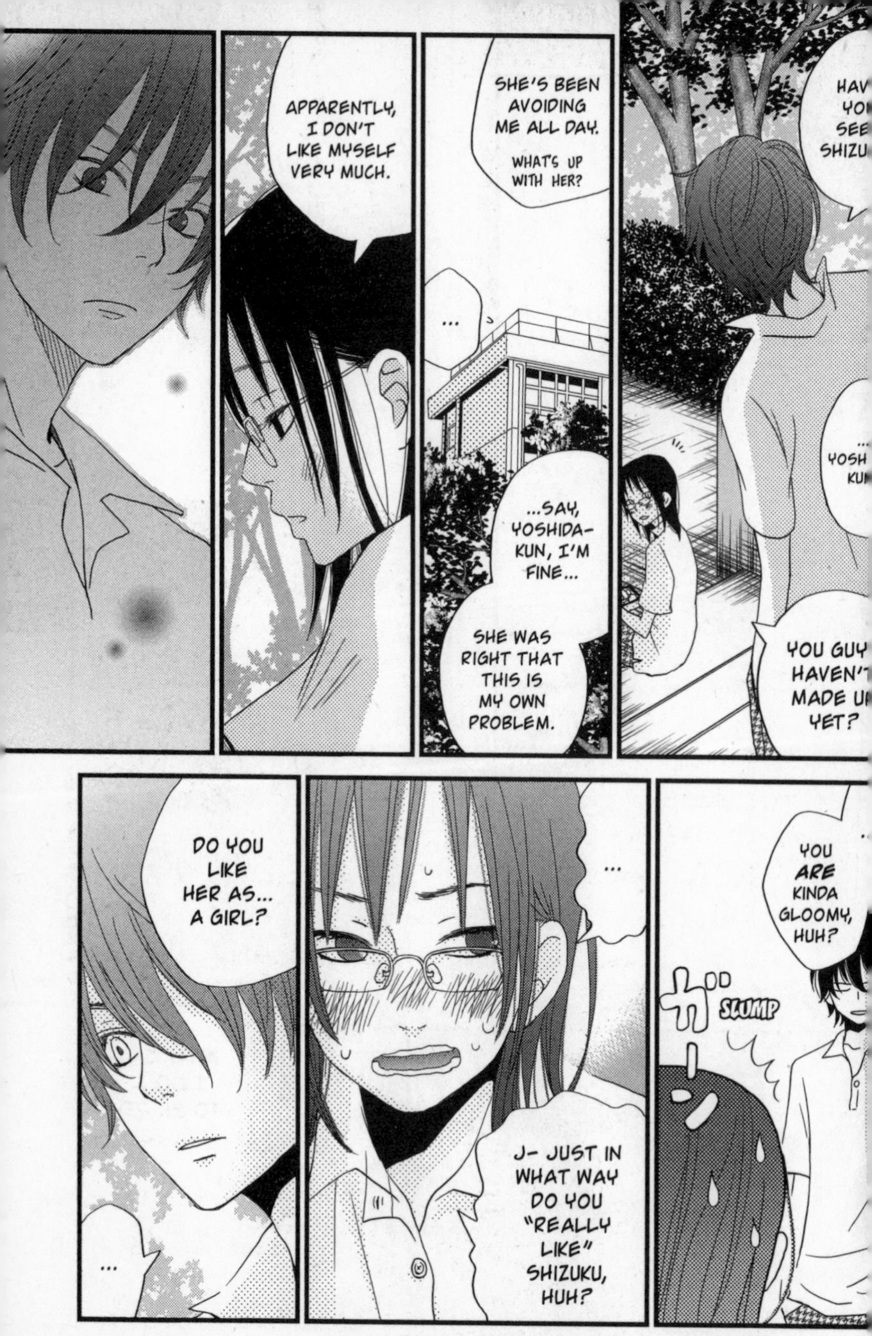

HAV
YO
SEE
SHIZU
...
YOSH
KU
YOU GUY
HAVEN'
MADE U
YET?
SHE'S BEEN AVOIDING ME ALL DAY.
WHAT'S UP WITH HER?
...
...SAY, YOSHIDA-KUN, I'M FINE...
SHE WAS RIGHT THAT THIS IS MY OWN PROBLEM.
APPARENTLY, I DON'T LIKE MYSELF VERY MUCH.
...
YOU ARE KINDA GLOOMY, HUH?
SLUMP
...
J- JUST IN WHAT WAY DO YOU "REALLY LIKE" SHIZUKU, HUH?
DO YOU LIKE HER AS... A GIRL?
...

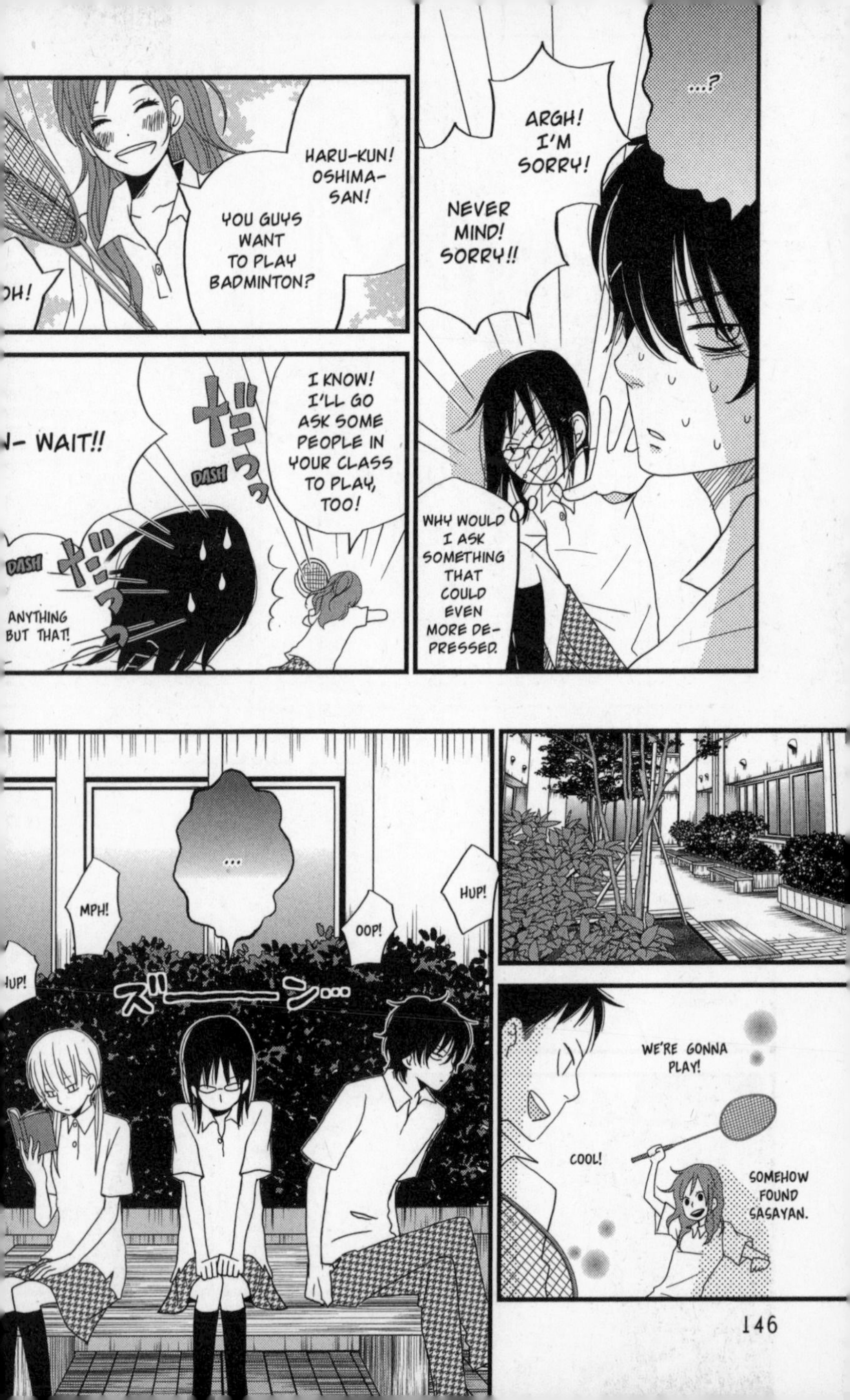
...?
ARGH! I'M SORRY!
NEVER MIND! SORRY!!
WHY WOULD I ASK SOMETHING THAT COULD EVEN MORE DE-PRESSED.
HARU-KUN! OSHIMA-SAN!
YOU GUYS WANT TO PLAY BADMINTON?
H!
I KNOW! I'LL GO ASK SOME PEOPLE IN YOUR CLASS TO PLAY, TOO!
DASH
- WAIT!!
DASH
ANYTHING BUT THAT!
WE'RE GONNA PLAY!
COOL!
SOMEHOW FOUND SASAYAN.
HUP!
OOP!
...
MPH!
UP!
ズーーーン…

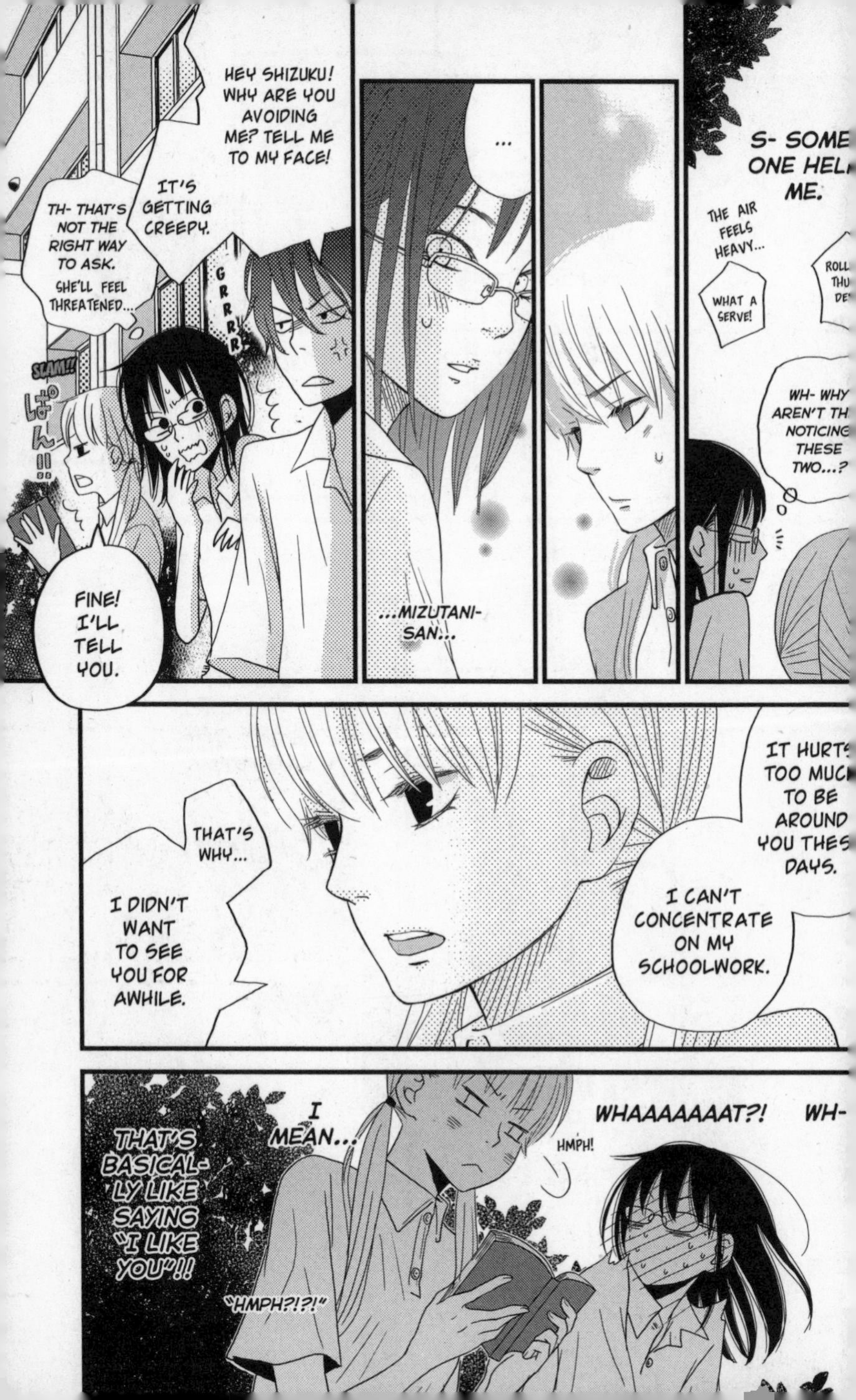
S- SOME ONE HEL ME.
THE AIR FEELS HEAVY...
ROLL THU DE
WHAT A SERVE!
WH- WHY AREN'T TH NOTICING THESE TWO...?
...
...MIZUTANI-SAN...
HEY SHIZUKU! WHY ARE YOU AVOIDING ME? TELL ME TO MY FACE!
IT'S GETTING CREEPY.
GRRRR
TH- THAT'S NOT THE RIGHT WAY TO ASK. SHE'LL FEEL THREATENED...
SLAM!!
ばん!!
FINE! I'LL TELL YOU.
IT HURTS TOO MUC TO BE AROUND YOU THES DAYS.
I CAN'T CONCENTRATE ON MY SCHOOLWORK.
THAT'S WHY...
I DIDN'T WANT TO SEE YOU FOR AWHILE.
WH-
WHAAAAAAAT?!
HMPH!
I MEAN...
THAT'S BASICAL-LY LIKE SAYING "I LIKE YOU"!!
"HMPH?!?!"

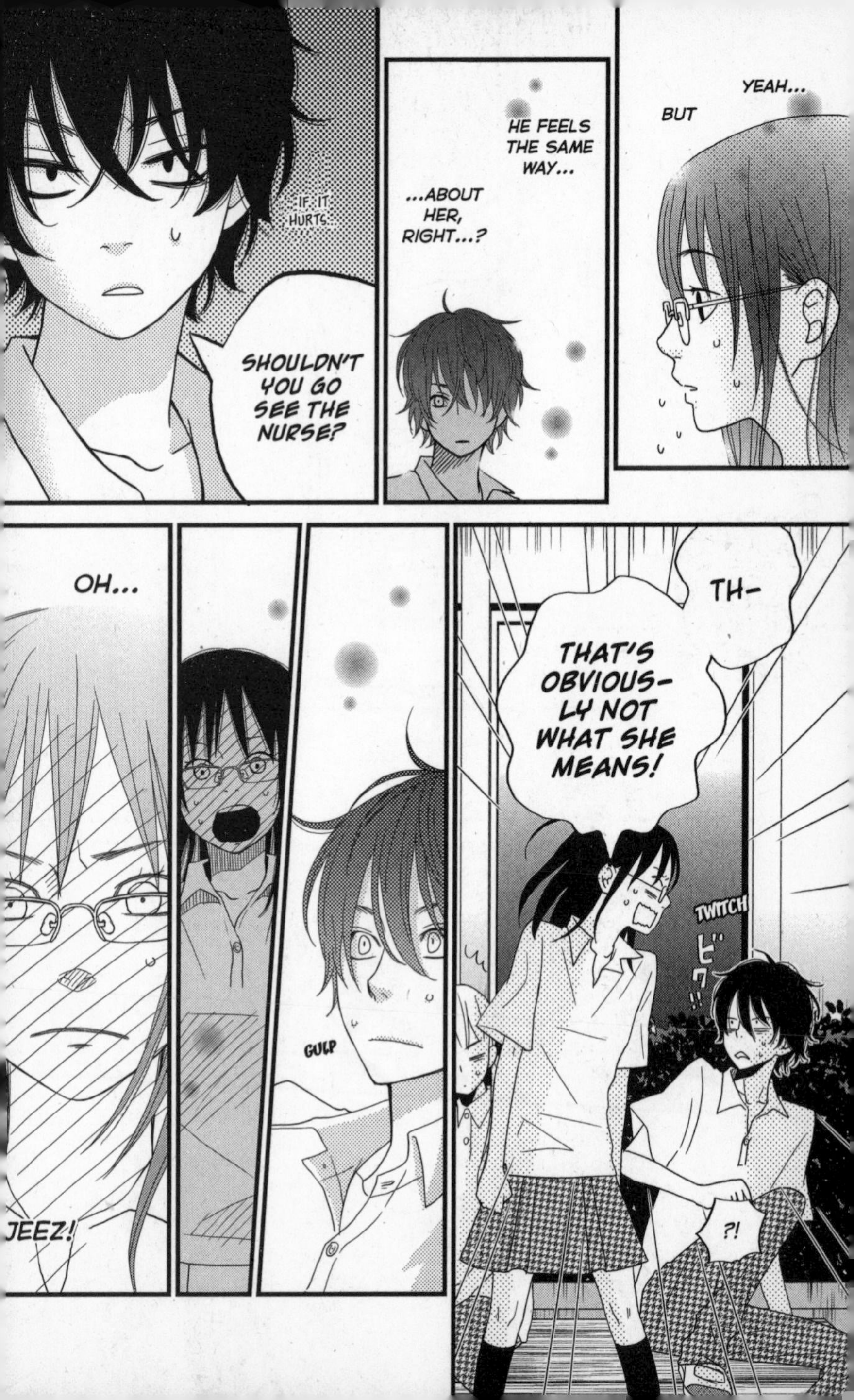
YEAH...
BUT
HE FEELS THE SAME WAY...
...ABOUT HER, RIGHT...?
...IF IT HURTS...
SHOULDN'T YOU GO SEE THE NURSE?
TH-
THAT'S OBVIOUSLY NOT WHAT SHE MEANS!
TWITCH
ビク!!
?!
GULP
OH...
JEEZ!

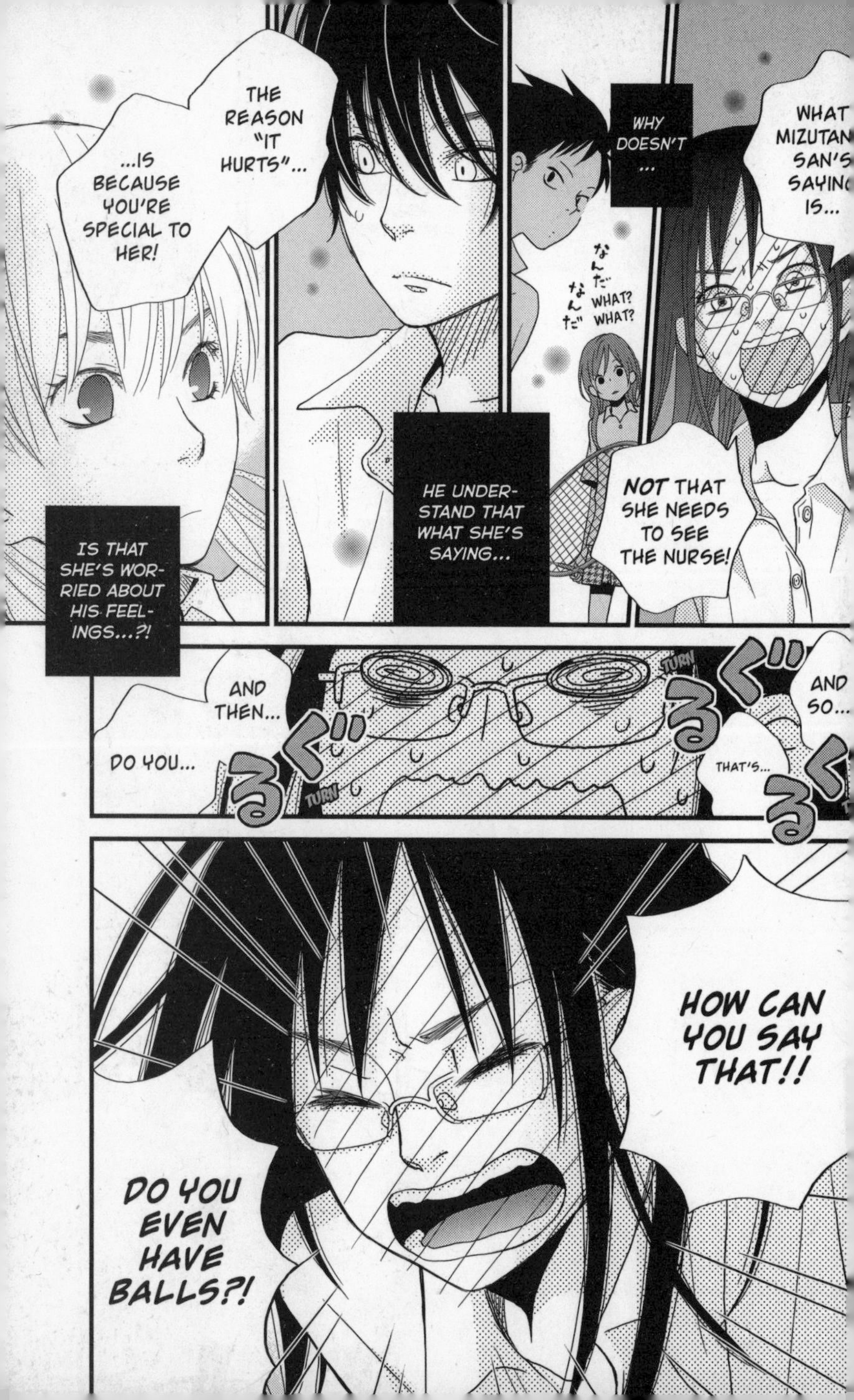
WHAT MIZUTAN SAN'S SAYING IS...
NOT THAT SHE NEEDS TO SEE THE NURSE!
WHY DOESN'T ...
なんだ なんだ
WHAT? WHAT?
HE UNDERSTAND THAT WHAT SHE'S SAYING...
THE REASON "IT HURTS"...
...IS BECAUSE YOU'RE SPECIAL TO HER!
IS THAT SHE'S WORRIED ABOUT HIS FEELINGS...?!
AND SO...
ぐるぐる
TURN
THAT'S...
AND THEN...
DO YOU...
ぐる
TURN
HOW CAN YOU SAY THAT!!
DO YOU EVEN HAVE BALLS?!

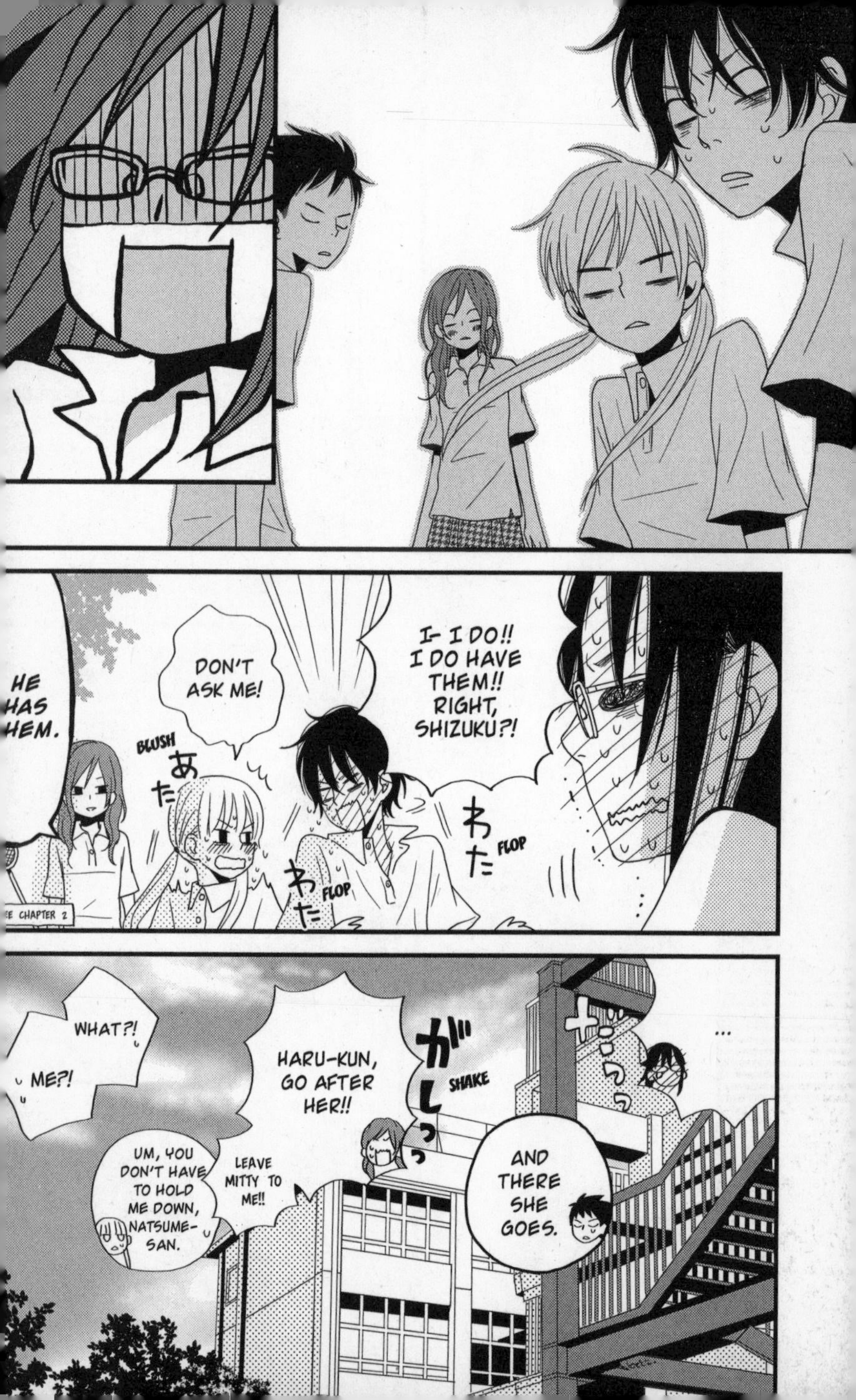
I- I DO!! I DO HAVE THEM!! RIGHT, SHIZUKU?!
わた
FLOP
わた
FLOP
DON'T ASK ME!
あた
BLUSH
HE HAS HEM.
EE CHAPTER 2
...
AND THERE SHE GOES.
がしっ
SHAKE
HARU-KUN, GO AFTER HER!!
LEAVE MITTY TO ME!!
UM, YOU DON'T HAVE TO HOLD ME DOWN, NATSUME-SAN.
WHAT?! ME?!

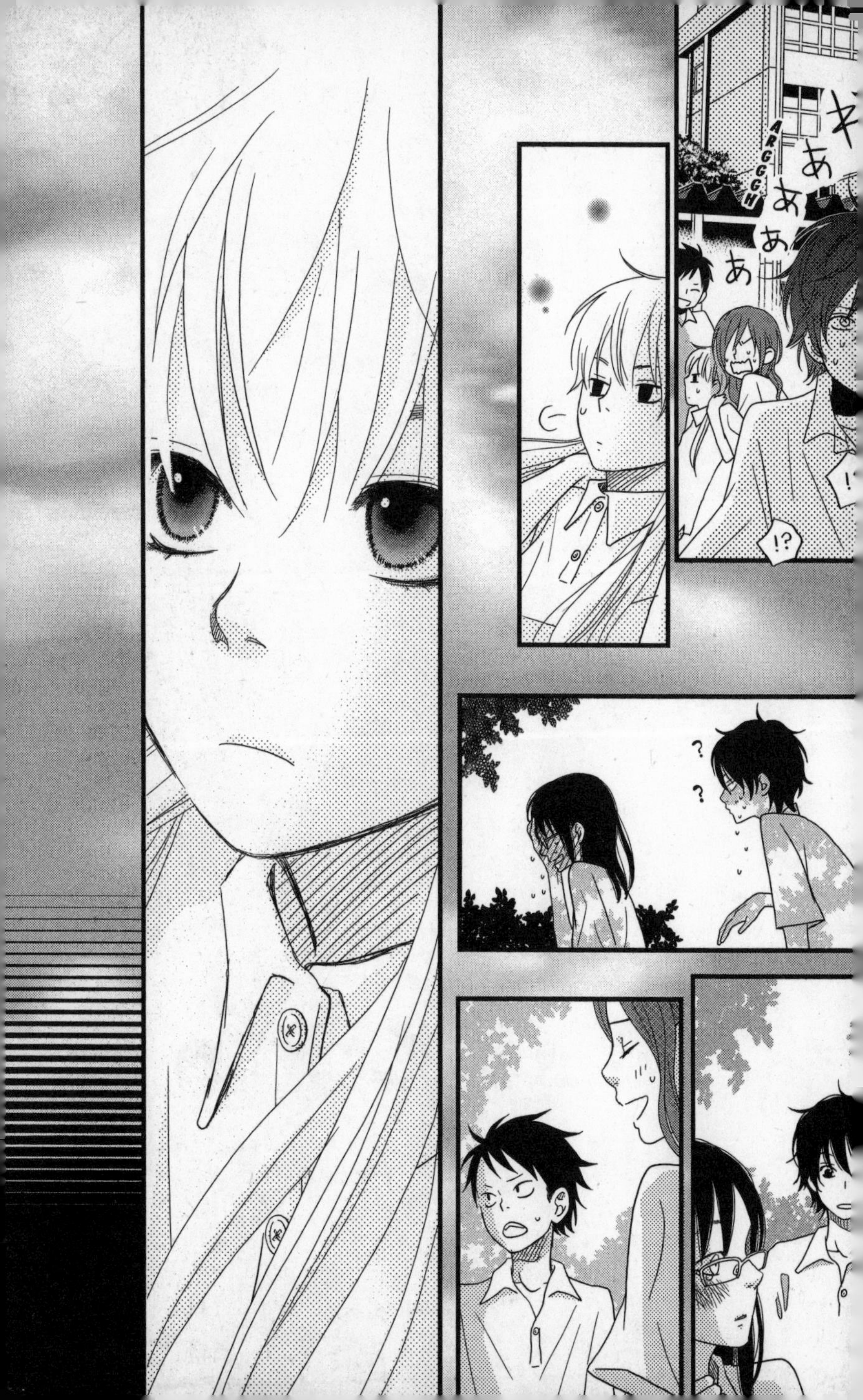
キあああああ
ARGGGGH
!
!?
?
?

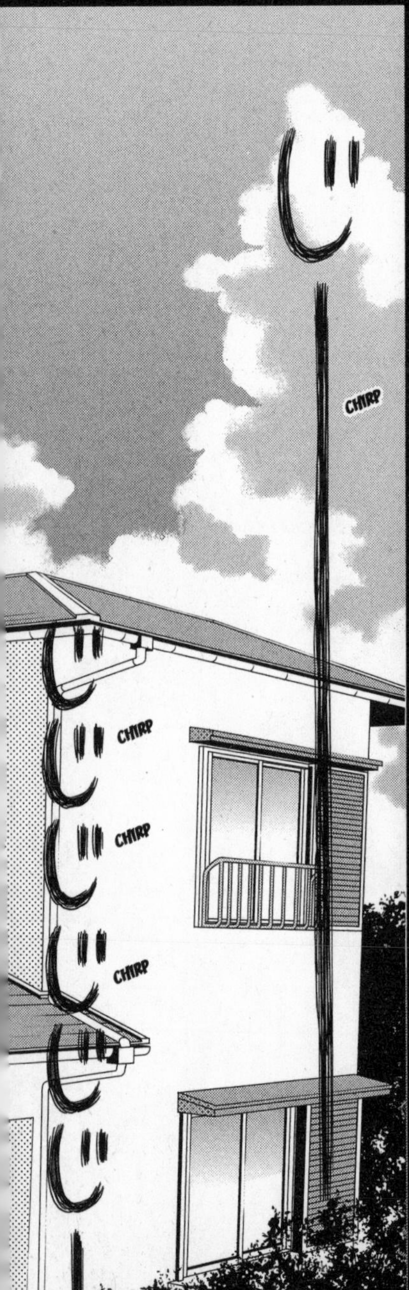
じー
CHIRP
じじじじじじー
CHIRP
CHIRP
CHIRP

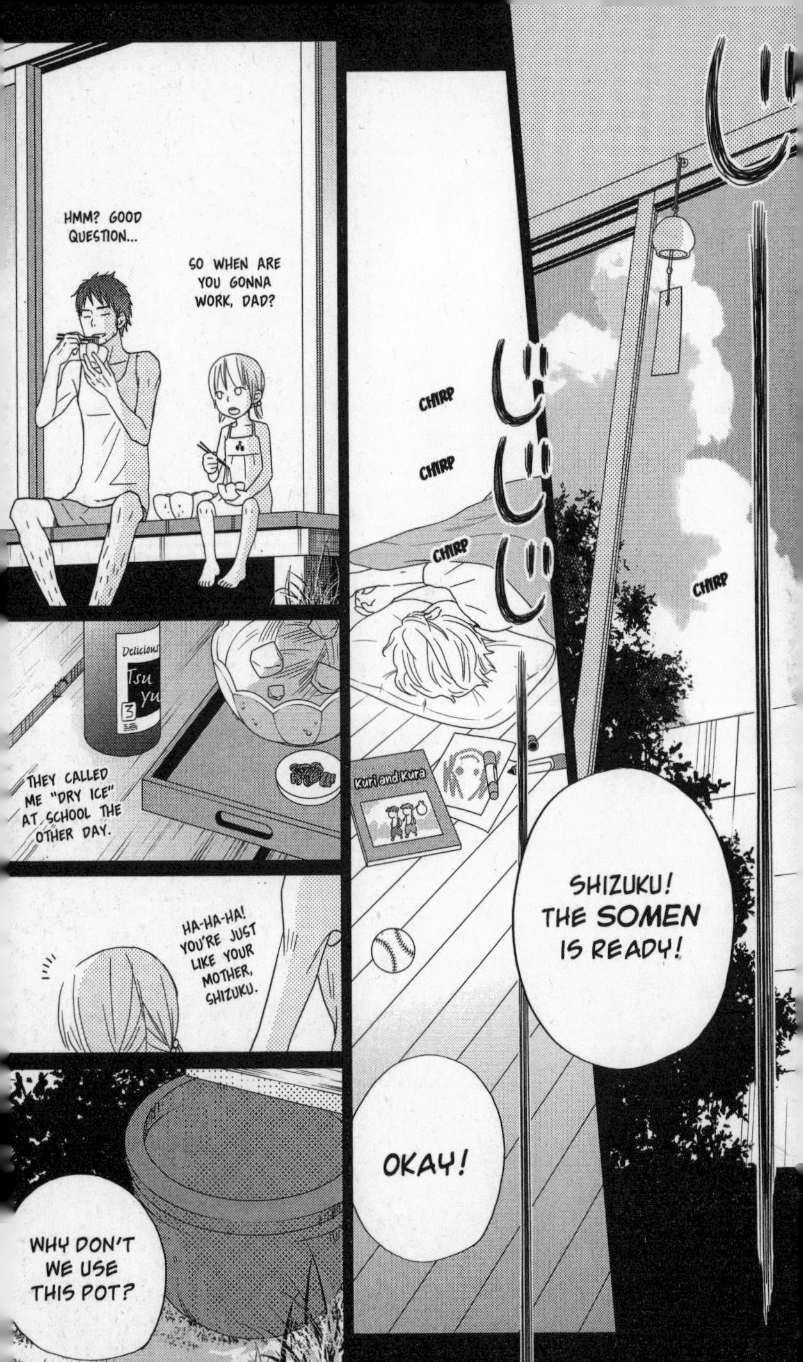
CHIRP
CHIRP
CHIRP
CHIRP
Kuri and Kura
SHIZUKU! THE SOMEN IS READY!
OKAY!
SO WHEN ARE YOU GONNA WORK, DAD?
HMM? GOOD QUESTION...
Delicious Tsu yu 3
THEY CALLED ME "DRY ICE" AT SCHOOL THE OTHER DAY.
HA-HA-HA! YOU'RE JUST LIKE YOUR MOTHER, SHIZUKU.
WHY DON'T WE USE THIS POT?

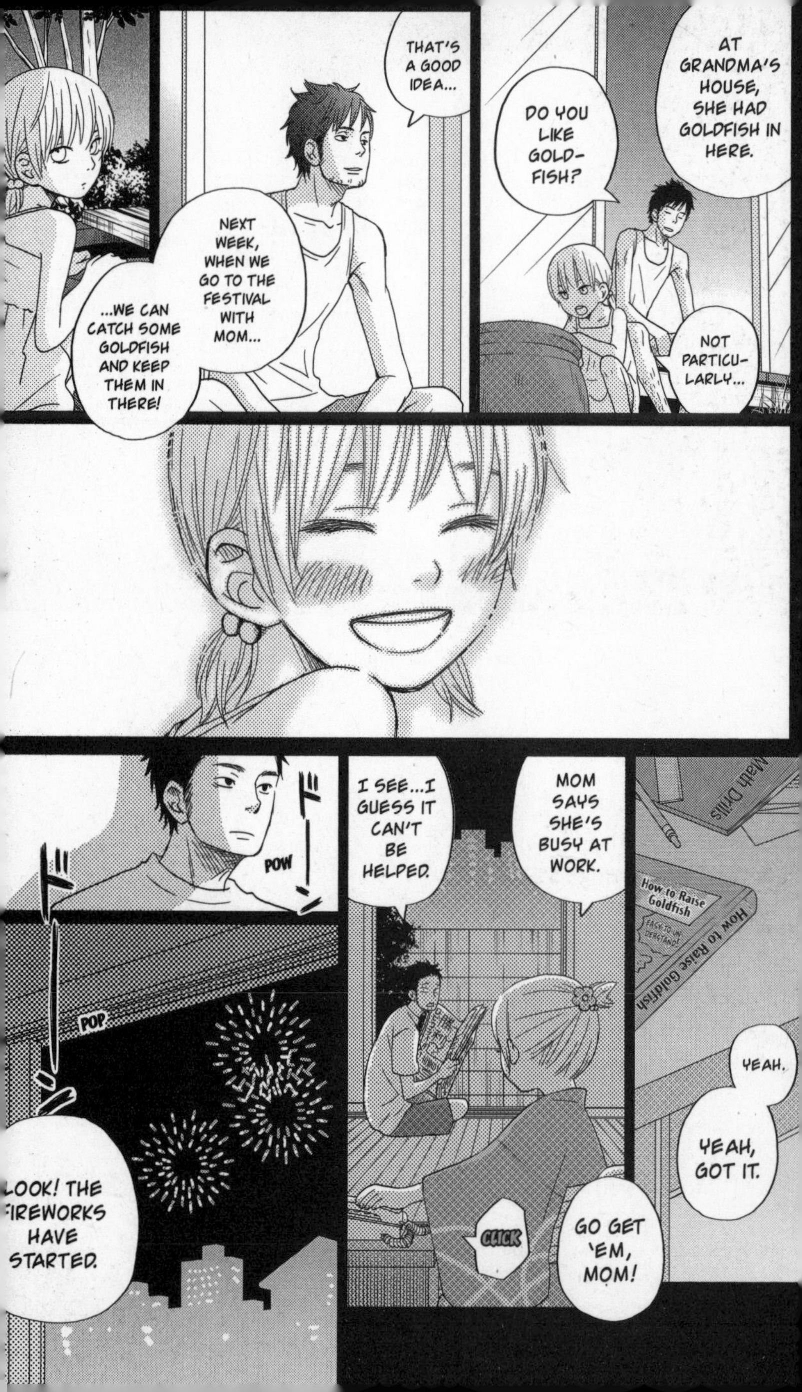
AT GRANDMA'S HOUSE, SHE HAD GOLDFISH IN HERE.
DO YOU LIKE GOLDFISH?
NOT PARTICULARLY...
THAT'S A GOOD IDEA...
NEXT WEEK, WHEN WE GO TO THE FESTIVAL WITH MOM...
...WE CAN CATCH SOME GOLDFISH AND KEEP THEM IN THERE!
Math Drills
How to Raise Goldfish
How to Raise Goldfish
YEAH.
YEAH, GOT IT.
MOM SAYS SHE'S BUSY AT WORK.
I SEE...I GUESS IT CAN'T BE HELPED.
CLICK
GO GET 'EM, MOM!
POW
POP
LOOK! THE FIREWORKS HAVE STARTED.

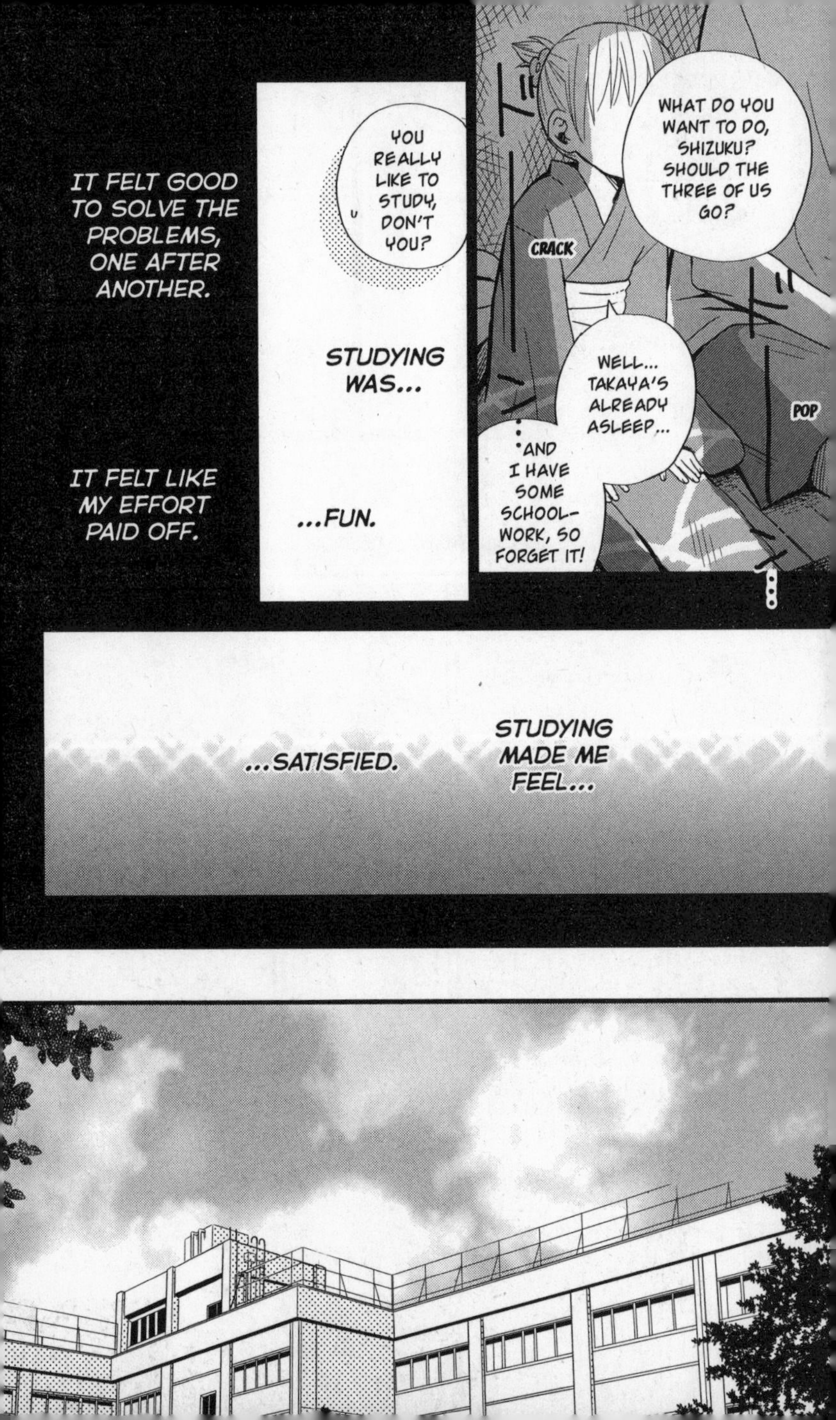
WHAT DO YOU WANT TO DO, SHIZUKU? SHOULD THE THREE OF US GO?
CRACK
WELL... TAKAYA'S ALREADY ASLEEP...
...AND I HAVE SOME SCHOOL-WORK, SO FORGET IT!
POP
YOU REALLY LIKE TO STUDY, DON'T YOU?
STUDYING WAS...
...FUN.
IT FELT GOOD TO SOLVE THE PROBLEMS, ONE AFTER ANOTHER.
IT FELT LIKE MY EFFORT PAID OFF.
STUDYING MADE ME FEEL...
...SATISFIED.

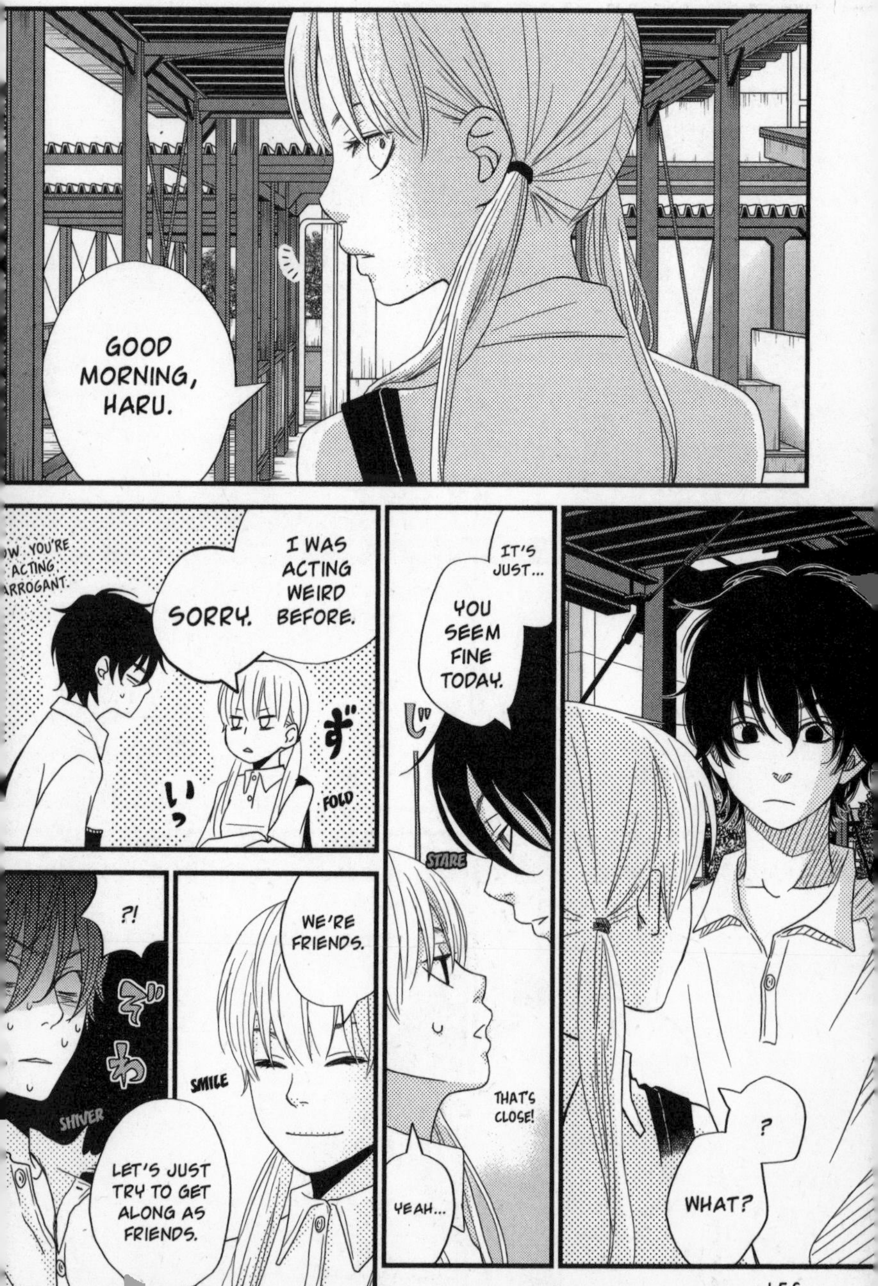
GOOD MORNING, HARU.
?
WHAT?
IT'S JUST...
YOU SEEM FINE TODAY.
じ
STARE
THAT'S CLOSE!
YEAH...
SORRY.
I WAS ACTING WEIRD BEFORE.
W. YOU'RE ACTING ARROGANT.
ず
いっ
FOLD
WE'RE FRIENDS.
SMILE
LET'S JUST TRY TO GET ALONG AS FRIENDS.
?!
ぞわ
SHIVER

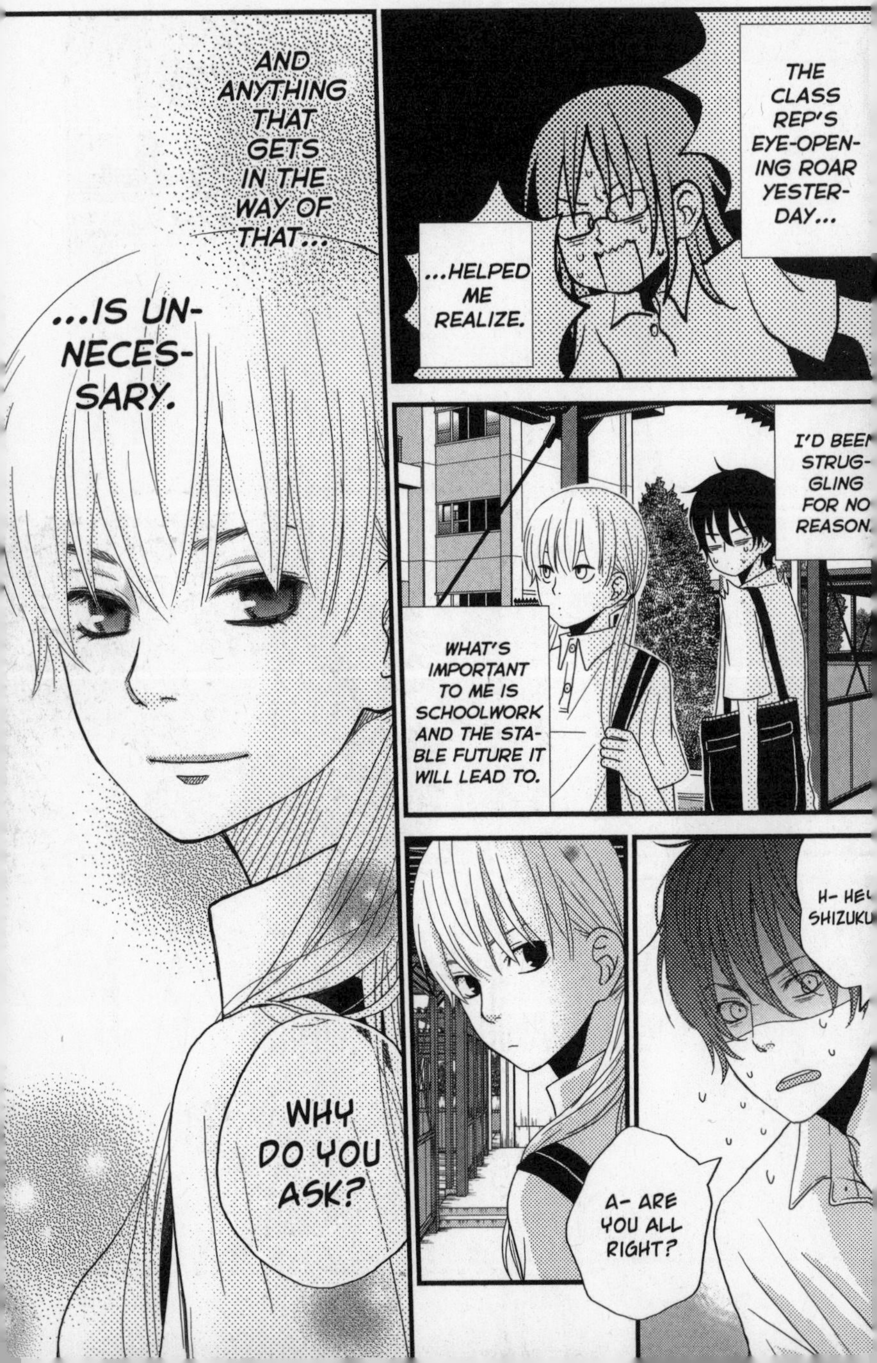
THE CLASS REP'S EYE-OPEN-ING ROAR YESTER-DAY...
...HELPED ME REALIZE.
I'D BEEN STRUG-GLING FOR NO REASON.
WHAT'S IMPORTANT TO ME IS SCHOOLWORK AND THE STA-BLE FUTURE IT WILL LEAD TO.
H- HE
SHIZUKU
A- ARE YOU ALL RIGHT?
AND ANYTHING THAT GETS IN THE WAY OF THAT...
...IS UN-NECES-SARY.
WHY DO YOU ASK?

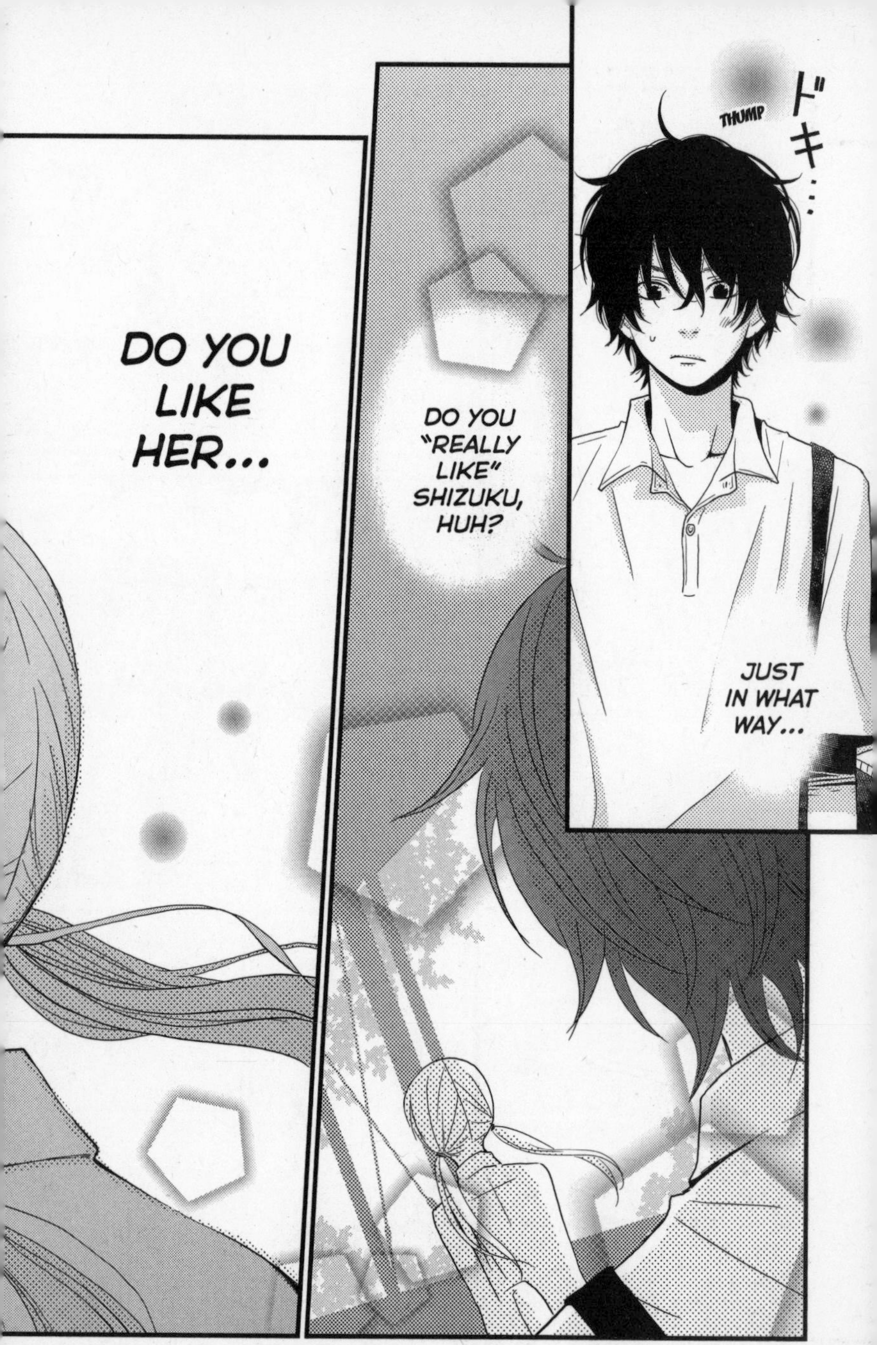
ドキ…
THUMP
JUST IN WHAT WAY...
DO YOU "REALLY LIKE" SHIZUKU, HUH?
DO YOU LIKE HER...

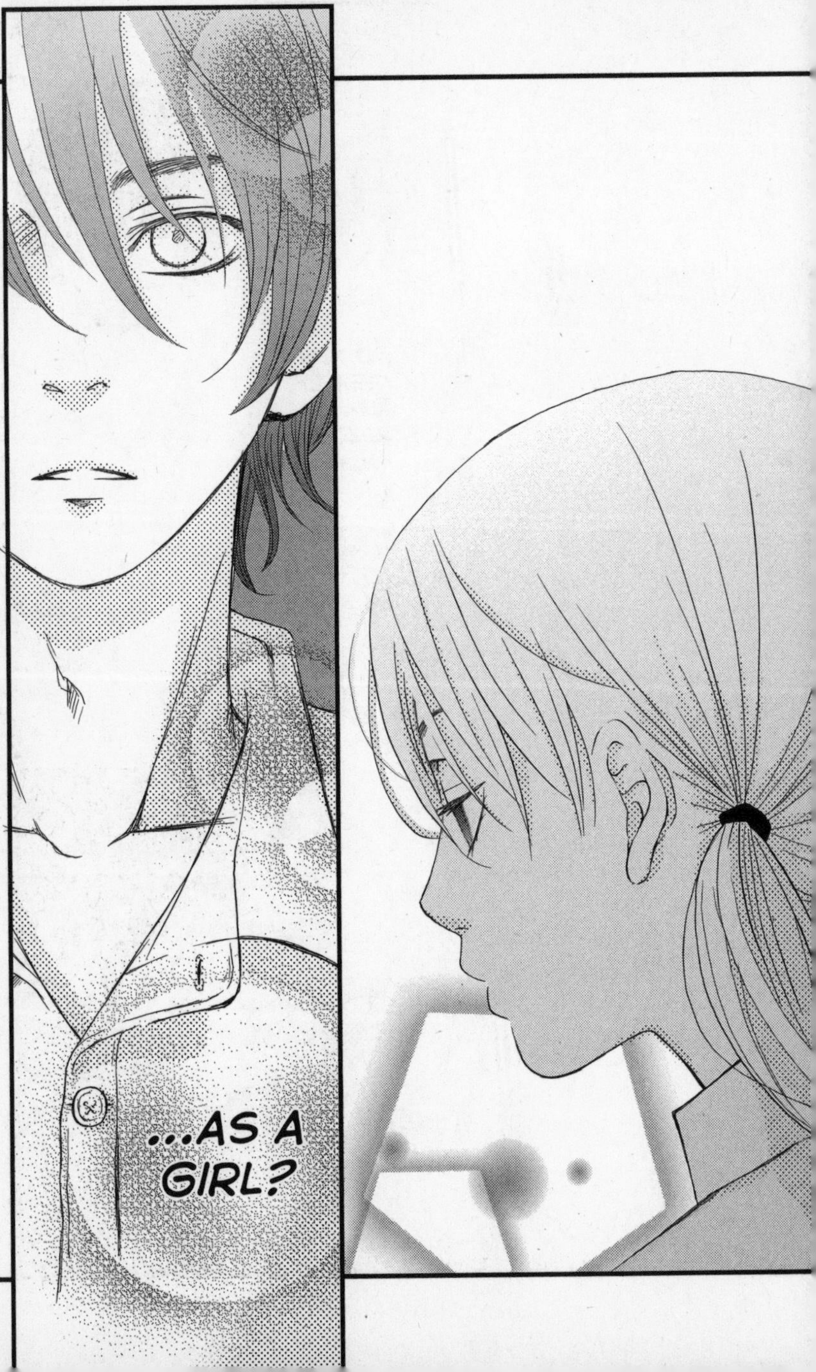
...AS A GIRL?

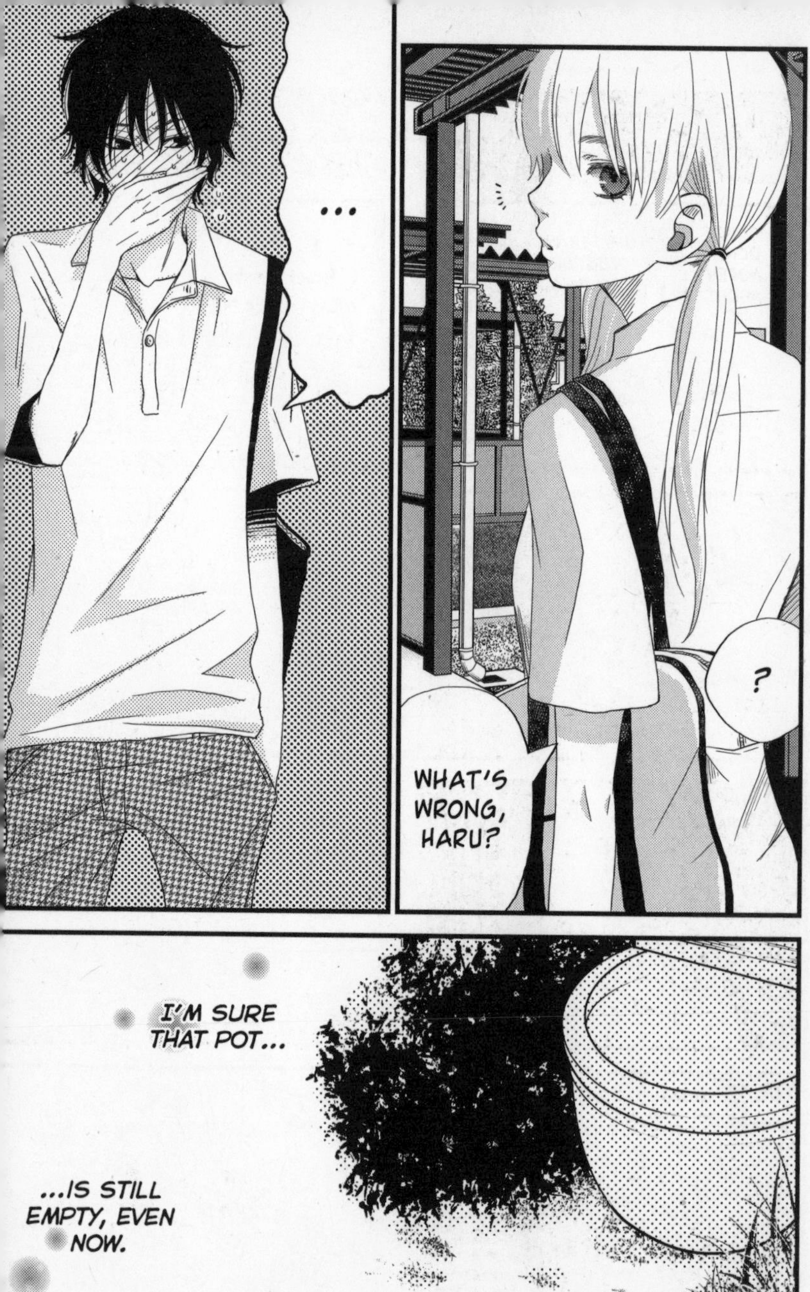
?
WHAT'S WRONG, HARU?
...
I'M SURE THAT POT...
...IS STILL EMPTY, EVEN NOW.

Continued in Volume 3!!

Strategy To Make Lots of Friends

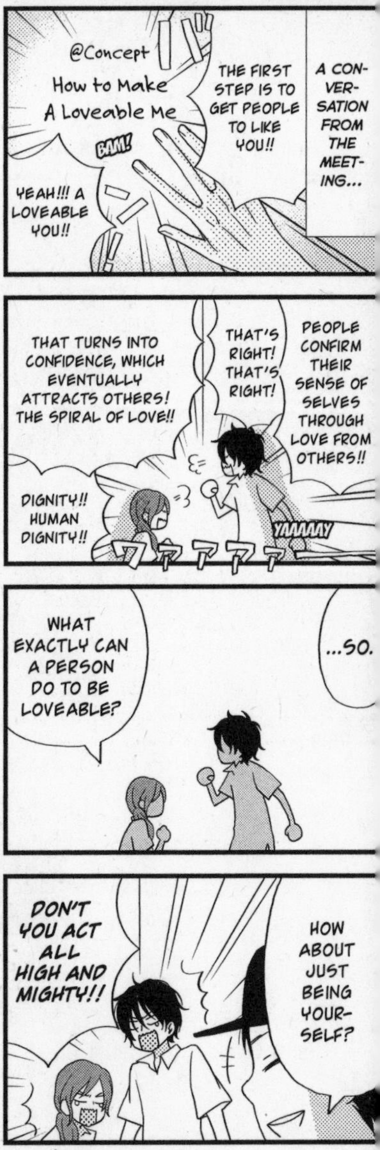
A CONVERSATION FROM THE MEETING...
THE FIRST STEP IS TO GET PEOPLE TO LIKE YOU!!
@Concept How to Make A Loveable Me
BAM!
YEAH!!! A LOVEABLE YOU!!
PEOPLE CONFIRM THEIR SENSE OF SELVES THROUGH LOVE FROM OTHERS!!
THAT'S RIGHT! THAT'S RIGHT!
THAT TURNS INTO CONFIDENCE, WHICH EVENTUALLY ATTRACTS OTHERS! THE SPIRAL OF LOVE!!
YAAAAAY
DIGNITY!! HUMAN DIGNITY!!
...SO.
WHAT EXACTLY CAN A PERSON DO TO BE LOVEABLE?
HOW ABOUT JUST BEING YOURSELF?
DON'T YOU ACT ALL HIGH AND MIGHTY!!

No Thank You

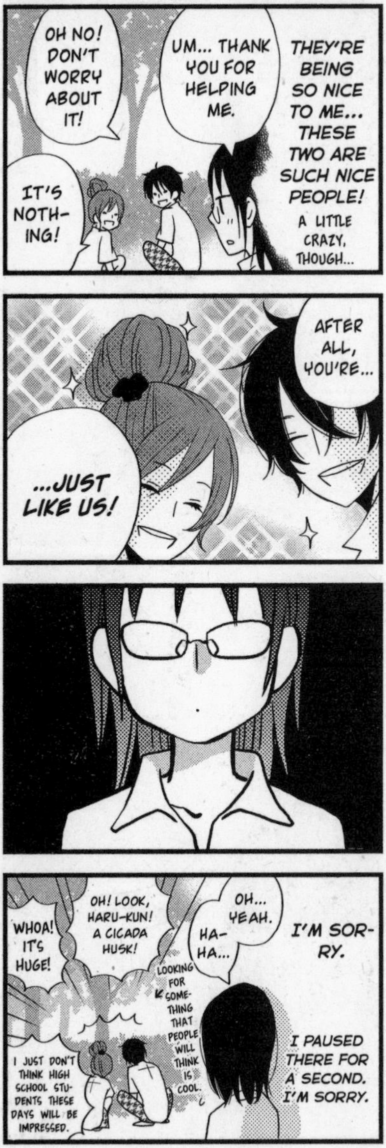
THEY'RE BEING SO NICE TO ME... THESE TWO ARE SUCH NICE PEOPLE!
A LITTLE CRAZY, THOUGH...
UM... THANK YOU FOR HELPING ME.
OH NO! DON'T WORRY ABOUT IT!
IT'S NOTHING!
AFTER ALL, YOU'RE...
...JUST LIKE US!
I'M SORRY.
I PAUSED THERE FOR A SECOND. I'M SORRY.
OH... YEAH.
HA-HA...
LOOKING FOR SOMETHING THAT PEOPLE WILL THINK IS COOL.
OH! LOOK, HARU-KUN! A CICADA HUSK!
WHOA! IT'S HUGE!
I JUST DON'T THINK HIGH SCHOOL STUDENTS THESE DAYS WILL BE IMPRESSED.

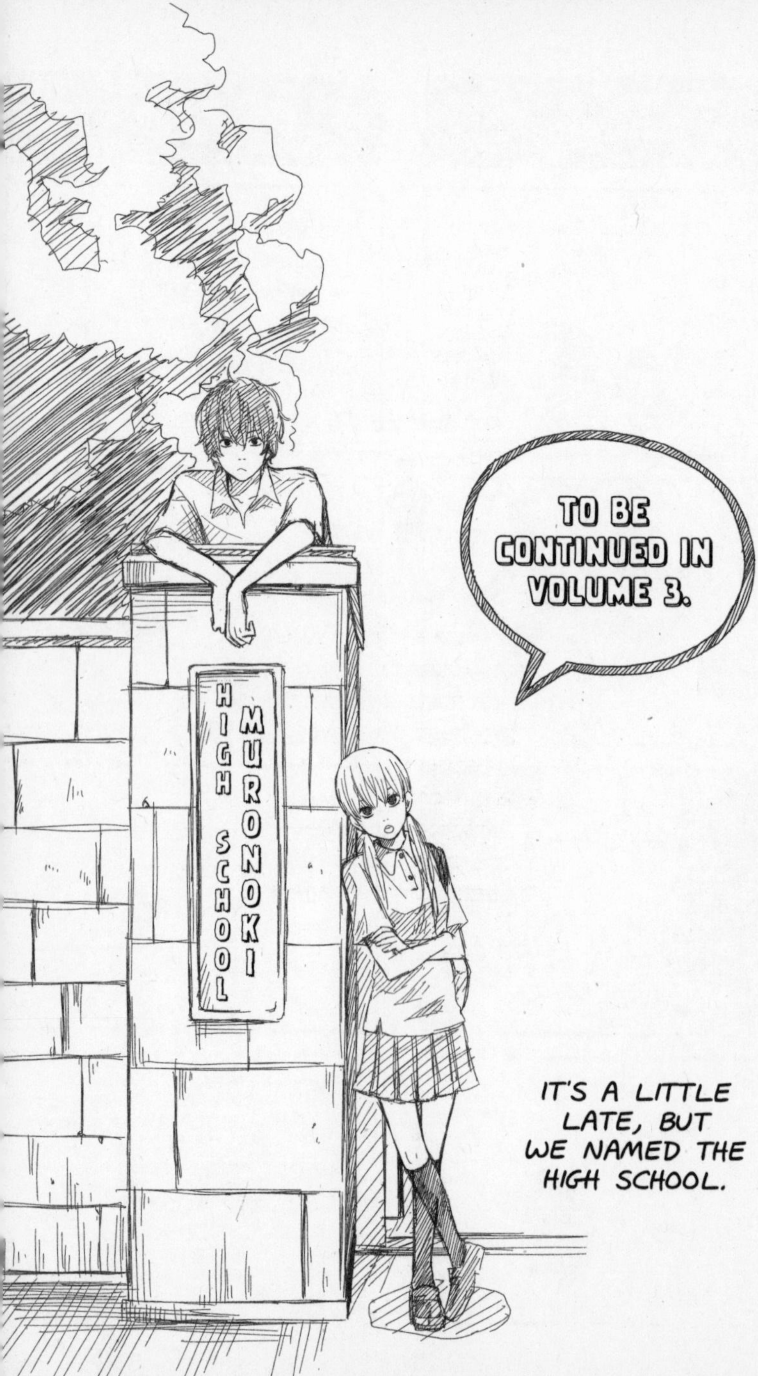
TO BE CONTINUED IN VOLUME 3.
MURONOKI HIGH SCHOOL
IT'S A LITTLE LATE, BUT WE NAMED THE HIGH SCHOOL.

COMMENT

Robico

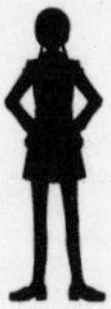

Every now and then when
I'm planning the storyline,
the plot starts to get fuzzy in
my head. Whenever
that happens, I tell myself,
"this is a romance manga!"
Which just confuses
me more...Anyway,
we seem to have made it
to Volume 2.
I'm so happy.

Translation Notes

Japanese is a tricky language for most Westerners, and translation is often more art than science. For your edificaiton and reading pleasure, here are note on some of the places where we could have gone in a different direction with our translation of this book, or where a Japanese cultural reference is used.

DHA, page 64

Docosahexaenoic acid (DHA) is an omega-3 fatty acid that is a primary structural component of the human brain, and other body parts. It can be synthesized or obtained directly from maternal milk or fish oil. While the importance of consuming DHA is debated, many believe it to be important for developing fetuses and healthy breast milk.

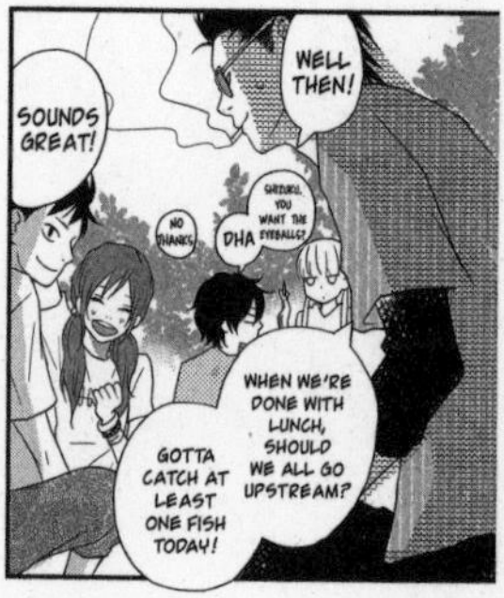
WELL THEN!
SHIZUKU, YOU WANT THE EYEBALLS?
DHA
NO THANKS.
SOUNDS GREAT!
WHEN WE'RE DONE WITH LUNCH, SHOULD WE ALL GO UPSTREAM?
GOTTA CATCH AT LEAST ONE FISH TODAY!

Suika-wari, page 69

Suika-wari, literally "watermelon-breaking," is a traditional Japanese game that involves splitting a watermelon with a stick while blindfolded, not unlike a piñata. Played in the summertime, suika-wari is most often seen at beaches, but also occurs at festivals, picnics, and other summer events.

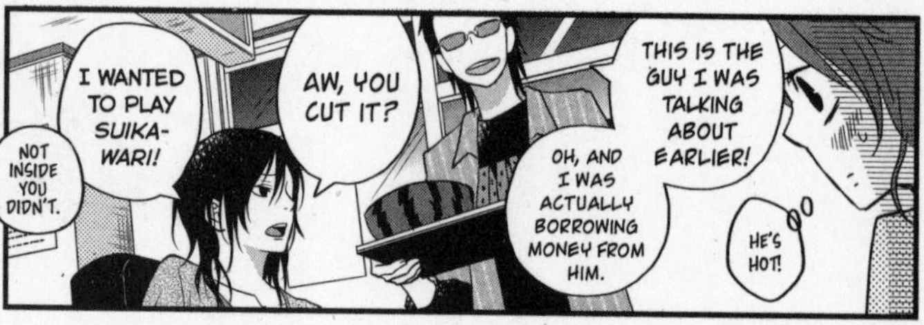
THIS IS THE GUY I WAS TALKING ABOUT EARLIER!
HE'S HOT!
OH, AND I WAS ACTUALLY BORROWING MONEY FROM HIM.
AW, YOU CUT IT?
I WANTED TO PLAY SUIKA-WARI!
NOT INSIDE YOU DIDN'T.

Brother Complex, page 70

The term "brother complex" is used in Japan to denote generally the strong feelings of love a sibling can develop for his or her brother, usually beyond what is considered "normal." It is a common theme in manga and anime.

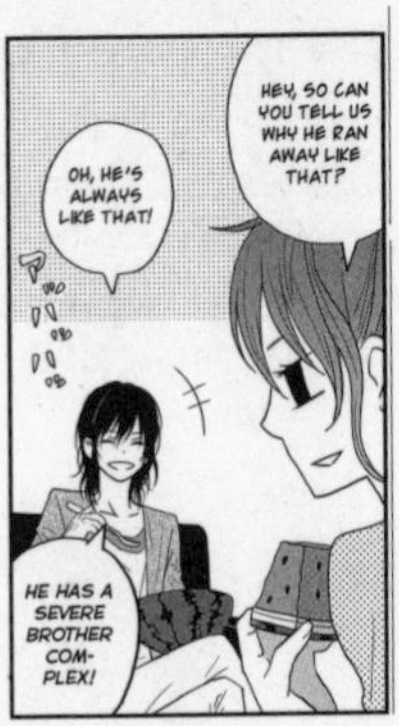
HEY, SO CAN YOU TELL US WHY HE RAN AWAY LIKE THAT?
OH, HE'S ALWAYS LIKE THAT!
HE HAS A SEVERE BROTHER COM-PLEX!

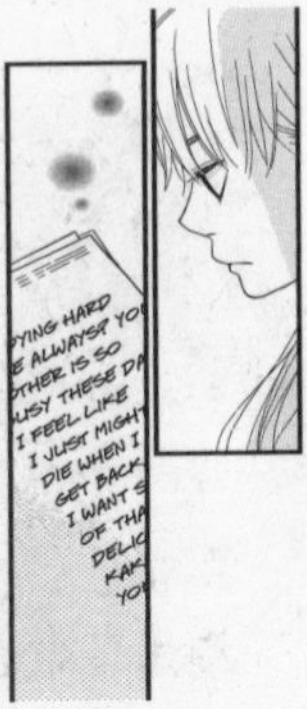

Kakuni, page 125

Kakuni, literally "square-simmered," is a Japanese braised pork dish, made of thick cubes of pork belly simmered in various sauces. It originates from the Nagasaki region.

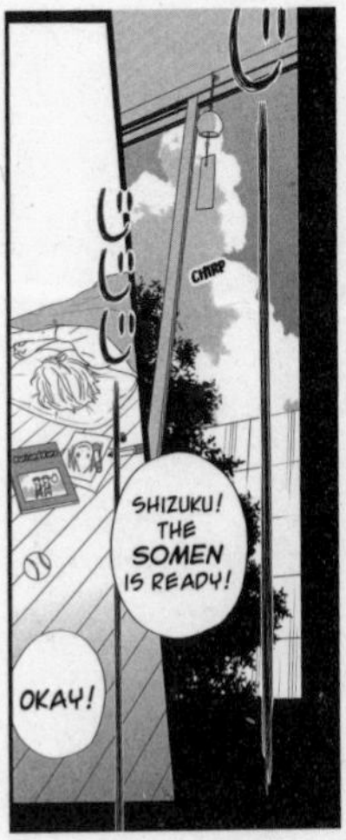
CHIRP
SHIZUKU! THE SOMEN IS READY!
OKAY!

Somen, page 153

Somen are very thin white Japanese noodles made of wheat flour, which are usually served cold and often eaten in the summer.

Mei Tachibana has no friends — and says she doesn't need them!
But everything changes when she accidentally roundhouse kicks the most popular boy in school! However, Yamato Kurosawa isn't angry in the slightest—in fact, he thinks his ordinary life could use an unusual girl like Mei. But winning Mei's trust will be a tough task. How long will she refuse to say, "I love you"?